What Your Fifth Grader Needs to Know

FUNDAMENTALS OF A GOOD FIFTH-GRADE EDUCATION

The Core Knowledge™ Series

Resource Books for Kindergarten Through Grade Six

DELL TRADE PAPERBACKS

What Your Fifth Grader Needs to Know

FUNDAMENTALS OF A GOOD
FIFTH-GRADE EDUCATION

(Revised Edition)

Edited by

E. D. HIRSCH, JR.

WHAT YOUR FIFTH GRADER NEEDS TO KNOW
A Delta Book

PUBLISHING HISTORY
Doubleday hardcover edition published October 2005
Delta trade paperback edition / July 2006

Published by
Bantam Dell
A Division of Random House, Inc.
New York, New York

Book design by Robert Bull

Library of Congress Catalog Card Number: 2004061858

Delta is a registered trademark of Random House, Inc.,
and the colophon is a trademark of Random House, Inc.

ISBN-10: 0-385-33731-0
ISBN-13: 978-0-385-33731-1
Printed in the United States of America
Published simultaneously in Canada

www.bantamdell.com

RRW 10 9 8 7 6 5

This book is dedicated to
Eliza Jane Hirsch
Born March 24, 2003

Contents

Acknowledgments   *xv*
A Note to Parents and Teachers   *xvii*
Introduction to the Revised Edition   *xix*
General Introduction to the Core Knowledge Series   *xxi*

I. Language and Literature

Introduction   3

Poetry   **4**
A Wise Old Owl   4
The Eagle   4
From Opposites   5
The Arrow and the Song   5
The Road Not Taken   6
The Snow-storm   7
I Hear America Singing   8
I, Too   9
Incident   9
Narcissa   10
I like to see it lap the Miles—   10
A Bird came down the Walk   11
The Tyger   12
A Poison Tree   13
Barbara Frietchie   14
O Captain! My Captain!   15
Casey at the Bat   16
Jabberwocky   18

Stories, Myths, and Legends   **19**
The Adventures of Tom Sawyer   19
Don Quixote   21
Little Women   24
Narrative of the Life
    of Frederick Douglass   28
The Secret Garden   29

The Red-Headed League   34
The Samurai's Daughter   38
The Sun Dance   40
Coyote Goes to the Land of the Dead   43

Learning About Literature   **45**
Literal and Figurative Language   45
Imagery   46
Simile and Metaphor   46
Symbols   48
Personification   48
Onomatopoeia   48
Alliteration   49
Drama   49
Shakespeare   50
Shakespeare's Comedies   51

Learning About Language   **52**
Subjects and Verbs   52
Sentence Fragments   53
Run-On Sentences   53
Direct Objects   54
Indirect Objects   54
Predicates   55
Nouns   56
Adjectives and Adverbs   56
Interjections   57
Personal Pronouns   57
Agreement in Case   57
Possessive Case   59

Agreement in Gender   59
Agreement in Number   59
The Versatile Comma   60
Colons and Italics   61
Writing   62
Researching and Writing a Report   62
Prefixes   63
Suffixes   64

Sayings and Phrases   **65**
Birthday suit   65
Bite the hand that feeds you   65
Catch forty winks   65
Chip on your shoulder   65
Count your blessings.   65
Eat crow   65
Eleventh hour   65
Eureka!   65
Every cloud has a silver lining.   65
Few and far between   66

The grass is always greener
  on the other side of the hill.   66
Kill two birds with one stone   66
Lock, stock, and barrel   66
Make a mountain out of a molehill   66
A miss is as good as a mile.   66
It's never too late to mend.   66
Out of the frying pan and into the fire   66
A penny saved is a penny earned.   66
Read between the lines   67
Sit on the fence   67
Steal his/her thunder   67
Take the bull by the horns   67
Till the cows come home   67
Time heals all wounds.   67
Tom, Dick, and Harry   67
Vice versa   67
A watched pot never boils.   67
Well begun is half done.   67
What will be will be.   67

II. History and Geography

Introduction   71

World Geography   **72**
Reference Points   72
Latitude and Longitude   73
Arctic and Antarctic   74
Tropical, Temperate, Frigid   75
The Seasons   76
It's About Time   76
Round Earth, Flat Map   78
The Mercator Projection   79
Conic and Plane Projection   79

Lakes   80
Salty Lakes and River Sources   81
Lakes of the World   81

**Early Civilizations
  of The Americas**   **82**
The Maya, Aztecs, and Incas   82
The Maya   82
Maya Life and Learning   83
Where Did They Go?   84
The Aztecs   84
A Fierce Religion   86

Fort Sumter: The Civil War Begins 134
Eager to Fight 135
The Confederacy 136
Robert E. Lee 136
Ulysses S. Grant 137
The Soldiers 138
Yanks and Rebs, Blue and Gray 138
Soldiers' Songs 139
Antietam and the Emancipation
    Proclamation 139
African-American Troops 140
The Misery of War 141
The Ironclads 142
Gettysburg 142
Lincoln's Gettysburg Address 143
Sherman's March to the Sea 144
Lincoln Is Reelected 145
Richmond Falls 145
Surrender at Appomattox 145
Lincoln Is Assassinated 147

Reconstruction 148
Repairing the "House Divided" 148
Johnson's Plan for Reconstruction 148
Black Codes 148
Scalawags and Carpetbaggers 149
The Freedmen's Bureau 150
The Impeachment of
    President Johnson 150
Three Important Amendments 150
The End of Reconstruction 152

Westward Expansion
    After the Civil War 153
"Go West, Young Man!" 153
Homesteaders 153
The Transcontinental Railroad 154
Buffalo Soldiers 155
Cowboys 156
The Wild West 156
Seward's Folly 158
The Closing of the American Frontier 158

Native Americans: Cultures
    and Conflicts 159
Natives and Settlers 159
Indians of the Southwest 159
Indians of the Pacific Northwest 160
Indians of the Great Basin
    and the Plateau 161
Indians of the Plains 161
The Buffalo Disappear 162
Reservations 163
The Sand Creek Massacre 163
Little Big Horn 164
"I will fight no more forever." 165
The Ghost Dance 165
Attempts to Assimilate the Indians 166
Splitting Up Reservations 166

U.S. Geography 168
Regions of the United States 168
Alaska and Hawaii 170

Two Worlds Meet   86
The Incas   88
Pizarro   89

European Exploration   **91**
The Discovery of the "New World"   91
Control of Trade   91
Early Portuguese Explorations   92
Christopher Columbus   92
Who Will Rule the Waves?   94
Da Gama   95
Cabral   96
Magellan Goes Around the World   97
The Dutch Head East   97
Where Are the English?   99
Europe's New World Colonies   99
Bartolomé de las Casas   100
Sugar, Plantations, and Slavery   101
The Transatlantic Slave Trade   101
The Middle Passage   102

**The Renaissance
    and Reformation**   **103**
Islamic Learning   103
The Renaissance   104
Florence and the Medici   104
Beyond Florence   105
Princes and Courtiers   106
Gutenberg   107
Martin Luther   108
Protestantism and Calvinism   110
The Counter-Reformation   111

England   **112**
Henry VIII   112
Protestant or Catholic?   112
Elizabeth I   113
The Spanish Armada   113
James I   114

Charles I   114
The Civil War   115
Charles II and the Restoration   115
James II and the Glorious Revolution   116
The Bill of Rights   116

Russia   **117**
Ivan the Great   117
Ivan the Terrible   118
Peter the Great   118
Catherine the Great   119

Feudal Japan   **120**
Land of the Rising Sun   120
Japanese Feudalism   121
Japanese Religions   122

**Westward Expansion
    Before the Civil War**   **123**
New Nation, New Lands   123
The Louisiana Purchase   123
The Fur Trade   124
Moving West   124
"There's Gold in Them Thar Hills!"   125
Getting There   126
Broken Treaties   127
Manifest Destiny   127
The Mexican-American War   128

The Civil War   **129**
North and South   12
The Missouri Compromise   12
Abolitionists   1
How Some Slaves Resisted   1
The Dred Scott Decision   1
The Lincoln-Douglas Debates   1
John Brown
States' Rights and Secession
Lincoln Elected:
    Southern States Secede

Fort Sumter: The Civil War Begins   134
Eager to Fight   135
The Confederacy   136
Robert E. Lee   136
Ulysses S. Grant   137
The Soldiers   138
Yanks and Rebs, Blue and Gray   138
Soldiers' Songs   139
Antietam and the Emancipation
    Proclamation   139
African-American Troops   140
The Misery of War   141
The Ironclads   142
Gettysburg   142
Lincoln's Gettysburg Address   143
Sherman's March to the Sea   144
Lincoln Is Reelected   145
Richmond Falls   145
Surrender at Appomattox   145
Lincoln Is Assassinated   147

Reconstruction   148
Repairing the "House Divided"   148
Johnson's Plan for Reconstruction   148
Black Codes   148
Scalawags and Carpetbaggers   149
The Freedmen's Bureau   150
The Impeachment of
    President Johnson   150
Three Important Amendments   150
The End of Reconstruction   152

Westward Expansion
    After the Civil War   153
"Go West, Young Man!"   153
Homesteaders   153
The Transcontinental Railroad   154
Buffalo Soldiers   155
Cowboys   156
The Wild West   156
Seward's Folly   158
The Closing of the American Frontier   158

Native Americans: Cultures
    and Conflicts   159
Natives and Settlers   159
Indians of the Southwest   159
Indians of the Pacific Northwest   160
Indians of the Great Basin
    and the Plateau   161
Indians of the Plains   161
The Buffalo Disappear   162
Reservations   163
The Sand Creek Massacre   163
Little Big Horn   164
"I will fight no more forever."   165
The Ghost Dance   165
Attempts to Assimilate the Indians   166
Splitting Up Reservations   166

U.S. Geography   168
Regions of the United States   168
Alaska and Hawaii   170

CONTENTS

Two Worlds Meet 86
The Incas 88
Pizarro 89

European Exploration 91
The Discovery of the "New World" 91
Control of Trade 91
Early Portuguese Explorations 92
Christopher Columbus 92
Who Will Rule the Waves? 94
Da Gama 95
Cabral 96
Magellan Goes Around the World 97
The Dutch Head East 97
Where Are the English? 99
Europe's New World Colonies 99
Bartolomé de las Casas 100
Sugar, Plantations, and Slavery 101
The Transatlantic Slave Trade 101
The Middle Passage 102

**The Renaissance
and Reformation** 103
Islamic Learning 103
The Renaissance 104
Florence and the Medici 104
Beyond Florence 105
Princes and Courtiers 106
Gutenberg 107
Martin Luther 108
Protestantism and Calvinism 110
The Counter-Reformation 111

England 112
Henry VIII 112
Protestant or Catholic? 112
Elizabeth I 113
The Spanish Armada 113
James I 114

Charles I 114
The Civil War 115
Charles II and the Restoration 115
James II and the Glorious Revolution 116
The Bill of Rights 116

Russia 117
Ivan the Great 117
Ivan the Terrible 118
Peter the Great 118
Catherine the Great 119

Feudal Japan 120
Land of the Rising Sun 120
Japanese Feudalism 121
Japanese Religions 122

**Westward Expansion
Before the Civil War** 123
New Nation, New Lands 123
The Louisiana Purchase 123
The Fur Trade 124
Moving West 124
"There's Gold in Them Thar Hills!" 125
Getting There 126
Broken Treaties 127
Manifest Destiny 127
The Mexican-American War 128

The Civil War 129
North and South 129
The Missouri Compromise 129
Abolitionists 130
How Some Slaves Resisted 131
The Dred Scott Decision 131
The Lincoln-Douglas Debates 132
John Brown 133
States' Rights and Secession 133
Lincoln Elected:
Southern States Secede 134

V. Mathematics

Introduction	219
Numbers and Number Sense	**220**
Billions	220
Place Value and Expanded Form	220
Comparing Large Numbers	220
Positive and Negative Numbers	221
Integers	221
Comparing Integers	222
Adding Integers	222
Subtracting Integers	224
Rounding	225
Squares and Square Roots	225
Exponents	225
Powers of Ten	226
Sets	226
Prime Numbers	227
Prime Factors	227
Greatest Common Factor	228
Least Common Multiple	228
Computation	**229**
Properties of Addition	229
Variables	229
Inverse Operations, Equations	229
Properties of Multiplication	230
Multiplication and Division as Inverse Operations	231
Multiplying Large Factors	232
Estimating a Product	232
Division and Divisibility	232
Short Division	233
Long Division	233
More Two-Digit Divisors	235
Three-Digit Divisors	236
Decimals, Fractions, and Mixed Numbers	**238**
Decimals	238
Decimals on a Number Line	238
Comparing Decimals	239
Decimal Sums and Differences	239
Multiplying Decimals	240
Multiplying Decimals by 10, 100, 1000	241
Estimating Decimal Products	242
Multiplying a Decimal by a Decimal	242
Checking Decimal Products	243
Decimal Division	243
Writing Zeros in the Dividend	244
Dividing Whole Numbers Without Remainders	245
Dividing by 10, 100, 1000	245
Rounding Decimal Quotients	246
Checking Inexact Division	247
Equivalent Fractions	249
Lowest Terms	249
Comparing Fractions	250
Comparing Fractions on a Number Line	250
Adding Fractions	251
Subtracting Fractions	253
Mixed Numbers and Fractions	253
Decimals, Mixed Numbers, and Fractions	254
Adding Mixed Numbers	255
Subtracting Mixed Numbers	256
Multiplying Fractions and Whole Numbers	258
Ratios, Percents, and Probabilities	**260**
Ratio	260
Scale	261
Rates and Speed	262
Percent	263
Percents and Fractions	263

III. Visual Arts

Introduction   173

The Renaissance   174
The Rebirth of the Arts   174
Beautiful Things   175
The Harmony of the Body   175
A New Perspective   176
Leonardo: Renaissance Man   177
The Last Supper   178
Michelangelo and the Sistine Ceiling   179
Raphael: Painter of Madonnas   180
Renaissance Sculpture   180

Renaissance Architecture   182
The Northern Renaissance   183
Bruegel: Painter of Peasants   184
The Proud Artist   185

American Art   186
The Lives of Americans   186
American Landscapes   189
The Civil War in Art   190

Japanese Art   191
Buddhism and Japanese Art   191

IV. Music

Introduction   195

Elements of Music   196
What All Music Has in Common   196
High Notes and Low Notes   196
Short Notes and Long Notes   197
Dotted and Tied Notes   198
Time for a Rest   198
Measures and Bar Lines   198
Could You Repeat That?   199
Time Signatures   199
The Treble Clef   200
From Sheet Music to Sound   201
Sharps and Flats   202
Italian for Composers   202
You Gotta Have Rhythm   203
Verse and Refrain   204
Harmony   204

Listening and Understanding   205
Polyphonic Music   205
Canons and Rounds   205
Renaissance Composers   205
Lute Music   206
John Dowland   207
Mendelssohn's Midsummer's Night   207

Beethoven: A Stormy Life Set
    to Music   208
Mussorgsky: Painting Pictures
    with Music   209

Spirituals   210
Sorrow Songs   210
Sometimes I Feel Like a
    Motherless Child   211
Down by the Riverside   211
Wayfaring Stranger   212
We Shall Overcome   212

**Songs About Westward
    Expansion**   213
Sweet Betsy from Pike   213
Shenandoah   214
Git Along, Little Dogies   214

American Songs   215
God Bless America   215
If I Had a Hammer   215

Songs About Love and Lovers   216
Danny Boy   216
Red River Valley   216

Percents and Decimals	264
Writing Fractions, Decimals, or Percents	264
Finding a Percent of a Number	265
Finding an Average	265
Probability	266

Graphs, Functions, and Word Problems — 267

Circle Graphs	267
Bar Graphs	268
Line Graphs	268
Functions and Inverse Operations	269
Graphing Functions	270
Writing and Solving Equations for Word Problems	271

Geometry — 273

Angles	273
Kinds of Angles	273
Kinds of Triangles	274
Polygons	276
Diagonals	278
Circles	278
Area	280
Finding the Area of a Triangle	282
Finding the Area of a Parallelogram	283
Finding Areas of Other Figures	283
Rectangular Prisms	284
Volume	285
Volume and Surface Area	286
Changing U.S. Customary Units of Volume	287
Changing Metric Units of Volume	288
Volume and Capacity	288

VI: Science

Introduction	291

Chemistry: Matter and Change — 292

Atoms	292
John Dalton	293
The Parts of Atoms	293
Mendeleev and the Periods	293
Explaining the Periods	295
Elements and Abbreviations	296
Metals and Non-Metals	296
Molecules	297
Compounds	297
Physical and Chemical Changes	298

Classifying Living Things — 300

Why Classify?	300
Classifying Organisms	301
Cells	302
The Parts of a Cell	302
Different Kinds of Cells	303
How Plant Cells Differ from Animal Cells	304
Fungi	305
Protists	306
Prokaryotes	307
Taxonomy	308
Latin Names	309
Meet the Vertebrates	309

Plants — 311

Plants and Photosynthesis	311
Vascular and Non-vascular Plants	313

Life Cycles and Reproduction — 314

The Replacements	314
Asexual Reproduction	315
Asexual Reproduction in Larger Animals and Plants	315

Sexual Reproduction in Mosses
  and Ferns   316
Conifer Seeds Are Naked   318
Seeds of Flowering Plants Have
  Clothes   318
Flowers   319
Flower Fertilization   320
Plant Development   321
Monocots and Dicots   322
Reproduction in Animals   323
Development of the Embryo   325
Care and Growth of Young   325
Growth Stages   326

The Human Body   327
Human Growth Stages   327
Adolescence and Puberty   327
The Human Reproductive System   328
The Endocrine System   331
Meet the Glands   331

Science Biographies   333
Galileo   333
Carl Linnaeus   334
Ernest Just   335
Percy Lavon Julian   336

Illustration and Photo Credits   339
Text Credits and Sources   342
Index   343

Acknowledgments

This series has depended on the help, advice, and encouragement of more than 2,000 people. Some of those singled out here already know the depth of our gratitude; others may be surprised to find themselves thanked publicly for help they gave quietly and freely. To helpers named and unnamed, we are deeply grateful.

Editor-in-Chief of the Core Knowledge Series: E. D. Hirsch, Jr.

Text Editor: Matthew Davis

Editorial Assistance: Diane P. Castro, Michael Marshall, Susan Tyler Hitchcock, John Holdren, Souzanne Wright, Robert D. Shepherd

Art, Photo, and Text Permissions Research: Matthew Davis, Susan Tyler Hitchcock, Peter Locke, Emily E. Reddick, Jeanne Siler, The Permissions Group

Writers: This revised edition involved careful reconsideration and sometimes reuse of material in the first edition of this book, as well as others in the series. In that spirit, we wish to acknowledge all who contributed to either edition. Writers for the revised edition: Rebecca Beall Barnes (music), Matthew Davis, Donna Lucey (American History), Michael Marshall, Michael Stanford (art), Souzanne Wright (math). Writers for the original edition: Nancy Bryson (science), Bernardine Connelly (history), Tricia Emlet (geography), Marie Hawthorne (science), E. D. Hirsch, Jr. (science), John Hirsch (math), John Holdren (history, language and literature), Jennifer Howard (history, science), Blair Longwood Jones (literature), Bethanne H. Kelly (literature), Elaine Moran (visual arts), A. Brooke Russell (geography, science), Peter Ryan (music), Lindley Shutz (language and literature), Helen Storey (language and literature), Steven M. Sullivan (history)

Advisors on Subject Matter: Richard Anderson, Wayne Bishop, Lucien Ellington, Andrew Gleason, Charles F. Gritzner, Eric Karell, Joseph Kett, Michael Lynch, Wilfred McClay, Joseph C. Miller, Anne Moyer, Kristen Onuf, Margaret Redd, Mark Rush, Gayle Sherwood, Michael Smith, Ralph Smith, James Trefil, Nancy Wayne, and others

Advisors on Multiculturalism: Minerva Allen, Barbara Carey, Frank de Varona, Mick Fedullo, Dorothy Fields, Elizabeth Fox-Genovese, Marcia Galli, Dan Garner, Henry Louis Gates, Cheryl Kulas, Joseph C. Miller, Gerry Raining Bird, Connie Rocha, Dorothy Small, Sharon Stewart-Peregoy, Sterling Stuckey, Marlene Walking Bear, Lucille Watahomigie, Ramona Wilson

Advisors on Elementary Education: Joseph Adelson, Isobel Beck, Paul Bell, Carl Bereiter, David Bjorklund, Constance Jones, Elizabeth LaFuze, J. P. Lutz, Sandra Scarr, Nancy Stein, Phyllis Wilkin, plus all the conferees at the March 1990 conference where the first draft of the curriculum was developed

Schools: Special thanks to the schools and individual teachers—too many to list here—that have offered their advice and suggestions for improving the *Core Knowledge Sequence*

Our grateful acknowledgment to these persons does not imply that we have taken their (sometimes conflicting) advice in every case or that each of them endorses all aspects of this project. Responsibility for final decisions rests with the editors alone. Suggestions for improvements are always welcome. We thank in advance those who send advice for revising and improving this series.

A Note
to Parents and Teachers

Most of this book is addressed to, and intended to be read by, fifth-grade students. However, at the beginning of each chapter, we have supplied a brief introduction with advice for parents and teachers. We hope these introductions will be useful for parents seeking to build on the foundation provided here and for teachers, whether or not they teach in the growing network of Core Knowledge schools.

If you are interested in learning more about the work and ideas of teachers in Core Knowledge schools, please contact the Core Knowledge Foundation for more information:

801 East High Street
Charlottesville, VA 22902
(434) 977-7550
coreknow@coreknowledge.org
www.coreknowledge.org

There you will find an online bookstore, lessons created by teachers in the Core Knowledge schools, a database listing additional resources, and other supporting materials developed by the Foundation.

Introduction
to the Revised Edition

This is a revision of the first edition of *What Your Fifth Grader Needs to Know*, first published in 1993. Almost nothing in that earlier book, which elicited wide praise and warm expressions of gratitude from teachers and parents, has become outdated. Why, then, revise the earlier book at all?

Because good work can be made better. In the intervening years since 1993, we at the Core Knowledge Foundation have had the benefit of a great deal of practical experience that can improve the contributions these books make to early education. We have learned from a growing network of Core Knowledge schools. At this writing, we can build on the experiences of hundreds of schools across the nation that are following the Core Knowledge curriculum guidelines. We have also received many suggestions from parents who are using the books. And besides conducting our own research, we have continued to seek advice from subject-matter experts and multicultural advisors. All these activities have enabled us to field-test and refine the original *Core Knowledge Sequence*—the curriculum guidelines on which the Core Knowledge books are based.

What kind of knowledge and skills can your child be expected to learn at school in fifth grade? How can you help your child at home? These are questions we try to answer in this book. It presents a range of knowledge and skills—in language arts, history and geography, visual arts, music, mathematics, and science—that should be at the core of an enriching, challenging fifth-grade education.

Because children and localities differ greatly across this big, diverse country, so do fifth-grade classrooms. But all communities, including classrooms, require some common ground for communication and learning. In this book, we present the specific shared knowledge that hundreds of parents and teachers across the nation have agreed upon for American fifth graders. This core is not a comprehensive prescription for everything that every fifth grader needs to know. Such a complete prescription would be rigid and undesirable. But the book does offer a solid common ground—about 50 percent of the curriculum—that will enable young students to become active, successful learners in their classroom communities and later in the larger world we live in.

In this revised edition, we have retold some stories in more detail and placed more emphasis on the story in history. We have also included many color reproductions in the visual arts section. Many people (see Acknowledgments) have worked to make the revised edition a better book than the original. As is customary with a chief editor, however, I accept responsibility for any defects that may still be found, and I invite readers to send criticisms and suggestions to the Core Knowledge Foundation.

   We hope you and your child will enjoy this book and that it will help lay the foundations upon which to build a lifetime of learning.

                                                          E. D. Hirsch, Jr.

General Introduction to the Core Knowledge Series

I. WHAT IS YOUR CHILD LEARNING IN SCHOOL?

A parent of identical twins sent me a letter in which she expressed concern that her children, who are in the same grade in the same school, are being taught completely different things. How can this be? Because they are in different classrooms; because the teachers in these classrooms have only the vaguest guidelines to follow; in short, because the school, like many in the United States, lacks a definite, specific curriculum.

Many parents would be surprised if they were to examine the curriculum of their child's elementary school. Ask to see your school's curriculum. Does it spell out, in clear and concrete terms, a core of specific content and skills all children at a particular grade level are expected to learn by the end of the school year?

Many curricula speak in general terms of vaguely defined skills, processes, and attitudes, often in an abstract, pseudo-technical language that calls, for example, for children to "analyze patterns and data," or "investigate the structure and dynamics of living systems," or "work cooperatively in a group." Such vagueness evades the central question: *what is your child learning in school?* It places unreasonable demands upon teachers and often results in years of schooling marred by repetitions and gaps. Yet another unit on dinosaurs or "pioneer days." *Charlotte's Web* for the third time. "You've never heard of the Bill of Rights?" "You've never been taught how to add two fractions with unlike denominators?"

When identical twins in two classrooms of the same school have few academic experiences in common, that is cause for concern. When teachers in that school do not know what children in other classrooms are learning on the same grade level, much less in earlier and later grades, they cannot reliably predict that children will come prepared with a shared core of knowledge and skills. For an elementary school to be successful, teachers need a common vision of what they want their students to know and be able to do. They need to have *clear, specific learning goals,* as well as the sense of mutual accountability that comes from shared commitment to helping all children achieve those goals. Lacking both specific goals and mutual accountability, too many schools exist in a state of curricular incoherence, one result of which is that they fall far short of developing the full potential of our children.

To address this problem, I started the nonprofit Core Knowledge Foundation in 1986.

This book and its companion volumes in the Core Knowledge Series are designed to give parents and teachers—and through them, children—a guide to clearly defined learning goals in the form of a carefully sequenced body of knowledge, based upon the specific content guidelines developed by the Core Knowledge Foundation.

Core Knowledge is an attempt to define, in a coherent and sequential way, a body of knowledge taken for granted by competent writers and speakers in the United States. Because this knowledge is taken for granted rather than being explained when it is used, it forms a necessary foundation for the higher-order reading, writing, and thinking skills that children need for academic and vocational success. The universal attainment of such knowledge should be a central aim of curricula in our elementary schools, just as it is currently the aim in all world-class educational systems.

For reasons explained in the next section, making sure that all young children in the United States possess a core of shared knowledge is a necessary step in developing a first-rate educational system.

II. WHY CORE KNOWLEDGE IS NEEDED

Learning builds on learning: children (and adults) gain new knowledge only by building on what they already know. It is essential to begin building solid foundations of knowledge in the early grades when children are most receptive because, for the vast majority of children, academic deficiencies from the first six grades can *permanently* impair the success of later learning. Poor performance of American students in middle and high school can be traced to shortcomings inherited from elementary schools that have not imparted to children the knowledge and skills they need for further learning.

All of the highest-achieving and most egalitarian elementary school systems in the world (such as those in Sweden, France, and Japan) teach their children a specific core of knowledge in each of the first six grades, thus enabling all children to enter each new grade with a secure foundation for further learning. It is time American schools did so as well, for the following reasons:

(1) Commonly shared knowledge makes schooling more effective. We know that the one-on-one tutorial is the most effective form of schooling, in part because a parent or teacher can provide tailor-made instruction for the individual child. But in a nontutorial situation—in, for example, a typical classroom with twenty-five or more students—the instructor cannot effectively impart new knowledge to all the students unless each one shares the background knowledge that the lesson is being built upon.

Consider this scenario: in third grade, Ms. Franklin is about to begin a unit on early explorers: Columbus, Magellan, and others. In her class, she has some students who were in Mr. Washington's second-grade class last year and some students who were in Ms. Johnson's second-grade class. She also has a few students who moved in from other towns.

As Ms. Franklin begins the unit on explorers, she asks the children to look at a globe and use their fingers to trace a route across the Atlantic Ocean from Europe to North America. The students who had Mr. Washington look blankly at her: they didn't learn that last year. The students who had Ms. Johnson, however, eagerly point to the proper places on the globe, while two of the students who came from other towns pipe up and say, "Columbus and Magellan again? We did that last year."

When all the students in a class *do* share the relevant background knowledge, a classroom can begin to approach the effectiveness of a tutorial. Even when some children in a class do not have elements of the knowledge they were supposed to acquire in previous grades, the existence of a specifically defined core makes it possible for the teacher or parent to identify and fill the gaps, thus giving all students a chance to fulfill their potential in later grades.

(2) Commonly shared knowledge makes schooling more fair and democratic. When all the children who enter a grade can be assumed to share some of the same building blocks of knowledge, and when the teacher knows exactly what those building blocks are, then all the students are empowered to learn. In our current system, children from disadvantaged backgrounds too often suffer from unmerited low expectations that translate into watered-down curricula. But if we specify the core of knowledge that all children should share, then we can guarantee equal access to that knowledge and compensate for the academic advantages some students are offered at home. In a Core Knowledge school, *all* children enjoy the benefits of important, challenging knowledge that will provide the foundation for successful later learning.

(3) Commonly shared knowledge helps create cooperation and solidarity in our schools and nation. Diversity is a hallmark and strength of our nation. American classrooms are often, and increasingly, made up of students from a variety of cultural backgrounds, and those different cultures should be honored by all students. At the same time, education should create a *school-based* culture that is common and welcoming to all because it includes knowledge of many cultures and gives all students, no matter what their backgrounds, a common foundation for understanding our cultural diversity.

III. THE CONSENSUS BEHIND THE CORE KNOWLEDGE SEQUENCE

The content in this and other volumes in the Core Knowledge Series is based on a document called the *Core Knowledge Sequence*, a grade-by-grade sequence of specific content guidelines in history, geography, mathematics, science, language arts, and the fine arts. The *Sequence* is not meant to outline the whole of the school curriculum; rather, it offers specific guidelines to knowledge that can reasonably be expected to make up about *half* of any school's curriculum, or perhaps a little more, thus leaving ample room for local requirements and emphases. Teaching a common core of knowledge, such as that articulated in the *Core Knowledge Sequence,* is compatible with a variety of instructional methods and additional subject matters.

The *Core Knowledge Sequence* is the result of a long process of research and consensus-building undertaken by the Core Knowledge Foundation. Here is how we achieved the consensus behind the *Core Knowledge Sequence:*

First, we analyzed the many reports issued by state departments of education and by professional organizations—such as the National Council of Teachers of Mathematics and the American Association for the Advancement of Science—that recommend general outcomes for elementary and secondary education. We also tabulated the knowledge and skills through grade six specified in the successful educational systems of several other countries, including France, Japan, Sweden, and West Germany.

In addition, we formed an advisory board on multiculturalism that proposed a specific knowledge of diverse cultural traditions that American children should all share as part of their school-based common culture. We sent the resulting materials to three independent groups of teachers, scholars, and scientists around the country, asking them to create a master list of the knowledge children should have by the end of grade six. About 150 teachers (including college professors, scientists, and administrators) were involved in this initial step.

These items were amalgamated into a master plan, and further groups of teachers and specialists were asked to agree on a grade-by-grade sequence of the items. That sequence was then sent to some one hundred educators and specialists who participated in a national conference that was called to hammer out a working agreement on an appropriate core of knowledge for the first six grades.

This important meeting took place in March 1990. The conferees were elementary school teachers, curriculum specialists, scientists, science writers, officers of national organizations, representatives of ethnic groups, district superintendents, and school principals from across the country. A total of twenty-four working groups decided on revisions in the *Core Knowledge Sequence.* The resulting provisional *Sequence* was further fine-tuned during a year of implementation at a pioneering school, Three Oaks Elementary in Lee County, Florida.

In only a few years, many more schools—urban and rural, rich and poor, public and private—joined in the effort to teach Core Knowledge. Based largely on suggestions from these schools, the *Core Knowledge Sequence* has been significantly revised: it was extended to seventh and eighth grades; separate guidelines were added for kindergarten; and a few topics in other grades were added, omitted, or moved from one grade to another, in order to create an even more coherent sequence for learning. A *Core Knowledge Preschool Sequence* was first published in 1997.

The Core Knowledge Foundation continues to work with schools and advisors to "fine-tune" the *Sequence*. The revised editions of this and other books in the Core Knowledge Series reflect the revisions in the *Sequence*. Current editions of the *Core Knowledge Sequence* and the *Core Knowledge Preschool Sequence* may be ordered from the Core Knowledge Foundation.

IV. THE NATURE OF THIS SERIES

The books in this series are designed to give a convenient and engaging introduction to the knowledge specified in the *Core Knowledge Sequence*. These are resource books, addressed primarily to parents, but which we hope will be useful tools for teachers, too. These books are not intended to replace the local curriculum or school textbooks, but rather to serve as aids to help children gain some of the important knowledge they will need to make progress in school and be effective in society.

Although we have made these books as accessible and useful as we can, parents and teachers should understand that they are not the only means by which the *Core Knowledge Sequence* can be imparted. The books represent a single version of the possibilities inherent in the *Sequence*. We hope that publishers will be stimulated to offer educational videos, computer software, games, alternative books, and other imaginative vehicles based on the *Core Knowledge Sequence*.

These books are not textbooks or workbooks, though when appropriate they do suggest some activities you can do with your child. In these books, we address your child directly and occasionally ask questions to think about.

Although fifth graders should be able to read this book on their own, you may also wish to read some passages aloud. You and your child can read the sections of this book in any order, depending on your child's interests or depending on the topics your child is studying in school. You can skip from section to section and reread as much as your child likes.

We encourage you to think of this book as a guidebook that opens the way to many paths you and your child can explore. These paths may lead to the library, to many other good books, and, if possible, to plays, museums, concerts, and other opportunities for knowledge and enrichment. In short, this guidebook recommends places to visit and describes what is important in those places, but only you and your child can make the actual visit, travel the streets, and climb the steps.

V. WHAT YOU CAN DO TO HELP IMPROVE AMERICAN EDUCATION

The first step for parents and teachers who are committed to reform is to be skeptical about oversimplified slogans like "critical thinking" and "learning to learn." Such slogans are everywhere, and unfortunately for our schools, their partial insights have been elevated to the level of universal truths. For example: "What students learn is not important; rather, we must teach students to learn *how* to learn." "The child, not the academic subject, is the true focus of education." "Do not impose knowledge on children before they are developmentally ready to receive it." "Do not bog children down in mere facts, but rather, teach critical-thinking skills."

Who has not heard these sentiments, so admirable and humane, and—up to a point—so true? But these positive sentiments in favor of "thinking skills" and "higher understanding" have been turned into negative sentiments against the teaching of important knowledge. Those who have entered the teaching profession over the past forty years have been taught to scorn important knowledge as "mere facts" and to see the imparting of this knowledge as somehow injurious to children. Thus it has come about that many educators, armed with partially true slogans, have seemingly taken leave of common sense.

Many parents and teachers have come to the conclusion that elementary education must strike a better balance between the development of the whole child and the more limited but fundamental duty of the school to ensure that all children master a core of knowledge and skills essential to their competence as learners in later grades. But these parents and teachers cannot act on their convictions without an agreed-upon, concrete sequence of knowledge. Our main motivation in developing the *Core Knowledge Sequence* and this book series has been to give parents and teachers something concrete to work with.

It has been encouraging to see how many teachers have responded to the Core Knowledge reform effort. If you would like more information about the growing network of Core Knowledge schools, please call or write the Core Knowledge Foundation.

Parents and teachers are urged to join in a grass-roots effort to strengthen our elementary schools. Start in your own school and district. Insist that your school clearly state the core of *specific* knowledge and skills that each child in a grade must learn. Whether your school's core corresponds exactly to the Core Knowledge model is less important than the existence of *some* core—which, we hope, will be as solid, coherent, and challenging as the *Core Knowledge Sequence* has proven to be. Inform members of your community about the need for such a specific curriculum, and help make sure that your local school board members are independent-minded people who will insist that children have the benefit of a solid, specific, world-class curriculum in each grade.

Share the knowledge!

E. D. Hirsch, Jr., Chairman
Core Knowledge Foundation

What Your Fifth Grader Needs to Know

FUNDAMENTALS OF A GOOD FIFTH-GRADE EDUCATION

I.

Language and Literature

Introduction

This chapter presents poems, stories, and sayings, as well as brief discussions of language and literature.

The best way to introduce children to poetry is to read it to them and encourage them to speak it aloud so they can experience the music of the words. A child's knowledge of poetry should come first from pleasure and only later from analysis. However, by fifth grade, children are ready to begin learning a few basic terms and concepts, such as metaphor and simile. Such concepts can help children talk about particular effects that enliven the poems they like best.

The stories in this book are excerpts, abridgments, and adaptations of longer works. If a child enjoys a story, he or she should be encouraged to read the larger work. *Don Quixote* and stories about Sherlock Holmes are available in child-friendly versions as part of the Foundation's Core Classics series. You can draw children into stories by asking questions about them. For example, you might ask, "What do you think is going to happen next?" or "What might have happened if . . . ?" You might also ask the child to retell them. Don't be bothered if the child changes events: that is in the best tradition of storytelling and explains why we have so many different versions of traditional stories!

The treatments of grammar and writing in this book are brief overviews. Experts say that our children already know more about grammar than we can ever teach them. But standard written language does have special characteristics that children need to learn. In the classroom, grammar instruction is an essential part, but only a part, of an effective language arts program. Fifth graders should also have frequent opportunities to write and revise their writing—with encouragement and guidance along the way.

For some children, the section on sayings and phrases may not be needed; they will have picked up these sayings by hearing them in everyday speech. But this section will be very useful for children from homes where American English is not spoken.

For additional resources to use in conjunction with this section, visit the Foundation's Web site: www.coreknowledge.org.

POETRY

A Wise Old Owl
by Edward Hersey Richards

A wise old owl sat on an oak,
The more he saw the less he spoke;
The less he spoke the more he heard;
Why aren't we like that wise old bird?

The Eagle
by Alfred, Lord Tennyson

He clasps the crag with crooked hands;
Close to the sun in lonely lands,
Ring'd with the azure world, he stands.

The wrinkled sea beneath him crawls;
He watches from his mountain walls,
And like a thunderbolt he falls.

From **Opposites**
by Richard Wilbur

What is the opposite of *riot?*
It's *lots of people keeping quiet.*

. . .

What is the opposite of *two?*
A *lonely me, a lonely you.*

. . .

The opposite of *doughnut?* Wait
A minute while I meditate.
This isn't easy. Ah, I've found it!
A *cookie with a hole around it.*

. . .

The opposite of a *cloud* could be
A *white reflection in the sea,*
Or *a huge blueness in the air,*
Caused by a cloud's not being there.

. . .

The opposite of *opposite?*
That's much too difficult. I quit.

The Arrow and the Song
by Henry Wadsworth Longfellow

I shot an arrow into the air,
It fell to earth, I knew not where;
For, so swiftly it flew, the sight
Could not follow it in its flight.

I breathed a song into the air,
It fell to earth, I knew not where;
For who has sight so keen and strong,
That it can follow the flight of song?

Long, long afterward, in an oak
I found the arrow, still unbroke;
And the song, from beginning to end,
I found again in the heart of a friend.

The Road Not Taken
by Robert Frost

Two roads diverged in a yellow wood,
And sorry I could not travel both
And be one traveler, long I stood
And looked down one as far as I could
To where it bent in the undergrowth;

Then took the other, as just as fair,
And having perhaps the better claim,
Because it was grassy and wanted wear;
Though as for that the passing there
Had worn them really about the same,

And both that morning equally lay
In leaves no step had trodden black.
Oh, I kept the first for another day!
Yet knowing how way leads on to way,
I doubted if I should ever come back.

I shall be telling this with a sigh
Somewhere ages and ages hence:
Two roads diverged in a wood, and I—
I took the one less traveled by,
And that has made all the difference.

The Snow-storm
by Ralph Waldo Emerson

Announced by all the trumpets of the sky,
Arrives the snow, and, driving o'er the fields,
Seems nowhere to alight: the whited air
Hides hills and woods, the river, and the heaven,
And veils the farm-house at the garden's end.
The sled and traveller stopped, the courier's feet
Delayed, all friends shut out, the housemates sit
Around the radiant fireplace, enclosed
In a tumultuous privacy of storm.

Come see the north-wind's masonry.
Out of an unseen quarry evermore
Furnished with tile, the fierce artificer
Curves his white bastions with projected roof
Round every windward stake, or tree, or door.
Speeding, the myriad-handed, his wild work
So fanciful, so savage, naught cares he
For number or proportion. Mockingly,
On coop or kennel he hangs Parian wreaths;
A swan-like form invests the hidden thorn;
Fills up the farmer's lane from wall to wall,
Maugre the farmer's sighs; and at the gate,
A tapering turret overtops the work.
And when his hours are numbered, and the world
Is all his own, retiring, as he were not,
Leaves, when the sun appears, astonished Art
To mimic in slow structures, stone by stone,
Built in an age, the mad wind's night-work,
The frolic architecture of the snow.

I Hear America Singing

by Walt Whitman

I hear America singing, the varied carols I hear,
Those of mechanics, each one singing his as it should be
    blithe and strong,
The carpenter singing his as he measures his plank or beam,
The mason singing his as he makes ready for work,
    or leaves off work,
The boatman singing what belongs to him in his boat,
    the deck-hand singing on the steamboat deck,
The shoemaker singing as he sits on his bench,
    the hatter singing as he stands,
The wood-cutter's song, the ploughboy's on his way
    in the morning, or at noon intermission or at sundown,
The delicious singing of the mother, or of the young wife
    at work, or of the girl singing or washing,
Each singing what belongs to him or her and to none else,
The day what belongs to the day—at night
    the party of young fellows, robust, friendly,
Singing with open mouths their strong melodious songs.

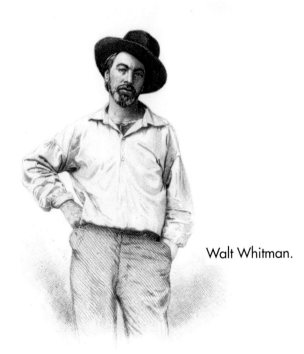

Walt Whitman.

I, Too
by Langston Hughes

I, too, sing America.

I am the darker brother.
They send me to eat in the kitchen
When company comes,
But I laugh,
And eat well,
And grow strong.

Tomorrow,
I'll be at the table
When company comes.
Nobody'll dare
Say to me,
"Eat in the kitchen,"
Then.

Besides,
They'll see how beautiful I am
And be ashamed—

I, too, am America.

Incident
by Countee Cullen

Once riding in old Baltimore,
    Heart-filled, head-filled with glee,
I saw a Baltimorean
    Keep looking straight at me.

Now I was eight and very small,
    And he was no whit bigger,
And so I smiled, but he stuck out
    His tongue, and called me, "Nigger."

I saw the whole of Baltimore
    From May until December;
Of all the things that happened there
    That's all that I remember.

Narcissa
by Gwendolyn Brooks

Some of the girls are playing jacks.
Some are playing ball.
But small Narcissa is not playing
Anything at all.

Small Narcissa sits upon
A brick in her back yard
And looks at tiger-lilies,
And shakes her pigtails hard.

First she is an ancient queen
In pomp and purple veil.
Soon she is a singing wind.
And, next, a nightingale.

How fine to be Narcissa,
A-changing like all that!
While sitting still, as still, as still
As anyone ever sat!

I like to see it lap the Miles—
by Emily Dickinson

I like to see it lap the Miles—
And lick the Valleys up—
And stop to feed itself at Tanks—
And then—prodigious, step

Around a Pile of Mountains—
And supercilious peer
In Shanties—by the sides of Roads—
And then a Quarry pare

To fit its Ribs
And crawl between
Complaining all the while
In horrid—hooting stanza—
Then chase itself down Hill—

And neigh like Boanerges—
Then—punctual as a Star—
Stop—docile and omnipotent
At its own stable door—

A Bird came down the Walk—

by Emily Dickinson

A Bird came down the Walk—
He did not know I saw—
He bit an Angleworm in halves
And ate the fellow, raw,

And then he drank a Dew
From a convenient Grass—
And then hopped sidewise to the Wall
To let a Beetle pass—

He glanced with rapid eyes
That hurried all around—
They looked like frightened Beads, I thought—
He stirred his Velvet Head

Like one in danger, Cautious,
I offered him a Crumb
And he unrolled his feathers
And rowed him softer home—

Than Oars divide the Ocean,
Too silver for a seam—
Or Butterflies, off Banks of Noon
Leap, plashless as they swim.

The Tyger
by William Blake

Tyger Tyger, burning bright,
In the forests of the night;
What immortal hand or eye,
Could frame thy fearful symmetry?

In what distant deeps or skies
Burnt the fire of thine eyes?
On what wings dare he aspire?
What the hand, dare seize the fire?

And what shoulder, & what art,
Could twist the sinews of thy heart?
And when thy heart began to beat,
What dread hand? & what dread feet?

What the hammer? what the chain?
In what furnace was thy brain?
What the anvil? what dread grasp,
Dare its deadly terrors clasp!

When the stars threw down their spears
And water'd heaven with their tears:
Did he smile his work to see?
Did he who made the Lamb make thee?

Tyger Tyger burning bright,
In the forests of the night;
What immortal hand or eye,
Dare frame thy fearful symmetry?

A Poison Tree
by William Blake

I was angry with my friend;
I told my wrath, my wrath did end.
I was angry with my foe:
I told it not, my wrath did grow.

And I waterd it in fears,
Night & morning with my tears:
And I sunned it with smiles,
And with soft deceitful wiles.

And it grew both day and night.
Till it bore an apple bright.
And my foe beheld it shine,
And he knew that it was mine.

And into my garden stole,
When the night had veild the pole;
In the morning glad I see;
My foe outstretched beneath the tree.

Barbara Frietchie
by John Greenleaf Whittier

Up from the meadows rich with corn,
Clear in the cool September morn,

The clustered spires of Frederick stand
Green-walled by the hills of Maryland.

Round about them orchards sweep,
Apple- and peach-tree fruited deep,

Fair as the garden of the Lord
To the eyes of the famished rebel horde,

On that pleasant morn of the early fall
When Lee marched over the mountain wall,—

Over the mountains winding down,
Horse and foot, into Frederick town.

Forty flags with their silver stars,
Forty flags with their crimson bars,

Flapped in the morning wind: the sun
Of noon looked down, and saw not one.

Up rose old Barbara Frietchie then,
Bowed with her fourscore years and ten;

Bravest of all in Frederick town,
She took up the flag the men hauled down;

In her attic-window the staff she set,
To show that one heart was loyal yet.

Up the street came the rebel tread,
Stonewall Jackson riding ahead.

Under his slouched hat left and right
He glanced: the old flag met his sight.

"Halt!"—the dust-brown ranks stood fast.
"Fire!"—out blazed the rifle-blast.

It shivered the window, pane and sash;
It rent the banner with seam and gash.

Quick, as it fell, from the broken staff
Dame Barbara snatched the silken scarf;

She leaned far out on the window-sill,
And shook it forth with a royal will.

"Shoot, if you must, this old gray head,
But spare your country's flag," she said.

A shade of sadness, a blush of shame,
Over the face of the leader came;

The nobler nature within him stirred
To life at that woman's deed and word:

"Who touches a hair of yon gray head
Dies like a dog! March on!" he said.

All day long through Frederick street
Sounded the tread of marching feet:

All day long that free flag tost
Over the heads of the rebel host.

Ever its torn fields rose and fell
On the loyal winds that loved it well;

And through the hill-gaps sunset light
Shone over it with a warm good-night.

Barbara Frietchie's work is o'er,
And the Rebel rides on his raids no more.

Honor to her! and let a tear
Fall, for her sake, on Stonewall's bier.

Over Barbara Frietchie's grave
Flag of Freedom and Union, wave!

Peace and order and beauty draw
Round thy symbol of light and law;

And ever the stars above look down
On thy stars below in Frederick town!

O Captain! My Captain!
by Walt Whitman

O Captain! my Captain! our fearful trip is done,
The ship has weather'd every rack, the prize we sought is won,
The port is near, the bells I hear, the people all exulting,
While follow eyes the steady keel, the vessel grim and daring;
But O heart! heart! heart!
O the bleeding drops of red,
Where on the deck my Captain lies,
Fallen cold and dead.

O Captain! my Captain! rise up and hear the bells;
Rise up—for you the flag is flung—for you the bugle trills,
For you bouquets and ribbon'd wreaths—for you the shores a-crowding,
For you they call, the swaying mass, their eager faces turning;
Here, Captain! dear father!
This arm beneath your head!
It is some dream that on the deck,
You've fallen cold and dead.

My Captain does not answer, his lips are pale and still,
My father does not feel my arm, he has no pulse nor will,
The ship is anchor'd safe and sound, its voyage closed and done,
From fearful trip the victor ship comes in with object won;
Exult, O shores! and ring, O bells!
But I with mournful tread,
Walk the deck my Captain lies,
Fallen cold and dead.

Casey at the Bat
by Ernest Lawrence Thayer

The outlook wasn't brilliant for the Mudville nine that day;
The score stood four to two with but one inning more to play.
And then when Cooney died at first, and Barrows did the same,
A sickly silence fell upon the patrons of the game.

A straggling few got up to go in deep despair. The rest
Clung to that hope which springs eternal in the human breast;
They thought if only Casey could but get a whack at that—
We'd put up even money now with Casey at the bat.

But Flynn preceded Casey, as did also Jimmy Blake,
And the former was a lulu and the latter was a cake;
So upon that stricken multitude grim melancholy sat,
For there seemed but little chance of Casey's getting to the bat.

But Flynn let drive a single, to the wonderment of all,
And Blake, the much despis-ed, tore the cover off the ball;
And when the dust had lifted, and the men saw what had occurred,
There was Johnny safe at second and Flynn a-hugging third.

Then from 5,000 throats and more there rose a lusty yell;
It rumbled through the valley, it rattled in the dell;
It knocked upon the mountain and recoiled upon the flat,
For Casey, mighty Casey, was advancing to the bat.

There was ease in Casey's manner as he stepped into his place;
There was pride in Casey's bearing and a smile on Casey's face.
And when, responding to the cheers, he lightly doffed his hat,
No stranger in the crowd could doubt 'twas Casey at the bat.

Ten thousand eyes were on him as he rubbed his hands with dirt;
Five thousand tongues applauded when he wiped them on his shirt.
Then while the writhing pitcher ground the ball into his hip,
Defiance gleamed in Casey's eye, a sneer curled Casey's lip.

And now the leather-covered sphere came hurtling through the air,
And Casey stood a-watching it in haughty grandeur there.
Close by the sturdy batsman the ball unheeded sped—
"That ain't my style," said Casey. "Strike one," the umpire said.

From the benches, black with people, there went up a muffled roar,
Like the beating of the storm-waves on a stern and distant shore.
"Kill him! Kill the umpire!" shouted some one on the stand;
And it's likely they'd have killed him had not Casey raised his hand.

With a smile of Christian charity great Casey's visage shone;
He stilled the rising tumult; he bade the game go on;
He signaled to the pitcher, and once more the spheroid flew;
But Casey still ignored it, and the umpire said, "Strike two."

"Fraud!" cried the maddened thousands, and echo answered fraud;
But one scornful look from Casey and the audience was awed.
They saw his face grow stern and cold, they saw his muscles strain,
And they knew that Casey wouldn't let that ball go by again.

The sneer is gone from Casey's lip, his teeth are clenched in hate;
He pounds with cruel violence his bat upon the plate.
And now the pitcher holds the ball, and now he lets it go,
And now the air is shattered by the force of Casey's blow.

Oh, somewhere in this favored land the sun is shining bright;
The band is playing somewhere, and somewhere hearts are light,
And somewhere men are laughing, and somewhere children shout;
But there is no joy in Mudville—mighty Casey has struck out.

Jabberwocky
by Lewis Carroll

'Twas brillig, and the slithy toves
    Did gyre and gimble in the wabe:
All mimsy were the borogoves,
    And the mome raths outgrabe.

"Beware the Jabberwock, my son!
    The jaws that bite, the claws that catch!
Beware the Jubjub bird, and shun
    The frumious Bandersnatch!"

He took his vorpal sword in hand:
    Long time the manxome foe he sought—
So rested he by the Tumtum tree,
    And stood awhile in thought.

And as in uffish thought he stood,
    The Jabberwock, with eyes of flame,
Came whiffling through the tulgey wood,
    And burbled as it came!

One, two! One, two! And through and through
    The vorpal blade went snicker-snack!
He left it dead, and with its head
    He went galumphing back.

"And hast thou slain the Jabberwock?
    Come to my arms, my beamish boy!
O frabjous day! Callooh! Callay!"
    He chortled in his joy.

'Twas brillig, and the slithy toves
    Did gyre and gimble in the wabe:
All mimsy were the borogoves,
    And the mome raths outgrabe.

STORIES, MYTHS, AND LEGENDS

The Adventures of Tom Sawyer

Mark Twain was the pen name, or pseudonym, of Samuel Clemens. Born in Missouri in 1835, Clemens worked as a Mississippi riverboat pilot, a journalist, and, finally, a novelist. He took his pen name from his days on the river. Twain means "two." Riverboat pilots would call out "Mark twain!" when a rope dropped overboard indicated that the water was two fathoms deep—deep enough for the boat to proceed.

Saturday morning was come, and the summer world was bright and fresh, brimming with life. There was a song in every heart and a spring in every step.

Tom Sawyer appeared on the sidewalk with a bucket of whitewash and a long-handled brush. He surveyed the fence, and all gladness left him and a deep melancholy settled down upon his spirit. He had been caught sneaking in late last evening, and Aunt Polly was punishing him by turning his Saturday into hard labor, whitewashing thirty yards of board fence nine feet high. Sighing, he dipped his brush and passed it along the topmost plank. Then he compared the whitewashed streak with the rest of the fence, and sat down discouraged.

Soon the free boys would come tripping along on all sorts of delicious expeditions, and they would make a world of fun of him for having to work—the very thought of it burnt him like fire. At this dark and hopeless moment an inspiration burst upon him! He took up his brush and tranquilly went to work.

Ben Rogers hove in sight presently—the very boy whose ridicule he had been dreading. Tom went on whitewashing. Ben stared a moment, then said:

"Hello, old chap, you got to work, hey?"

Tom wheeled and said: "Why, it's you, Ben! I warn't noticing."

"*I'm* going in a-swimming, *I* am. But of course you'd druther *work*—wouldn't you?"

Tom contemplated the boy a bit, and said: "What do you call work?"

"Why, ain't that work?"

Tom resumed his whitewashing, and answered carelessly: "Well, maybe it is and maybe it ain't. All I know is, it suits Tom Sawyer."

"Oh come, you don't mean to let on that you *like* it?"

"Well, I don't see why I oughtn't to like it. Does a boy get a chance to whitewash a fence every day?"

That put the thing in a new light. Tom swept his brush daintily back and forth, stepped back to note the effect, and added a touch here and there. Ben watched every move, more and more absorbed. Presently he said:

"Say, Tom, let *me* whitewash a while."

"No—no—I reckon it wouldn't hardly do, Ben. You see, Aunt Polly's awful particular about this fence. I reckon there ain't one boy in a thousand, maybe two thousand, that can do it the way it's got to be done."

"Oh come, now—lemme just try. Only just a little. I'll give you my apple!"

Tom gave up the brush with reluctance in his face, but alacrity in his heart. And while Ben worked and sweated in the sun, Tom sat on a barrel in the shade, dangled his legs, and munched his apple.

Boys happened along every little while; they came to jeer, but remained to whitewash. By the time Ben was tired out, Tom had traded the next chance to Billy Fisher for a kite. Johnny Miller bought in for a dead rat and a string to swing it with. By the middle of the afternoon, Tom was rolling in wealth. He had twelve marbles, a fragment of chalk, a tin soldier, a couple of tadpoles, six firecrackers, a kitten with only one eye, and a dog collar—but no dog. If he hadn't run out of whitewash, he would have bankrupted every boy in the village.

Tom had discovered a great law of human action, without knowing it—namely, that in order to make a man or boy covet a thing, it is only necessary to make the thing difficult to attain.

Don Quixote

The novel Don Quixote (DON key-HOH-tay) was written during the Renaissance by the Spanish writer Miguel de Cervantes. The main character, Don Quixote, is a man with a fantastic imagination, who confuses his own experiences with the adventures of a bold and brave knight. Today, if a person believes in things most people view as impossible, we say the person is "quixotic" (kwik-SOT-ic].

Once upon a time, in a village in La Mancha, there lived a lean, thin-faced old gentleman whose favorite pastime was to read books about knights in armor. He loved to read about their daring exploits, strange adventures, bold rescues of damsels in distress, and intense devotion to their ladies. In fact, he became so caught up in the subject of chivalry that he neglected every other interest and even sold many acres of good farmland so that he might buy all the books he could get on the subject. He would lie awake at night, absorbed in every detail of these fantastic adventures. He often argued with the village priest or the barber over who was the greatest knight of all time. Was it Amadis of Gaul or Palmerin of England? Or was it perhaps the Knight of the Sun?

As time went on, the old gentleman crammed his head so full of these stories and lost so much sleep from reading through the night that he lost his wits completely. He began to believe that all the fantastic tales he read about enchantments, challenges, battles, wounds, and wooings were true histories. At last he resolved to become a knight errant himself, to travel through the world in search of adventures.

First he got out some rust-eaten armor that had belonged to his ancestors, then cleaned and repaired it as best he could. Although the head-piece of the helmet was intact, unfortunately, the visor that would have protected his face was gone. Not to be discouraged, he fashioned another out of some pieces of stiff paper and strips of iron. In his eyes it was the most splendid helmet ever fashioned.

Next he considered what glorious, high-sounding name he might give his horse, who was to bear him on his quest. For though his horse was but a tired hack, practically skin and bones, to him it appeared as magnificent as Bucephalus, the horse of Alexander the Great. After four days of inventing and rejecting various names, he at last settled on Rocinante, which he thought sounded suitably grand.

He then set about to choose a suitable name for himself. After eight days of hard consideration, he decided that he would be known as Don Quixote. Following the example of many knights he admired, he decided to proclaim his native land as well, and so he called himself Don Quixote de la Mancha.

Now he needed to find a lady whom he might adore and serve, for a knight without a lady is like a body without a soul. In a neighboring village there lived a nice-looking farm girl whom he had admired from a distance. He decided that she would be the lady of his fancy, and that she should be known as Dulcinea del Toboso, a name that to his ears sounded musical and anything but ordinary.

With all these preparations made, Don Quixote was eager to sally forth. A whole world awaited, full of injustices to be made right, and great deeds to be performed. So, clad in his rusty armor, with his improvised helmet tied to his head, Don Quixote mounted Rocinante and started out through the back of the stable yard.

But then he had a terrible thought: he had not yet been dubbed a knight! He took comfort, however, in his memory of the many books of chivalry he had read, and determined that, like many of the heroes in those books, he would simply have himself knighted by the first person that came along. So he rode on until at nightfall he came upon a simple country inn.

Everything that Don Quixote saw, or thought he saw, came out of the fantastic books he had read; so, when he neared the inn, he saw not a plain inn but a gleaming castle, with turrets thrusting to the sky, and a drawbridge and a moat. He reined in Rocinante and awaited the blast of a trumpet to signal his arrival, for that is what always happened in the books he read. But no trumpet sounded. Just as he was getting impatient, a swineherd came along with a bunch of grunting hogs, which he called together by blowing his horn. With great satisfaction, Don Quixote took this to be the signal he awaited, and rode forth.

The innkeeper, in Don Quixote's eyes, was certainly the keeper of the castle. Don Quixote dismounted and told the innkeeper to take special care of his steed, which was surely the finest horse in the world. The innkeeper looked doubtfully at the bony hack, but decided to humor his guest.

As Don Quixote had not eaten all day, he requested some food. The innkeeper served him a meal of badly cooked fish and moldy bread, but Don Quixote remained firm in his belief that this was a brilliant castle, and the food a gourmet feast.

When the meal was over, Don Quixote dropped to his knees before the surprised innkeeper. "Never," he said, "shall I rise from here until you have consented to grant me the favor I ask, which will bring you great praise and benefit all mankind. I ask that you dub me a knight." The innkeeper obliged the Don by whacking him on the shoulder with a sword and mumbling a few words.

The next day, Don Quixote, joyous in having been quite officially made a knight, set forth. His destination was his own village, for he planned to return home for some money and clean clothes (details which had been overlooked in all the books about knights and their adventures). And he planned to find a good man who could serve as his squire.

He set about with all his powers of persuasion to convince a laborer, whose name was Sancho Panza, to accompany him. At last, with the promise that Don Quixote would someday make him governor of his very own island, the country bumpkin agreed to leave his wife and children and follow the knight. The tall, lean knight sat upon bony Rocinante, while the plump Sancho Panza climbed astride his donkey named Dapple, a leather wine bottle and well-stocked saddlebags at his side. And so this unlikely pair set off in search of adventures.

As they crossed the plain of Montiel, they spied dozens of windmills. "Fortune has smiled on us," said Don Quixote to his squire. "Yonder stand more than thirty terrible giants. I will fight them and kill them all, and we shall make ourselves rich with the spoils."

"What giants?" asked Sancho Panza.

"Those giants there, with the long arms," said the knight.

"Be careful, sir," said the squire. "Those are not giants, but windmills, and what seem to be their arms are the sails that turn the millstone."

"If you are afraid of them, then go say your prayers," said Don Quixote. "But I shall engage them in battle." Immediately he spurred his horse forward, and, paying no attention to Sancho Panza's shouted warnings, he cried, "Do not run, you cowards, for a lone knight assails you!" Just then a slight wind caused the windmills to begin turning. "I fear you not, though you have more arms than the giant Briareus," cried the knight. Covering himself with his shield, and thrusting forth his lance, he spurred Rocinante toward the nearest windmill. His lance pierced one of the whirling sails, which immediately wrenched it with such force that the horse was dragged along and the knight sent rolling across the ground. He lay without moving as Sancho Panza trotted to his side.

"Oh dear," said Sancho, "didn't I warn your worship to watch what you were doing when attacking those windmills?"

"I believe," replied the knight, "that some evil enchanter turned those giants into windmills to rob me of a glorious victory."

"As God wills," said Sancho, helping the knight to his feet. They climbed upon Rocinante and Dapple once more, and continued on their way.

Just as Don Quixote desired, he and Sancho Panza encountered many dangerous and unusual adventures, for so often did the knight mistake shepherds, holy men, and peasant girls for miscreant knights, evil enchanters, and ladies in distress, that he was continually involved in ridiculous quarrels and brawls. No matter how frantically Sancho urged him to see things as they really were, Don Quixote paid no attention to him. But although these absurd encounters were matters of great seriousness to the knight, many who witnessed them were delighted and amused.

Gradually his exploits became known all over the countryside, and there were few who had not heard of that flower of chivalry, Don Quixote de la Mancha.

Little Women

Louisa May Alcott's novel Little Women *introduces us to the March family—the sisters Meg, Jo, Beth, and Amy, and their parents. At the beginning of the novel, Mr. March is away, serving as a chaplain with the Union army during the Civil War. The girls meet their young neighbor, a boy named Laurie, with whom they become fast friends.*

"Where are you going?" Amy asked Jo and Meg, when she found them getting ready to go out. There was an air of secrecy about them that excited her curiosity.

"Never mind," returned Jo sharply.

Amy bridled at this, and determined to find out the secret. Turning to Meg, she said coaxingly, "Do tell me! Oh, wherever you're going, you might let me go, too."

Meg told Amy she wasn't invited, and Jo added impatiently, "You can't go, Amy, so don't whine about it."

"You are going somewhere with Laurie, I know you are. Aren't you going with him?"

"Yes, we are. Now stop bothering us," said Jo.

"I know! I know! You're going to the theater!" she cried. "Let me go, too!"

Meg reminded Amy that she was still recovering from a cold and couldn't risk going out in the winter weather. But Amy begged even more passionately.

Meg started to give in: "I don't believe Mother would mind," she said to Jo, "if we bundle her up well."

But Jo was having none of it. "If she goes I won't, and if I don't, Laurie won't like it, and it will be very rude, after he invited only us, to drag in Amy. I should think she'd hate to poke herself where she isn't wanted," she said crossly.

Jo's tone and manner angered Amy, and she began to cry.

The older girls hurried downstairs, leaving their sister wailing. Amy called

over the banister in a threatening tone, "You'll be sorry for this, Jo March, see if you aren't."

"Fiddlesticks!" returned Jo, slamming the door.

Meg and Jo and Laurie had a charming time at the theater. The play they saw was as brilliant and wonderful as any heart could wish, but in spite of the sparkling elves and gorgeous princes and princesses, Jo's pleasure had a drop of bitterness in it. The fairy queen's yellow curls reminded her of Amy, and between the acts she found herself wondering what her sister would do to make her "sorry for this." She and Amy had had many lively skirmishes in the course of their lives, for both had quick tempers. Although she was the oldest, Jo had the least self-control, and had a hard time curbing her fiery spirit. But her anger never lasted long, and her repentance was always sincere. Poor Jo tried desperately to be good, but her temper was always ready to flame up and defeat her.

When they got home, they found Amy reading in the parlor. She assumed an injured air as they came in and never lifted her eyes from her book. Jo went straight to her bureau, for in their last quarrel Amy had turned Jo's top drawer upside down on the floor. Tonight, though, everything was in its place, and Jo decided that Amy had forgiven her.

There Jo was mistaken, for next day she made a discovery that produced a tempest. Jo burst into the living room, looking excited, and demanded, "Has anyone taken my book?"

Meg and Beth said, "No" at once, and looked surprised. Amy poked the fire and said nothing.

"Amy, you've got it!" cried Jo.

"No, I haven't."

"You know where it is, then!"

"No, I don't."

"That's a fib!" cried Jo, taking her by the shoulders and looking fierce. "You know something, and you'd better tell at once."

"You'll never see your silly old book again," cried Amy, getting excited in her turn. "I burned it up."

"What! My little book I was so fond of, and worked over, and meant to finish before Father got home? You really burned it?" said Jo, turning very pale.

"Yes, I did! I told you I'd make you pay for yesterday, and I have."

Jo's hot temper got the best of her, and she shook Amy, crying, "You wicked girl! I'll never forgive you as long as I live."

Then Jo stormed out of the room.

Soon Mrs. March came home, and, having heard the story, gradually brought Amy to a sense of the wrong she had done her sister. Jo's book was the pride of her heart. It was only half a dozen little fairy tales, but Jo had worked over them patiently, putting her whole heart into her work, hoping to make something good enough to print. Amy's bonfire had consumed the loving work of several years. It seemed a small loss to others, but Jo felt that it never could be made up to her.

At length Amy realized that she had done wrong and would have to apologize.

When the tea bell rang, Jo appeared, looking so grim and unapproachable that it took all Amy's courage to say meekly, "Please forgive me, Jo. I'm very, very sorry."

"I will never forgive you," was Jo's stern answer, and she ignored Amy entirely for the rest of the day.

When Mrs. March gave Jo her good-night kiss, she whispered gently, "My dear, don't let the sun go down upon your anger. Forgive your sister and begin again tomorrow."

Jo felt so deeply injured that she couldn't quite forgive yet. Because she knew Amy was listening, she said, "She doesn't deserve to be forgiven." Then she marched off to bed, and there was no merry or confidential gossip among the sisters that night.

It was bitter cold in the morning and Jo still looked like a thundercloud. "Everybody is so hateful," she said to herself. "I'll ask Laurie to go skating. He is always kind and jolly." And off she went.

Amy heard the clash of skates and exclaimed: "She promised I could go next time, for this is the last ice we shall have!"

"You were very naughty," Meg answered her, "but I think she might do it, if you try her now. Go after them. Don't say anything till Jo has got good natured with Laurie, then take a quiet minute and just kiss her, or do some kind thing, and I'm sure she'll be friends again."

"I'll try," said Amy, and after a flurry to get ready, she ran after Jo and Laurie.

They were already skating by the time Amy caught up with them. Jo saw her coming, and turned her back on purpose. Laurie did not see, for he was carefully skating along the shore, testing the ice. There had been a warm spell a few days earlier and he wanted to make sure the ice would bear the weight of the skaters.

Jo heard Amy behind her, trying to put her skates on, but she never turned around, for her anger had grown strong and taken possession of her, like a demon.

Laurie shouted, "Keep near the shore. It isn't safe in the middle."

Jo heard, but Amy did not catch a word. Jo glanced over her shoulder, and the little demon she was harboring said in her ear, "Let her take care of herself!"

Laurie had vanished round the bend. Jo was just at the turn, and Amy, far behind, was striking out toward the smoother ice in the middle of the river. For a minute Jo stopped skating, with a strange feeling in her heart. Something turned her round just in time to see Amy throw up her hands and go down. The sudden crash of rotten ice and Amy's cry made Jo's heart stand still with fear. For a second, she could only stand motionless, staring with a terror-stricken face at the little blue hood floating above the black water. Something rushed swiftly by her, and Laurie's voice cried out.

"Bring a rail. Quick, quick!"

For the next few minutes Jo obeyed Laurie blindly. He was quite self-possessed. Lying flat on the ice, he held Amy up till Jo dragged a rail from the fence, and together they got the child out of the freezing water, more frightened than hurt.

"Now pile some clothing on her," Laurie said.

Shivering, dripping, and crying, Amy was hurried home, where she fell asleep under a blanket and in front of a hot fire. Jo's dress was torn, and her hands cut and bruised by ice and rails. When Amy was finally asleep, Mrs. March began to bandage Jo's hurt hands.

"Are you sure she is safe?" whispered Jo.

"Quite safe, dear. She is not hurt, and won't even take cold, I think. You were sensible to cover her and get her home so quickly."

"Mother, if she should die, it would be my fault!" Jo broke out sobbing. "It's my dreadful temper! I try to cure it, I think I have, and then it breaks out worse than ever. Oh, Mother, what shall I do?"

"You must never get tired of trying, Dear, and never think it is impossible to conquer your fault." She kissed her daughter's cheek so tenderly that Jo cried even harder.

"Oh, Mother, you don't know, you can't guess how bad it is! It seems as if I could do anything when I'm in a passion."

"Jo, dear, we all have our temptations, and it often takes us all our lives to conquer them. You think your temper is the worst in the world, but mine used to be just like it."

"Yours, Mother? Why, you are never angry!"

"I've been trying to cure it for forty years, and have only succeeded in controlling it. I am angry nearly every day of my life, Jo, but I have learned not to show it, and I still hope to learn not to feel it."

The patience and the humility of her mother's face was a better lesson to Jo than the sharpest reproof. She felt comforted, too, knowing that her mother had a fault like her own, and tried to mend it. It strengthened her resolution to cure it.

"Oh, Mother, if I'm ever half as good as you, I shall be satisfied," cried Jo.

Narrative of the Life of Frederick Douglass

Frederick Douglass was born a slave in Maryland in 1817. In the South before the Civil War, it was against the law for a slave to learn to read and write. But a few, like Douglass, managed to learn. When Douglass was twenty-one, he escaped and made his way to Massachusetts, where he began making powerful speeches against slavery. In 1845, he wrote an autobiography from which this selection is adapted.

From the time that I was very young, I knew that I would not remain a slave for the whole of my life. I was born in Tuckahoe, Maryland. Like most of those who were born into slavery, I have no knowledge of the year I was born, as masters did not like to provide slaves with any such information. Some people have told me that my father was my white slave owner. This was a common practice, as it increased the owner's slave holdings, but it boded ill for the child. My mother was traded to another plantation early on, and I only saw her a few times in my life, and then only at night.

As a young man I learned to sing slave songs. Every tone of these songs was a prayer to God for deliverance from chains. I have been utterly astonished to hear that people in the North often mistake that singing for happiness. A slave's songs represent the sorrows in his heart, and he finds relief through them as if they were tears.

I have been owned and leased by several masters in my life and worked as a house servant, a field hand (the most cruel of

Frederick Douglass.

labors), and a ship carpenter. When I was twelve or so, I was leased to my master's relative. For a time, my mistress taught me my ABCs, and would have gone further had her husband not forbidden it. He thought that education would make a slave unruly and discontented. He was right: the more I learned, the more determined I was to be free. I carried books with me whenever I was sent on an errand, and traded bread for reading lessons from the little white boys playing in the street. When my master's son left school, I secretly copied the handwriting in his practice book, and then challenged the street boys to handwriting competitions. I learned to read and write in the only way possible for a slave: I stole the knowledge.

At sixteen, I was leased to a Mr. Covey, an overseer with a reputation of breaking untamed slaves. I lived with Mr. Covey for one year. During the first six months, hardly a week passed without his whipping me. I was seldom free from a sore back. I was somewhat unmanageable when I first went there, but a few months of his discipline tamed me.

Then came the turning point in my life as a slave. One morning, Mr. Covey met me with a rope, intent on punishment. For the first time in my life, I resisted. I tossed him to the ground and fought. When he saw that I meant to persist, he walked off and my long-crushed spirit rose. From then on, I let it be known of me that the white man who succeeded in whipping me must also succeed in killing me. I had several more fights, but I was never beaten again, though I remained a slave for four more years.

After one failed attempt, I finally succeeded in escaping in 1838. I settled in New Bedford with my wife (who was already free), where I have lived with a pleasure never known before. Here, people are far wealthier than any plantation owner—they are rich with freedom. Until I die, I will strive for the abolition of slavery and the freedom of all my brethren.

The Secret Garden

Frances Hodgson Burnett's novel The Secret Garden *tells the story of a young orphan girl named Mary Lennox who is sent from India to England to live with relatives. At first, Martha, the housemaid, and Ben Weatherstaff, the gardener, are her only acquaintances. But eventually she discovers a mysterious secret garden and a charming new friend.*

When Mary Lennox arrived in England, everyone agreed she was as sour and cross and contrary a girl as they had ever known. Nothing pleased her, and she would do nothing for herself.

The day she arrived, she asked her nurse, Martha, "Who is going to dress me?"

Martha stared. "Can't you put on your own clothes?"

"No," answered Mary, quite indignantly. "I never did in my life. My nurse dressed me, of course."

"Well," said Martha, "it's time tha' should learn. It'll do thee good to wait on thyself a bit."

At first Mary sat inside all the time, moping. Then, one foggy day, Martha said, "You wrap up warm an' run out an' play you. It'll do you good."

"Out?" Mary replied in her contrary fashion, "Why should I go out on a day like this?" But eventually she went out just the same.

While she was outside, a wonderful thing happened. She heard a soft little rushing flight through the air. A bird with a bright red breast landed on the ground near her and burst into song. She stopped and listened to him and somehow his cheerful, friendly little whistle gave her a pleased feeling. The bright-breasted little bird brought a look into her sour little face that was almost a smile.

Mary went a step nearer to the robin and looked at him very hard. She thought his black dewdrop eyes gazed at her with great curiosity.

"I'm lonely," she said.

She had not known before that this was one of the things that made her feel sour and cross. She seemed to find it out when the robin looked at her and she looked at the robin.

Just that moment the robin gave a little shake of his wings and flew away towards a garden that was surrounded by an ivy-covered wall and seemed to have no door.

"He has flown over the wall!" Mary cried out, watching him. "He has flown into the garden!"

"He lives there," said old Ben the gardener, "among th' old rose-trees there."

"I should like to see them," said Mary. "There must be a door somewhere."

Ben drove his spade deep and said, "There was ten year' ago, but there isn't now. None as any one can find—an' none as is any one's business. Don't you be a meddlesome wench an' poke your nose where it's no cause to go."

The robin sang loudly. "It's in the garden no one can go into," Mary said to herself. "It's in the garden without a door. He lives in there. How I wish I could see what it is like!"

After a few days Mary went out into the gardens again. Ben Weatherstaff caught sight of her and called out, "Springtime's comin'! Cannot tha' smell it?"

Mary sniffed the air and said, "I smell something nice and fresh and damp."

"That's th' good rich earth," he answered. "It's in a good humor makin' ready to grow things. In th' flower gardens out there things will be stirrin' down below in th' dark. Th' sun's warmin' 'em."

As they talked, the robin that lived in the locked garden flew to them. Mary asked, "Are things stirring down below in the garden where the robin lives?"

"Ask him," said Ben Weatherstaff. "He's the only one as knows. No one else has been inside it for ten years."

Ten years was a long time, Mary thought. She had been born ten years ago.

The robin let her come very close as he scratched for worms. After a few moments Mary saw that the robin's scratching had made a hole, and that in the newly turned soil lay a piece of rusty metal. She knelt to pick it up, and found a key.

"Perhaps it has been buried for ten years," she said in a whisper. "Perhaps it is the key to the garden!"

She walked to the wall and looked at the ivy growing on it. She could not find a door beneath the dark green leaves. She made up her mind to keep the key with her always, so that if she ever found the door she would be ready.

In the morning, as Mary skipped all around the garden, the robin appeared again and she followed him down the walk with little skips.

"You showed me where the key was yesterday," she said. "You ought to show me the door today; but I don't believe you know!"

Mary had heard a great deal about magic in stories, and she always said that what happened at that moment was magic.

A gust of wind swept down the walk and swung aside some loose ivy. Mary jumped forward and caught it, because underneath she saw the round knob of a door and a rectangular key plate. Her heart began to thump and her hands to shake a little. The robin sang and twittered as if he, too, were excited. It was the door that had been closed for ten years. Mary drew out the key from her pocket, put it in the lock, and turned it. She took a deep breath and looked to see if anyone was coming. No one was, so she pushed back the door, which opened very slowly.

Then she slipped through it, and shut it behind her, and stood with her back against it, looking about her and breathing quite fast with excitement, and wonder, and delight.

She was standing *inside* the secret garden.

It was the most mysterious-looking place anyone could imagine. The high walls that shut it in were covered with the leafless stems of climbing roses. All the ground was covered with grass of a wintry brown and out of it grew clumps of bushes that were surely rose bushes if they were alive. There were other trees in the garden, and climbing roses had run all over them and swung down long tendrils which made light swaying curtains. Mary did not know whether they were dead or alive, but their thin gray branches looked like a sort of hazy mantle spreading over everything. This hazy tangle from tree to tree made it all look so mysterious. It was different from any other place Mary had ever seen in her life.

"It isn't quite dead," she cried out softly to

herself. "Some of these roses may be alive. Oh! I can't tell; but so many other things are alive."

She did not know anything about gardening, but it looked to her as if the small green plants she saw poking through the dirt needed to breathe. She searched about until she found a rather sharp piece of wood and knelt down and dug and weeded until she had made little clear places around all the plants. She went from place to place, digging and weeding, until it was past the time for dinner. She had been actually happy the whole time.

For the next week the sun shone on what Mary now called the Secret Garden. It seemed like a fairy place, different from the rest of Mary's world. Mary was a determined little person, and now that she had something interesting to be determined about, she was very much absorbed. She got a spade and set to work. She dug and pulled up weeds; it seemed to her a fascinating sort of play. Sometimes she stopped digging to look at the garden and tried to imagine what it would be like when it was covered with thousands of lovely things in bloom.

One day as she skipped round the laurel-edged walk, she heard a low, whistling sound, and wanted to find out what it was. It was a very strange thing indeed. A funny-looking boy of about twelve was sitting under a tree, playing a wooden pipe. His cheeks were red as poppies, and never had Mistress Mary seen such round and blue eyes in any boy's face. A brown squirrel was watching him from the tree trunk, a pheasant peeked out from a nearby bush, and quite near him two rabbits were sitting up, as if they and the other animals were drawing near to watch and listen to him. He got up slowly, so as not to frighten the animals, and said, "I'm Dickon. I know tha'rt Miss Mary."

Dickon was Martha's younger brother. Mary had heard about him but had never met him, and yet he spoke to her as if he knew her quite well. She felt a little shy. Soon they began to talk about gardening and seeds and plants. She wished she could talk as easily and nicely as he did. He showed her mignonette seeds, and poppy seeds, and seeds for all kinds of lovely flowers.

"See here," said Dickon. "I'll plant them for thee myself. Where is tha' garden?"

Mary did not know what to say. She had never thought of anyone asking her about this. "I don't know anything about boys," she said slowly. "Could you keep a secret, if I told you one? If anyone should find out, I believe I should die!" She said the last sentence quite fiercely.

Dickon looked puzzled, but answered quite good-humoredly, "I'm keepin' secrets all th' time. If I couldn't keep secrets from the other lads about birds' nests, an' wild things' holes, there'd be naught safe on th' moor. Aye, I can keep secrets."

"I've stolen a garden," said Mary, very fast. "It isn't mine. It isn't anybody's. Nobody wants it, nobody cares for it, nobody ever goes in to it. Perhaps everything in it is dead already; I don't know." She began to feel as contrary as she had ever felt in her life.

"Nobody has any right to take it from me when I care about it and they don't." She burst out crying.

"Where is it?" asked Dickon softly.

Mistress Mary felt quite contrary still, but she said, "Come with me and I'll show you."

She led him to the walk where the ivy grew so thickly. Dickon felt as if he were being led to some strange bird's nest and must move softly. When she stepped to the wall and lifted the hanging ivy he started. There was a door. Mary pushed it slowly open and they passed in together, and then Mary stood and waved her hand round defiantly.

"It's this," she said. "It's a secret garden, and I'm the only one in the world who wants it to be alive."

While Mary watched him, Dickon looked and took in all the grey trees with their grey creepers, and the tangle on the walls. "I never thought I'd see this place," he said in a whisper. "Martha told me about it, once. The nests'll be here come springtime. It'd be th' safest nestin' place in England."

Mary put her hand on his arm without knowing it. "These rosebushes—are they alive? Is that one quite alive—quite?"

Dickon smiled. "It's as wick as you or me," he said, and Mary remembered that Martha had said "wick" meant "alive." They ran eagerly from bush to bush, and then Dickon noticed the clearings around the young plants, and asked Mary if she had done that work.

"Yes," she said. "But I don't know anything about gardening."

"Tha' did right," said Dickon. "A gardener couldn't have told thee better. Now they'll come up like Jack's beanstalk. There's a lot of work to do here!"

Mary thought that she had never seen such a funny boy, or a nicer one. "Will you come and help? Oh! Do come, Dickon!"

"I'll come every day if tha' wants me, rain or shine," he answered. "But I don't want to make it look all clipped. It's nicer like this, all runnin' wild."

"Don't let us make it tidy," said Mary. "It wouldn't seem like a secret garden if it all was tidy."

Then Mary did a strange thing. She leaned forward and asked him a question she had never before dreamed of asking anyone. And she tried to ask it in Yorkshire because that was his language, and in India a person was always pleased if you knew his dialect.

"Does tha' like me?" she said.

"That I does; I likes thee wonderful!"

They worked then harder than ever, and when it was time for Mary to go, she went slowly to the wall. Then she stopped and went back.

"Whatever happens, you—you never would tell?" she said.

He smiled encouragingly. "If tha' was a missel thrush an' showed me where thy nest was, does tha' think I'd tell anyone? Not me," he said. "Tha'art as safe as a missel thrush."

And she was quite sure she was.

The Red-Headed League

This is one of many stories by Arthur Conan Doyle about a fictional detective named Sherlock Holmes, whose amazing powers of observation and deduction enable him to solve crimes that perplex the police. Like Doyle's other stories about Holmes, this story is told by Holmes's friend, Dr. James Watson. The setting is London, England, around 1890.

One day last fall I called upon my friend, Mr. Sherlock Holmes, in his lodgings at 221B Baker Street. I found him in conversation with a stout gentleman with fiery red hair.

"You could not possibly have come at a better time, my dear Watson," he said cordially. "Mr. Wilson, this is Dr. Watson, who has been my partner in many of my most successful cases." The stout gentleman gave a little bob of greeting.

"Your cases have been of great interest to me," I observed.

"Now, Mr. Jabez Wilson here has called upon me with a story which promises to be one of the most singular I have listened to for some time. Perhaps, Mr. Wilson, you would recommence your narrative."

The portly client pulled a wrinkled newspaper from the pocket of his greatcoat. I took a good look at the man and endeavored, as Holmes might, to learn something about him from his appearance. Our visitor wore baggy gray trousers, a dirty black coat, and a drab vest. There was nothing remarkable about him except his blazing red head.

Sherlock Holmes smiled as he noticed my questioning glances. He said, "Beyond the obvious facts that he has done manual labor, and that he has done much writing lately, I can deduce nothing else."

Mr. Wilson look startled. "How did you know all that, Mr. Holmes?"

"Your hands, my dear sir. Your right hand is larger than your left. The muscles are more developed from hard work."

"Ah, of course. But the writing?"

"Your right cuff is so shiny, and your left sleeve shows a smooth patch near the elbow where you rest it upon the desk."

Mr. Wilson laughed in surprise. Holmes asked, "But won't you let Watson read the advertisement, Mr. Wilson?"

He gave me the paper and I read as follows:

TO THE RED-HEADED LEAGUE: *On account of the bequest of the late Ezekiah Hopkins, there is now another vacancy open which entitles a member of the League to a salary of four pounds a week for purely nominal services. All red-headed men are eligible. Apply in person to 7 Pope's Court, Fleet Street.*

"What on earth does it mean?" I asked.

"Well, as I have been telling Mr. Holmes," said Mr. Wilson, "I have a small pawnbroker's business at Coburg Square. I keep one assistant. His name is Vincent Spaulding, and I should not wish a smarter assistant. I know he could better himself, but if he is satisfied, why should I put ideas into his head?"

"Why, indeed? You are fortunate to have such an employee."

"Oh, he has his faults, too," said Mr. Wilson. "Never was there such a fellow for photography. Always diving down into the cellar to develop his pictures. But on the whole he's a good worker, and we go about our business quietly. The first thing that put us out was this advertisement. Spaulding came into the office eight weeks ago with this very paper in his hand, and he says: 'I wish that I was a red-headed man.' 'Why?' I ask. 'Why,' says he, 'here's another vacancy on the League of the Red-Headed Men. It's worth quite a little fortune to any man who gets it.' 'What is it?' I asked. 'Have you never heard of the League of the Red-Headed Men? Why, you yourself are eligible for one of the vacancies. As far as I can make out, the League was founded by a millionaire, Hopkins. He was red-headed, and he had a great sympathy for red-headed men. When he died he left instructions that the interest from his enormous fortune be applied to provide easy jobs for men whose hair is red. I hear it is splendid pay and very little to do.'

"Now, gentlemen, as you may see for yourselves, my hair is of a very rich tint, so it seemed to me I stood as good a chance as any man. So we shut the business up and started off for the address given.

"What a sight! From every direction tramped every man who had a shade of red in his hair: orange red, brick red, Irish setter red. I would have given up, but Spaulding pushed me right up the steps and into the office. Behind a table sat a small man with a head even redder than mine. He found some fault to disqualify each candidate before us, but when our turn came, he closed the door, looked me over, then suddenly shook my hand in congratulations. He explained that he was Mr. Duncan Ross, a member of the League himself. 'When shall you be able to begin?' he asked. 'What would be the hours?' I asked. 'Ten to two.' Now a pawnbroker's business is mostly done of an evening, Mr. Holmes, so it suited me well to earn a little in the mornings. He told me that the job required me to stay in the office the entire time each day, and that I would forfeit my position if I left for any reason. The work was to copy out the Encyclopaedia Britannica.

"I feared that the whole affair might be a hoax, but to my delight the next morning I found the table set out for me, and Mr. Duncan Ross there to see I got to work. He started me off upon the letter A, and then he left me. This went on day after day for eight weeks, and every Saturday Mr. Duncan Ross came in and planked down four gold coins for my week's work. I had written about Abbots, and Archery, and Armor, and Architecture, and hoped that I might get on to the Bs before very long. Then suddenly the whole business came to an end. This morning I went to work and found this tacked to the door." He held up a card, which read: THE RED-HEADED LEAGUE IS DISSOLVED.

"Well, Mr. Holmes, I was staggered. I went to the landlord to ask what had become of Mr. Duncan Ross and the Red-Headed League, but he had never heard of them. The red-haired gentleman was known to him as Mr. Morris, who had rented the room temporarily. When I went to his new address, I found it was a manufactory. Now I want to know who played this prank on me, and why."

"You were wise to come to me," said Holmes. "This assistant of yours—how did you find him?"

"He answered an advertisement. I picked him because he was willing to work for half wages."

"What is he like?"

"Small, quick in his ways, no hair on his face, with a white scar on his forehead."

Holmes asked in excitement, "Are his ears pierced?"

"Yes, sir. He told me a gypsy had done it for him."

"That will do, Mr. Wilson. I shall give you an opinion in a day or two."

"Well, Watson," said Holmes, when our visitor had left us, "what do you make of it all?"

"I make nothing of it," I answered, frankly. "It is a most mysterious business."

"As a rule," said Holmes, "the more bizarre a thing is, the less mysterious it proves to be."

Then he curled up in his chair, with his pipe in his hand and his thin knees drawn up to his hawk-like nose, and there he sat with his eyes closed. I believed that he had fallen asleep, when he suddenly sprang up with the gesture of a man who had made up his mind.

He invited me to accompany him to St. James Hall to hear a violin concert. On the way we walked through Coburg Square, where we found Mr. Wilson's pawnshop. Holmes thumped vigorously on the pavement three times with his cane, then knocked upon the door. It was opened by a clean-shaven fellow and Holmes asked directions to the Strand.

"Third right," answered the assistant, closing the door.

"Smart fellow, that," said Holmes, "I know something of him."

"I take it you asked your way in order that you might see him," I said.

"Not him," said Holmes, "but the knees of his trousers."

Holmes next led me around the corner to look at the row of businesses that lined the back of Coburg Square. "Let me see," said Holmes, "there's the tobacconist, the newspaper shop, the City and Suburban Bank, and the carriage depot. And now, Doctor, we've done our work. Let us go to the concert."

My friend was himself a capable performer on the violin and all afternoon he sat listening to the concert in perfect happiness. But as we emerged, he returned to the business regarding Coburg Square. He feared a serious crime was about to take place. I was to meet him at Baker Street at ten and to bring my revolver.

When I arrived, I found Sherlock Holmes in the company of two men. He introduced Mr. Peter Jones of Scotland Yard and Mr. Merryweather, a banker. Mr. Merryweather said that he hoped he had not given up his weekly card game to come on a wild goose chase. "You play for a higher stake tonight than you have ever done yet," said Sherlock Holmes. "For the stake will be 30,000 pounds. For you, Mr. Jones, it will be John Clay, the murderer, thief, and forger."

"John Clay is a cunning man," said Jones. "I've been on his track for years and have never set eyes on him yet."

"I hope I introduce you to him tonight," said Holmes. The four of us drove to the same row of businesses we had seen earlier in the day, and followed Mr. Merryweather through a number of locked doors and gates into a huge vault, piled all around with massive boxes. Holmes cautioned us to be quiet, then got down on his knees and began examining the stones in the floor with his lantern and a magnifying glass. After a few seconds he sprang to his feet. "We have at least an hour to wait," he said, "for they can hardly take any steps until the pawnbroker is safely in bed."

He then explained to me that we were in the cellar of Mr. Merryweather's bank, where a large amount of gold was being stored temporarily. John Clay and his accomplice, Holmes believed, would appear shortly to attempt to steal it. He warned that we must be ready to shoot, if necessary, for these were daring men.

After we had waited for what seemed hours, my eyes suddenly caught a glint of light on the floor. It lengthened into a yellow line, then suddenly one of the stones turned over and left a hole. Over the edge peeped a boyish face, then his two hands emerged to draw himself up. Next he hauled up a red-haired companion. Suddenly Sherlock Holmes seized the first intruder by the collar. The second dived down the hole. "It's no use, John Clay," said Holmes to the boyish-looking man. "You have no chance, and there are three men waiting for your companion at the door."

Later Holmes told me how he had solved the mystery: "You see, Watson, it was obvious that the only possible purpose of this fantastic business of the League was to get the pawnbroker out of the way every day. When I heard that the assistant came for half wages, I knew he had some strong, secret motive."

"But how could you guess what the motive was?"

"I thought of the assistant's fondness for photography, and his trick of vanishing into the cellar. He was doing something down there—something which took many hours a day for months on end. I could think of nothing save that he was running a tunnel to some other building. Our glimpse of him confirmed this, for the worn, stained knees of his pants spoke of hours of burrowing. You'll remember I tapped on the pavement with my cane and heard no hollow sound. I then knew the tunnel led in the other direction. I saw the location of the bank, and felt that I had solved my problem."

"You reasoned it out beautifully!" I exclaimed admiringly.

"It saved me from boredom," he answered, yawning.

The Samurai's Daughter

This story is set in feudal Japan around the year 1300. The samurai were the knights of feudal Japan.

Many years ago in Japan, there lived a samurai named Oribe Shima. By some misfortune, Oribe Shima had offended the emperor and been banished to one of the Oki Islands, off the west coast of Japan.

Oribe had a beautiful daughter, eighteen years old, named Tokoyo. When Oribe was sent away, Tokoyo wept from morning till night, and sometimes from night till morning. At last, unable to stand the separation any longer, she decided to try to reach her father or else die in the attempt, for she was a brave girl.

Tokoyo sold everything she owned and set off for the province closest to the Oki Islands. She tried to persuade the local fishermen to take her to the islands, but no one was allowed to land there.

The fishermen laughed at Tokoyo and told her to go home. But the brave girl was not to be put off. She went down to the beach, found an abandoned boat, and pushed it into the water. Then she started rowing. After several hours, Tokoyo reached the Islands. Cold and exhausted, she stumbled ashore and lay down to sleep.

In the morning, she began asking if anyone knew of her father's whereabouts. The first person she asked was a fisherman.

"I have never heard of your father," he said, "and you should not ask for him if he has been banished, for it may lead you to trouble and him to death!"

Poor Tokoyo wandered from one place to another, asking about her father but never hearing any news of him. One evening she came to a little shrine near the edge of the ocean. After bowing before a statue of the Buddha and imploring his help, Tokoyo lay down, intending to pass the night there, for it was peaceful and sheltered from the winds.

She was awakened by the sound of a girl wailing. As she looked up, she saw a young girl sobbing bitterly. Beside the girl stood the priest who kept the shrine. He was clapping his hands and mumbling a prayer. Both the man and the girl were dressed in white. When the prayer was over, the priest led the girl to the edge of the rocks and was about to push her into the sea, when Tokoyo ran and caught the girl's arm in a nick of time. The old priest looked surprised, but not angry.

"You must be a stranger to our island," said the priest. "Or you would know that this business is not at all to my liking. We are cursed with an evil god called Yofuné-Nushi. He lives at the bottom of the sea, and demands, once a year, the sacrifice of a girl. If we do not do this, Yofuné-Nushi causes great storms that drown many of our fishermen."

Tokoyo said, "Holy priest, let this girl go, for I will willingly take her place. I am the sorrowing daughter of Oribe Shima, a samurai of high rank, who has been exiled to this island. I came here to find my father, but I cannot even find out where he has been hidden. My heart is broken, and I have no desire to go on living."

Saying this, Tokoyo took the white robe off the girl and put it on her own body. She knelt before the figure of Buddha and prayed. Then she drew a small dagger, which had belonged to one of her ancestors, and, holding it between her teeth, she dove into the roaring sea.

When she was young, Tokoyo had spent many days diving with the women in her village to look for pearls. Because of this, she was a perfect swimmer. She swam down, down, down, until at last she reached the bottom, where she found an underwater cave. As Tokoyo peeped in, she thought she saw a man seated in the cave. Fearing nothing, willing to fight and die, she approached, holding her dagger ready. Tokoyo took the man for the evil god Yofuné-Nushi. However, she soon saw that it was not a god, but only a statue of the emperor, the man who had exiled her father.

Tokoyo took hold of the statue and was about to lift it when a horrible creature appeared. It was pale and scaly and shaped like a snake, but with a head and claws like a dragon. It was twenty feet long, and its eyes burned with hatred.

Tokoyo gripped her dagger, feeling sure that this was Yofuné-Nushi. No doubt Yofuné-Nushi took Tokoyo for the girl that was sacrificed to him each year.

When the creature was within six feet of her, Tokoyo ducked sideways and slashed his right eye. Now the monster was half blind, so Tokoyo was able to strike him again, this time near the heart. Yofuné-Nushi gave a hideous

Tokoyo gripped her dagger, feeling sure that this was Yofuné-Nushi.

gurgling shriek and sank lifeless on the ocean floor. Tokoyo placed her dagger between her teeth, took the monster in one hand and the statue in the other, and swam up towards the surface.

Meanwhile the priest and the girl were still gazing into the water where Tokoyo had disappeared. Suddenly they noticed a struggling body rising towards the surface.

When the priest realized it was Tokoyo, he climbed down the cliff to help her. He helped lug the hideous monster onto the shore and placed the carved image of the emperor on a rock. Soon other people arrived, and everyone was talking about the brave girl who had killed Yofuné-Nushi.

The priest told the story to the lord who ruled the island, and he reported the matter to the emperor. The emperor had been suffering from a strange disease that his doctors could not cure, but as soon as the statue of him was recovered, he got better. Then it was clear to him that he had been under the curse of someone he had banished to the Oki Islands— someone who had carved a statue of him, put a curse on the statue, and sunk it in the sea. Now the curse had been broken. On hearing that the girl who had recovered the statue was the daughter of Oribe Shima, the emperor ordered the noble samurai released from prison.

Now the islanders were no longer afraid of storms, and no more girls were thrown into the sea. Tokoyo and her father returned to their homeland, where they lived happily ever after.

The Sun Dance

For Plains Indians, the Sun Dance is a way to ask for or repay a favor granted to them by one of the great forces, or gods. The Blackfoot Indians tell versions of the following story to explain the origin of the dance.

One summer night long ago, a young woman named Feather Woman left her hot, airless teepee to sleep in the sweet-smelling breeze of the plains, with no covering but the sky. She awoke just before dawn and saw the morning star rising. The star was beautiful and bright in the clear morning air, and the woman whispered, "I love the morning star, for he is more beautiful than any man." Then she rose and thought no more about the morning star until several weeks later, when she was out walking and met a beautiful young man. His head was crowned with eagle feathers, and his hands and face glistened as though he had passed through a spiderweb.

"Feather Woman," the young man said, "I am Morning Star. One night in summer I looked down and saw you lying in the grass. As I was looking down, you looked up and said you loved me. I knew then that it was you I wanted as my wife. You must leave your people and come with me to my home in Star Country."

Feather Woman wanted to say goodbye to her family, but Morning Star said, "There must be no leave-taking. Come at once." So Feather Woman took his hand and stepped onto the silk gloss of a spiderweb. Then the two of them flew into the sky as magically as the spider casts his silken threads.

In Star Country, Feather Woman discovered a country much like her own. The prairie grasses sang in the wind, the star people stitched soft, white deerskins, and the women spent their days digging for roots.

Morning Star took Feather Woman to the teepee of his father and mother, Sun and Moon. Since it was daytime, Sun was out doing his work, but Moon was home and welcomed Feather Woman with smiles. When Sun returned in the evening, weary from his passage across the sky, he spoke to Feather Woman sternly, saying that if she wished to remain in Star Country she would have to learn the ways of his people and obey the rules. He said that Moon would teach her.

Morning Star and Feather Woman were married, and soon had a child, Star Boy. Whenever Morning Star went out to dig up roots with Moon and the other star women, she would bundle her child in soft clothes and carry him with her.

Moon told Feather Woman, "You may dig up any roots that grow in the sky, but I warn you not to dig up the giant turnip. If you do, unhappiness will follow."

One afternoon, Feather Woman went digging for roots without Moon and came upon the giant turnip. She remembered Moon's warning but could not see the reason for it. Curiosity got the better of her and she began to try to dig up the giant turnip. She had made little progress, when two cranes alighted beside her. They cooed, "Can we help you? Our bills are sharp. We can unearth the root for you." Not knowing that there was a terrible history between the cranes and the star people, Feather Woman consented. The cranes tore at the turnip's roots, and finally uprooted the giant plant.

Now, Moon had been very wise when she warned Feather Woman not to dig up the giant turnip, for the turnip plugged up the hole through which Morning Star had brought Feather Woman to the Star Country. Feather Woman peered down through the hole and saw the world below, the world she had left behind. She saw her sisters running on the prairie and her father returning from a hunt, and she heard her mother singing. Suddenly she felt terribly homesick, and she began to weep.

When Feather Woman returned

home, Morning Star saw her face and knew at once what had happened. When Sun came home and learned what had happened, he was very angry. He announced: "She has disobeyed and must go back to her people—she and the child. There can be no sorrow in the Country of the Stars." Morning Star and Moon begged Sun to allow Feather Woman and Star Boy to stay, but he refused.

That night, as members of Feather Woman's old family lay in the prairie grass, they saw a star falling towards them. They ran to the place where it fell and found Feather Woman, who had vanished many months ago, along with her child.

Feather Woman returned to live with her people, but she was never happy. One day, when Star Boy tried to wake her, he found that her spirit had gone.

Ever since his passage from Star Country to earth, Star Boy had been blemished by a strange scar on his face. People called him Scar Face and made fun of him.

When Scar Face was a young man, he fell in love with the daughter of the chief. Unlike other people, she talked to him kindly when they met and smiled and looked in his eyes. Scar Face wanted to marry her, but she said she would not marry him until he removed the strange scar from his face. Scar Face did not know what to do. How could he make the scar vanish? At last he consulted an old medicine-woman. She told him that his scar had been created by the Sun and there was only one way to remove it: he must return to Sky Country and convince his grandfather, the Sun, to remove the mark.

"But how shall I reach him?"

The medicine-woman gave him moccasins and a new shirt. "You will find him," she said.

Scar Face traveled far into the mountains until one night the Milky Way seemed to reach down to where he was sitting and then stretch upward, like a bridge from the earth to the sky. Scar Face stepped into the air and followed the Milky Way up into the Sky Country, to the home of his grandparents, Sun and Moon.

At first Sun did not recognize Scar Face and wanted to kill him, for earth-dwellers were not supposed to enter the Sky Country. But Moon, being kind, prevented it and saved the boy's life. Then Morning Star, the boy's father, came from his teepee. He recognized his child at once.

Scar Face lived with Sun and Moon and Morning Star. One afternoon when he and Morning Star were hunting together, several cranes appeared and began swooping down on them. Scar Face attacked the cranes with his spear and felled them one by one.

When Sun heard of the brave deed Scar Face had done, he removed the scar from the young man's face and made him Star Boy again. He also made his grandson a messenger to the Blackfeet people of the Plains. Sun promised that, if the people would honor him by doing the Sun Dance, he would heal those that were sick among them. He taught Star Boy the secrets of the dance and the songs to be used in it, and he gave him raven feathers to wear, and a wonderful robe and a magic flute.

Then Star Boy returned to his people, the Blackfoot of the Plains, running along the Milky Way. When he had taught them the Sun Dance, he married the girl he loved, and Sun allowed them to come and live with him and Moon and Morning Star in the Sky Country. Sometimes, even today, if you get up very early, you can catch a glimpse of Morning Star and Star Boy side by side in the sky.

Coyote Goes to the Land of the Dead

A trickster character who appears in many Native American tales is called Coyote. The following adaptation draws on stories told by the Nez Percé and Zuni peoples.

It had been a bitter winter, filled with sickness and death. Coyote's wife died, and he wept.

Eagle tried to cheer him. "Spring will soon be here," he said. But still Coyote wept. His lonely howls filled the night.

One day the Death Spirit came to Coyote and said, "I will take you where your wife has gone. Follow me. But listen: you must do exactly what I tell you."

"Whatever you say," promised Coyote. "But it is very hard to see you." It was hard, because the Spirit was invisible in daylight.

"I will carry something for you to follow," said the Spirit. "Give me something your wife loved." Coyote hated to give away anything that reminded him of his wife. Reluctantly he gave the Spirit a feather she wore when she danced.

They set off. In the daytime Coyote could see the feather. At night, he could not see the feather but he could see the Death Spirit shimmering.

Soon they were in a vast plain. The wind blew swirls of snow. Then the Spirit stopped. "Now," it said, "do as I do." The Spirit pointed ahead and said, "What a fine group of horses there."

Coyote saw nothing, but pointed and said, "What a fine group of horses there."

In the daytime Coyote could see the feather.

They walked on, until the Spirit said, "There is the longhouse."

Coyote saw nothing, but he said, "There is the longhouse."

The Spirit then bent down as if to lift a skin-covered door and crawl into a longhouse. Coyote did the same.

"Take a seat there, next to your wife," the Spirit ordered. Coyote sat, though he saw nothing around him but open plain.

"Now, your wife will serve us something warm," the Spirit said. Coyote looked around eagerly but could see nothing. He cupped his hands before his chest, as the Spirit did. Then both drank from their hands. Strangely, Coyote felt warmed.

"Now we must wait for nightfall," said the Spirit. Coyote slept. When he woke, he heard drums. When he looked around, he saw shadowlike figures dancing. He recognized his old friends who had died. Then he saw his wife and greeted her with joy. Then they all talked and danced till the sun rose, when the spirits disappeared.

By day, Coyote slept fitfully on the open ground in the bitter air. At night, he woke to find himself surrounded by the spirits of his loved ones. Night after night they talked and danced.

Then the Death Spirit came to Coyote and said, "It is time for you to go." Coyote began to protest but the Spirit silenced him. "Your wife may go with you to the Land of the Living, but only if you do exactly as I say. Follow your wife for five days over five mountains. On the sixth day, when you have crossed all five mountains and see the fires of home, only then may you touch her. Do not touch her before then. If you do anything foolish, then the spirits of the dead will never again be able to return to the Land of the Living."

The Death Spirit tied the feather that had belonged to Coyote's wife to her hair so Coyote could follow her spirit in the daytime. On the first day they crossed the first mountain. On the second day they crossed the second mountain. As they went on, Coyote no longer needed to watch the feather, for the farther they went, the more clearly he could see his wife.

On the fifth night they camped on the fifth mountain. Coyote sat and watched the glow of the fire on his wife's face and hair. Then—who can say why Coyote did this—he jumped across the fire and gathered his wife into his arms. As he touched her, she vanished. He cried out as her feather dropped to the ground.

The Death Spirit appeared before Coyote and said sternly, "Because of you, no spirit will ever again return from the dead."

Coyote ran howling back over the five mountains till he came again to the open plain. Though he saw nothing but swirling dust and snow, he stopped and said, "What a fine group of horses there." Then he went on and said, "There is the longhouse." Then he bent as though to lift a skin-covered door and crawled in on his knees. Then he cupped his hands and drank from them but felt nothing. He waited through the night to hear drums and see spirits dancing. But he heard only wind, and saw only darkness.

The next day, he began the long walk home.

LEARNING ABOUT LITERATURE

Literal and Figurative Language

When you speak or write, you use language in different ways. Sometimes you use *literal* language; you say exactly what you mean. But sometimes you use *figurative* language, which is a more colorful way of expressing yourself when you don't say exactly what you mean. After a really tough game of basketball or soccer, you might say:

> *literal*: I'm exhausted.
> or
> *figurative*: I'm dead.

The game might have worn you out, and you might be lying flat on your back out of breath, but you're still alive! In saying, "I'm dead," you are using figurative language to express how tired you feel.

Look at the verb *floated* in the following sentences. Which use is literal and which is figurative?

> (1) The graceful ballerina floated across the stage.
> (2) The leaf floated on the water.

Have you ever heard someone say, "That's a figure of speech"? A *figure of speech* is an expression that is not meant to be taken literally. You may know this old joke: "Why did the little boy throw the clock out the window? Because he wanted to see time fly." That's funny because the boy in the joke takes a figure of speech literally. What does it really mean to say that "time flies"?

Scientists often use the literal meanings of words because they need to be clear and precise. Poets and storytellers often use figurative language to stir our emotions and to help us see things in new ways. The American poet Emily Dickinson used figurative language when she compared a book to a frigate (a sailing ship) that can take us on imaginary voyages:

> There is no frigate like a book
> To take us lands away. . . .

Imagery

The words writers use to create mental pictures and other imaginary sensations are called *imagery*. The American writer Ernest Hemingway used imagery in the title of a story called "Hills Like White Elephants." It's his way to give us a mental picture of hills in the distance.

The English writer Christina Rossetti used images of animals in this poem:

> White sheep, white sheep,
> On a blue hill,
> When the wind stops
> You all stand still.

That seems like a straightforward description, but when you know that the title of the poem is "Clouds," you can see how imaginatively Rossetti is using imagery.

Simile and Metaphor

When writers use imagery, they often put their images into special kinds of figurative language called *simile* [SIM-uh-lee] and *metaphor* [MET-uh-for]. If you've ever said something like "She's fast as lightning" or "He's an angel," then you've used similes and metaphors yourself.

Similes and metaphors help us see things in unusual or imaginative ways by comparing one thing to another. Sometimes they bring together things you normally would not think of comparing. For example, fog might not make you think of an animal, but notice the surprising comparison Carl Sandburg makes in a poem called "Fog":

> The fog comes
> on little cat feet.
> It sits looking
> over harbor and city
> on silent haunches
> and then moves on.

A simile is a figure of speech that compares unlike things but makes the comparison obvious by including the word *like* or *as.* You've probably heard people use common similes in conversation: for example, "busy as a bee" or "sweet as honey" or "proud as a peacock." The great boxer Muhammad Ali described himself with some vivid similes: he said he would "float like a butterfly, sting like a bee" in the boxing ring.

Like a simile, a metaphor is a figure of speech that brings together unlike things. But a metaphor doesn't use *like* or *as*, so the comparison is not so obvious. For example, in talking about someone who's really stubborn, you might say:

> SIMILE: He's stubborn as a mule.
>
> or
>
> METAPHOR: He's a mule.

In the poem mentioned above, "Clouds," Christina Rossetti uses metaphors to describe the clouds and the sky. The poem compares clouds to white sheep and the sky to a blue hill. The metaphors help us see the clouds and sky in a way that we might not have seen them before. The metaphor makes the sky seem more solid to us, and the clouds almost alive.

Here is a poem you may know, called "Dreams," by Langston Hughes. It has two powerful metaphors. Can you find them?

> Hold fast to dreams
> For if dreams die
> Life is a broken-winged bird
> That cannot fly.
>
> Hold fast to dreams
> For when dreams go
> Life is a barren field
> Frozen with snow.

Think how dull this would have been if Hughes had written something literal like, "If you let go of your dreams, life will be very disappointing."

Sometimes a metaphor may be almost hidden in the words. For example, there's a metaphor lurking in this sentence: *The snow blanketed the town.* Do you see how the snow is being compared to a blanket? Now find the metaphor in this sentence: *Darkness swallowed the explorers as they entered the cave.*

Figurative language creates an emotional effect different from a literal statement such as "The explorers entered the dark cave." When you use a metaphor to compare the darkness to a hungry animal waiting to "swallow" the explorers, the cave becomes a place that most of us would rather not enter!

Ready for a metaphor challenge? Emily Dickinson's poem "I like to see it lap the Miles—" (p.10) is based on an elaborate metaphor. Read the poem several times and see if you can figure out what Dickinson is comparing with what.

Symbols

A *symbol* is something that stands for or suggests something else beyond itself. You're probably familiar with certain symbols for the United States of America: the bald eagle, the American flag, Uncle Sam. Another familiar symbol is a heart. Especially on Valentine's Day, what does a heart symbolize? In contrast, what do the skull and crossbones on a pirate's flag symbolize?

Works of literature often contain symbols. In his poem "The Road Not Taken" (p. 6), Robert Frost uses two paths in a wood as symbols of the choices we make in life. The two roads are literal roads but also symbols for something more.

Sometimes the significance of a symbol is not so clear-cut. For example, what do you think the tree suggests in the poem called "A Poison Tree" on page 13?

A symbol can mean different things to different readers, and not everything in a work of literature is a symbol. For example, let's say you're reading a poem about a bird: the bird may be a symbol, suggesting a quality like freedom. Or, the bird may simply be a bird. When you're reading stories and poems, you don't need to search for symbols, but when you do notice them, it's interesting to think about how they enrich what you're reading.

Personification

Imagine you're trying to sharpen a pencil but the lead keeps breaking. Frustrated, you exclaim, "This pencil sharpener refuses to work!" Did the pencil sharpener actually *refuse?* Did it say, "I won't sharpen your pencil"? Of course not. When you said that the pencil sharpener refused to work, you used a kind of figurative language known as *personification*.

To personify is to give a thing or an animal the qualities of a human being. In a poem called "Trees," the poet Joyce Kilmer personifies a tree by giving it certain human qualities. He describes how the tree "lifts her leafy arms" and wears "a nest of robins in her hair."

Onomatopoeia

Onomatopoeia [ON-uh-maht-uh-PEA-uh] is a Greek word for a special effect that writers use. In a comic book, when something explodes, you read, "BOOM!" Or when a superhero punches a villain, you read "BIFF!" or "POW!" Onomatopoeia refers to words that sound like the things they describe. If you drop a coin in a metal bowl, it goes "clink." If a car speeds by, it goes "varroom." *Clink* and *varroom* are examples of onomatopoeia. Try to think of what might produce these sounds: buzz, hiss, clack, gurgle, whoosh.

Now, think of some words that might capture the following sounds: bacon frying, thunder in the distance, windshield wipers going back and forth, a car door closing, fingernails scratching a blackboard.

Alliteration

Another special effect that poets use is *alliteration*. Alliteration means starting several words in a row with the same sound. The first two lines of "The Eagle," by Alfred, Lord Tennyson, are an example:

> He clasps the crag with crooked hands;
> Close to the sun in lonely lands,

Do you hear the repetition of the hard *c* sound in the first line? Can you find more alliteration in the second line of the poem?

Drama

A *drama*, or play, is a special kind of story meant to be acted out on stage. Instead of telling you what happened, the dramatist, or playwright, shows you. If you see a play performed in a theater, the action unfolds in front of you.

The first plays were written by the ancient Greeks, as part of religious festivals. At first, a group of men called a "chorus" sang songs together and danced around the altar of the Greek god Dionysus. Gradually, the performances became more complex. First a single actor from the chorus was allowed to speak as an individual. Then more actors were added, so the characters on stage could talk to each other and act out stories. Eventually these religious ceremonies began to look a lot like modern plays.

The Greeks developed two kinds of plays: comedies and tragedies. Comedies are funny, happy stories, in which everything works out well in the end. Tragedies are sad stories, in which things turn out badly. A comedy often ends with a marriage or a celebration; a tragedy often ends with the death of the main character, or with several deaths.

The Greeks used these two masks to stand for comedy and tragedy. Can you guess which one stands for comedy?

Shakespeare

One of the most famous dramatists of all time was the Englishman William Shakespeare. Shakespeare's plays are among the most popular of all time and are still performed today.

Shakespeare lived near the end of the great age called the Renaissance, which you can read about in the history and art sections of this book. His plays, written between 1592 and 1611, were performed in theaters around London, including the famous Globe Theater.

One of the greatest things about Shakespeare is his ability to describe all kinds of characters: kings and queens, soldiers, merchants, servants, and beggars—and everyone in between. Shakespeare seems to understand all kinds of people: good and bad, heroic and selfish, brave and cruel. He helps us to understand them as well.

Another reason for Shakespeare's greatness is the beauty and power of his poetry. Although the people in his plays think and act like real people, they speak an almost magical language. Listen to a character called Caliban tell you about his island, which is haunted by music.

> Be not afeard: the isle is full of noises,
> Sounds and sweet airs, that give delight, and hurt not.
> Sometimes a thousand twangling instruments
> Will hum about mine ears, and sometimes voices,
> That, if I then had waked after long sleep,
> Will make me sleep again.

Shakespeare loved to use unusual words like *twangling* to describe things. In fact, Shakespeare invented many words, and we still use some of them today. As far as we can tell, words like *gloomy, suspicious, countless, bump, hurry, lonely, monumental,* and many others first appeared in Shakespeare's works!

Shakespeare probably had more influence on the English we speak than any other writer. Many of his phrases describe things so well that we still use them: expressions like "elbow room," "fair play," and "catching a cold," and famous phrases like "to be or not to be" and "all's well that ends well" come from his plays.

The Globe Theater, where many of Shakespeare's plays were originally performed.

Shakespeare's Comedies

Shakespeare wrote both comedies and tragedies. His comedies are usually divided into five acts, each containing several scenes. In the early scenes of a Shakespeare comedy, there is often an obstacle of some kind that keeps two young lovers from getting married. Sometimes the woman's father does not approve of the man she loves, or the lovers' families are enemies, or there is an unfair law that prevents the marriage. The later acts of the play then tell the story—often a funny story—of how the lovers get around these obstacles. The road from thwarted love to happiness and marriage is seldom smooth. Usually there is a period of confusion in which it is not clear who loves whom. Sometimes there are quarrels and breakups, but the comedy usually ends with a wedding.

One of Shakespeare's most famous comedies is called *A Midsummer Night's Dream.* You can read this play in a version edited for young readers. But to really get the feeling of a Shakespeare play, you should see one performed or try to act out some scenes by yourself.

The south bank of the River Thames, in 1647, showing the Globe Theater to the right.

LEARNING ABOUT LANGUAGE

Subjects and Verbs

Every sentence needs a subject and a verb to be complete. In the following sentences, the subjects are underlined and the verbs are printed in color.

> The bird **ate** the worm.
> The pitcher **throws** the ball.

One good way to find the verb is to look for a word that can change tense. Take the word *ate* in the example above. You could say "the bird ate the worm," "the bird eats the worm," or "the bird will eat the worm." The first of these sentences is in the past tense, the second is in the present tense, and the third is in the future tense. Since the word *ate* can change tense, it's a verb. The same thing is true of *throws*.

Once you've found the verb, you can find the subject by asking who or what is doing what the verb describes. *Who ate the worm?* The bird did. So *bird* is the subject of the sentence. *Who throws the ball?* The pitcher does. So *pitcher* is the subject of the sentence.

See if you can identify the subject and the verb in the sentences below.

> The judge banged his gavel.
> The bells tinkled in the wind.

The subject and verb of a sentence must always agree. If the subject of your sentence is singular—like *judge*—use the singular form of the verb. If your subject is plural—like *bells*—use the plural form of the verb.

> An antelope **runs** quickly.   Antelopes **run** quickly.
> He **teaches** Spanish.   They **teach** Spanish.

The singular forms of verbs generally have an s at the end.

In most cases it's easy to tell if your subject is singular or plural. But in some cases it can be a little tricky. Which of the verbs below would you use to complete the sentence?

> A flock of seagulls **flies/fly** overhead.

Since there are many seagulls, you might think that the subject must be plural. But in fact, the subject is *flock*, and there's only one flock, so we say, "A flock of seagulls flies overhead."

Which verb would you choose for these sentences?

A band of gypsies **was/were** singing for us.
One of my best friends **like/likes** to dance.
Two of my best friends **like/likes** to dance.

Sentence Fragments

A complete sentence has a subject and a verb. If either of these is missing, you've got a *sentence fragment*. We use fragments all the time when we're talking. For instance, your mother might call you, saying, "Mary!" And you might answer, "Coming!" Neither of these is a complete sentence, and yet you and your mom understand each other perfectly.

Even though we use lots of fragments in everyday speech, fragments are generally considered inappropriate in formal writing. You should repair the sentence fragments you find in your own writing. See if you can find and repair the sentence fragments in the following passage.

> I read a story yesterday. A mystery story about Sherlock Holmes. Holmes is
> an English detective. Very smart. Solves the mystery easily.

There are three fragments in all. The first sentence is a complete sentence, but "A mystery story about Sherlock Holmes" is a fragment. You might fix it by adding a subject and verb: "It was a mystery story about Sherlock Holmes." The third sentence is fine. But the two phrases that follow are fragments. Most sentence fragments can be fixed in more than one way. One way would be to combine the two fragments and add a subject and verb: "He is very smart and solves the mystery easily." Or you might write, "Because he is very smart, he solves the mystery easily."

Run-On Sentences

A *run-on* is the opposite of a sentence fragment. A fragment lacks something it needs; a run-on sentence has more than it needs. It contains enough materials for two or more complete sentences crammed into one sentence. Often these materials are separated by commas:

The next chapter is very difficult, you should start studying right away.

This kind of run-on sentence is called a *comma splice*. The easiest way to fix it is to divide it into two separate sentences:

The next chapter is very difficult. You should start studying right away.

Another way to fix the run-on would be to combine the two parts of the sentence with a conjunction. A *conjunction* is a word that connects words, phrases, and clauses. In this case you would use what's called a *coordinating conjunction*. Don't let the fancy name scare you: you already know most of the coordinating conjunctions. There are seven: *for, and, or, nor, but, yet, so*. When you use a coordinating conjunction, it's okay to use a comma, like this:

> The next chapter is very difficult, so you should start studying right away.

Each coordinating conjunction has a slightly different meaning, so pick the right one for the job.

The following items remind you of some important rules you've learned, but they don't always obey those rules themselves. See if you can fix them.

> Verbs has to agree with their subjects.
> No incomplete sentences.
> Do not write run-on sentences they are hard to understand.

Direct Objects

Some sentences add another element to their subject and verb—a direct object. In the sentence "Dad cooked hamburgers," *hamburgers* is the direct object of the verb *cooked*. A *direct object* is a noun or pronoun that the verb does something to. It is the object of the verb. It is called a direct object, because the verb acts directly on it.

> Michelangelo painted <u>the ceiling</u> of the Sistine Chapel.
> Harriet Tubman led <u>slaves</u> to freedom.

To find a direct object, first find the subject and the verb. Then ask yourself who or what the verb is acting on.

Indirect Objects

Sometimes when a sentence has a direct object, it also has an indirect object. The *indirect object* answers the question *to whom?* or *to what?* An indirect object is the person or thing that receives the direct object from the subject.

> Jim threw Tina the ball.

In the sentence above, *ball* is the direct object and *Tina*, who received the ball, is the indirect object. Here's another example. If you had lived in 1920, you might have read this headline:

Nineteenth Amendment gives women the vote!

To find the indirect object in this sentence, remember to find the direct object of the verb first. You would ask "gives what?" and the answer would be "the vote." And then you would ask, "gives the vote to whom?" The answer would be "women." So *vote* is the direct object and *women* is the indirect object.

Predicates

The *predicate* is the part of a sentence that states something about the subject. The predicate always includes the verb. It may also include a direct object, an indirect object, and other words related to the verb. In the sentences below, the predicates are in bold print.

The fireman **pointed his hose at the blazing fire.**
A bird **came down the walk.**
The Oki Islands **are part of Japan.**

In some sentences, the predicate is very short. The shortest sentence in the King James Bible is just two words, one of which is the subject and the other the predicate:

Jesus **wept.**

On the other hand, in some sentences the predicate can be quite long, as it is in this sentence from the *Narrative of the Life of Frederick Douglass*:

I **carried books with me whenever I was sent on an errand and traded bread for reading lessons from the little white boys playing in the street.**

In English, the subject often comes at the beginning of the sentence and the predicate comes later. But this is not always true. Here's a sentence from a poem, in which the predicate comes at the beginning of the sentence and the subject comes at the end:

Into the valley of Death rode <u>the six hundred</u>.

Can you find the subject and the predicate in each of the following sentences?

The skunk left a terrible smell.
In the morning wind were flapping forty flags.

Nouns

A *noun* is a word that names a person, place, or thing. How many nouns can you find in the following sentence from *The Adventures of Tom Sawyer?*

> Tom had twelve marbles, a fragment of chalk, a tin soldier, a couple of tadpoles, six firecrackers, a kitten with only one eye, and a dog collar—but no dog.

There are lots of nouns here: *marbles, fragment, eye,* and *collar* are what we call common nouns, and *Tom* is a proper noun. Proper nouns name a specific person, place, or thing. Proper nouns are always capitalized. Here are some examples:

common nouns	proper nouns
friend	Susan
city	New York
sandwich	Big Mac
queen	Queen Victoria

Adjectives and Adverbs

Adjectives are words that modify nouns. When you ask for a green shirt, you are using the adjective *green* to modify the noun *shirt.* Adjectives are helpful when you want to describe something in detail. Notice how the adjectives in the following sentence from *The Secret Garden* help us visualize the scene:

> There were **other** trees in the garden, and **climbing** roses had run all over them and swung down **long** tendrils which made **light swaying** curtains.

What an adjective does for a noun, an adverb does for a verb—it modifies the verb, telling you *how* an action is performed. Remember how Tom Sawyer came up with a plan to trick other kids into whitewashing the fence for him? When Tom comes up with his plan, Mark Twain writes that he "took up his brush and *tranquilly* went to work." *Tranquilly* is an adverb that means "calmly, without any worries." Tom works tranquilly because he has a plan: he is confident that he can get the other kids to do his work for him if he makes it seem as if it isn't really work at all. In this case, the adverb not only tells you how Tom performs the action but also gives you a glimpse inside his head.

Interjections

An *interjection* is a word added to a sentence to convey emotion. When Jo in *Little Women* discovers that her sister has destroyed her book, she cries out, "What! My little book I was so fond of?" Here *what* is used as an interjection.

Here are some more interjections:

Yikes, I'm late for work!
Hey, come back here!
Gee, I didn't know that.

Use interjections in your own writing when you are trying to capture the way people talk in everyday life.

Personal Pronouns

Pronouns take the place of nouns. There are several kinds of pronouns, but the kind we use most often is the *personal pronoun*—the pronoun that can replace the name of a person or thing in a sentence:

When Louis Armstrong played <u>his</u> trumpet, <u>he</u> moved <u>our</u> hearts with <u>his</u> rhythm and shattered glasses with <u>his</u> pitch.

Using personal pronouns makes our sentences shorter and less cumbersome. But how do you know which pronoun to use? Most people use the pronoun that fits without knowing its name or the rule for its use. They say, "Give me the book," not "Give I the book." But the rule for choosing personal pronouns is easy to learn: The personal pronoun must agree with the noun it replaces in case, gender, and number. Let's see what that means.

Agreement in Case

Think of the various pronouns you can use to refer to yourself: *I, me, my,* or *mine.* Which form of pronoun you use depends on how you use it in a sentence. A pronoun takes the place of a noun, and the particular form a pronoun takes—that is, the *case* of the pronoun—must agree with the function of the noun that the pronoun replaces in the sentence. There are three cases: nominative, objective, and possessive. Let's look at the nominative and objective cases by considering the following sentence:

The nurse held the babies.

If you were to replace "the nurse" with a pronoun, which one would you use? Here are the pronouns you could choose, each in a different case:

> nominative case: she
> objective case: her

What is the function of "the nurse" in the sentence? It is the subject. When the noun acts as the subject, you replace it with a pronoun in the nominative case:

> She held the babies.

Now, what pronoun would you use to replace "the babies" in that sentence? Here are your choices:

> nominative case: they
> objective case: them

What is the function of "the babies" in the sentence? It is a direct object. When the noun to be replaced is either a direct object or an indirect object, the pronoun must be in the objective case.

> She held them.

Here are the personal pronouns in the nominative case: *I, we, you, he, she, it, they.* Any of these nominative pronouns will work as the subject of a sentence like the following:

> _____ danced to the music.

Here are the personal pronouns in the objective case: *me, us, you, him, her, it, them.* Any of the objective pronouns will work as the object in a sentence like the following:

> He threw the ball at _____.

Often you will use the nominative and objective case correctly without thinking about it, although there are some tricky cases to watch out for. Sometimes people use the objective case when they should use the nominative case:

> My brother and me are going to the market.

What is the function of the word *me* in that sentence? It's part of the subject. If you take away the other part of the subject—my brother—you'll see how odd it sounds to say "Me am going to the market." So the correct form is the nominative:

> My brother and *I* are going to the market.

Be on the lookout for the mistake people occasionally make when they use a nominative pronoun instead of an objective pronoun, as in the following:

Dad is taking Mark and I to see the parade.

You wouldn't say "Dad is taking I to see the parade." So use the objective pronoun:

Dad is taking Mark and me to see the parade.

Possessive Case

Here are the personal pronouns you use when the noun is showing possession: *mine*, *ours*, *yours*, *his* and *hers*, *its*, *theirs*. These are called the *possessive pronouns*.

Jane's story is more exciting than _____.

Mine, *ours*, *yours*, *his*, *hers*, and *theirs* will all fit in the blank.

But we can also change Jane's story to *her* story. The possessives that come before a noun are a little different from those that stand by themselves. The ones that come before a noun are *my*, *our*, *your*, *his*, *her*, *its*, and *their*.

_____ story is more exciting than mine.

The *her* in "her story" is still called a possessive personal pronoun. But you see that it doesn't stand alone. It's a word that modifies the noun *story*, just as an adjective would. Notice that you can use *mine*, *ours*, *yours*, *his*, *hers*, and *theirs* all by themselves, but *my*, *our*, *your*, *her*, and *their* always come before the thing they possess, as in "my dog" or "her cap." *His* and *its* can be used all by themselves or to modify a noun.

Agreement in Gender

Pronouns also need to agree in *gender* with the noun they replace—whether female, male, or neither. If you were describing Casey's failure in "Casey at the Bat," you wouldn't say, "She struck out." You would say, "He struck out," because Casey is a man, and *he*, *him*, and *his* are the pronouns we use for nouns that are masculine. Do you know the pronouns we use for feminine nouns?

While people always have a gender, things often don't. *It* is the pronoun we use for things that are gender-neutral, such as a heart, a painting, or a hammer. For instance, when describing the heart, we might say, "It is an amazing muscle."

Agreement in Number

Agreement in *number* means the pronoun must be singular or plural like the noun it replaces. Use singular pronouns when talking about one thing and plural pronouns when talking about more than one thing.

Here are the singular pronouns we use for one person:

nominative	objective	possessive
I	me	my, mine
you	you	your, yours
he	him	his
she	her	her, hers
it	its	its

Here are the plural pronouns we use for more than one person:

nominative	objective	possessive
we	us	our, ours
you	you	your, yours
they	them	their, theirs

The Versatile Comma

You know to use a period (.) at the end of a sentence that makes a statement, a question mark (?) at the end of a sentence that asks a question, and an exclamation point (!) at the end of a sentence or phrase that is exclaimed, or shouted out, like "My foot hurts!" You have also learned to use commas in certain situations, such as when you want to separate items in a list:

Lemonade is made from water, sugar, and lemon juice.

You also need a comma when you write a sentence with a coordinating conjunction like *but, and,* or *or* separating two phrases that could otherwise stand on their own:

We went to the store, but they didn't have any bread.
I took the test, and I think I did well.

Commas are used after the words *yes* and *no:*

Yes, I can hear you, my dear!
No, I don't want another slice of pizza.

Commas are used in dates to separate the day and the year, and in addresses to separate the names of cities and states:

> The Civil War began on April 12, 1861.
> Our trip took us to London, England.

Commas are also used to set off appositives. So what's an appositive? An *appositive* is a noun or noun phrase that renames another noun right beside it. For instance, look at the following sentence.

> My best friend, Susan Scott, is coming to my house tonight.

"Susan Scott" renames "my best friend." Therefore, it is an appositive, and it is set off with commas.

Sometimes appositives can be quite long, as in this case.

> Don Quixote, a poor, skinny man from an insignificant town somewhere in Spain, thinks he is a knight in shining armor.

Here the first and last commas set off the appositive, which renames Don Quixote, while the second comma separates two adjectives, *poor* and *skinny*.

Colons and Italics

The colon looks like two periods stacked on top of each other. Use a colon any time you want to introduce a list.

> I had to choose one of three sports: tennis, football, or soccer.
> Mom told me to buy three things: milk, flour, and cheese.

Sometimes colons are also used to introduce quotations.

> Later Holmes told me how he had solved the mystery: "You see, Watson, it was obvious from the beginning."

If you want to write down the title of a book, you should either underline the title or italicize it. (Italics are letters that slant a little to the right, *like this*.)

> I read <u>The Adventures of Tom Sawyer</u>.
>   or
> I read *The Adventures of Tom Sawyer*.

If you're writing about a poem, a short story, a song, or a magazine article, you'll want to place the title inside quotation marks.

We sang "The Yellow Rose of Texas."

I memorized Robert Frost's poem "The Road Not Taken."

Writing

Nobody is born knowing how to write, and the only way to get good at it is to practice. Here's a list of different kinds of documents you can create in your own writing:

- A letter to a friend or relative
- A description of a person or place
- A summary of what you did yesterday
- A short story
- A poem

Why not try some of the kinds of writing you haven't already tried?

Researching and Writing a Report

Sometimes, in school, you may be asked to write a report. For instance, suppose you were asked to write a report on Frederick Douglass. The first thing you would do would be to learn about Douglass. You could look for information on the Internet, but you should look at some printed books and articles, too.

To find books and articles, go to your school library or to the local public library and ask a librarian to help you find the books you need. The librarian will be glad to help you.

You might start by reading an encyclopedia article, a biography of Douglass, or his own autobiography. You might also want to look at books on slavery or on the Civil War.

To see if a particular book contains any information on Douglass, look at the index, at the back of the book. An *index* is an alphabetical list of topics discussed in the book. If Douglass is covered, he will be listed in the index by his last name, and the index will tell you which pages to look at.

As you read, try to focus in on a particular aspect of the subject that interests you. For instance, you might decide to write about Douglass's experiences as a slave or his achievements as a free man working to get rid of slavery.

When you read something you think you might like to use in your report, jot it down. Also be sure to jot down some important information about the book you've been reading. For example, suppose you were reading *War, Terrible War*, a history of the Civil War by Joy Hakim, and you came across Douglass's reaction to the Emancipation Proclamation, Abraham Lincoln's declaration that freed slaves in the South. You would want to write down what Douglass had to say: "We shout for joy that we live to record this righteous decree!" You'd also want to write down some information on the book where you found this quotation, including the author's name, the book's title, the place of publication, the publisher, the date, and the page where you found the quotation:

Hakim, Joy. *War, Terrible War*. New York: Oxford University Press, 1999, p. 100.

If you decide to use this quotation in your report, you'll need to list Hakim's book in your bibliography. A *bibliography* is a list of books you've used in making your report. The bibliography goes at the end of the report.

When you write your report, try to think of it as a series of paragraphs, each of which has a specific job to do. The first paragraph's job is to introduce the topic. Each of the next paragraphs should also have a clear job. For instance, the second paragraph's job might be to tell how Douglass worked for the abolition of slavery. The third paragraph could describe Douglass's reaction when slavery finally was abolished, and the fourth could tell what Douglass did after it was abolished. The final paragraph is called the *conclusion*. This is where you wrap up your report and explain why it matters.

Learning to write a good report is hard in the same way that learning to excel in a sport is hard. Before you can be a good baseball or softball player, you have to learn how to hit, run, throw, and catch. You also have to learn rules like *three strikes and you're out* and *four balls make a walk*. Then you have to combine all your knowledge and all your skills to score runs and keep the other team from scoring. Writing a report is just the same: you have to learn how to use nouns and verbs and adjectives, how to follow punctuation rules, and how to do research. Then you have to bring all these skills together, turning your ideas into sentences, your sentences into paragraphs, and your paragraphs into a report. Remember: practice makes perfect!

Prefixes

A *prefix* is a set of letters that can be attached to the front of a word to make a new word. For instance, you probably know that *unfriendly* means "not friendly," and a *replay* is what happens when a TV station plays a bit of videotape a second time. Here are some more prefixes that will help you make sense of unfamiliar words.

anti- means "against," "in opposition to," or "opposed to." An *antibacterial* soap fights against bacteria.

inter- means "between" or "among." *International* trade is trade between nations, and an *interstate* highway is one that allows you to travel rapidly among the various states in the United States.

co- means "together with" or "joint." If your sports team has *cocaptains*, it has two captains who serve jointly. When two groups don't like each other but try to get along, they try to *coexist*.

mid- is short for "middle," so *midnight* is the middle of the night. Shakespeare's play *A Midsummer Night's Dream* takes place in the middle of the summer.

fore- means "before" or "the front part of." A *forefather* is someone from an earlier time or an ancestor. If you *forewarn* a friend, you warn her ahead of time. (But if your friend has *foresight*, she won't need to be *forewarned!*)

post- means "after." In football and other sports, the *postseason* comes after the regular season, and the *postgame* report comes after the game.

il-, *ir-*, *in-*, and *im-* are four prefixes that mean "not." An *illegal* play is not legal. An *irregular* edge is not regular. An *intolerant* person is not tolerant or understanding toward other people. An *immature* person is not mature.

semi- means "half," "incomplete," or "partial." In some cases, it can also mean twice within a period of time. A *semicircle* is half a circle. A *semiannual* event happens twice a year.

Suffixes

A *suffix* is a set of letters that can be attached to the end of a word. The suffixes *-ly* and *-ily* can be added to adjectives to make adverbs, like *desperately* and *angrily*.

-ist is a suffix that is very useful when you want to describe what somebody does or believes. It can be added to nouns to indicate a person associated with that noun: a *pianist* is someone who plays the piano; an *artist* is someone who makes art; a *biologist* is someone who studies biology; a Buddhist is a person who follows the teachings of the Buddha.

-ish is a suffix that is often added to nouns to make them into adjectives. Is your brother a fool? Then he is *foolish*. Does your best friend have style? Then she's *stylish*. Sometimes this suffix can also mean "approximately or somewhat," as when we say something is not exactly green, but *greenish*.

-ness is a suffix that indicates the state, condition, or quality of something. *Redness* is the state or quality of being red. *Sadness* is the condition you experience when you are sad.

-tion and *-sion* are two suffixes that are often used to make verbs into nouns. If you decide to do something, you make a *decision*. If you react to a referee's decision, you have a *reaction*. If you tense up, you experience *tension*.

Sayings and Phrases

Every culture has sayings and phrases that can be difficult for outsiders to understand. In this section we introduce a handful of common English sayings and phrases. As you study these phrases, try to imagine a situation in which you might use each one.

Birthday suit

When you were born, you weren't wearing any clothes. When we say someone is wearing his or her "birthday suit," we mean that person is naked.

Bite the hand that feeds you

An ill-tempered dog might bite his master, even though he depends on his master for food. When you harm someone who supports you, you are "biting the hand that feeds you."

Catch forty winks

To "catch forty winks" is to take a nap.

Chip on your shoulder

When someone has "a chip on his shoulder," it means that he seems eager to pick a fight.

Count your blessings.

People use this saying to mean "Be thankful for what you have."

Eat crow

If you "eat crow," you have to take back something that you once said. It is usually a humbling experience and is similar to "eating your words."

Eleventh hour

This phrase means "at the last possible moment."

Eureka!

"Eureka" is a Greek word that means, "I have found it!" The Greek mathematician Archimedes once sat in his bathtub, thinking about a problem. When he hit on the solution, he called out "Eureka!"

Every cloud has a silver lining.

Even bad things usually have a hidden good side.

Few and far between

Things that are "few and far between" are rare or not easily available.

The grass is always greener on the other side of the hill.

This saying is often used to console a person who feels that what other people have is better than what she has. It points out that appearances can be deceiving.

Kill two birds with one stone

When you do one thing but manage to accomplish two goals, you are "killing two birds with one stone."

Lock, stock, and barrel

The lock, the stock, and the barrel were the essential parts of guns in earlier times. If you bought the whole gun, you would want the lock, the stock, and the barrel. The phrase "lock, stock, and barrel" has come to mean "the whole package" or "every last thing."

Make a mountain out of a molehill

When someone makes a big deal out of something that is not very important, we often say the person is "making a mountain out of a molehill."

A miss is as good as a mile.

This saying reminds us that missing by a little bit is no better than missing by a whole lot.

It's never too late to mend.

There is always time to improve yourself or change your ways.

Out of the frying pan and into the fire

This expression describes what happens when you go from a bad situation to an even worse one.

A penny saved is a penny earned.

When you save money instead of spending it, it is almost the same as earning money, because you'll have extra cash instead of an empty pocket.

Read between the lines

When you "read between the lines," you go beyond the surface of what someone says to find out what the person really means.

Sit on the fence

To "sit on the fence" is to avoid taking sides in a debate or argument.

Steal his/her thunder

If you are planning on doing something that will impress other people, but another person does it first, that person is "stealing your thunder."

Take the bull by the horns

This phrase means to stop hesitating and take action.

Till the cows come home

Cows may sleep in their pastures and not come home to the barn until the very end of the day. When we say that something won't happen until the cows come home, we mean that it won't happen for a long time.

Time heals all wounds.

When people say "time heals all wounds," they are usually talking about feelings. Sometimes after something bad happens, you feel better only when a lot of time passes.

Tom, Dick, and Harry

If you invite "every Tom, Dick, and Harry," to a party it means you are inviting just about everyone.

Vice versa

When people use this Latin term, they mean something is exactly the same but the other way round. "He's angry with her, and vice versa" means both are angry at each other.

A watched pot never boils.

When you wait anxiously for something to happen, it always seems to take longer.

Well begun is half done.

If you start something off well, it will be easier to finish.

What will be will be.

Some things are beyond our control, so there's no point in worrying about them.

II.

History and Geography

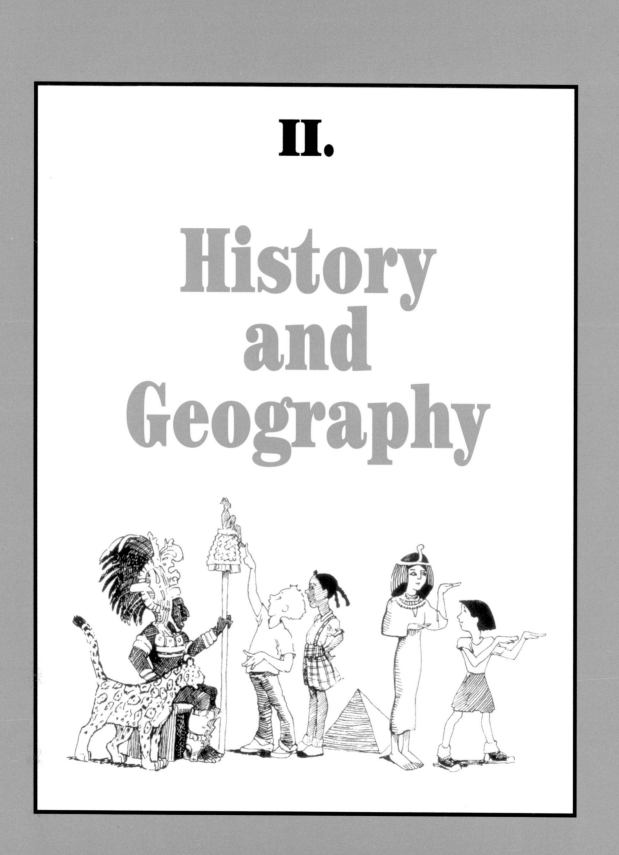

Introduction

This chapter treats geography, world history, and American history. Geography has been described as the study of "what's where, why it's there, and why we should care." It looks at how humans are challenged by, culturally adapt to, utilize, and change the natural environments in which they live. Fifth-grade students should know the rudiments of geography. They should be able to read maps and make simple maps of their own. In this book we discuss reference points, latitude and longitude, climate zones, time zones, and lakes. Children can learn more about geography in many ways—by studying atlases and books on foreign lands, by subscribing to geography magazines like *National Geographic for Kids,* and even by collecting stamps.

In both world and American history, we have tried to emphasize the *story* in history, without an undue emphasis on dates. Some crucial dates—like 1492, 1861, and 1865— should be memorized. Most others serve a useful purpose without being committed to memory, for they help to reinforce the child's sense of chronology and establish a foundation for more sophisticated historical understanding in years to come.

The world history topics for grade 5 build on the topics introduced in grade 4. In grade 4, students studied the Middle Ages. In grade 5, they move on to the Renaissance, the Reformation, the Age of Exploration, and concurrent developments in Russia and Japan. In addition, they learn about early American civilizations that were discovered and conquered by European explorers and conquistadors.

In American history, children build on their knowledge of early American history by studying the Civil War, westward expansion, and the consequences of westward expansion for Native Americans.

This chapter can be supplemented with readings elsewhere in this book. Renaissance history goes hand in hand with the section on Renaissance art, as well as the section on Shakespeare and the selections from *Don Quixote.* Japanese history connects with Japanese art and "The Samurai's Daughter," an excerpt in Language and Literature. Various stories, poems, and songs connect to the Civil War (Frederick Douglass, spirituals, "Barbara Frietchie," "O Captain! My Captain,") and westward expansion ("Shenandoah," "Git Along, Little Dogies").

Parents and teachers are encouraged to build on the foundation provided here by discussing history with children and seeking out additional books. We especially recommend the Pearson Learning/Core Knowledge history series, described on our Web site, www.coreknowledge.org.

WORLD GEOGRAPHY

Reference Points

One of the most important concepts in geography is the idea of a reference point. If you want to tell a friend how to get to a particular movie theater, you'll give her directions starting from a place you both know, such as city hall or your school. She will be able to understand the directions because she will have the same reference point.

To describe locations on Earth's surface, geographers use agreed-upon reference points such as the equator and the prime meridian.

The equator is an imaginary line that encircles Earth halfway between the two poles. It divides Earth into two halves, called hemispheres. Everything north of the equator is in the Northern Hemisphere, and everything south of the equator is in the Southern Hemisphere

The prime meridian is an imaginary line that runs from the North Pole to the South Pole, passing through Greenwich, England. On the opposite side of Earth, the prime meridian becomes the 180 degree (°) meridian. The prime meridian and the 180° meridian form a circle that divides the world into the Eastern and Western Hemispheres.

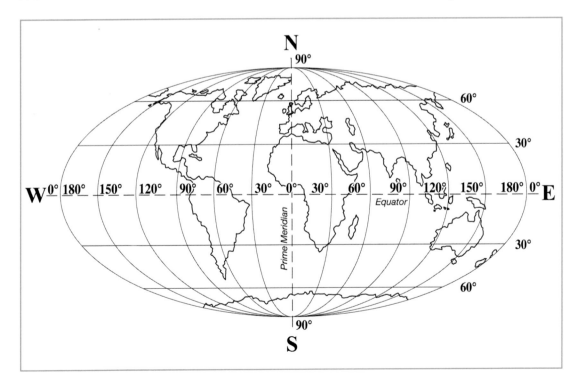

Latitude and Longitude

Latitude tells you how many degrees north or south of the equator a place is located. The lines that measure degrees of latitude are called "parallels," because they run parallel to the equator and to one another. For example, the 40th parallel (north) is the line of latitude 40 degrees north of the equator that passes through Spain, Italy, and northern Turkey.

Longitude tells you how many degrees east or west of the prime meridian a place is located. Lines of longitude, which connect the poles, are called meridians.

The prime meridian is 0° longitude. Here, the word *prime* means "first or most important." The prime meridian is important because locations are designated according to how far east or west of this meridian they are.

The location of the prime meridian was agreed upon by geographers from around the world who met in 1884 in Washington, D.C. They could have chosen another meridian, but this one passed through the location of the famous Royal Observatory, where for centuries astronomers prepared charts for navigators. Because many people were familiar with the location of Greenwich (a suburb of London, England), it was chosen as the reference point for all other meridians.

By combining longitude and latitude, you can specify any location on earth. For instance, Mecca, the holiest city in the Islamic world, is located very close to 20° N latitude and 40° E longitude. The numbers that tell you the location of a place are called coordinates. It's useful to be able to read coordinates, since the indexes of some atlases use coordinates to indicate locations.

What continent are you in if you are at 20° S, 40° W? 20° S, 20° E? 50° N, 10° E?

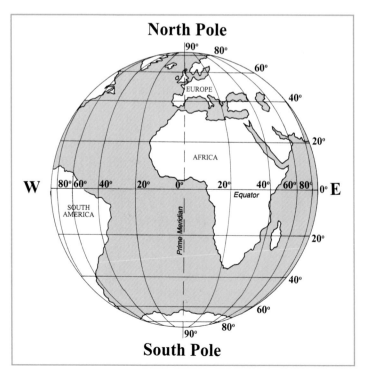

Arctic and Antarctic

Geographers use latitude to divide the earth into bands that run parallel to the equator. These bands tell us a lot about the climate of those regions. The farther from the equator in either direction, the colder the climate tends to be.

Far to the north, at about 67° N latitude, there is an imaginary boundary called the Arctic Circle. The lands and waters north of the Arctic Circle are called the Arctic Region. You can see the lands inside the Arctic Circle as if you are looking from above the North Pole on the map to the right. Notice that these lands form a ring around the Arctic Ocean. Much of this ocean is frozen in a thick pack of ice called the polar ice cap.

In the Southern Hemisphere, there is another imaginary circle called the Antarctic Circle, located at about 67° S latitude. The Antarctic climate is even colder than that of the Arctic. Most of Antarctica is buried under a permanent ice cap big enough to cover the entire United States in a layer two miles thick! This southern polar ice cap contains over 75 percent of the world's fresh water.

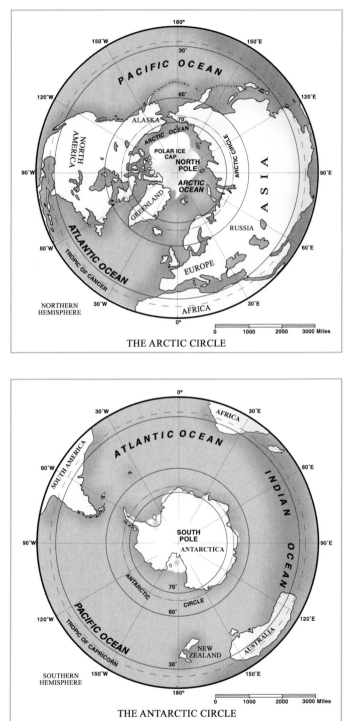

THE ARCTIC CIRCLE

THE ANTARCTIC CIRCLE

Tropical, Temperate, Frigid

Now let's find two more imaginary circles, the Tropic of Cancer and the Tropic of Capricorn. Both of these circles lie parallel to the equator at about 23° latitude: the Tropic of Cancer to the north and the Tropic of Capricorn to the south. These circles mark the northern and southern boundaries of the region known as the tropics.

Ancient Greek astronomers used these lines to develop a simple model of climate zones. They called the area between the two tropics the torrid, or tropical, zone. To the north and south of the tropical zone are two temperate zones, and beyond these are two frigid zones. Weather in the tropical zones tends to be very hot, weather in the temperate zones tends to be moderate, and weather in the frigid zones tends to be very cold.

The ancient Greeks believed that climate remained constant along any parallel (line of latitude). This rule turns out to be only somewhat true, because there are many exceptions. Geographers today argue that an area ought to be considered part of the frigid zone if the average summer temperature is fifty degrees or lower. According to this revised definition, some places south of the Arctic Circle are considered part of the frigid zone.

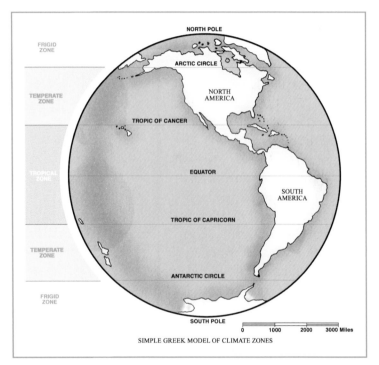

SIMPLE GREEK MODEL OF CLIMATE ZONES

It's important to remember that latitude is only one of the factors that determines climate. The tropical zones include lands as varied in climate as snow-capped mountains in Ecuador, dry desert, and lush rain forest. Even the temperate zones contain lands as different as cold Siberia, hot, humid Florida, and the hot, dry Gobi Desert. Temperature, rainfall, elevation, and distance from the sea can be as important to climate as latitude.

Differences in climate have a tremendous effect on people, animals, and plants. Climate influences what kinds of animals will survive in a region, how much and what kind of housing and clothing human beings will need, and how much food people can grow.

The Seasons

Latitude is also connected with the seasons. Remember that Earth revolves around the sun and also rotates on a slightly tilted axis. Because Earth's axis is tilted, there are certain times during the year when the North Pole is pointed a little more toward the sun and other times when the South Pole is pointed a little more toward the sun. In June, July, and August, the North Pole is tilted toward the sun. This means that the Northern Hemisphere gets more light and heat from the sun and experiences summer. At the same time, the South Pole is tilted away from the sun, so it is winter in the Southern Hemisphere. Six months later, in December, January, and February, the situation is exactly reversed. The South Pole is pointing toward the sun, so that the Southern Hemisphere experiences summer and the Northern Hemisphere experiences winter.

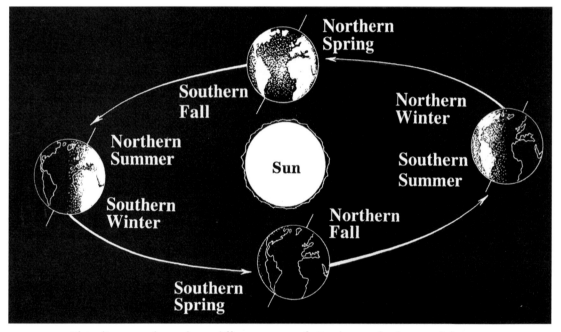

This diagram shows how different parts of Earth are tilted toward the sun
at different times of the year.

It's About Time

Longitude is connected with time of day. As Earth rotates (spins) on its axis, different parts of Earth point toward the sun. Only half of Earth faces the sun at any given time. That half experiences daytime, while the other half experiences nighttime. When it's noon at the prime meridian, it is midnight at the 180° meridian on the other side of Earth.

Suppose you want to call a friend in China on her birthday. When should you call her? Remember, China is halfway around the world from the United States. It is about half a day ahead of the United States in time. To reach your friend in China at 8 o'clock at night, you would have to call her from the United States early in the morning—at 7 A.M. if you live in New York, or at 4 A.M. if you live in Seattle.

Just as the prime meridian is the reference point from which distance east and west is measured, it is also the reference point for measuring time. Using the prime meridian as the starting point, we divide the world into 24 hourly time zones, to match the 24-hour cycle of Earth's rotation on its axis.

Find the 180° meridian on the Time Zones map below. This line is halfway around the world from the prime meridian. Now look at the sometimes zigzagging line that generally

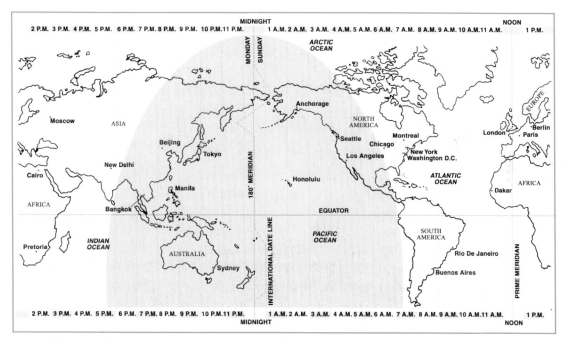

This map shows time zones all around the world. The shaded area shows the areas of Earth that are experiencing darkness.

Why do we tell time using the abbreviations A.M. and P.M.? A.M. stands for the Latin term *ante meridiem*, which means "before noon." P.M. stands for *post meridiem*, which means "after noon." The English word *meridian* comes from the Latin word *meridiem*, and both words mean "midday," or "noon." The hours before the sun shines directly on the meridian are labeled A.M., and the hours after are labeled P.M.

follows the 180° meridian: this is called the international date line. If you cross the date line going east, Monday becomes Sunday. If you cross it going west, Sunday becomes Monday.

Round Earth, Flat Map

Have you ever compared a globe and a flat map, noting the differences in size of the world's landmasses? If you do, you will notice that some landmasses seem larger on the flat map than on the globe. For example, the island of Greenland looks very large on some maps. Sometimes it even looks larger than South America. But in fact, South America is more than eight times as large as Greenland. What's going on?

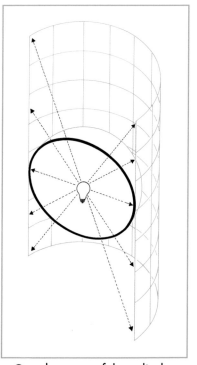

These differences in size result from distortions that occur when mapmakers represent our round Earth on a flat piece of paper. Here's one way to understand this: take a large sheet of paper and wrap it around the globe so that the paper touches the globe along the equator. The paper forms a tube or cylinder that does not touch the globe at the poles. Now, pretend your globe is hollow and made of clear plastic. On the plastic are opaque outlines of the world's landmasses. If you put an electric lightbulb in the middle of this hollow, clear globe, the light would cast the shadows of the globe's features onto the tube. Where the paper fits fairly closely to the globe, the sizes and the shapes of the shadows would be accurate. However, where the paper is far away from the globe, there will be some distortion.

On what part of the cylinder will the shadows cast by the lightbulb most accurately represent the globe's features? Where will there be the most distortion?

Think in particular about how areas near the poles are represented on the globe and the tube. On the globe all the lines of longitude meet in a single point at the pole, but on the paper tube the lines of longitude are stretched apart to look vertical and parallel. That's why Greenland and Alaska look so big on many flat maps.

Mapmakers are known as cartographers. They use the mathematics that go along with simple geometric shapes—such as the sphere, cylinder, cone, or plane—to draw maps on flat pieces of paper. Different kinds of maps are called "projections."

The Mercator Projection

The Flemish cartographer Gerhardus Mercator was the first to project Earth's surface onto a flat map. Made in the 1500s, his is still the best-known map projection of the world. Mercator's projection was made onto a cylinder like the one in the description opposite.

Generally speaking, you can trust the Mercator projection between the Tropics of Cancer and Capricorn. Direction on Mercator's map is also accurate, so the map is helpful in ship navigation. However, the Mercator projection makes landmasses near the poles look larger than they are. Thus, Alaska looks larger than Mexico on the Mercator projection shown below, when in fact Mexico is slightly larger.

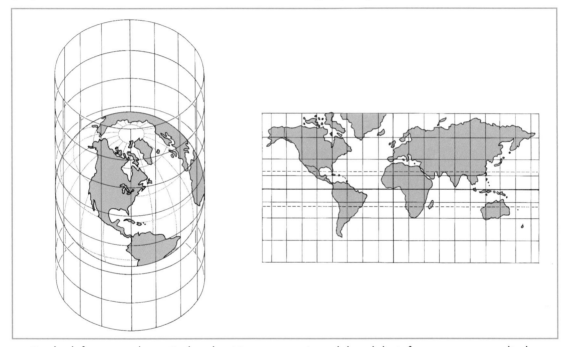

On the left you see how Gerhardus Mercator projected the globe's features onto a cylinder. On the right, a finished Mercator projection map laid out flat.

Conic and Plane Projection

If you twisted a paper into the shape of a cone and put it over a part of a globe, you would end up with a conic projection. This projection is most accurate where the cone touches the sides of the globe. As you move away from places where the cone touches the paper, however, distortion increases, so conic projections are rarely used for world maps. Instead, they focus on smaller parts of the globe, such as the United States.

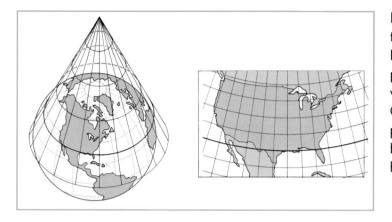

Look back at the diagram of the Mercator projection map. Notice that the meridians and parallels on that map run vertically and horizontally. Compare that to the conic projection map you see here. How are the maps different? How are they similar?

If you put a flat piece of paper against the globe, it would touch the globe at one point only, like the polar projection in the diagram below. This method is called plane projection. Maps of this sort are accurate only in the center, near where the plane touches the globe.

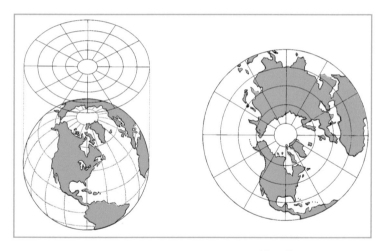

Would this polar projection be your first choice if you wanted to learn about the geography of Mexico? Why or why not?

Lakes

Lakes are bodies of water that collect in large depressions in the land called basins. Lakes are surrounded on all sides by land. They collect water from rainfall, melting snow, glaciers, rivers, and streams, as well as underground springs and groundwater.

Lakes are formed in many different ways. A glacier can scour out a basin, which later fills with water. In other cases, rocks and soil deposited by glaciers or landslides block a river's flow, causing a lake to form behind the natural dam. Sometimes a river flows so fast it overruns bends in the riverbed, leaving behind a lake the shape of a crescent moon or a horseshoe. These are known as oxbow lakes, because they are in the shape of an old-fashioned yoke that was used to harness oxen. Lakes are also created when cracks open in

Earth's crust and fill with water, when craters of extinct volcanoes fill with water, and when groundwater dissolves limestone, creating sinkholes.

Salty Lakes and River Sources

In places that receive a lot of rainfall, water overflows lake basins and runs out at the lowest point or outlet, forming a river either above or below ground. This water eventually flows to the ocean or sea, unless it dries up before it gets there.

In some desert climates, lakes lose water rapidly due to evaporation, and no outlets form. Minerals dissolved in the water begin to build up as more water evaporates, making very salty lakes. An example of this is the Great Salt Lake in Utah. Sometimes these salty lakes dry up completely.

Lakes of the World

See if you can find the following lakes on a globe or map of the world: in Africa, Lake Chad, Lake Victoria, and Lake Tanganyika; in South America, Lake Titicaca and Lake Maracaibo; in Asia, the Aral Sea; and, right on the border between Asia and Europe, the Caspian Sea. The Caspian and the Aral seas are salty lakes like the Great Salt Lake, but they are so large they are called seas.

The United States and Canada are home to the five lakes known as the Great Lakes. See if you can find all five on a map: Superior, Huron, Michigan, Erie, and Ontario. These lakes occupy deep basins that were scoured out by glaciers. The lakes are connected by rivers and falls. Water from Lake Erie flows over Niagara Falls to reach Lake Ontario. Water from Lake Ontario enters the Saint Lawrence River and flows to the Atlantic Ocean.

These Chicago skyscrapers look out over Lake Michigan.

EARLY CIVILIZATIONS OF THE AMERICAS

The Maya, Aztecs, and Incas

Centuries before Europeans came to the New World, great civilizations had already arisen in the Americas—the civilizations of the Maya, Aztecs, and Incas. The Maya civilization was the earliest of the three, starting as far back as 500 B.C. The Aztec Empire developed much later, beginning in the 1300s, and flourished in what is now central Mexico. The Incas thrived about the same time as the Aztecs and lived in the Andes Mountains in South America.

The Maya

In Guatemala and parts of Mexico, you can still meet people who call themselves Maya and speak a Mayan language. They are descendents of the ancient Maya, who built dozens of impressive cities in Central America.

One of the most impressive Maya cities was Tikal [teh-KAAL]. You can still see the ruins of Tikal in the jungles of Guatemala. Tikal had soaring temples and palaces decorated with sculptures, colorful paintings, and a kind of writing called hieroglyphs. In recent years scholars have decoded many of these hieroglyphs and learned a great deal about Tikal and the Maya.

EARLY CIVILIZATIONS
OF THE AMERICAS

The great plaza at Tikal, a Mayan site in Guatemala.

The hieroglyphs tell us that the people of Tikal believed their rulers were descended from the gods. The hieroglyphs also tell us when rulers took control, when they died, and how leadership was passed from one ruler to another.

For the ancient Maya, ancestors were very important. Who your ancestors were determined whether you would spend your life as a laborer in a quarry, as a priest performing religious ceremonies, or as a soldier.

Maya Life and Learning

Most of the Maya were peasants. They lived outside the cities in the rain forests. A peasant family would chop down a patch of rain forest, burn the cuttings, and plant corn in the ashes. After farming one place for a few years, they would move to a different section of the forest, burn the new area, and let the forest take over the old field. This kind of farming, known as slash-and-burn agriculture, is still practiced in parts of Mexico and Central America today.

We don't know a lot about the Mayan religion. We do know that the Maya believed in many gods who controlled the natural elements, such as the rain, the wind, the sun, the moon, and the stars. We also know they believed that they had to please the gods by shedding blood. In Mayan artwork, you can see both princes and slaves piercing themselves with thorns or even pulling ropes through their tongues. The Maya believed that offering blood to the gods was necessary to ensure that their crops grew and their children were born healthy.

The Maya's knowledge of math was unequaled for hundreds of years after their civilization collapsed. They discovered the concept of zero and developed an extremely accurate calendar.

Where Did They Go?

Most Mayan cities, including Tikal, seem to have been abandoned in the 800s. During those years, the Mayan scribes, who had dutifully recorded important dates and events for many years, stopped carving hieroglyphs into buildings and temples. Some cities were taken over by new peoples, and others were overgrown by the dense tropical vegetation.

Nobody knows what caused this great collapse. Some archeologists—scientists who study the remains of ancient cultures—think that the Mayan cities collapsed because their lands were farmed so heavily that they became worn out. Others think that the peasants revolted against the rulers and chaos followed. Still others suggest droughts, diseases, and foreign invasions as possible causes.

This stele, or carved pillar, is covered with hieroglyphs carved by the ancient Maya.

The Aztecs

The Aztecs were a warrior nation that ruled a large empire in central Mexico from the late 1300s until Hernando Cortés arrived on their shores from Spain in 1519. The Aztecs concentrated their power in the magnificent city of Tenochtitlán [Te-NOCH-tee-TLAHN], which now lies under modern-day Mexico City.

According to Aztec legend, the Aztecs lived as hunter-gatherers until a god told their people to stop moving from place to place when they found an eagle holding a snake in its beak. The Aztecs came across the eagle sitting on a prickly pear cactus on an island in a shallow lake, and they built their city right there. They called it *Tenochtitlán*, which means "the place of the prickly pear cactus."

Tenochtitlán was founded in the 1300s. Eventually, the city grew to nearly 150,000 inhabitants. It had avenues that led out from a massive pyramidlike temple in its center. Causeways connected the island city with the mainland, and aqueducts brought in fresh water. The Aztecs also built a maze of canals. The main thoroughfares had a water lane for canoes and rafts and a dry lane for people traveling on foot. The inhabitants scooped mud from the lake, piled it up into gardens, and grew corn and other vegetables. In the center of the city were palaces, ball courts, and a large bustling market.

The city amazed the first Spaniards who set eyes on it. One of them wrote, "Some of the soldiers among us who had been in many parts of the world, in Constantinople, and all over Italy and Rome, said that so large a marketplace and so full of people and so well regulated and arranged, they had never beheld before."

The Aztecs increased their power by conquering neighboring tribes and demanding tribute from them. The fierceness with which the Aztecs made war and exacted tribute made them many enemies. At the height of its power, the Aztec Empire stretched from the Pacific Ocean to the Gulf of Mexico.

This reconstruction shows how Tenochtitlán might have looked at the height of the Aztec civilization.

A Fierce Religion

Religion touched every aspect of Aztec life. The emperor was considered a kind of god, and the high priests who advised him had great power. These priests studied the stars to predict future events. A comet might mean good fortune, for example, while any babies born on the day of an eclipse were considered doomed.

The Aztecs believed in powerful gods who could bring good or evil upon the people. Two of their most important gods were the god of the sun and the god of rain. Many of their gods were depicted in the shapes of animals such as jaguars or serpents. The most distinguished warriors belonged to the knightly orders of the Jaguars and the Eagles. In battle they wore jaguar pelts and eagle feathers to give them fighting prowess.

The Aztecs also practiced human sacrifice. They believed that they had to offer their gods human blood. The victims were mostly prisoners of war and slaves. To perform these sacrifices, a priest would plunge a knife into the victim's chest and rip out the still-beating heart.

An Aztec priest performs a sacrificial offering of a living human's heart to the war god Huitzilopochtli.

Two Worlds Meet

In 1519, the ruler of the Aztec Empire was Montezuma (sometimes spelled Moctezuma or Motecuhzoma). Aztec history books describe him as a brave warrior and a wise ruler, knowledgeable about astrology and greatly respected by his subjects. During his reign, Montezuma conquered several neighboring peoples and strengthened the power of the emperor and the Aztec nobility, but he himself would ultimately be toppled by an even more powerful conqueror.

In 1519, Montezuma's messengers brought news that pale-skinned men had landed on the coast. These were Spanish conquistadors led by Hernando Cortés. Cortés had sailed to Mexico seeking gold and new subjects for Spain. He had arrived with only 600 men, many of whom were afraid to be in the New World and wanted to go back. Cortés, however, intended to march to the Aztec capital. He burned his boats to make his men understand that there would be no turning back.

Soon after he landed, Cortés began plotting with some of the Aztecs' enemies. One chief was so eager to get revenge on the Aztecs that he gave Cortés a young slave girl named Malinche [mah-LEEN-chay], who was very smart and could speak several languages. She quickly learned Spanish and soon became Cortés's translator and trusted spy.

Cortés recruited more allies and began marching toward Tenochtitlán. Montezuma followed their advance closely and ordered his subjects to ambush the Spaniards several times along the road to Tenochtitlán, but the ambushes proved unsuccessful. Despite their great numbers and skill as warriors, the Aztecs were at a disadvantage when they encountered the Spaniards. The Spaniards had various tools and weapons the Indians had not developed and could not easily understand. When the Spaniards first arrived in their ships, the Aztecs reported seeing "floating islands." When the Spaniards rode horses, animals unknown in the Americas, the Aztecs gazed in astonishment. Even more astonishing were the Spaniards' guns. The Aztecs were amazed that the Spaniards seemed able to control thunder and lightning.

But the most dangerous thing the Spaniards brought with them was not gunpowder: it was germs. Without knowing it, the Spaniards carried many germs that the Aztecs had no protection against. Ultimately many Aztecs would die of European diseases.

After trying unsuccessfully to ambush the Spaniards, Montezuma changed his tactics. He decided to allow Cortés to enter Tenochtitlán without further resistance. No one is quite sure why Montezuma did this. Perhaps he thought the Spaniards would impose gentler terms if he cooperated with them.

Once admitted to the city, Cortés and his men took Montezuma hostage. Eventually Montezuma was killed. The Spaniards claimed the emperor was killed by a mob of Aztecs; the Aztecs claimed the Spaniards did it.

The Spaniards ordered the Aztecs to stop sacrificing human beings and start worshiping the Christian god. But the Aztecs worried that their old gods would be angered if they neglected them.

In this atmosphere of growing tension, the Spaniards opened fire on a gathering of unarmed Aztecs, killing hundreds. The Aztecs fought back, killing three-quarters of the Spaniards. Cortés and his remaining men had to fight their way out of Tenochtitlán and barely escaped with their lives.

Cortés recruited more troops from the Aztecs' many enemies and attacked Tenochtitlán. He surrounded the city with cannons and cut off its fresh water. The Aztecs fought back for three months, but eventually too many of them died in battle or from diseases caught from the Spaniards. Tenochtitlán fell in August 1521, and the Aztec Empire collapsed.

The Incas

At the time that the Aztecs controlled much of Central America, the Incas ruled an even larger empire along the Pacific coast of South America. Even without a system of writing, the Incas administered a highly organized empire.

Among the cliffs and valleys of the Andes Mountains, the Incas built cities like Machu Picchu. They also built more than 14,000 miles of roads, some connected with tunnels and rope bridges. They fished in the waters off the coast and raised llamas and alpacas for wool on the hillsides. They grew crops in the green valleys between mountain ranges and used terraces to turn steep hills into good, level farmland. They even developed irrigation canals. Inca farming was so successful that warehouses were built to store extra food.

The Incas' most important crop was the potato. The Incas grew more than 200 different kinds of potatoes. Potatoes were unknown in Europe until the 1500s, when Spanish explorers brought them back from the Inca Empire.

The ancient Inca city of Machu Picchu was built among the high peaks of the Andes Mountains.

The Incas were also skilled stonemasons. Many of their walls were so well built that they still stand today, even though no mortar cements them. The stones fit together so perfectly, like the pieces of a jigsaw puzzle, that even now a sharp knife cannot pass through the cracks.

Like the Aztecs, the Incas believed that their rulers descended from the gods. According to legend, the founders of the Inca dynasty were sent down to Earth by the sun god.

This wall, with stones carefully fitted together, was crafted by ancient Inca stonemasons.

Pizarro

The Inca Empire rose to power in the 1430s, when a powerful ruler conquered neighboring tribes both through battle and by dominating trade routes through the mountains. In a short time, this emperor created a huge empire that included parts of modern-day Peru, Ecuador, Chile, Bolivia, and Argentina. The empire stretched almost 1,000 miles from end to end.

The Spanish conquistador Francisco Pizarro [pih-ZAHR-oh] heard stories about the mighty Inca Empire. Pizarro had been on the expedition led by Vasco Núñez de Balboa that hacked through the dense rain forests of Panama to become the first known Europeans to see the eastern shore of the Pacific Ocean. In 1532, Pizarro launched an expedition to contact and possibly conquer the Incas. He sailed from the west coast of Panama to Peru in one ship, with 180 men and thirty-seven horses. Two ships carrying ammunition and reinforcements later joined him in Peru. What allowed Pizarro to overpower the Incas was not only soldiers, guns, and horses, but also European diseases and a long civil war among the Incas.

Disease had ravaged Inca territories ever since the first Spanish ships visited the coast years earlier. Indeed, the previous Inca emperor, Manco Capac, had died of smallpox without ever seeing a Spaniard. He died without naming a successor, and this led to a civil war. Two brothers, Atahualpa [ah-ta-WHAL-pa] and Huáscar [WHAH-scar], fought to be the supreme ruler of the empire. Atahualpa won, but not before tens of thousands of Incas died in the fighting.

Pizarro arrived just as this civil war was reaching its climax. Pizarro and his men marched inland until they made contact with Atahualpa. He agreed to meet the Spaniards in a nearby town and left his soldiers—more than 30,000 of them—outside the town. He was carried to the meeting on a golden litter, escorted by several thousand unarmed men.

The Spaniards had decided on a treacherous plan: they would try to capture the Inca emperor, just as Cortés and his men had captured the Aztec emperor Montezuma a few years earlier. But first a priest stepped forward and, with the help of an interpreter, made a speech. He demanded that Atahualpa and his followers obey the Christian god, the Pope, and the King of Spain. Then he offered the Inca emperor a prayer book. Insulted, Atahualpa threw the book down. At that moment, bugles sounded and Spaniards charged out of nearby buildings. Some rode horses and carried lances; others fired guns. They took Atahualpa prisoner. Seven thousand Incas died that day, but not a single Spaniard perished.

Atahualpa promised to fill his prison cell with silver and gold in exchange for his freedom. Pizarro agreed, and the order went out: bring silver and gold! But when the ransom was collected, Pizarro did not keep his promise. Instead, he executed Atahualpa.

The Incas continued to fight, but they grew weaker and the Spanish eventually took over the Inca Empire and most of South America.

The Execution of the Inca, by A. B. Greene.

EUROPEAN EXPLORATION

The Discovery of the "New World"

Conquistadors like Cortés and Pizarro were part of a wave of Europeans who explored the world. Beginning in the fifteenth century, ships sailed from Portugal and Spain, and later from the Netherlands and England, on voyages to the fabled East described by Marco Polo. Explorers also sailed to continents that the Europeans called a "New World." Until the late 1400s, Europeans did not know that North and South America existed.

The Europeans didn't explore just to find out what was there. Their first interest was in making money from trade. Once they discovered new regions, they often became interested in conquest. Many explorers also hoped to convert the residents of newfound lands to Christianity.

Control of Trade

In medieval Europe, trade with the East had been dominated by merchants from Italian cities, especially Venice and Genoa. The Venetians and Genoese had set up a network of trading centers in port cities across the Mediterranean—on the coast of North Africa, in the Middle East, and along the shores of the Black Sea. The Venetians and Genoese brought raw materials, such as fur, fish, timber, and wool, from northern Europe into the Mediterranean. Then they bought luxury goods from the East, such as silk and spices. Later they resold these goods to other Europeans, at a large profit. The Italians did not go regularly to China, Africa, or the Indies themselves. Instead, they relied on other traders, mostly Muslim merchants, who dominated both the land and the sea routes to Asia.

Muslims are followers of Islam, a religion started in the seventh century by Mohammed. Arabic Muslims spread the new religion from the Arabian Peninsula westward across North Africa to Spain and eastward to India. As Arabs spread their religion, they also set up trade routes. By the thirteenth century, Muslim traders were transporting spices from the islands now called Indonesia, gold from Africa, silk and porcelain from China, and grain from Egypt.

By 1400, however, this trading system was under new pressure. The Ottomans, or Turks, another Muslim group, were moving west into the Mediterranean. In 1453, the Turks captured Constantinople, putting an end to the Byzantine Empire. By the sixteenth century, their European holdings stretched from Greece to Hungary. The Italians worried that the Turks might conquer their lands, or seize control of the trade routes and push them out of business.

Although the expansion of the Ottoman Turks was a threat for Italian traders, it was an opportunity for Spanish and Portuguese merchants. Since these lands were located far to the west, there was little danger of them being invaded by the Turks. From their coastal ports, Portuguese and Spanish traders could launch expeditions in search of alternate trading routes. They hoped to find new routes that would bypass the Turks as well as the Venetians and Genoese.

Early Portuguese Explorations

Portugal led the way. The Portuguese developed new ships that could travel farther, sail faster, and carry more cargo. In the early 1400s, Prince Henry the Navigator sent Portuguese sailors to explore the western coast of Africa.

In 1434, a Portuguese ship became the first European vessel to sail beyond Cape Bojador [BAJ-uh-door] on the west coast of Africa. Soon, Portuguese ships passed Cape Bojador often and returned with cargo from Africa, mostly gold, ivory, and slaves. These expeditions brought great wealth, but the Portuguese were still impatient to find a way around Africa to India.

Prince Henry the Navigator.

In 1487, a Portuguese captain named Bartolomeu Dias set out with two ships to follow the west coast of Africa. Dias kept close to the shore, but then winds and currents drove him into unknown waters, out of sight of land. His ships were pounded by storms, and one ship went down before Dias turned north and finally saw land again. To his amazement, the land was on the left side of the ship as he sailed north. Dias knew that meant he had sailed around the tip of Africa. Pressured by his weary sailors, he did not sail on to India but turned around to head home. He left a stone pillar to mark the tip of Africa, which he called the Cape of Storms. The Portuguese king renamed it the Cape of Good Hope because he thought "Cape of Storms" might scare off would-be explorers.

Christopher Columbus

The Portuguese soon found themselves challenged by the Spanish. The most famous explorer to sail for the Spanish rulers was Christopher Columbus. Columbus was actually an Italian, born in Genoa. He was fascinated by the tales of Marco Polo's travels to China. Like most educated people of his day, Columbus believed Earth was round. But he also believed that it was significantly smaller than most people thought. Putting these two ideas together, he concluded that he could reach the East by sailing west. There were only two problems with his plan. First, Earth was actually bigger than Columbus had reckoned, and second, the continents of North and South America stood between Columbus and the Indies. At the time, nobody in Europe knew that these continents existed.

Columbus first took his ideas to King John of Portugal. But just as Columbus arrived, Dias returned with news of the sea route around Africa to India, so King John was not inclined to gamble on Columbus's idea of reaching the East by sailing west.

Columbus then took his idea to King Ferdinand of Aragon and Queen Isabella of Castile. These two kingdoms would later combine to form the Kingdom of Spain. Isabella and Ferdinand had been working to extend Christian rule throughout the Iberian Peninsula by pushing out Muslims (often called Moors) who had controlled parts of the peninsula since the eighth century. In 1492, Isabella had just captured Granada, the last Moorish stronghold. Columbus had seen the city fall. Now the peninsula had only Christian rulers. Ferdinand and Isabella decided to unify the religion of the kingdoms and ordered all Jews and Muslims to become Christians or leave the country.

In order to sell his idea, Columbus appealed to the two monarchs' desire for wealth from trade. He also appealed to their desire to continue their success in taking power from the Moors and their desire to help spread the Christian religion. Ferdinand and Isabella agreed to fund his journey.

Columbus made four voyages. His first voyage in 1492 involved three ships—the *Niña*,

Columbus explains his plan to Ferdinand and Isabella.

the *Pinta*, and the *Santa María*. After two months of sailing west, the crew grew fearful and threatened to mutiny. Columbus promised they would turn back if they did not sight land in three days. On the third day, October 12, 1492, Columbus and his men landed at an island in the Bahamas, which he called San Salvador.

Columbus was convinced he was near India or China. When he encountered native people, he called them "Indians" because he thought he had reached the islands south of China called the East Indies. He was wrong, but the name stuck. Even today, the islands where Columbus first landed are called the West Indies.

The first people Columbus encountered were the Tainos [TIE-nos]. The Tainos received Columbus with friendly greetings. Another native people, the Caribs [CA-reebs], proved hostile. They were warlike people who often raided neighboring tribes. When Columbus returned to Spain, he took six Tainos with him as "proof" that he had reached Asia.

Queen Isabella honored Columbus with the title "Admiral of the Ocean Sea" and agreed to finance another voyage. More than a thousand Spaniards accompanied Columbus on his next voyage. Columbus was placed in charge as governor, but he could not keep peace and order among the adventurers who came to the "New World" seeking fortunes.

Columbus made two more voyages before he died in 1506. He went to his death still believing that he had reached Asia. Though Columbus did not "discover America," as people used to say, his voyage in 1492 begins the story of different peoples forming the nations of the Americas.

The sense that Columbus defines a hugely important moment is why, in the United States, October 12 is set aside as Columbus Day. For many people, it is a day of mixed emotions. For many years, Americans have been awed by the vision and bravery of Columbus, whose voyage changed the course of history. However, in recent years we have also come to understand that Columbus and the European explorers who followed him often acted violently against native peoples and that they (unknowingly) brought with them diseases that wiped out great numbers of the original inhabitants of the New World.

Who Will Rule the Waves?

After Columbus's voyage in 1492, the Spanish and Portuguese began competing to claim new lands. To prevent a fight, the rulers of the two countries turned to the pope, who often served as an international arbitrator. The pope, Alexander VI, had both sides sign the Treaty of Tordesillas [tor-de-SEE-yas] in 1494. This treaty drew an imaginary line through the Atlantic Ocean and said that all newly discovered land east of that line was open to Portugal, including India and the African lands Portugal had claimed. All lands west of that line, including those Columbus found, were open for conquest and colonization by the Spanish realms of Ferdinand and Isabella.

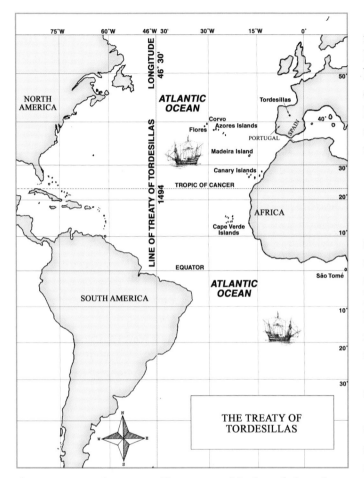

THE TREATY OF
TORDESILLAS

The Treaty of Tordesillas did not anticipate that countries like England, France, and the Netherlands would begin their own explorations some years later. They were not part of the agreement and had no reason to obey it.

Da Gama

With the Treaty of Tordesillas in mind, the Portuguese continued to send expeditions south. Vasco da Gama, a Portuguese nobleman and businessman, knew he would be rich if he could find a route around Africa to India. In 1497, he set out with four ships and 170 men.

After sailing around the Cape of Good Hope, da Gama sailed north, up the eastern coast of Africa, into an area that was entirely new to Europeans. He found that the coast was dotted with trading cities, including Mogadishu, Mombasa, Malindi, Zanzibar, and Kilwa. For hundreds of years, Arab traders had been trading with the people of the East African coast. They brought silk and cotton cloth, spices, and porcelain from China and India and returned with African goods, including animal skins, gold, and especially ivory, much in demand in Asia.

Some East Africans adopted Islam as their religion and added Arabic words to their Bantu language. They came to call themselves the Swahili, meaning "people of the coast," from the Arabic word *sahil*, meaning "coast."

In Malindi, an experienced Muslim sailor joined da Gama and showed the Portuguese the route to India. The

Vasco da Gama.

voyage was costly: the Portuguese were harassed by Arabs fearful of losing their trade monopoly, and more than half of da Gama's sailors died of scurvy, a disease caused by the sailors' poor diet, especially a lack of vitamin C from fresh fruits and vegetables. Finally, in May 1498, da Gama reached India.

Cabral

Vasco da Gama brought back great wealth from India, wealth that paid for another Portuguese explorer and trader, Pedro Cabral [cuh-BRAHL], to set out for India. On his way, he went far west of his planned course and landed on the coast of South America! He claimed the new land, which he called Brazil, for Portugal, because it lay east of the line established by the Treaty of Tordesillas. That's why today, while most people in South America speak Spanish, the language of Brazil is Portuguese.

When Cabral finally arrived in India, he did not negotiate well with the Muslim traders there, and violence erupted. The Portuguese ships had an advantage over most others sailing the seas: they were heavily armed with cannons, for Europeans had developed firearms in the fifteenth century. The Portuguese eventually used this military advantage to establish a headquarters at Goa, in India, and a network of fortified trading posts from the Swahili coast all the way to China. The Portuguese took over many trade routes that had previously been controlled by Muslims. The Portuguese often allowed Muslims to continue trading, but forced them to pay taxes to the Portuguese.

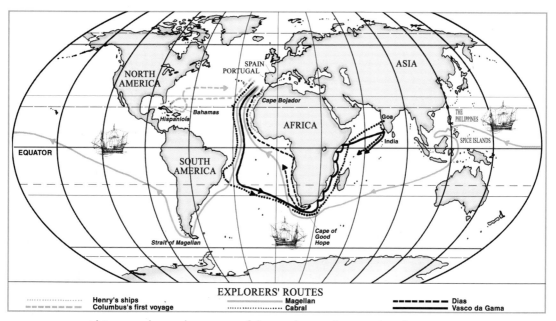

This map shows the routes of the explorers discussed in this section.

Magellan Goes Around the World

In 1519 (the same year Cortés encountered the Aztecs), a Portuguese seaman named Ferdinand Magellan set out on what became the first journey around the world. Magellan's trip was financed by King Charles of Spain. Magellan convinced the Spanish king that he could claim vast lands by exploring the area given to Spain by the Treaty of Tordesillas.

Magellan's five boats and 240 men sailed along the coast of Brazil, looking for a strait (a narrow waterway) leading west to the Pacific Ocean. No one had yet sailed the length of South America. When Magellan did indeed find a strait at the very tip of South America, he named it for himself, and we still call it the Strait of Magellan. Magellan also gave the Pacific Ocean its name.

Like Columbus, Magellan hoped that by sailing west he could avoid having to go around Africa and instead would reach the Moluccas [moh-LOO-cahs], or "Spice Islands," from the east. The name "Spice Islands" tells you what he was after: cloves, nutmeg, cinnamon, and other spices desired by Europeans.

Once Magellan got around South America, he thought it would take only a few days to sail across the Pacific. It took almost four months. Magellan and his men suffered terribly on the Pacific crossing. One survivor remembered, "We were three months and twenty days without getting any kind of fresh food. We ate biscuit, which was no longer biscuit, but powder of biscuit swarming with worms. . . . It stank strongly of the urine of rats."

Finally they reached the Philippines, where Magellan was killed during a fight with the native peoples. But his men sailed on. Eventually they reached the Moluccas, sailed across the Indian Ocean, and rounded the Cape of Good Hope. In 1522, the first ship to sail around the world returned to Spain. Only eighteen sailors came home alive.

The *Victoria* was the only ship to survive Magellan's voyage around the earth.

The Dutch Head East

The Netherlands soon joined the Portuguese and the Spanish in sending ships to sea. People from the Netherlands are called Dutch. In the early 1500s, the Dutch had been ruled by Spain, and Amsterdam and several other Dutch cities had grown into important centers of trade and exchange. However, when the Protestant Reformation began (see page 110), many Dutch followed the ideas of the Protestant reformer John Calvin, while the Spanish king rejected those ideas. Religious differences led to a rebellion in which the Dutch won independence from Spain.

The Pacific Islands and the Ring of Fire

The Spice Islands are in the island group south of the Philippines and southeast of Indochina and the Malay Peninsula. Look for them on the map. These are the islands that Columbus was trying to reach. The Portuguese were the first to colonize the islands, but most were later taken over by the Dutch.

Today the Spice Islands are part of the Republic of Indonesia. There are more than 13,000 islands in Indonesia, strung out from Sumatra to New Guinea. A large group of islands like these is called an archipelago [ar-keh-PEL-uh-go].

Volcanoes dot the rim of the Pacific Ocean from Asia to South America. Some are quiet; others are ready to spew out lava in fiery eruptions. This circle of volcanoes around the Pacific is called the Ring of Fire. The same areas are prone to earthquakes as well.

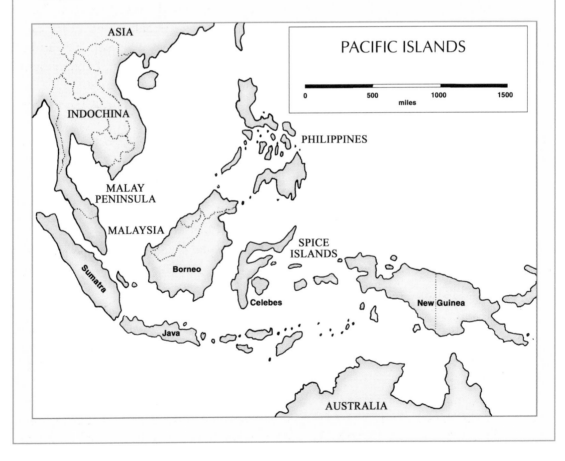

After breaking with Spain, the newly independent Dutch could not use Spanish trade routes, so they ventured out on their own. Dutch merchants set up the Dutch East India Company in 1602. Investors provided money to finance more voyages, and the Dutch government ordered the Dutch navy to help as well. With navy ships along to help fight the Spanish or Portuguese when necessary, Dutch traders made many profitable journeys. Dutch ships traveled to Indonesia, Japan, and the land that is now Vietnam. The Dutch became Europe's leading suppliers of spices, silk, and indigo (a popular blue dye).

The halfway point between Amsterdam and Indonesia is the Cape of Good Hope in South Africa. The Dutch founded Cape Town there as a supply station. The people in South Africa today who are called Afrikaners are descendents of the early Dutch settlers, and their language, Afrikaans, is a form of Dutch.

Where Are the English?

Although England was not a great sea power during the time of Columbus and Magellan, the English became aggressive traders and explorers (and pirates) by 1600. That year, Queen Elizabeth I made the English East India Company the only English company that could trade in the East Indies. The monopoly meant that the English East India Company grew very quickly. The English competed against the Dutch in Indonesia and began establishing trading posts in India, a country they would later take over entirely.

Because the Portuguese—and afterward the Dutch—controlled the southerly trade routes in the Indian Ocean, the English looked for a northerly route to Asia. They searched in vain for a "northwest passage," a route that would allow them to sail above North America to Asia. While the Spanish took the lead in exploring Central and South America, the English dominated exploration of the Atlantic coast of North America.

Europe's New World Colonies

Most European explorers sailed in search of gold and spices. But some Europeans were also interested in settling in the new lands. These lands became *colonies*: regions under the control of governments in distant lands.

After Cortés forced the Aztecs to submit to Spanish rule, he colonized them. In later years, the Spanish created colonies in South America, as well as in the Caribbean islands claimed by Columbus. When Cabral bumped into Brazil, he made it a Portuguese colony. The United States also started this way. When the English came to North America, they established colonies. These later became the first thirteen states.

In some colonies, Europeans settled to farm and raise their families. In others, the Europeans raised crops on large estates or plantations and sold those crops on the market. In other colonies they set up mines to dig for precious metals such as silver. The Europeans in charge of these plantations and mines did not expect to do the farming or mining themselves. At first, they often forced the native people to work for them. Many colonists treated the natives poorly.

Bartolomé de las Casas

A few Europeans spoke out against mistreatment of the Indians. One was the Spanish priest Bartolomé de las Casas. Las Casas studied religion and law in Spain before sailing to the New World in 1502. In the West Indies, he witnessed mistreatment of the native peoples and eventually dedicated his life to combating it. Las Casas preached sermons, wrote books, and traveled to Spain to speak before the king and the universities. He condemned the Spanish settlers for "waging cruel and bloody wars" and enslaving all who survived these wars.

According to las Casas, Spanish settlers were motivated by greed: "Their reason for killing and destroying such an infinite number of souls is that [they] have an ultimate aim, which is to acquire gold. Their insatiable greed and ambition, the greatest ever seen in the world, is [sic] the cause of their villainies."

Las Casas blamed the Spaniards for depopulating the West Indies, but disease probably played an even larger role in this tragedy. The same diseases that devastated the Aztec and Inca civilizations ravaged other parts of the Americas as well. When the native peoples died out, the European colonists began to look for new laborers. Eventually many began importing slaves from Africa.

Bartolomé de las Casas fought for decent treatment of the native peoples.

Sugar, Plantations, and Slavery

Slavery itself had existed for centuries, in many cultures. What was new in the 1500s was the development of a transatlantic slave trade. By the time Columbus sailed, there were already a few colonies in the Atlantic using slave labor. The Portuguese had colonized lands as early as 1419, even before they sailed beyond Cape Bojador. They claimed islands in the Atlantic, such as Madeira [muh-DEAR-uh] and the Azores [AAY-zorz]. These islands, along with the island of São Tomé [SOW toe-MAY], became sites for a new sugar industry. Portuguese citizens set up homes and businesses in these new lands, while still following the rule of the Portuguese king.

Growing sugarcane and turning it into sugar became a big business for the first time in the 1400s. By the early 1500s, the Portuguese island colony of São Tomé—where African slaves did the work—became the model for plantations in the Americas and in the Caribbean.

The Transatlantic Slave Trade

European settlers were quick to exploit the wealth of the New World, setting up gold and silver mines in the Andes Mountains and sugar plantations on the Caribbean islands. At first, Europeans forced the native peoples to work in the mines or on the plantations. When diseases decimated the native peoples, the Europeans looked to Africa for new laborers. The demand for slave labor increased as more plantations were established. In South America and the West Indies, slaves were imported to grow sugar and coffee, and in the English colonies, they grew rice, tobacco, and, later, cotton.

By the mid-1600s, there were many colonies in the Americas. Spain had colonies in the West Indies, Mexico, and South America. The Portuguese were in Brazil. The English and French were in North America and the West Indies. All of these colonies imported Africans to work as slaves.

For the most part, European traders purchased Africans who had been taken captive in wars between African states. A few powerful African rulers became very rich by selling war prisoners into slavery. Part of the coast of West Africa became known as the Slave Coast because so many slaves were sold from there. African traders marched chained captives to the busy trading ports. There, European merchants offered manufactured goods such as textiles, metal goods, and alcohol in exchange for enslaved people. In the late 1600s, European traders also began offering guns, and some African states, like Ashanti and Dahomey, became wealthy when they used European guns to attack neighboring states for the purpose of taking captives.

The European traders profited from a network of buying and selling known as the triangular trade. It was called triangular because ships often made a circuit of three journeys. Ships left Europe stocked with manufactured goods to exchange for slaves in Africa. From Africa, loaded with slaves, the ships crossed the Atlantic to the colonies in the Caribbean and the Americas. There, the traders sold the slaves for sugar, cotton, and tobacco—all goods produced by slave labor. The traders then returned to Europe and sold those goods.

The Middle Passage

Africans sold into slavery had to endure an agonizing voyage across the Atlantic called the Middle Passage. Large ships that carried from 150 to 600 slaves were built to make this terrible voyage, which could take more than ninety days. Slaves were forced to lie on their backs, crammed like sardines in a can, one person's head at the next one's feet. Slave traders used red-hot irons to brand their captives like cattle and shackled male slaves with heavy chains. So many slaves died during the Middle Passage—one out of every ten—that sharks followed the ships waiting to eat the corpses thrown overboard.

Between 1520 and 1870, more than ten million Africans were taken across the Atlantic to work as slaves. Most went to the Caribbean colonies and Spanish colonies in South and Central America. Beginning in 1619—when a Dutch ship left about twenty blacks at Jamestown, Virginia—the institution of slavery began to take hold in the English colonies that became the United States.

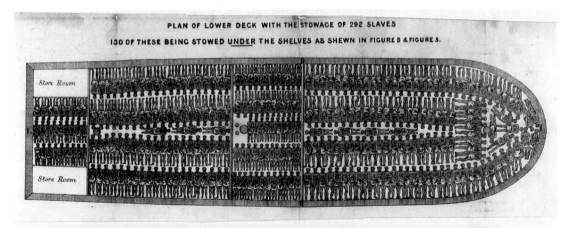

PLAN OF LOWER DECK WITH THE STOWAGE OF 292 SLAVES
130 OF THESE BEING STOWED UNDER THE SHELVES AS SHEWN IN FIGURE D & FIGURE 5.

This diagram shows how hundreds of slaves were packed into slave ships.

THE RENAISSANCE AND REFORMATION

Islamic Learning

Around the year 1000, Europeans began once again to rebuild their schools and revive the world of learning. They turned first to books from Ancient Rome—books that had been saved and painstakingly copied in monasteries. By the later twelfth century, they were looking for more books. They knew that even the ancient Romans had written most of their science and philosophy in Greek, not Latin. But few Europeans could read Greek.

Fortunately, many books by Greek philosophers and scientists had been preserved and translated into Arabic by Islamic scholars. Muslim scholars also wrote commentaries to explain these ancient Greek books, and in some cases they went beyond the ancient Greeks to make new discoveries.

Around A.D. 1000, a remarkable Muslim thinker and writer named Ibn Sina (in Europe he was called Avicenna) wrote commentaries on works of the Greek philosopher Aristotle and made especially important contributions to the field of medicine.

The scholar Ibn Sina is received by the Governor of Isfahan, in what is now Iran.

Other Muslim scholars made important advances in math. Even today, when you do math, you use Arabic numerals, not Roman numerals. When you study the kind of math called algebra, you learn principles explored by a ninth-century Muslim scholar who wrote a number of books on math, including one with the Arabic title *al jabr*.

Many cities on the Iberian Peninsula and in Sicily had been medieval centers of Islamic learning. Christian scholars from around 1150 to 1250 traveled to these centers. There they worked with Muslim and Jewish scholars to translate books from Arabic into Latin, the language of European scholarship.

These works of science, medicine, and philosophy helped form the curriculum of the first universities. Universities arose in Europe in the thirteenth century, and soon they became prominent centers of learning and scholarship. Bologna, Paris, Oxford, Cologne, and Padua were all important university cities. University students studied the liberal arts and might go on to receive a doctorate in law, medicine, or theology.

The Renaissance

Interest in the writings of the ancient Greeks and Romans continued to grow and eventually led to the period in European history we call the Renaissance. The Renaissance lasted from about 1300 to 1600. It was a time of great accomplishments in science, literature, and the arts. The Renaissance began in the city-states of northern and central Italy, especially Florence. Later it spread to other parts of Europe.

The word *renaissance* means "rebirth." During this period there was a rebirth of interest in the literature, learning, philosophy, art, and ideas of ancient Greece and Rome. A group of scholars called humanists led the way. They were called humanists because they were interested in the humanities—subjects like poetry, history, rhetoric, and moral philosophy. The humanists wanted to write as beautifully as the ancients did. They also thought that many ancient writers had good ideas about how to live a virtuous life.

The humanists began to study ancient Greek and collected manuscripts by ancient writers. When printing appeared, they published these works. Thanks to the humanists, we can read ancient authors like Livy, Cicero, Homer, and Plato. The humanists also wrote about the world around them. They wrote poetry and literature, history and politics.

Most humanists were very interested in religion. They read the works of early Christian thinkers, as well as other Greeks and Romans. Some studied Greek and Hebrew so that they could read the Bible in its original languages. They began the field of biblical scholarship. Desiderius Erasmus, from the Netherlands, was an important Dutch humanist and biblical scholar.

Humanist scholars also studied art and architecture. They discovered a book on architecture by an ancient Roman named Vitruvius, which showed Renaissance architects how to make new buildings in the ancient style. One humanist, Leon Battista Alberti, wrote a book on painting in which he described how to make a flat painting seem to have depth. The process is called *linear perspective*. This new way of painting became very popular and spread quickly.

Florence and the Medici

In Florence, the humanist movement was supported by the Medici [MED-ih-chee], a family that had grown wealthy through trade and banking. In the fifteenth century,

Cosimo de Medici (1389–1464) used his family's wealth and influence to transform Florence into a center of learning and art. Cosimo paid for paintings and sculptures to display in churches and public buildings. He built churches and started a new library, where ancient books and modern ones were collected and made available.

Cosimo also worked to attract the best humanist scholars. One Florentine scholar, Marsilio Ficino, wanted to translate the works of Plato from Greek into Latin. Cosimo gave Ficino a house, and he and his friends who visited Ficino called themselves "the Academy" after Plato's school in ancient Athens.

Cosimo's grandson, Lorenzo de Medici (1449–1492), carried on the family tradition of supporting artists and scholars. Lorenzo was so impressed with the work of the young Michelangelo that he invited the teenager to come and live in the Medici Palace. Lorenzo was also a patron, or supporter, of other great artists, including Leonardo da Vinci and Botticelli.

Lorenzo's son Giovanni de Medici (1475–1521) pursued a religious career and eventually became Pope Leo X. As pope, he brought many great artists to Rome to decorate the buildings in the Vatican. One of his favorite artists was the painter Raphael.

You can learn more about Raphael, Michelangelo, Leonardo, and Botticelli in the art section of this book. As you read about the wonderful things these artists achieved and look at their creations, remember that it might not have happened without the support of wealthy patrons like the Medici.

Michelangelo was one of many artists supported by the Medici family.

Beyond Florence

Although Florence was the birthplace of the Renaissance, Renaissance painters and scholars also worked in other Italian cities, including Rome, Milan, Mantua, Naples, Urbino, Bologna, and Venice.

Eventually the Renaissance spread to other parts of Europe as well. In the literature section of this book, you can read about the English poet and dramatist William Shakespeare and the Spanish novelist Miguel de Cervantes. In the art section, you can learn about Northern European Renaissance painters like Pieter Bruegel, Albrecht Dürer, and Jan van Eyck.

Princes and Courtiers

During the Renaissance, the courts of princes and other rulers were very important both to government and to culture. Those who spent their days in the courts and served the prince were called "courtiers." They had to know how to dress well and behave politely.

Baldassare Castiglione, a courtier in the Italian city of Urbino, wrote one of the most famous books of advice on how to succeed at court, called *The Courtier*. This book helped set the standard for proper behavior. Castiglione wrote that a courtier should be polite but also witty. He should be knowledgeable about politics and able to give good advice to the ruler, without giving offense. In addition, he should be able to sing and talk about the arts and discuss classical and modern literature. Above all, the courtier should make it all look easy. He should exhibit a quality known as *sprezzatura*. A person who has *sprezzatura* makes even the most difficult tasks look effortless.

Castiglione.

About the time Castiglione wrote his book explaining how a courtier should act, Niccolò Machiavelli wrote a book explaining how a prince should act. Machiavelli was a Florentine who had served his city as an official and a diplomat. But by 1500, the Italian states were at war. Some had been invaded by foreign powers, and many were riddled with corruption. What was needed, Machiavelli thought, was a prince who would be willing to act decisively and ruthlessly to restore order.

Machiavelli studied the politics of his day and also the politics of ancient Rome to discover how power really worked. In his book *The Prince* he described how a prince gains power and stays in power. While princes could not know what the future would bring, Machiavelli argued that they would be more likely to succeed if they were prepared and understood the world *as it really is*, not as we wish it might be.

If a prince wanted to remain in power, Machiavelli wrote, it would be better for him to be *feared* than *loved*. Also, the prince might need to do some things that would be immoral for a regular person to do. He might need to lie or to break agreements. In some cases, he might need to use violence. Although this might seem dishonorable, Machiavelli believed that the goal of keeping power—and keeping the peace—was more important than always playing by the rules.

Over the centuries, people have attacked Machiavelli's ideas as wicked and immoral. Even today, the adjective "Machiavellian" is used to describe sneaky, untrustworthy, power-hungry people. But Machiavelli's defenders say he was only being realistic about how people behave. The controversy has only helped sales of Machiavelli's book, which was a best seller in its time and is still widely read today.

Gutenberg

In the Middle Ages, books were rare and expensive because every book had to be copied by hand, by people called scribes. Around 1440, Johannes Gutenberg invented a way of making books that used a printing press and small pieces of movable type that could be arranged to make words. This meant that books could be made faster, more cheaply, and in greater numbers.

In less than one hundred years, more than ten million books were printed and sold. At first most of the books were printed in Latin, the language of scholars, but eventually the presses produced books in English, German, French, and Italian.

These two prints show stages of the printing process. On the left, a printer's boy is putting ink on the raised letters, while two workers behind him set type. On the right, a worker pulls down the press, while another on the right sets type.

The first book Gutenberg printed was the Bible. Soon printing became big business. Printers sold prayer books and cookbooks, books for scholars and books for average people. Printing helped the humanists share their findings by making new editions of ancient and modern authors available. It also helped religious reformers spread their ideas and rally people to their causes. One reformer who would make especially good use of this new technology was a German priest named Martin Luther.

Martin Luther

Martin Luther studied and taught at the University of Wittenberg. As a young man, he had a spiritual crisis about sin, confessing sin, and receiving forgiveness. He found reassurance in Saint Paul's letters in the Bible. Based on his reading of Paul's letters, Luther decided that people are saved not because of their prayers or good works or because they confess their sins to a priest regularly, but only because of the grace of God, made available by Jesus Christ's sacrifice of himself and death on the cross. Luther concluded that good works could do nothing to save a man; justification was *by faith alone.*

This conclusion set Luther up for a run-in with the church, which placed great emphasis on works and the confession and forgiveness of sins. When a person committed a sin, that person was in a sinful state. In order to be justified (put back in a state of being "just" or right with God), the person had to have the sin forgiven. To do that, the person would go to a priest and confess the sin. The priest had the power to grant forgiveness, but, even after confessing, the person would be expected to do certain acts of penance to fix the harm done by his or her sins. The average person might build up a long list of penitential tasks—so many that it might not be possible to accomplish them all during his or her lifetime. If a person died without having performed all of the necessary tasks, the person would be expected to work off the remaining tasks after death, in a place

Martin Luther points to the Bible, his source of religious authority.

called purgatory. Once the debt of penance had been paid in full, the person would be released from purgatory and would go to heaven.

To help people work off their penitential tasks, the Church gave extra credit for some acts, such as going on a pilgrimage to a holy place. These credits were called indulgences. The idea behind indulgences was that Christ and the saints had performed so many good works that they had built up more credits than they needed for themselves; the church could therefore draw on this "treasury of merits" to help others.

In the early 1500s, the popes needed money to rebuild St. Peter's church in Rome. Some German officials cooked up a scheme to raise money for the pope and for themselves. They decided to sell indulgences. They began their aggressive fund-raising campaign in 1517. A monk named Johann Tetzel sold the indulgences in Wittenburg, where Martin Luther lived. Tetzel promised buyers that if they purchased the indulgences for their relatives, those relatives would not have to work off their penitential tasks in purgatory but would go directly to heaven.

Luther was one of many people upset about the sale of indulgences. He prepared a list of ninety-five points against the Church's teachings on indulgences and other issues. In 1517, he nailed his "Ninety-five Theses" to the door of the Castle Church in Wittenberg, along with an offer to debate these points with anyone. In the debate that followed, Luther argued that if church officials would not fix the abuses he had identified, they were not really church officials at all and they should not be obeyed. Luther also denied the whole idea of a "treasury of merits." This went too far. Pope Leo X, the Medici pope discussed earlier, ordered Luther to take back what he had written. Luther refused. In 1520, Luther was excommunicated (thrown out of the church) and declared an outlaw.

Luther was discouraged, but he did not give up. A German prince offered him a hiding place, and Luther published a series of pamphlets defending and developing his ideas. With the help of the printing press, his ideas quickly spread across Germany. Luther argued that people could not obtain salvation by buying indulgences, going on pilgrimages, or confessing to priests. Salvation was by faith alone. He argued that God's word, as found in the Bible, was the true authority in all religious matters, not the pope or other religious leaders. Prior to Luther's time the church had seven sacraments, or religious practices, that it considered very important. Luther could find a biblical basis for only two of these, so he denied that the others were really sacraments.

Because people need leaders, Luther did not reject the clergy, but he insisted that clergymen were more like guides and shepherds, so he called them pastors. Luther saw no need for monks and nuns, and he rejected the rule that said priests could not marry. He himself married a former nun.

Luther's followers came to be known as Lutherans. Many German princes became Lutherans. Some of them liked the idea of closing the monasteries and nunneries, because they could then keep the land for themselves. Luther's reforms spread through German regions and led to a series of horrific wars between Catholics and Protestants. Finally, the German emperor agreed that the local prince or ruler could decide whether his region would follow Luther or Rome.

Protestantism and Calvinism

Luther and other religious reformers were called Protestants because they protested, or publicly declared their disagreement, with Church practices and beliefs. The movement these reformers spearheaded is known as the Protestant Reformation, or just the Reformation.

John Calvin was another Protestant reformer. Calvin was a Frenchman who began to read the writings of the reformers at the University of Paris. When the German wars of religion broke out, the king of France banned reformers. Calvin fled to the Swiss city of Geneva and spent most of the rest of his life there.

Like Luther, Calvin rejected the idea of salvation by works and insisted on salvation by faith. Like Luther, he believed that the Bible was the revealed word of God and the ultimate source of religious authority. One of the ideas Calvin is best known for is *predestination*, the idea that certain people have been pre-selected to be saved and others to end up in hell. Calvin believed that the Bible showed God to be all-powerful and all-knowing and showed humans to be weak and sinful. The Bible says that some people are saved by God, while some are not saved. Since God is all-knowing, Calvin reasoned, He must know in advance which people will be saved and which will not be.

Calvin also believed that the Bible explains how God wants people to live. In Geneva, Calvin and his followers set up a strict religious community based on their understanding of the Bible. Their church services were based on the singing of Psalms and the preaching of sermons. Calvinist churches were plain, with no statues or stained glass, because the Calvinists believed the biblical commandment against graven images prohibited such decorations.

Followers came to Geneva to study Calvin's reforms and to train to be ministers. These followers carried Calvinist ideas to France, the Netherlands, England, and Scotland.

The Protestant reformers continued to think of the Christian church as a single body that needed repair. Yet no single reformer could convince everyone that his set of repairs was exactly the right one. The result of the Reformation was that Christianity split into a number of different groups, or sects: Catholics, Lutherans, Calvinists, Baptists, Mennonites, Anglicans, etc. Each group saw itself as the real church and the others as heretics, or Christians whose beliefs were so wrong that they were doomed to hell. These divisions caused a series of wars in Europe that lasted over a century.

The Counter-Reformation

In the 1540s, Rome finally responded to these reformers. The pope called a meeting of all church leaders at Trent in northern Italy. The Council of Trent reformed abuses in the church. It also issued papers stating that many of the teachings of Luther, Calvin, and other Protestants were wrong. The council argued that the correct way to reform the church was from within, not from outside. The church leaders who met at Trent believed that traditional practices and observances did have value, and they worked to protect them. The movement inaugurated by the Council of Trent is called the Counter-Reformation or the Catholic Reformation.

One of the movement's leading figures was Saint Ignatius of Loyola. Born in Spain, he grew up loving adventure and became a soldier. In 1521, during a battle, a cannonball seriously wounded both of his legs. It took a long time for his wounds to heal, and he suffered great pain. During this time, Ignatius studied religion and became a Catholic priest. While some church officials lived in luxury, Ignatius set a different example: he lived in poverty and devoted himself to study and self-discipline. He founded an order of priests called the Society of Jesus, whose members are known as Jesuits. Jesuits became missionaries all around the world, as well as leaders in education. Thanks to their efforts, some regions returned to Catholicism. The Jesuits also brought their ideas to the Americas, where they established many schools.

Ignatius of Loyola, depicted as a saint, with a halo over his head.

ENGLAND

Henry VIII

What was happening in England during the Renaissance and Reformation? King Henry VIII was born in 1491, one year before Columbus sailed to America, and took the throne in 1509. Remembered as the ruler who established England as a major power, he ruled England until his death in 1547.

Henry VIII was also responsible for England's break with the Roman Catholic Church. His reasons for breaking from Catholicism were more personal and political than religious: he wanted to have his marriage annulled, or declared invalid. Henry's wife, Catherine of Aragon, was the daughter of Queen Isabella and King Ferdinand, who had sponsored the voyage of Christopher Columbus. Catherine had given birth to several children, but no son had survived past infancy—and Henry wanted a son to inherit his throne. Henry had also fallen in love with a court lady named Anne Boleyn. When the pope refused to grant the annulment, Henry declared himself head of the Church of England and ordered his archbishop to declare his marriage null and void. He then proceeded to marry Anne. Eventually Henry would run through a total of six wives, several of whom he had executed.

Henry VIII established the Church of England and declared himself its supreme head on earth. He followed Luther's lead in taking over Catholic monasteries and dividing the land among his followers.

Protestant or Catholic?

Under Henry VIII, the Church of England wasn't all that different from the Roman Catholic Church, except that Henry was in charge instead of the pope. Some people in England wanted the church to become more Protestant. Others wanted England to return to Catholicism.

Henry was succeeded by his son, Edward VI. During Edward's brief reign, England became more Protestant and Catholics were persecuted. When Edward died and Henry's eldest daughter, Mary I, took the throne, all this changed. Mary was a passionate Catholic and tried, unsuccessfully, to

Henry VIII.

restore the old religion. She had several hundred Protestants burned at the stake, thus earning the nickname "Bloody Mary."

When Henry's younger daughter, Elizabeth I, took over in 1558, it was still not clear whether England would end up a Protestant or a Catholic country. Elizabeth ruled England for forty-five years and ruled so well that many consider her one of the most intelligent and able rulers of all time.

Elizabeth I

Elizabeth was a Protestant, but she didn't want to see England torn apart over religion, so she tried to make the Church of England a moderate Protestant church. Although the English church refused to take orders from Rome and introduced a number of Protestant reforms, it also kept some old-fashioned church practices. For instance, the English church was still run by bishops, many churches were still decorated with stained-glass windows, and priests continued to wear robes called vestments.

English Calvinists felt that the English church was not Protestant enough. These people were called Puritans, because they wanted to *purify* the church by getting rid of traditions left over from the Catholic period, like bishops, stained glass, and vestments. Throughout her reign, Elizabeth had to deal with Puritans on one hand and Catholics on the other.

Queen Elizabeth I.

Many people expected Elizabeth to marry and hand over the throne to her husband, but Elizabeth remained unmarried all her life. She said she was "married to England." Elizabeth filled her court with poets, playwrights, and musicians and encouraged their talents. The great English playwright William Shakespeare lived during the time of Queen Elizabeth.

The Spanish Armada

Under King Philip II of Spain, Spanish ships were bringing in great riches from trade and plunder in the New World. Elizabeth's response was to encourage British ships to pirate the Spanish ships and claim their cargoes for England.

There were also religious differences between the two countries. Spain was Catholic; Elizabeth upheld Protestantism. In the 1580s, Protestants in the Netherlands fought to win their independence from Spain. Elizabeth supported the Dutch Protestants. The Spanish responded by assembling a huge fleet, known as the Spanish Armada, complete with 130 ships and over 30,000 men, to invade England.

The Spanish Armada seemed invincible, but the smaller English boats sailed into the heart of the Spanish fleet, broke it up, and sank ships at close range. The Spanish retreated, only to sail into a terrific storm that blew them onto rocks off Ireland and Scotland. England had defeated the unbeatable Armada!

The defeat of the Spanish Armada marked the beginning of British dominance of the seas. Leading the British fleet against the Armada was Sir Francis Drake, a favorite of Queen Elizabeth's. Drake had made his name attacking Spanish merchant ships and had also sailed around the world. Drake's voyages opened the seas to British exploration and set the stage for the first British settlements in America.

James I

Because Elizabeth had no children, she was succeeded by a distant relative, James Stuart, the King of Scotland. James I was a Protestant who commissioned a new translation of the Bible. The King James Bible appeared in 1611 and has had a tremendous influence on religious life and on English language and literature ever since.

During James's reign, England established its first colonies in the New World— Jamestown in Virginia and Plymouth in Massachusetts. Although Jamestown was named for James I, the king did not approve of its major export crop, tobacco. He called smoking "a custom loathsome to the eye, hateful to the nose, harmful to the brain, [and] dangerous to the lungs."

James I believed in the divine right of kings. He believed that the king was God's agent on Earth and that it was unlawful to disobey him. James passed this idea on to his son, Charles I, who succeeded him in 1625.

Charles I

Since the 1300s, the kings and queens of England had ruled with the help of the English national assembly, the Parliament. Whenever the king needed money, he asked Parliament to levy new taxes. Usually Parliament agreed. Parliament sometimes refused to grant the money that James I requested, however, and this did not sit well with a monarch who believed in the divine right of kings. Under Charles I, the situation got even worse. Eventually, Charles decided he would rule without getting approval from Parliament. This angered many members of Parliament, who felt that Charles was turning into a tyrant.

Religious disagreements also heated up. After Charles married a Catholic, many Puritans thought he was secretly plotting to reintroduce Catholicism, so thousands of

Puritans emigrated to Massachusetts. In 1637, Charles (who was king of Scotland as well as England) tried to force Scottish Calvinists (Presbyterians) to use a new prayer book. The Scots rebelled. Charles was forced to call on Parliament for money, but Parliament refused him. Soon England tumbled into a Civil War, with Parliament and the Puritans on one side and the king and his supporters on the other.

The Civil War

The English Civil War lasted from 1642 to 1649. Englishmen who supported the king were known as Royalists or Cavaliers. Those who supported Parliament were known as Roundheads, because many of them wore a short, bowl-shaped haircut. Eventually the Roundheads won, in large part because of the leadership of their general, Oliver Cromwell.

Charles I was taken prisoner and placed on trial for treason. He was found guilty and, in January of 1649, beheaded. For a nation that had heard so much about the divine right of kings, this was a truly shocking event.

King Charles I, with a priest, just before his execution.

Cromwell became the new leader, with the title of Lord Protector. He and other Puritans closed all the theaters in London, crusaded against gambling and card playing, persecuted Catholics, replaced old-fashioned Church of England priests with zealous Puritans, and passed strict rules outlining what people could not do on Sundays.

By the time Cromwell died in 1658, the English people were tired of strict Puritan laws. Some wanted to restore the monarchy. Charles I had lost his head, but his son was still alive and living in France. What if the English invited him back?

Charles II and the Restoration

In 1660, the English restored the monarchy and crowned a new king, Charles II. Charles II reestablished the Church of England and punished the men who had tried his father for treason. But he was careful to cooperate with Parliament and not do anything too drastic. He explained that he had no desire to "go on his travels" again.

Charles II.

Known as the Merry Monarch, Charles II enjoyed gambling, drinking, and watching plays in the reopened theaters. Although Charles had several children with his mistresses, he had no children with his wife. When he died in 1685, he was succeeded by his brother, James II.

James II and the Glorious Revolution

James II was a Catholic. By now, most of the English were Protestants, and Catholic rulers made them nervous. Although more than a hundred years had passed, people still remembered the reign of Bloody Mary.

When King James began making laws favoring Catholicism, members of Parliament decided to take action. They contacted the Dutch prince, William of Orange, and his wife, Mary. Both were descended from English kings and both were strong Protestants. The parliamentary delegates asked William and Mary to come to England with an army to make the country safe for Protestants. In 1688, William and his troops landed in England. King James panicked and fled to France. William and his troops marched into London without fighting a single battle.

Parliament declared that James II had "vacated" the throne by running away. The crown was offered to William and Mary, and they accepted. Because this change was accomplished with so little bloodshed, those who supported it called it the "Glorious Revolution."

Parliament presenting the crown to William and Mary.

The Bill of Rights

Shortly after the Glorious Revolution, Parliament passed a Bill of Rights to make sure the problems England had experienced in recent years would not happen again. The bill said that English rulers must be Protestants and could not marry Catholics. It also said that rulers could not set aside laws made by Parliament, keep Parliament from meeting, interfere with free speech or debates in Parliament, or collect taxes without the consent of Parliament. The king's subjects were also protected against excessive fines and cruel and unusual punishment. The leaders of the American Revolution would cite the Bill of Rights in their struggles with King George III during the 1770s, and representatives later drew on the English Bill of Rights when making one for the United States.

RUSSIA

Ivan the Great

In 1462, as the Renaissance was gaining momentum in western Europe, a Russian prince named Ivan III took the throne in Moscow. At the time, Russians were worried about freeing themselves from the Mongols and building their own nation. Ivan III, who came to be known as Ivan the Great, did just that. In 1480, he ended Mongol control and began to conquer provinces around Moscow, extending Russia's borders in every direction.

By the end of Ivan's reign, Moscow had become the most important city in Russia. In 1453, when the Turks conquered Constantinople, many leaders of the Eastern Orthodox Church fled to Moscow, bringing their religion, art, and culture. Under Ivan the Great, Moscow became an important center of the Eastern Orthodox Church.

Ivan the Great adopted the two-headed eagle, an old Byzantine symbol, as the symbol of Russia. He also began to call himself "czar," from the Latin word *Caesar*. This was Ivan's way of comparing himself to the great emperors of Rome, men like Augustus Caesar and Marcus Aurelius.

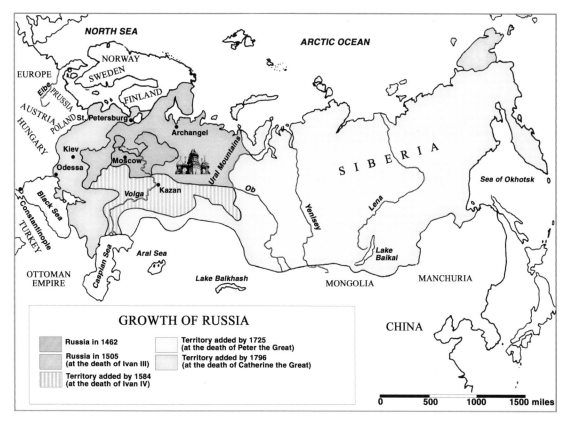

GROWTH OF RUSSIA

- Russia in 1462
- Russia in 1505 (at the death of Ivan III)
- Territory added by 1584 (at the death of Ivan IV)
- Territory added by 1725 (at the death of Peter the Great)
- Territory added by 1796 (at the death of Catherine the Great)

0   500   1000   1500 miles

Ivan the Terrible

Ivan the Great's grandson, Ivan IV, continued the work of his predecessor. During his reign, Russia expanded to the south and east, especially along the Don and Volga rivers. Russians also crossed the Ural Mountains to farm the treeless grasslands of Siberia, which are much like the Great Plains in the American Midwest.

Ivan IV also worked to increase his own power by limiting the power of the Russian nobles. He ruled with an iron fist, executing nobles and church leaders who opposed him. He even set up a special police force to enforce his reign of terror. They promised to arrest their own family members if the czar gave the order.

As he grew older, Ivan grew increasingly paranoid and moody. During one temper tantrum, he struck his own son with a staff and killed him. Because he struck terror into the hearts of foreign enemies and Russians alike, Ivan IV is known to history as Ivan the Terrible.

Ivan the Terrible.

Peter the Great

When Peter the Great took control of Russia in 1682, he was determined to make Russia into an international power. He visited western Europe in 1697 and decided to follow European ways. He reorganized the government, set up factories, brought in foreign scientists, and modernized the army. Peter even ordered Russian men and women to dress like Europeans. Noblemen were required to shave their beards or pay a steep tax.

Peter the Great.

With the help of western advisors and weapons, Russia fought the Swedes for more than a decade, and in the end pushed the Russian border all the way to the Baltic Sea, where Peter built a new capital city, St. Petersburg.

Catherine the Great

Catherine the Great was a German princess who married into the Russian royal family. She took over the throne in 1762 at age thirty-three and proved to be a strong ruler. Just as Peter the Great captured Swedish territory to get to the Baltic Sea, so Catherine attacked the Turks to get access to the Black Sea. Russia was victorious and built the port of Odessa, which, unlike the Russian ports in the north, does not freeze in the winter. Catherine's army also took part of Poland.

Catherine separated the powers of church and state and seized the church's lands, much as Henry VIII had done in England. During Catherine's reign, Russian nobles acquired lavish wealth, but it was based on the labor of peasants who had been forced into serfdom, a condition in which they could be bought and sold like slaves. The gap between rich and poor continued to grow and played a major role in later Russian history.

Catherine the Great.

FEUDAL JAPAN

Land of the Rising Sun

Japan is the easternmost country in Asia and has long been called "the land of the rising sun." Japan is a densely populated country made up of islands that are actually the tops of a great mountain range. There are four major islands. Honshū is the largest and the home of the capital city of Tokyo. Hokkaidō lies to the north and Shikoku and Kyūshū to the south.

Japanese weather is influenced by monsoons, wind systems that bring heavy rains in summer and winter. The summer monsoons bring rain, crucial for growing rice and other crops, to southern and central Japan. The winter monsoons blow cold air from Siberia across the Sea of Japan and dump snow on Hokkaidō and Honshū.

In late summer, storms called typhoons strike the eastern coast of Japan. Typhoons have swirling winds of over seventy-five miles per hour. In the United States, such storms are called hurricanes. Japan is also subject to tsunamis [soo-NAH-meez], gigantic waves caused by earthquakes beneath the ocean floor.

Japanese Feudalism

At the time of Columbus's voyages, Japan was not yet a unified nation. Powerful nobles controlled large portions of the country, much as they did in Europe during the Middle Ages.

By the 1500s, there had already been a long line of emperors in Japan. The emperors were mainly religious and cultural leaders. Real political power was in the hands of major landholders called *daimyos* [DIME-yos], who fought each other for more power. The most powerful *daimyo* would pressure the emperor to name him "shogun," which means "great general."

Because warfare was so important to this way of life, a special class of swordsmen arose—the samurai. They followed a strict code called *bushido* [bush-EE-do], which required bravery, self-control, and loyalty to their *daimyo*. You can read a story about a samurai warrior and his daughter on page 38.

Feudal Japan had a very rigid class system. The samurai class—from which the *daimyos* and shoguns came—was on top. Then came peasants, followed by artisans. Peasants were ranked higher than artisans because they fed people. Merchants were on the lowest rung of the social ladder because they did not produce anything; they only traded.

The Japanese did not always welcome foreigners. For a few decades in the 1500s, the Japanese welcomed some European traders and even a few Catholic missionaries. However, in the early 1600s, the shogun closed all Japanese ports to Europeans, except Nagasaki, where the Dutch were allowed to land on a small island in the bay and trade. Japan continued its isolationist policy of excluding European traders for more than 250 years.

A samurai warrior. When the samurai went into battle, the hundreds of tiny wooden and leather plates that made up his armor clattered against each other, making an alarming sound.

Japanese Religions

Unlike Europe, where Protestants and Catholics fought bloody battles, in Japan different religions managed to coexist. One of the most important religions in Japan is Buddhism. Buddhism began in India in the middle of the sixth century B.C., when a prince gave up his riches to teach the poor. He was called the Buddha, which means "the enlightened one." The essence of the Buddha's teaching is the Four Noble Truths:

1. All life, from birth to death, is filled with suffering.
2. This suffering is caused by a craving for worldly things.
3. Suffering will stop when one learns to overcome desire.
4. We can learn to overcome desire by following the eightfold path.

The eightfold path is a list of eight things Buddhists must to do to escape from desire and suffering. Among other things, Buddhists are expected to practice right speech, which means never lying or using bad language; right behavior, which means never doing anything one might later regret; and right effort, which means always working for the good and avoiding what is evil. By following the eightfold path, Buddhists believe they can attain a state known as nirvana and be released from suffering.

Shintoism, or just Shinto, is a religion that began in Japan. Its followers worship nature spirits called kami [KAH-mee] who are believed to live all around—in rocks, trees, lakes, even in blades of grass. The Japanese also honor their ancestors, emperors, and great heroes.

The Japanese people have built elaborate gardens on the grounds of their Buddhist temples and Shinto shrines. You can learn more about these gardens on page 191.

A bronze statue of the Buddha.

WESTWARD EXPANSION BEFORE THE CIVIL WAR

New Nation, New Lands

Now let's turn to American history. In the previous grades you should have learned how the British colonies in North America rebelled against the British king and Parliament and established themselves as an independent nation, the United States of America.

During the colonial period, settlers had moved farther and farther west, until the Appalachian Mountains stopped them. In 1775, the frontiersman Daniel Boone led a group of men through a mountain pass called the Cumberland Gap and blazed the Wilderness Trail into Kentucky. Over twenty years, about 200,000 pioneers poured over this route. Many settled along the Ohio River, because a great river is like a highway for boats and trade.

The Louisiana Purchase

In 1803, the country doubled in size when President Thomas Jefferson purchased a vast territory from France called the Louisiana Purchase. The deal included the Mississippi River and the wilderness that stretched beyond it to the Rocky Mountains. All this was

The Louisiana Purchase doubled the size of the United States.

Rocky Mountains

Louisiana Purchase 1803

Mississippi River

Appalachian Mountains

United States before 1803

bought for $15 million. Eager to find out exactly what was there, Jefferson sent out a party of explorers led by Meriwether Lewis and William Clark.

In the spring of 1804, Lewis and Clark set off from St. Louis, near where the Mississippi and Missouri rivers meet. The expedition traveled up the Missouri's tributaries until it reached the Rocky Mountains. Then they climbed the mountains and crossed the Continental Divide—the backbone of the continent. (East of the divide, rivers flow to the Atlantic or Arctic oceans; west of it, rivers flow to the Pacific.) The expedition reached the Columbia River and followed it to the Pacific Ocean. Lewis and Clark had the help of Native Americans along the way—including a young woman named Sacagawea [sak-a-juh-WEE-a] who accompanied them for most of the rugged journey with an infant strapped to her back. She supplied critical help as a translator when the expedition encountered new tribes.

The Fur Trade

Returning from the Pacific, Lewis and Clark met a pair of American trappers heading west on the Missouri River. Beaver hats were the height of fashion then, and these trappers wanted to make their fortune by catching beavers. The English, French, and Spanish had long traded with western Indians for furs. The Lewis and Clark Expedition and other exploring parties helped attract frontiersmen to the West. In 1806, army officer Zebulon Pike and his soldiers explored the southwestern section of the new Louisiana Purchase. They sighted a majestic peak in the Colorado Rockies that was later named Pike's Peak.

The mountain men in the fur trade led rugged lives in the wilderness. Many married Indian women who helped them survive. Transportation was the key to success in the fur trade. Luckily, the United States and Canada share a vast inland network of lakes: the Great Lakes reach from Minnesota to New York State. Lake Ontario feeds into the St. Lawrence River, which flows into the Atlantic Ocean. Taken together, they form a 2,300-mile waterway from the Midwest to the Atlantic. In 1825, the Erie Canal, a 363-mile manmade waterway linking Lake Erie to the Hudson River and New York City, was opened. As a result, New York City became the most important business center in the country.

Moving West

The promise of the West seemed endless. In the 1820s, American traders blazed another trail across 800 miles of forbidding desert to reach the Mexican city of Santa Fe (now the capital of New Mexico). Next, word spread of farmland available in California and Oregon Country. Pioneer families rushed to claim land, traveling overland on the Oregon Trail. Religious intolerance drove others. Mormons (followers of the Church of Jesus Christ of

Latter-day Saints) kept moving from place to place to escape persecution. Mormon Leader Brigham Young read of a remote valley located near the Great Salt Lake (an ancient inland lake of salt water), a dry, treeless area that offered the privacy that Mormons wanted. Beginning in 1846, thousands of Mormons traveled to this distant valley and built a city of their own, Salt Lake City.

In the early years, Mormons practiced polygamy. This picture shows a Mormon man with his six wives.

"There's Gold in Them Thar Hills!"

In 1848, something happened that changed the West forever. James W. Marshall was building a sawmill by a river in California. When he looked into the water running through the mill, Marshall saw little yellow flakes: gold!

News of this discovery spread quickly. Soon thousands of Americans, as well as people from other countries, headed to California hoping to strike it rich. The Gold Rush had begun. Most fortune seekers reached California in 1849, so they were called forty-niners.

Most forty-niners prospected (looked for gold) by sifting soil in a pan. Most of them, however, found only heartache. The work was hard and dirty, and life in crowded mining camps was miserable. One miner wrote home, "We all live more like brutes than humans." Gamblers tried to cheat miners out of their money, and shopkeepers charged high prices for food and everything else. Some disappointed forty-niners returned home, but others kept looking.

A forty-niner heads west.

Getting There

Many pioneers began their journey in St. Louis, Missouri. Boats loaded with goods and passengers traveled up the Missouri River to Montana.

Other pioneers loaded their possessions into canvas-covered wagons called prairie schooners, because on the vast grasslands they looked like ships bobbing on the sea. Oxen, horses, or mules pulled the heavily loaded wagons for over 2,000 miles. Usually, pioneers walked alongside. Since it was safer to travel in a group, families banded together in a wagon train to make the trek. The trip lasted six months or more through heat, rain, and hailstorms. Sometimes wagon trains got lost, and many travelers died along the way.

A westbound wagon train.

As pioneers moved west, the terrain changed. The early part of the trip was across the treeless, rolling grasslands of the Great Plains. This vast area stretches all the way to the Rocky Mountains and from Canada into Texas.

Except for a few missionaries and traders, the only people who lived there were Native Americans who hunted and lived off the buffalo that thundered across the plains. In the early days, the natives often were helpful. White settlers bartered with them, exchanging calico cloth for salmon, trout, and buffalo meat. As more wagons rolled across the plains, however, some Indians grew disgusted. Newcomers disrupted the buffalo herds and brought diseases like cholera, smallpox, and measles that native people had no resistance to. Many died. Angry at the invasion of their land, some Native Americans began to attack wagon trains.

The United States made a series of treaties with tribes to allow its citizens to settle on Indian land. But eventually the settlers wanted even more land and broke treaties to get it. This had happened before in the east.

Broken Treaties

In the early 1800s, the United States government made treaties with tribes in the Midwest that opened millions of acres to settlement. A Shawnee tribal leader named Tecumseh [te-KUM-sa] opposed these treaties. He claimed that the land was owned in common by all Native Americans and no tribe could give away land that belonged to everyone. Tecumseh was a brilliant leader who convinced tribes to fight together against white takeover of their lands. In 1811, at the Battle of Tippecanoe, his forces were defeated by the Americans and the native alliance was broken.

Another important Indian leader was Osceola [os-ee-O-la], a member of the Seminole tribe in Florida. Settlers took over Seminole land and forced the native people to move to what is now Oklahoma. Osceola resisted. He killed several white officials and began fighting. For two years the United States Army tried to capture him, but he knew how to hide in Florida's swamps and forests. Finally the army offered peace talks, but when Osceola arrived he was arrested and thrown in prison. He died shortly thereafter. The Seminoles were forced to leave their lands.

Manifest Destiny

Americans began to believe that it was their natural right to control all the land between the Atlantic and Pacific oceans. This idea became known as manifest destiny. Settlers eager for land looked to what is now the state of Texas. Mexico owned the entire area, but only a small number of settlers lived there.

Stephen Austin led a group of Americans to East Texas in 1821. At first, the Mexican government was eager to have Americans live there and gave land to newcomers. But so many Americans arrived that the Mexican government began to fear losing control of the region. After Mexico outlawed new immigration, Americans in Texas began to push for independence. In the fall of 1835, settlers attacked a group of Mexican soldiers, and the Texas Revolution began.

In February 1836, the Mexican army under General Antonio López de Santa Anna surrounded the Alamo, an old Spanish mission. Inside were about 180 men eager to fight for Texas's independence. For ten days they fought. Finally, the Mexicans broke through the walls and killed all the Texans in hand-to-hand combat, including two famous frontiersmen— Davy Crockett and Jim Bowie, creator of the broad-bladed bowie knife. This massacre made Texans furious. Six weeks later, they defeated the Mexicans at the Battle of San Jacinto. During the fighting Texans yelled, "Remember the Alamo!" The Texans captured General Santa Anna and created the Republic of Texas.

The Alamo, in San Antonio, Texas.

The Mexican-American War

In 1845, the United States admitted Texas as the twenty-eighth state. Texas claimed its border with Mexico was the Rio Grande. Mexico claimed it was the Nueces River, farther north. President James Polk sent General Zachary Taylor and his troops into the disputed area, and war broke out in the spring of 1846.

President Polk not only wanted the Rio Grande to be the border, he also wanted other Mexican lands so that the United States could reach all the way to the Pacific. Many people said the Mexican War was just an excuse to grab land. One American writer, Henry David Thoreau, opposed the war so strongly that he refused to pay his taxes and was jailed. He wrote a famous essay called "Civil Disobedience" in which he argued that an individual has the right to protest an unjust government action by breaking the law, or committing "civil disobedience."

In 1846, President Polk persuaded the British to give up their claim to the Pacific Northwest (now the states of Washington, Oregon, and Idaho). Two years later, the United States won the Mexican War and forced Mexico to give up what is now California, Nevada, Utah, and parts of Arizona, New Mexico, Colorado, and Wyoming. In 1853, the government purchased from Mexico the southern part of Arizona and New Mexico. The United States' boundaries now stretched from sea to sea. But a bitter debate over these new areas divided the country. Would the western states allow slavery or not?

THE CIVIL WAR

North and South

In the mid-1800s, America's population and industry grew rapidly. But the country was also growing apart. The economy of the North was becoming industrial, with factories producing iron, steel, machinery, and cloth. The South's economy was mostly agricultural and relied especially on tobacco and cotton crops. Most Southern farmers owned small farms and did not own slaves. But much of the South's cotton grew on large plantations, and these relied heavily on slave labor. Slaves did almost all of the hardest work and most of the skilled labor as well. A way of life developed in the South that depended on slavery.

Slavery existed in the North as well during colonial times, but as the Northern economy developed, it relied less on slave labor. In the North, people made their

A poster for a slave sale.

living as small farmers, shopkeepers, craftsmen, merchants, or factory workers. Because they did not rely on slave labor, many Northerners opposed slavery. Some saw it as a threat to the jobs of white workers. Others, however, considered slavery morally wrong and a threat to the principles of American government.

The Missouri Compromise

As more people moved to the West, more territories became eligible for statehood. The South wanted new states to be slave states, where slavery was legal. The North wanted the new states to be free states, where slavery was forbidden. If either side gained a majority in Congress, then it could pass laws against the wishes of the other side.

In 1819, the country was equally balanced between slave states and free states, with eleven of each. Then Missouri applied to become a new state—a new slave state. This triggered long, angry debates in Congress.

Finally, in 1820, the Missouri Compromise was reached. Missouri was admitted to the union as a slave state, and Maine was admitted as a free state. This balancing act was part of a larger agreement. Congress drew a line across the American territories; all lands north of the line (except Missouri) would be free, while settlers south of the line could own slaves.

The Mason-Dixon Line

During the colonial period, two Englishmen, Charles Mason and Jeremiah Dixon, surveyed the boundary between Maryland and Pennsylvania to settle a dispute over it. This boundary became known as the Mason-Dixon Line. Around the time of the Missouri Compromise in 1820, people began to speak of it as an unofficial boundary between the North and the South.

Abolitionists

Northern reformers called abolitionists worked to abolish, or get rid of, slavery. One was a journalist named William Lloyd Garrison. For more than thirty years, Garrison published a newspaper called *The Liberator*, dedicated to ending slavery. Another important abolitionist was the former slave Frederick Douglass (page 28).

Abolitionists like Garrison and Douglass persuaded some people, but nobody stirred up opposition to slavery more than Harriet Beecher Stowe. In 1852, Stowe published a novel called *Uncle Tom's Cabin*. The novel tells the story of Uncle Tom, a kind and religious slave who saves the life of a white girl but later is sold to a cruel master, Simon Legree. When Tom refuses to tell where two escaped slaves are hiding, Simon Legree whips him until he dies.

PICTURES AND STORIES from UNCLE TOM'S CABIN

Published by John P. Jewett & Co., Boston.

Over 300,000 copies of *Uncle Tom's Cabin* sold in one year, an amazing number for that time. Some Northerners felt so outraged they wanted to force the South to end slavery.

How Some Slaves Resisted

Slaves responded to their bondage in different ways. Some ran away. Others deliberately broke tools. Some organized rebellions. Some tried to kill themselves. Many slaves suffered quietly. Most slaves became Christians, and they often hoped they would find their reward in heaven. Many slaves still held on to some of their African beliefs. They made a new kind of music, songs called spirituals, that brought together African music and the Christian religion. These spirituals are moving songs, often based on stories in the Bible about how the people of Israel were delivered from slavery in Egypt. You can read more about them in the music section of this book (page 210).

The Dred Scott Decision

In 1857, the Supreme Court decision in the Dred Scott case pushed the North and South closer to war. Dred Scott was a slave whose owner moved Scott from the slave state of Missouri to the free territory of Wisconsin. In Wisconsin, Scott got married and had two daughters. But then Scott's owner decided to move back to Missouri, and he took Scott and his family with him—as slaves. Dred Scott went to court to argue that he and his family were free because they had lived in free territory.

Dred Scott.

The Supreme Court didn't give Scott and his family their freedom. With a majority of justices from the South, the Court used Dred Scott's case to take an extreme pro-slavery stand. The Chief Justice wrote a racist opinion: all black people, he said, were "so far inferior" to whites "that they had no rights which the white man was bound to respect." For many white people at the time, the idea that "all men are created equal" with "unalienable rights" did not apply to African Americans. Then the Court went even further and declared the Missouri Compromise unconstitutional, claiming that Congress had no right to exclude slavery from *any* territory.

The Lincoln-Douglas Debates

When people want to be elected to Congress, they usually explain to the voters their beliefs about important issues. In Illinois in 1858, one issue dominated the election for senator: slavery.

Senator Stephen A. Douglas was trying to get reelected. His opponent was Abraham Lincoln, already known as Honest Abe. Lincoln was a member of the Republican Party, which took a strong stand against slavery. In 1858, Lincoln made a speech calling slavery a great threat to the United States. Lincoln quoted from the Bible: "A house divided against itself cannot stand." He made clear what that meant for America: "I believe this government cannot endure, permanently half slave and half free."

Lincoln challenged Douglas to public debates on slavery. Douglas said that the people in the territories should decide whether to own slaves. Lincoln said this proved that Douglas was pro-slavery. In the final debate, Lincoln spoke of "the eternal struggle between . . . right and wrong." He went on to condemn the principle that says, "You toil and work and earn bread, and I'll eat it." "No matter in what shape it comes," Lincoln continued, "whether from the mouth of a king who seeks to bestride the people of his own nation and live by the fruit of their labor, or from one race of men as an apology for enslaving another race, it is the same tyrannical principle."

Douglas was reelected, but Lincoln was the big winner. He gained national attention because of the debates, which put him on the road to the presidency.

Abraham Lincoln as a young man.

John Brown

A year before the presidential elections of 1860, a violent event scared Southern slaveholders. An abolitionist named John Brown tried to capture a large supply of weapons at Harpers Ferry, Virginia. His goal was to give guns to slaves and urge them to rebel against their owners. Cornered by federal troops, Brown was captured and sentenced to hang. In the North, abolitionists made a hero of Brown: on the day of his death, church bells tolled and cannons were fired. Southerners were amazed and angered by the Northern sympathy for a man they saw as a dangerous fanatic.

Southerners began to think that the whole North was like John Brown: ready to use violence against the South. Southerners began to say that the only way to protect their way of life was to secede (break away) from the United States.

John Brown.

States' Rights and Secession

The tenth amendment to the Constitution says that if the Constitution doesn't forbid the states to do something, then the states have the right to do as they choose, so long as it does not conflict with the Constitution.

The Southern states claimed that slavery was a matter of states' rights. Southerners believed that, since the Constitution did not forbid slavery, each state had the right to decide whether to allow slavery, without the involvement of the federal government.

Southern leaders also claimed that states have the right to secede from the Union. They said they joined the United States voluntarily when they ratified the Constitution. And so they had the right to leave the Union, or secede, if the national government failed to respect the states' rights or made laws unfavorable to slave owners.

Talk of secession increased during the months before the election of 1860. One of the candidates, Abraham Lincoln, was a strong opponent of slavery. Many Southerners threatened to leave the union if he was elected.

Lincoln Elected: Southern States Secede

Lincoln was narrowly elected President, without the support of a single Southern state. Even though Lincoln promised not to interfere with slavery where it existed, many Southerners did not believe him. They no longer wanted to have anything to do with a government that they saw as an enemy. In December 1860, South Carolina became the first state to secede. By February 1861, six other Deep South states had seceded. When Lincoln took over in March 1861, five states in the upper South still had not seceded: Virginia, North Carolina, Kentucky, Tennessee, and Arkansas. Some people in these states were against slavery, but they didn't want to fight their neighbors to bring them back into the Union. Some Northerners agreed that states that seceded should be left alone.

Fort Sumter: The Civil War Begins

The fighting, so long in coming, began in 1861 at Fort Sumter, South Carolina. By this time, Southerners considered themselves a separate country. They wanted U.S. soldiers to get out of the South. Lincoln knew the South would probably resist any government attempt to send supplies to Fort Sumter. But he sent them anyway.

When the Southerners heard that supply ships were on the way, they began shelling Fort Sumter. On April 12, 1861, the Civil War began.

Lincoln called for a Union army to stop the South's rebellion. The South, Lincoln said, had fired the first shots. Southerners said they were forced to. Days after the firing on Fort Sumter, Virginia seceded from the Union, and three other Southern states quickly followed. Each side expected a quick victory. They were horribly wrong.

Southern forces open fire on Fort Sumter.

Eager to Fight

When Fort Sumter fell, Lincoln asked for 75,000 volunteers to join the Union army. The Confederate states, as the southern states were called, planned to assemble an army of about 100,000 men. Before the Civil War was over, the Union would send more than two million soldiers to fight almost a million Confederate troops.

Few Americans at this time had firsthand experience of the horrors of war. They didn't think about bloodshed and death. Instead they thought of war as an adventure, like stories they had read about famous battles and heroes. Each side expected the fighting to end quickly.

This map shows which states belonged to the Union and which to the Confederacy. It also shows some cities and battles mentioned in this section.

Some people in Washington, D.C., packed picnic baskets and lined up, like spectators at a football game, to watch the first major battle. On July 21, 1861, Union troops attacked Confederate troops by a creek called Bull Run, near Manassas, Virginia (about 30 miles west of Washington, D.C.). It appeared that the Union soldiers were winning, but then Confederate General Thomas J. Jackson arrived. His troops held their ground "like a stone wall," thus earning their general the nickname "Stonewall" Jackson. (For more on Jackson, see "Barbara Frietchie" on page 14.) The Confederate troops then turned the tables, and the Union soldiers retreated in a panic—along with the frightened sightseers. The Confederates won most of the major battles from 1861 to the summer of 1863.

The Confederacy

Eleven states seceded from the Union: South Carolina, Florida, Georgia, Alabama, Mississippi, Louisiana, Texas, Virginia, Arkansas, North Carolina, and Tennessee. They formed the Confederate States of America. Many Southerners wanted the Confederacy to be a loose collection of states, without much central government. The Confederacy adopted a constitution that contained strong rules in favor of slavery and states' rights.

The Confederates established a capital at Richmond, Virginia, only a hundred miles from Washington, D.C., and chose Jefferson Davis as their first president. Davis had been a Senator and had fought in the Mexican War. But he was not an effective leader. One member of the Confederate government called Davis "the most difficult man to get along with" he'd ever met. At the beginning of the war, most Southerners looked up to Jefferson Davis, but as the war went on, they blamed Davis for the South's problems.

Jefferson Davis.

Robert E. Lee

The commander of the Confederate army was General Robert E. Lee. A graduate of the military academy at West Point, Lee had served in the United States Army for more than thirty years. He was a hero of the Mexican War and had led the federal troops that put down John Brown's raid on Harpers Ferry.

When the Civil War broke out, Lee faced a painful decision. He was asked to command all Union forces and lead the fight against the Confederacy. But Lee was from Virginia. "With all my devotion to the Union, and the feeling of loyalty and duty of an American citizen," Lee said, "I have not been able to make up my mind to raise my hand against my relatives, my children, my home." Lee resigned from the federal army and joined the Confederate army.

By 1862, Lee was President Davis's top military advisor. Lee proved himself a master of planning and a strong leader. Soldiers who served under Lee liked and respected him. He set a good example for his men: he did not curse, smoke, or drink alcohol.

Ulysses S. Grant

On the Union side, the first years of the war were disappointing. Union troops failed to capture Richmond. Several times Lincoln replaced generals in hopes of finding someone who could lead the Union army to victory. As the war went on, a few officers proved themselves in battle, especially Ulysses S. Grant.

Like Lee, Grant attended West Point and fought in the Mexican War. Otherwise, they had little in common. Grant was fifteen years younger than Lee. Unlike Lee, Grant sometimes drank too much alcohol. Grant was not an army officer when the Civil War began. Instead, Grant was working in his father's leather shop in Illinois.

As soon as he learned of the firing on Fort Sumter, Grant began to organize volunteers in his town. He entered the war as a colonel in charge of an Illinois regiment, but he was soon promoted to general. In February 1862, his troops captured Fort Henry and Fort Donelson in Tennessee. When the commander at Fort Donelson sent Grant a message to see if he would make a deal, Grant answered, "No terms except an unconditional and immediate surrender can be accepted." In other words, give up completely and immediately. After a three-day battle, the Confederates surrendered unconditionally. Northerners joked that Grant's initials—U.S.G. —stood for "Unconditional Surrender" Grant.

Grant's leadership impressed Lincoln. "I can't spare this man," Lincoln said, "he fights." In 1864, Lincoln placed Grant in charge of the entire Union army.

Ulysses S. Grant.

Robert E. Lee.

The Soldiers

Most people who fought in the Civil War had never been soldiers. Most were farmers. They fought alongside workers and shopkeepers from cities and small towns. About one out of every four Union soldiers was born in a foreign country; for example, a large number of Irish immigrants joined the Union army.

Men of all ages became soldiers. One was as old as eighty; one was as young as nine. Most soldiers were young men, but some were boys. Usually, the boy soldiers didn't fight. Instead, they helped the adult soldiers by doing chores.

Boy soldiers did fill two important roles, as bugle boys and drummers. Since there were no radios or loudspeakers at this time, Civil War soldiers relied on the sound of bugles or drums to tell them when to wake up, when to march,

A youthful Union soldier.

when to attack, and when to retreat. On a battlefield clouded with smoke, a soldier could listen for the sound of bugles or drums to find out where to go and what to do.

Sometimes boys did fight with the men. Johnny Clem was eleven years old when he became a drummer for the Union army. When a Confederate cannon shot destroyed his drum, Johnny picked up a gun and fired back. From then on he fought alongside the adults. He even became a sergeant—at the age of thirteen!

Yanks and Rebs, Blue and Gray

Soon after the war began, Southerners started calling Northerners "Yankees" and Northerners called Southerners "Rebels." These nicknames were often shortened to "Yanks" and "Rebs," or sometimes turned up as "Billy Yank" and "Johnny Reb."

Early in the war, soldiers on both sides tended to wear the militia uniform of their home state or city. But this made it hard to tell who was on which side. Eventually, the Union army settled on blue uniforms, and the Confederates chose gray.

A Confederate soldier.

Soldiers' Songs

To forget the dangers of war and pass the time, soldiers on both sides sang songs. Southerners sang "Dixie":

> O, I wish I was in the land of cotton;
> Old times there are not forgotten.
> Look away! Look away! Look away! Dixie Land.

In December of 1861, an abolitionist named Julia Ward Howe visited a Union camp in Virginia, where she heard soldiers singing a song called "John Brown's Body," about the abolitionist. A few days later, Howe wrote new lyrics to be sung to the same tune. Howe's song, "The Battle Hymn of the Republic," combined images from the Bible with descriptions of what she had seen in the Union camp.

> Mine eyes have seen the glory of the coming of the Lord:
> He is trampling out the vintage where the grapes of wrath are stored;
> He hath loosed the fateful lightning of His terrible swift sword:
> His truth is marching on.
> Glory! Glory! Hallelujah!

"The Battle Hymn of the Republic" became one of the most popular songs on the Union side, and it is still sung today.

Antietam and the Emancipation Proclamation

When the war began, Lincoln insisted that the purpose of the war was not to end slavery. According to Lincoln, the North was fighting for one reason: to keep the United States united.

Lincoln wanted slavery to end, but first he wanted to hold the nation together. He was careful how he expressed opposition to slavery because some states fighting for the Union —the border states of Delaware, Maryland, Kentucky, and Missouri—allowed slavery. Lincoln was concerned that if he took too strong a stand against slavery, the border states would join the Confederacy.

Some Northerners urged Lincoln to use his power to end slavery. At first he refused, but eventually Lincoln began to think that freeing the slaves in the South might help the Union win. He wrote a presidential order that declared all slaves in Confederate territory free, but he kept this order locked up in his desk. Lincoln wanted the North to win a major battle before he made his announcement.

In 1862, Lee and his troops invaded the North. At first Lee's invasion went well, but then a Union soldier found a copy of Lee's plans wrapped around three cigars. Now Union generals knew where Lee was heading, and they confronted him at the Battle of Antietam in Maryland.

Antietam wasn't much of a victory: the Union army actually suffered higher casualties than the Confederate army, but Lee's invasion was stopped. Five days after the battle, Lincoln issued his Emancipation Proclamation. *To emancipate* means to set someone free; a proclamation is an official announcement. The Emancipation Proclamation announced that all slaves in areas under Confederate control were free beginning January 1, 1863.

Of course, neither the Congress nor Lincoln could force Southerners to free their slaves. But news of the Emancipation Proclamation brought hope and joy to African Americans. In the North, Frederick Douglass wrote, "We shout for joy that we live to recall this righteous moment."

African-American Troops

When the Civil War began, neither the Union nor the Confederacy allowed blacks to be soldiers. Prejudice still gripped the minds of many whites who thought blacks were not smart enough or brave enough to be good soldiers. But blacks wanted a chance to fight against the Confederacy. Some helped the Union army by spying. The Underground Railroad conductor, Harriet Tubman, was one of many African Americans who sneaked behind the battle lines to gather information about Confederate armies.

Meanwhile, the Union army

A recruiting poster for "colored" regiments in the Union army.

needed more soldiers and drafted thousands of whites, some of whom did not want to fight. Frederick Douglass called the Union foolish for not using black soldiers. This, said Douglass, was "no time to fight only with your white hand, and allow your black hand to remain tied." In 1862, the Union government passed laws to allow blacks to become soldiers. African Americans rushed to volunteer. The Emancipation Proclamation also encouraged Southern blacks to escape and join the Union cause. By the end of the war, one out of ten Union soldiers and one out of four Union sailors was African American.

The first Union army regiment to be made up entirely of African-American troops was the Fifty-fourth Massachusetts Volunteers. Their leader was Colonel Robert Gould Shaw, a young white officer who was the son of an abolitionist. In 1863, the Fifty-fourth went into action near Charleston, South Carolina. In their first battle, the soldiers of the Fifty-fourth defeated a Rebel charge. Later they were ordered to attack Fort Wagner, a Confederate fortress with thick walls and many guns. Although the fort remained in Confederate hands, the soldiers of the Fifty-fourth Massachusetts proved that African Americans were capable of great courage and sacrifice for their country.

Despite their bravery, black soldiers usually were not treated as well as white soldiers. For example, African Americans received less pay. Many black soldiers refused to accept any wages until the government agreed to pay them the same as white soldiers. Finally, Congress passed a law requiring equal pay for all soldiers, regardless of color.

The Misery of War

As the fighting dragged on, soldiers and citizens learned that war brings hunger, illness, suffering, and death. Soldiers were often hungry. Usually they ate cold salted pork or perhaps beans. When their supplies ran out, soldiers searched for whatever food they could find. On the march, soldiers might go several days without food.

For a Union soldier, an important part of meals was a biscuit called hardtack. It was so hard to chew, soldiers had to soak it in water or coffee, or fry it, before they could eat it. Confederate soldiers ate hard black cakes of fried cornmeal called pone.

Diseases spread quickly. Today you wouldn't eat or drink from a plate or cup used by someone who was sick. But at the time, doctors didn't understand that diseases are caused by germs. Civil War soldiers saw nothing wrong with sharing a cup with a sick man or using a dirty bandage.

Most of the medicines we have today had not been invented. If a soldier was sick or wounded, there was little anyone could do. Even soldiers with only minor injuries or illnesses would sometimes die. Surgery was crude: a severely wounded arm or leg was usually amputated. Twice as many soldiers died of disease as were killed in battle. In fact, an illness we no longer consider serious in this country, diarrhea, was the leading cause of death during the war.

The Ironclads

In March 1862, a ship unlike any other steamed out of Norfolk, Virginia, and attacked Union ships. The ship's name was the *Virginia*, but today it is better known as the *Merrimack*. What made this ship different were the four inches of iron armor that protected her. Cannonballs bounced harmlessly off her sides. On her first day in action, the *Merrimack* sank one Union ship and disabled three more. When the sun went down, the *Merrimack* sailed back to Norfolk, expecting to destroy more ships the next day.

The Confederates didn't know that the Union navy also had an ironclad ship, called the *Monitor*. The *Monitor* was much smaller than the *Merrimack* and had fewer guns, but its size made it hard to hit and its guns were in a rotating turret.

When the *Merrimack* came out to destroy more wooden ships, she was met by the *Monitor*. The two ships fought for four hours with neither victorious, but they changed naval warfare forever. Wooden ships were obsolete.

Gettysburg

By the summer of 1863, the Union was attacking the Confederacy from all sides. The Union navy bombarded cities and forts all along the Southern coast. Thanks to Grant's leadership and a fleet of ironclads, the Union controlled all of the Mississippi River except Vicksburg, Mississippi, which was surrounded.

Lee knew that he must do something to draw Union forces away from the weary South. If Lee could capture a Northern city, Grant might take troops away from Vicksburg to fight Lee's army. So, Lee led 75,000 men into Pennsylvania. On July 1, 1863, just outside Gettysburg, the Confederates were surprised to find Union soldiers. They fought all day long, until the Union soldiers took cover on ridges south of the town.

Confederate General James Longstreet issues orders at the Battle of Gettysburg.

Against Lee stood 90,000 Union troops. For two days, Lee attacked again and again. But Union troops had the advantage of being on hilltops, and each time the Confederates charged, cannonballs and bullets rained down on them.

Finally, on the afternoon of July 3, the Union cannons held their fire. It was a trick, and the Confederates fell for it. Lee ordered 15,000 men to make one massive attack, led by General George Pickett. General Pickett rallied his troops, calling out, "Up, men, and to your posts. Don't forget today that you are from old Virginia."

But many of the Confederate soldiers who took part in what is known as Pickett's Charge never made it back to old Virginia. Nearly half of the Confederates who took part in it were killed. When Pickett and his surviving troops returned to the Confederate lines, General Lee asked Pickett to gather his division and prepare for a possible Union counterattack. "General Lee," replied Pickett, "I have no division."

The next day, July 4, 1863, Lee expected Union troops to attack him, but an attack never came. That night, Lee began the long retreat back to Virginia. Earlier in the day, a thousand miles away, the Confederate fort at Vicksburg, Mississippi, fell, and the entire Mississippi River was under Union control.

At the Battle of Gettysburg, each side suffered over 20,000 casualties. Still, the Union had stopped Lee's invasion of the North. It was a turning point in the war: although there were many months of fighting ahead, the Union could see the possibility of victory.

Lincoln's Gettysburg Address

To honor their fallen soldiers, the governors of the Northern states decided to create a national cemetery at Gettysburg, and they asked Lincoln to speak at the dedication ceremony. First Edward Everett, then the most famous speaker in America, gave a speech that lasted two hours. Then Lincoln spoke. It took only two minutes to deliver his speech. But what a speech it was! The Gettysburg Address, as we call it, is one of the most famous speeches in American history:

Fourscore and seven years ago, our fathers brought forth upon this continent a new nation, conceived in liberty, and dedicated to the proposition that all men are created equal.

Now we are engaged in a great civil war, testing whether that nation, or any nation so conceived and so dedicated, can long endure. We are met on a great battlefield of that war. We have come to dedicate a portion of that field as a final resting place for those who here gave their lives that that nation might live. It is altogether fitting and proper that we should do this.

But in a larger sense we cannot dedicate, we cannot consecrate, we cannot hallow this ground. The brave men, living and dead, who struggled here, have consecrated it far above our poor power to add or detract. The world will little note, nor long remember, what we say here, but it can never forget what they did here. It is for us, the living, rather to be dedicated here to the unfinished work that they have thus far nobly advanced. It is rather for us to be here dedicated to the great task remaining before us— that from these honored dead we take increased devotion to that cause for which they gave the last full measure of devotion; that we here highly resolve that these dead shall not have died in vain; that this nation, under God, shall have a new birth of freedom, and that government of the people, by the people, for the people, shall not perish from the earth.

The Arithmetic of the Gettysburg Address

In the Gettysburg Address, Lincoln refers to an event that happened "Four score and seven years ago." *Score* is another word for "twenty." So "four score and seven" = (4 x 20) + 7 = 87. What happened 87 years earlier? 1863 – 87 = 1776—the year of the Declaration of Independence! In 1776, the signers of the Declaration asserted that "all men are created equal." In the Gettysburg Address, Lincoln described the Civil War as a test of that ideal.

Sherman's March to the Sea

In the spring of 1864, the Confederates continued to block Union troops in Virginia. But elsewhere the Union was winning. General William Tecumseh Sherman led Union troops into the heart of the Confederacy. Sherman's army advanced from Chattanooga, Tennessee, to Atlanta, Georgia, one of the South's largest cities. By the end of the summer, Sherman's troops marched into Atlanta and many citizens fled. When they left two months later, soldiers started fires that burned down much of the city.

Captain William Tecumseh Sherman.

Sherman told General Grant his plan was "to cut a swath to the sea." Sherman believed that seeing the horror of war would convince Southerners to give up. On their march, Sherman's troops, spread out in a line sixty miles long, destroyed houses, barns, and crops all the way from Atlanta to Savannah. Wherever Sherman's troops went, they left behind them starving men, women, and children. Years afterward, Sherman said, "War is hell."

Lincoln Is Reelected

After Sherman captured Atlanta, Northerners were convinced they could win the war. They showed their new faith by reelecting Lincoln. At his inauguration, Lincoln gave another short, powerful speech urging his listeners in the North to work hard to win the war but also to be merciful in victory. His closing words are especially famous:

> *With malice toward none, with charity for all, with firmness in the right as God gives us to see the right, let us strive on to finish the work we are in, to bind up the nation's wounds, to care for him who shall have borne the battle and for his widow and his orphan, to do all which may achieve and cherish a just and lasting peace among ourselves and with all nations.*

Richmond Falls

By the time of Lincoln's reelection, Union troops controlled part of every Confederate state. Lee's tired and hungry Confederate troops spent the winter in trenches outside Petersburg, Virginia, waiting to be attacked. In March, Lee surprised the Union troops by attacking them first, but there was little they could do against Grant's larger, better-supplied army.

General Lee sent an urgent telegram to Jefferson Davis in Richmond, telling him that the army could no longer protect the capital. Confederate officials boarded trains headed to Danville, Virginia, to set up a new capital. As they left, they set fire to warehouses and burned much of Richmond.

On April 3, 1865, Union troops led by black soldiers marched into Richmond, where they were greeted by crowds of cheering African Americans, many of them slaves.

Surrender at Appomattox

Lee's dwindling army hurried west to escape pursuing Union forces. Lee made it to a small town called Appomattox Courthouse, where the war came to an end for his weary soldiers. Grant sent a note to Lee asking him to surrender.

Lee sent back a note asking what terms Grant would offer. This time, Grant did not ask for unconditional surrender. Instead, he asked that Lee's soldiers stop fighting until they could be exchanged for Union soldiers captured by the Confederates.

General Lee learned from his scouts that his troops had no way to escape. "Then there is nothing left for me to do but go and see General Grant," Lee said. Then he added, "and I would rather die a thousand deaths." On April 9, 1865, Lee met Grant in a house in the village of Appomattox Courthouse. When Grant arrived, he and Lee shook hands. Grant had fought long and hard to defeat the Confederates. But now that he had won, he was kind to them. Grant agreed to allow Lee's soldiers to return to their homes and let them keep their horses and personal weapons.

Lee surrendering to Grant at Appomattox.

As Lee rode away, Grant removed his hat to show his respect for Lee. Union soldiers started to celebrate the surrender, but Grant ordered them to be quiet. Grant did not want the Southern soldiers to feel even worse. "The war is over," Grant said. "The rebels are our countrymen again."

Lee's orders to his troops were simple: "Boys, I have done the best I could for you. Go home now, and if you make as good citizens as you have soldiers, you will do well, and I shall always be proud of you."

Lincoln Is Assassinated

Northerners rejoiced at the news of Lee's surrender. But the celebrations would soon end.

Only five days after Lee surrendered, President Lincoln and his wife attended a play at Ford's Theatre, not far from the White House. As Lincoln watched the play from a seat high above the stage, an actor named John Wilkes Booth crept up behind the President and shot him in the head. Then Booth jumped down onto the stage, breaking his leg, and shouted to the audience, "*Sic semper tyrannis*"—Latin words meaning "Thus ever to tyrants." Booth ran from the theater and rode away on a fast horse. Lincoln was carried to a house across the street, where he died the next morning.

A week later, soldiers trapped Booth in a barn in Virginia. When he refused to give up, the barn was set on fire and Booth was killed as he ran from it.

This photograph of Lincoln was taken just a few days before his assassination.

The joy Northerners felt after Lee's surrender turned to deep sadness. As Walt Whitman wrote in a poem called "O Captain! My Captain!" (see page 15), it was as though a brave captain had brought a ship through a terrible storm—but then died.

RECONSTRUCTION

Repairing the "House Divided"

Even while the Civil War was going on, Lincoln began planning what is known as the Reconstruction, the process of bringing the Confederate states back into the Union. Americans disagreed on how to reunite the country. Lincoln wanted to make it easy for the Southern states to rejoin. In his second inaugural address, he called on all Americans to carry out the work of reconstruction "with malice toward none, with charity for all." But many Northerners looked upon Confederates as traitors who should be punished.

Within Lincoln's Republican Party, there was a group called the Radical Republicans that wanted the government to force changes upon the South. As the Radical Republicans saw it, white Southerners couldn't be trusted to treat blacks fairly. Some Radicals wanted the government to take land away from white Southerners and give it to freed slaves. All Radicals insisted that blacks must have the right to vote. Now, all eyes turned to Lincoln's successor, Andrew Johnson. How would the new president handle the problem of Reconstruction?

Johnson's Plan for Reconstruction

Andrew Johnson—a native of North Carolina who had been governor of Tennessee—was a Southerner at heart. Johnson announced a plan to grant amnesty—forgiveness—to Southerners. Most Southerners could qualify for amnesty simply by swearing to be loyal to the United States.

Johnson wanted to return control to Southern state governments as soon as possible. He insisted that slavery must be abolished, but he believed the states should decide what rights freed blacks would have. Under Johnson's plan, as soon as a Southern state amended its state constitution to abolish slavery, the people of that state could set up their own government with the same rights and powers as any other state in the Union.

Most white Southerners were happy with Johnson's plan. But every former Confederate state denied blacks the right to vote, angering blacks and Radical Republicans.

Black Codes

Southern legislatures went even further and passed laws known as Black Codes that limited a black citizen's ability to own property and engage in certain businesses. Some Black Codes gave whites the right to treat black workers almost like slaves. Many African-American Southerners felt angry and cheated. The Black Codes made them less than free.

The Black Codes also angered Radical Republicans in Congress. The same Confederate leaders who had lost the war were now serving in state legislatures across the South, passing laws that denied blacks their basic rights. Radicals saw the Black Codes as proof that Johnson's plan for Reconstruction must be overturned.

In 1867, Congress passed laws that forced nearly all the former Confederate states to start Reconstruction over. States must allow all male citizens to vote, including blacks. Until these Southern states satisfied all of Congress's requirements, they remained under the control of the federal army.

Scalawags and Carpetbaggers

Under the Radicals' Reconstruction plan, many former Confederate leaders could not hold public office. Federal military officials worked hard in the South to get blacks registered to vote. With fewer old Confederate leaders, and with more blacks voting, more Republicans were elected to state legislatures. These changes led to the development of two stereotypes, scalawags and carpetbaggers.

A scalawag is a rascal. Southerners who cooperated with the new state governments were called scalawags by other Southerners who rejected the post-war political changes. Maybe some scalawags were rascals, but just as many were genuinely working to improve the South's future.

Southerners who disliked scalawags felt the same way about another group, called carpetbaggers. Carpetbaggers were Northerners who came south to take part in Reconstruction. They were called carpetbaggers because they sometimes arrived with their belongings in a suitcase made out of carpet fabric. Many Southerners were convinced that carpetbaggers were greedy Northerners who came to the South looking to get rich quickly.

A carpetbagger.

The Freedmen's Bureau

For the millions of former slaves, freedom was a hard blessing. With no property of their own, how would they survive? Would there be schools for them? Who would protect their rights? The federal government tried to solve these problems by creating an agency known as the Freedmen's Bureau.

The Freedmen's Bureau tried to give African Americans plots of land from the vast areas the Union army seized during the war. During the war, Sherman distributed land and mules to blacks who followed his march to the sea. Later, word spread across the South that the federal government intended to give every freed slave "forty acres and a mule." Congress did give the Freedmen's Bureau control of millions of acres of land for freed slaves, but President Johnson opposed the giveaway and ordered the land returned to its former owners.

The Freedmen's Bureau did help to educate African Americans by building freedmen's schools and colleges across the South.

The Impeachment of President Johnson

Do you remember the three branches of American government and how the Constitution set up a system known as checks and balances? This system gives each of the branches—executive, legislative, and judicial—the power to check (stop) the other branches and so keep power balanced. The system of checks and balances gives Congress the power to remove the president from office if he is found guilty of "treason, bribery, or other high crimes and misdemeanors." The process of formally accusing a president is called impeachment. Once impeached by a vote of the House of Representatives, the president must have a trial, with the Senate serving as the jury and the Chief Justice of the Supreme Court presiding as judge. The president cannot be removed from office unless two-thirds of the Senators find the president guilty.

Because of his attempts to block Radical Republicans' plans for Reconstruction, in 1868 Andrew Johnson became the first president to be impeached. The trial dragged on for more than two months, and Johnson eventually promised that he would no longer oppose the Radicals' plans for Reconstruction. Johnson was found not guilty, but by just one vote.

Three Important Amendments

The Constitution, the highest law of our land, is not permanently fixed. Changes to the Constitution are called amendments. After the Civil War, the country adopted three new amendments to the Constitution in order to end problems caused by slavery.

- The Thirteenth Amendment outlaws slavery.
- The Fourteenth Amendment says that all persons born in this country are automatically citizens of the United States and of the states where they live. Further, no state may "deprive any person of life, liberty, or property, without due process of law." Due process of law usually requires the government to give every person a chance to defend his rights in court. The Fourteenth Amendment also says that no state may deny to any person "equal protection of the laws." The "equal-protection clause" has helped achieve fairness for all citizens.
- The Fifteenth Amendment prevents the state and federal governments from denying or limiting a person's rights on account of race, color, or the fact that the person was once a slave.

Following the ratification of the Fourteenth Amendment, polls were opened to blacks in Southern states.

The End of Reconstruction

Reconstruction lasted from 1865 to 1877. During that period, the South suffered from hunger and hard times. Angry whites across the South began trying to regain control of their state governments and their lives. Many Southerners claimed that the new state governments were corrupt, and some were. But mostly, white Southerners were fighting because they did not believe that blacks were their equals and did not believe them capable of responsible citizenship.

Some whites formed secret organizations to scare blacks and also whites who were friendly to blacks. The worst of these was the Ku Klux Klan. Members of the Klan wore white hoods to hide their faces when they went on raids to burn black churches, schools, and houses, and even kill innocent black people.

In elections in the 1870s, whites found underhanded ways of denying blacks their right to vote. Some states imposed a poll tax, which required a payment before voting. Many blacks couldn't afford to pay, so they couldn't vote.

By 1877, all federal troops were removed from the South. By then most Northern voters were willing to let white Southerners govern themselves, even if it meant blacks would suffer. In the next decades, Southern whites took more steps to deny blacks their basic rights. Not until the middle of the twentieth century would African Americans begin to achieve the equality promised by the Thirteenth, Fourteenth, and Fifteenth Amendments.

WESTWARD EXPANSION AFTER THE CIVIL WAR

"Go West, Young Man!"

After the Civil War, many Americans looked to the West as the place for new beginnings. In 1865, a newspaperman named Horace Greeley wrote, "Go West, young man, and grow up with the country." Many people read Greeley's advice, and the phrase "Go West, young man" became popular across the country.

Homesteaders

When pioneers began to move West in the 1840s, they headed to the Pacific Northwest and California in search of good land and gold. They saw no point in staying in the Great Plains where there were few trees and little water. No one could imagine farming there. On maps the region was called the "Great American Desert."

That changed in 1862 when Congress passed the Homestead Act. According to that law, a United States citizen could claim 160 acres of government land, called a "homestead," in the West. It was practically free—there was just a ten-dollar sign-up fee. Homesteaders had to live on their claim for five years, and then it became theirs forever.

Overnight, cabins and houses appeared on the Great Plains. A new kind of house was made out of sod (grass-covered earth) cut into strips and laid like bricks. Sod walls were very thick. They held heat well in the winter and stayed cool (like a basement) in the summer. But if the walls began to leak, the house became a muddy mess. Also, sometimes creatures emerged from the sod. One sod house pioneer wrote:

> How happy am I when I crawl into bed;
> A rattlesnake hisses a tune at my head!
> A gay little centipede, all without fear,
> Crawls over my pillow and into my ear.

The Homestead Act gave small farmers a fresh start. People tired of city life and immigrants from other countries rushed to the West. Women could claim land, too. This was an amazing opportunity. At that time women did not generally own property—whatever they had was actually owned by their husbands or fathers.

A sod house.

The Transcontinental Railroad

As more people moved west, people wanted faster ways to move people and goods out west. The country needed a railroad across the entire continent. The project was too expensive for any private business to attempt. So in 1863, Congress passed a law that paid for a transcontinental railroad by giving companies federal land and lending them money.

In 1863, the Central Pacific Railroad started laying track east from California. Most of the workers were Chinese. Through two winters, workers laid track through the Sierra Nevada, where snow drifts were up to six stories high. The Chinese worked twelve-hour days and had to supply their own food, even though white workers were fed by the company.

In 1864, the Union Pacific Railroad started laying track west from Iowa. Their crews were mostly Irish immigrants eager to leave crowded city slums. There were few trees, so wood for railroad ties had to be brought out from the East. Indians, angry at the invasion of their lands, sometimes attacked the workers. Finally, on May 10, 1869, at Promontory Point, Utah, the Central Pacific track was linked to the Union Pacific. One of the last spikes hammered in was made of gold. The nation had its first transcontinental railroad! Soon six others were under construction.

A Chinese worker working on the railroad.

Buffalo Soldiers

After the Civil War, Congress ordered the creation of all-black army units to be sent out West. Because white military leaders did not trust African-American soldiers, the officers in charge of these units were white. Native-American warriors gave the African-American

troops a special name: "Buffalo Soldiers." This was a sign of respect, because Indians believed that buffalo were sacred.

Buffalo Soldiers helped build forts and roads, explored huge areas in the Southwest, strung telegraph lines across hundreds of miles, and protected railroad crews and settlers from Indian attacks. They worked seven days a week (their only holidays were the Fourth of July and Christmas) and put up with very difficult conditions. Despite all the hardships, the Buffalo Soldiers remained on the job, and a number of them earned congressional Medals of Honor for bravery in battle.

Cathay Williams was a woman who disguised herself as a man (under the name William Cathay) and became a Buffalo Soldier. She served for two years before her secret was discovered by a doctor and she was forced to leave the army.

Cowboys

Cowboys became a familiar sight in the West after the Civil War. The East needed beef. In southern Texas, millions of beef cattle roamed free. Some businessmen gathered Texas cattle to sell back East, but they faced one big problem: the railroad had not reached Texas. The cattle had to walk to the nearest train depot—in Missouri, 1,500 miles away! The trip was called the "Long Drive," because cowboys would ride alongside the cattle and drive them in the right direction.

Newspapers exaggerated the amount of money to be made in cattle ranching. Soon many people rushed into the cattle business, just as the forty-niners had rushed west to hunt for gold. Cattle ranches sprang up wherever there was grass for pasture, and the cowboy became a familiar sight on the frontier.

This photo of a cowboy was taken in 1867, two years after the Civil War ended.

The Wild West

Because the West seemed much less civilized than the East, people often called it the "Wild West." Some stories about the West stretched the truth. Sometimes newspaper writers would spice up stories to make more people buy the newspaper. By the time the report traveled east, the story might have very little truth left in it.

The West became famous for outlaws like Jesse James. Many of these outlaws had served in the Civil War. They had learned to kill without hesitation and to steal to survive. When the war was over, some men continued to kill and rob as a way of life. Jesse and his brother Frank formed a gang to rob banks and trains. It seemed as if they would never be caught. But one morning, Jesse James was killed by a member of his own gang. His brother Frank was captured and put on trial, but he was found not guilty.

Another famous outlaw was Billy the Kid, whose real name was William Bonney. Before he reached his eighteenth birthday, Billy may have killed as many as twelve men. His gang stole cattle and killed anyone who tried to stop them. Then Billy's friend Pat Garrett became a sheriff. Within a few months, Garrett tracked Billy to his hideout. Garrett fired a shot into a dark bedroom, and at the age of twenty-one, Billy the Kid was dead.

So many colorful stories were told about Billy the Kid that some people admired him for his daring acts. But an editor for Billy's hometown newspaper wanted everyone to know what he was really like: "Despite the glamour of romance thrown about his daredevil life by sensational writers, the fact is, he was a low-down vulgar cutthroat, with probably not one redeeming quality."

The most famous character of all from the West was William F. Cody, better known as Buffalo Bill. He was a buffalo hunter, army scout, gold-seeker, and rancher whose adventures were exaggerated in popular books called "dime novels." Cody organized outdoor Wild West shows that were extremely popular. He hired cowboys and Indians, and he used real horses and buffalo to re-create scenes of western life. The audience loved it. One of his most popular attractions was Annie Oakley, a sharpshooter who could shoot a gun more accurately than any man. His Wild West show traveled the world and even performed for Queen Victoria of England.

On the left, Buffalo Bill; on the right, his star, Annie Oakley, with a gun Buffalo Bill gave her.

Seward's Folly

The federal government remained eager to add to the country. Russia needed money, so in 1867 the Russians agreed to sell Alaska to the United States. The Secretary of State, William H. Seward, made the deal secretly. The price was unbelievably low—only about two cents an acre. But Americans made fun of the purchase, calling it "Seward's Folly" or "Seward's Icebox." Seward believed that the Alaska purchase was his most important achievement—and he was right. In 1880, gold was discovered in Juneau, and gold fever helped settle the state.

The Closing of the American Frontier

In 1890, the United States government took a census (a count) of all of the people in the country. Nearly 17 million people lived between the Mississippi River and the Pacific Ocean. That was three times more than the number of people who lived in the entire country before the Louisiana Purchase in 1803. So the frontier was considered officially closed. But to Americans, the idea of the frontier is even more important than the West itself. That's one reason why there have been so many Western movies. To Americans, the frontier is about making a fresh start. It is a place of opportunity—a place to get rich or get land or have adventures or be alone in the wilderness. Americans still love the idea of the frontier.

NATIVE AMERICANS: CULTURES AND CONFLICTS

Natives and Settlers

Before Europeans arrived in North America, more than 500 languages were spoken among Native Americans. The land west of the Mississippi was home to over one hundred major Indian tribes, each with its own customs and beliefs. No one asked the Native Americans who had lived in the West for hundreds of years what they thought about the arrival of settlers. Since Indians were not citizens of the United States, they had no rights as far as the government was concerned. For Native Americans, the westward expansion of millions of settlers was not an opportunity but a catastrophe that disrupted and in many cases destroyed their way of life.

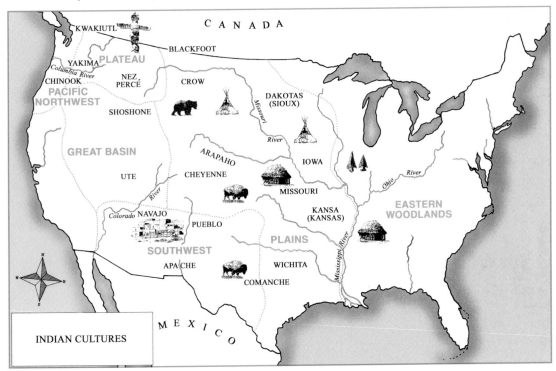

Indians of the Southwest

In the desert Southwest, some Indians had lived in organized towns for centuries before the Europeans arrived. Spanish conquistadors found Indians living in "apartment buildings" up to six stories high. These buildings were made mostly of adobe—a mixture of clay, sand, and straw. The explorers called the Indians *Pueblos*, the Spanish word for "towns."

Other southwestern Indians were not settled. The Apache tribe roamed the mountains, hunting and gathering wild foods. They were some of the fiercest fighters in the West. Because the desert was very dry, the Apache learned to go long distances without water. In one game, an

A pueblo in New Mexico, circa 1920.

Apache boy would fill his mouth with water, and then run four miles—without swallowing a drop!

The Navajo [NAV-a-hoe] at first roamed like the Apache. But they learned how to grow crops from the Pueblo Indians, got flocks of sheep from the Spanish, and began living in settlements across present-day Arizona and New Mexico. Navajo women made beautiful weavings that were prized by tribes all over the West.

Indians of the Pacific Northwest

In the Northwest, along the shores of the Pacific Ocean, lived the Chinook, Yakima, and the Kwakiutl, who devoted themselves to fishing and hunting for seals, sea lions, and otters. Some tribes hunted whales from canoes made from huge cedar trees that grew along the coast.

A totem pole.

The northwestern tribes had grand feasts called *potlatches,* where the host showered presents on his guests. The coastal tribes also created enormous totem poles—cedar trees carved with the likenesses of animals and mythical creatures. The carvings indicated the local chief's family history and were believed to protect their households from danger.

Indians of the Great Basin and the Plateau

East of the Sierra Nevada and west of the Rocky Mountains is a mostly barren area called the Great Basin. Few animals or plants can survive on the dry, rocky soil. But some Indians managed to live there. To survive, they spent hours looking for food every day. If they were lucky, supper might include an antelope, a rabbit, a bird, a snake, or a rat. But more often the Indians of the Great Basin ate grasshoppers and other insects and the seeds, roots, and leaves of plants. Two of the major tribes in the Great Basin were the Shoshone [sho-SHOW-nee] and the Ute. Sacajawea, who guided Lewis and Clark on their journey, was a Shoshone. The state of Utah takes its name from the Ute.

North of the Great Basin is high, level land that extends into Canada, called the Columbia Plateau. The Plateau Indians lived by hunting,

Five Ute women.

fishing, and gathering berries, nuts, seeds, and roots. Among the Plateau Indians were the Nez Percé, which in French means "pierced nose." The French who traded with the Nez Percé gave the Indians this name because some of them wore rings in their noses.

Indians of the Plains

Thirty million buffalo once roamed the Great Plains. Before the Spanish brought horses to America, Plains Indians hunted buffalo on foot using a lance or bow and arrow.

Sometimes groups of Indians would stampede buffalo over a cliff. Once Plains Indians learned to hunt on horseback, they raced fearlessly among the buffalo.

Indians did not waste any part of a buffalo. They ate the meat and made tools and weapons from buffalo bones and sinews. The hide was made into clothing and cone-shaped tents called tepees. Even buffalo dung was used as fuel.

The Lakota [la-COAT-a] (also called the Sioux) and the Crow lived on the northern Plains. The Arapaho [a-RAP-a-hoe] and Cheyenne [shy-ANNE] lived on the central Plains. To the south lived the Comanche [ko-MAN-chee] and the Wichita [WHICH-i-tah]. Many of the tribes were nomadic, moving often to keep up with wandering herds of buffalo. Other tribes close to the Missouri River raised crops in addition to hunting.

The Plains Indians spoke many different languages. To facilitate trade among tribes, they developed an elaborate system of sign language.

Plains Indians hunting buffalo.

The Buffalo Disappear

By the 1840s, Native Americans trading for guns, tobacco, whiskey, and other supplies delivered about 100,000 buffalo skins a year to white traders. Soon whites would kill buffalo on a much larger scale. To feed their workers, railroad companies hired teams of hunters. Others killed buffalo simply for sport. Many hunters took the valuable buffalo hide and left the carcass to rot. One hunter killed nearly 6,000 animals in two months. By 1883, only about 200 buffalo remained in the entire West. Only through the efforts of conservationists were buffalo saved from extinction.

The decimation of the buffalo herds was a terrible blow to the Indians of the Great Plains, for whom the buffalo was not only a source of food and other necessaries but also a sacred animal. One Lakota explained what the loss of the buffalo herd meant to his people: "The buffalo gave us everything we needed. Without it we were nothing."

Reservations

In 1840, the United States government promised Indians that the land west of Missouri and Iowa would remain closed to whites except for trading purposes. When this promise was made, most Americans thought of the Great Plains as a wasteland: the Indians were welcome to live on such undesirable land. But this changed when the Gold Rush, homesteading, and railroads began to bring settlers to the West.

When Indians resisted attempts by settlers to take their land, the government broke its earlier promises and began pressuring the Indians to give up some of their land. The government sometimes made a new promise: if a tribe agreed to live within an area called a reservation, the Indians could stay there forever, free from the threat of more settlers.

Reservations were usually much smaller than the areas the tribes formerly lived in. Indians were uprooted from homelands that had great spiritual importance for them and marched to reservations in unfamiliar territory, far away. Some Indians who had been farmers were forced to accept dry, rocky lands not suited for farming. Indians who had hunted buffalo over vast stretches of the Plains were put on small reservations where hunting was poor.

The government sometimes broke its promise that Indians could stay on their reservation forever. A federal agency called the Bureau of Indian Affairs administered government policies toward Indians. The bureau was supposed to protect Native American rights and help Indians adjust to reservation life. Sometimes the bureau did help Indians; but many bureau officials had no understanding of Native American life, and some were corrupt.

The Sand Creek Massacre

Some Indians decided to fight to keep their lands and their way of life. A series of wars pitted Indians against settlers and the United States Army.

In 1859, miners poured into Colorado looking for gold on Cheyenne and Arapaho land. Federal officials tried to force the Indians to accept a smaller reservation away from the miners. But the land was too poor to farm, and it had no game for hunting. Angry Indians took to the warpath and fought for over three years. Then they tried to make peace. Led by Chief Black Kettle of the Cheyenne, the Indians offered their surrender at a federal army outpost.

The Indians thought the war was over, but a band of white volunteers led by Colonel J. M. Chivington attacked them at a place called Sand Creek. Black Kettle waved an American flag and a white flag as a sign of peace. But Chivington's men attacked anyway, killing virtually all of the Indians. Not even children were spared: a visitor who came after the massacre recalled seeing infants lying dead in their mothers' arms. Later, the United

States government apologized for "the gross and wanton outrage" of the Sand Creek Massacre.

Little Big Horn

In 1874, gold was discovered in the Black Hills (in present-day South Dakota), part of the Great Sioux Reservation. Once again, miners moved into the area. The Lakota considered the Black Hills sacred ground and were ready to fight for it. By the spring of 1876, large numbers of Lakota, Cheyenne, and Arapaho joined in a war against the United States Army.

Two of the Indian leaders were Sitting Bull and Crazy Horse, both proud warriors determined to defeat the white men. For a time, it seemed they might succeed.

Sitting Bull was a Lakota leader who led resistance to westward expansion.

In June, a brash army colonel named George Armstrong Custer led a column of soldiers along a stream called Little Big Horn. Custer was under orders not to attack until more soldiers arrived. But he was confident that his small unit of cavalry could defeat any number of Indians. Ignoring orders, Custer tried a surprise attack against the camp where Sitting Bull and Crazy Horse were staying.

As it turned out, the Indians surprised Custer. A force of 2,500 warriors quickly surrounded Custer's 265 soldiers. In a few hours, Custer and all his men lay dead. The Battle of Little Big Horn became famous as "Custer's Last Stand."

Despite their victory at Little Big Horn, a few months later most of the Indians were forced to surrender. Sitting Bull and a small group escaped to Canada, but starvation later forced them to return.

Custer, several years before the battle of Little Big Horn.

"I will fight no more forever."

In 1877, the United States government ordered Chief Joseph, a Nez Percé, to bring his people onto a reservation. The Indians were furious. Three young warriors slipped away and murdered several whites. This meant war. The United States Army came after the Indians, but the Nez Percé kept managing to escape. Traveling for months over mountains and plains, nearly 800 men, women, and children tried to outrun the army. Finally, the army caught up with the Nez Percé. Chief Joseph was sick of fighting and running. He sent a message to the commander of the U.S. troops:

Chief Joseph.

Tell General Howard I know his heart. What he told me before, I have it in my heart. I am tired of fighting. Our chiefs are killed. . . . The old men are all dead. . . . It is cold, and we have no blankets. The little children are freezing to death. My people, some of them, have run away to the hills, and have no blankets, no food. No one knows where they are—perhaps freezing to death. I want to have time to look for my children, and see how many of them I can find. Maybe I shall find them among the dead. Hear me, my chiefs! I am tired. My heart is sick and sad. From where the sun now stands, I will fight no more forever.

The Ghost Dance

As the 1800s ended, American Indians were losing the West. They expressed their frustrations at being driven from their homelands and their longing for the old ways of life in a new sacred dance, called the Ghost Dance. Indians believed that if they kept dancing, white men and all they brought with them (railroads, telegraph wires, fences, etc.) would be swept away, dead Indians would return to life, and herds of buffalo would again wander the Plains. Belief in the power of the Ghost Dance spread across the northern Plains.

Among the Lakota, Ghost Dancers began wearing guns when dancing. The Lakota were angry because the government had not sent food it had promised. Fearing an uprising, the federal government sent troops to stop the dancing and arrest the Lakota chief, Sitting Bull. He did not put up a fight, but another Indian shot one of the arresting officers. That officer in turn shot and killed Sitting Bull.

Two weeks later, at a place called Wounded Knee, the Lakota prepared to surrender to federal troops. Soldiers surrounded the Indian camp and ordered the warriors to give up their weapons. A medicine man began to dance and chant. "You have nothing to fear," he assured the Indians. "The Ghost Dance has turned your shirts to iron. No bullet can harm you." One Indian held a gun over his head and screamed. Soldiers grabbed the gun, but a shot from another rifle rang out. The soldiers opened fire. Cannons fired exploding shells into the camp. The cries of the Ghost Dance came to a sad end as Indian men, women, and children died in the bloodstained snow.

Attempts to Assimilate the Indians

Many white Americans felt compassion for the Indians and wanted to help them, but they did not understand Indian ways of life and were not interested in preserving or protecting them. For most Americans, helping Indians meant assimilating them—trying to make them more like whites.

Schools were started to assimilate young Indians. In 1879, the Carlisle Indian School opened in Carlisle, Pennsylvania. Young Indians from western reservations were sent there for mechanical and agricultural training, as well as lessons in citizenship. While many Indians understood the need for education, they distrusted the new schools, which often taught them to reject the ways of their own people. At the Carlisle School, students were forbidden to wear tribal clothes, speak tribal languages, or practice tribal customs. The aim of the school was to "kill the Indian and save the man," said its founder.

Splitting Up Reservations

Indians and settlers also had different ideas about the land. Traditionally, an Indian tribe believed that its lands belonged to all the members of the tribe, jointly. By contrast, white settlers brought with them the European idea of property ownership, in which each piece of land can be owned by an individual person.

In the 1880s, many Americans believed that the Indians could make progress only if they accepted the idea of property ownership. This was another example of the whites trying to help Indians by making them more like whites. One Senator declared that the Indians "have got as far as they can go because they own their land in common."

The U.S. Congress agreed and passed a new law. Under this law, tribal lands would be divided among the Indians. Opponents of the law said that it would simply allow whites to take over more Indian land. They were right. Once an individual Indian owned land, he could also sell it. Since most Indians were poor, they sold their lands to white people for money. So the allotment system eventually caused Indians to lose most of their remaining lands. Not until 1934 did Congress pass a law to stop the breakup of the reservations.

Native American men and a boy at the Carlisle School.

U.S. GEOGRAPHY

Regions of the United States

The map on this page shows the fifty U.S. states and their capitals. It also shows eight regions within the continental United States. Each region has certain things it is known for.

New England is known for its role in American history, when it welcomed the Pilgrims and Puritans and hosted the first Thanksgiving. It is famous for lobsters, maple syrup, white churches, and splendid, multicolored autumn leaves.

The Mid-Atlantic contains some of the most densely populated areas in the

A winter scene in New England.

United States and several of its most important cities, including Philadelphia, Washington, D.C., and New York City.

In the South, winters are mild and the growing season is longer. This climate allowed plantation owners to grow tobacco, cotton, and rice, and it allows modern farmers to grow peaches in Georgia and oranges in sunny Florida. The Gulf Stream, a current of warm water that flows along the southeastern coast, helps make beaches in Florida and other southern states popular. Jazz, blues, and country music were born in the South.

The Midwest and the Great Plains are known for their rich fields of corn, soybeans, and wheat that stretch as far as the eye can see. While the Great Plains are relatively thinly populated, the Midwest includes a number of large cities: Chicago, Detroit, and Cleveland along the shores of the Great Lakes, and Minneapolis and St. Louis along the mighty Mississippi.

Much of the West is dominated by the Rocky Mountains, but this region also includes the lowest spot in the United States: Death Valley, California. Utah is home to many Mormons, while Las Vegas, Nevada, is a gambler's paradise. California is the most heavily populated state. In northern California are stands of ancient redwood forests; in the south are the sunny beaches and crowded freeways of Los Angeles and the movie studios of Hollywood.

The Northwest is close to Canada, while the Southwest borders Mexico and exhibits many aspects of Mexican culture. The coastal Northwest is one of the wettest areas in the United States. The Southwest is dry and contains many deserts. In the Northwest, you can see salmon swimming upstream toward their mating grounds. In the Southwest, you can see the Colorado River running through the spectacular Grand Canyon.

A highway runs through a desolate stretch of the Southwest.

Alaska and Hawaii

Because Alaska and Hawaii are separate from the continental United States, they are not considered parts of a region.

Hawaii is a group of volcanic islands in the Pacific Ocean. Hawaii's weather is warm, with daytime temperatures close to 80°F most of the year.

Alaska, by contrast, is very cold. The coldest weather ever recorded in the United States was in Prospect Creek, Alaska, in 1971, when the temperature dropped to -80° F. Alaska has a small population but is a rich source of oil and other natural resources.

A Hawaiian landscape.

III.

Visual Arts

Introduction

This chapter complements the history and geography chapter by discussing examples of Renaissance, American, and Japanese art. Parents and teachers can build on the brief treatment offered here by exposing children to additional books and pictures and by taking them to visit museums and interesting buildings. Although books are delightful and informative, there is no substitute for the experience of seeing works of art in person. Many museums make this experience possible for all by offering free admission once a week.

Children should experience art not only as viewers but also as creators. They should be encouraged to draw, cut, paste, mold with clay, and take photographs, to imitate styles and artists they have encountered and to develop a style of their own.

The Core Knowledge Foundation sells a popular interdisciplinary history of the Renaissance for fifth graders, *Rats, Bulls and Flying Machines*, as well as a set of art prints for the artworks in this grade. Visit our Web site (www.coreknowledge.org) for details on these and other products.

THE RENAISSANCE

The Rebirth of the Arts

The European Renaissance, which lasted from about 1400 to 1600, saw deep changes in European culture. Enriched by trade, Europeans prospered and embarked on the voyages of exploration that led to the discovery of the New World. Education spread, scholarship flourished, and new ideas abounded.

The Renaissance also saw a great flowering of painting, sculpture, and architecture. In Italy, where the Renaissance began, wealthy people paid artists to decorate palaces, churches, and public squares. Florence and Rome were centers of the arts because the Medici family in Florence and the popes in Rome both supported artists. It felt as if the arts were being "reborn." (The word *Renaissance* is French for "rebirth.") The Renaissance is perhaps the most glorious period in the history of European art.

Botticelli's *Birth of Venus.*

Beautiful Things

In European history, the period just before the Renaissance is called the Middle Ages. During the Middle Ages, almost all art was religious. Painters and sculptors decorated churches and cathedrals with scenes from the Bible to express the Christian idea that people should live their lives serving God and their neighbor, trusting in a heavenly reward after they die.

The artists of the Renaissance were Christians, too, and often took their subjects from the Bible. But they also glorified life on earth. During the Renaissance, artists and scholars rediscovered the cultures of classical Greece and Rome. The Renaissance began in Italy partly because the Italians were influenced by Roman ruins. Renaissance artists admired Greek and Roman art because it focused on the beauty of nature and of the human body.

In the late 1400s, an Italian artist named Sandro Botticelli [bot-ih-CHELL-ee] painted a work called *The Birth of Venus*. In Roman mythology, Venus, the goddess of love and beauty, was born miraculously from the sea. Botticelli shows the goddess riding a scallop shell toward shore and arriving in a shower of roses, because according to the myth, roses were born at the same time as Venus. The flying male figure on the left represents the zephyr, a warm, westerly wind that blows in spring, the season of rebirth. The painting's main colors—pale blues, pinks, and greens—also suggest the color of plants in spring.

The Harmony of the Body

Botticelli borrowed Venus's pose from an ancient Roman sculpture. Renaissance artists were fascinated by how Greeks and Romans depicted the human body as a beautifully balanced and harmonious form. In fact, some Renaissance artists used the human body as a symbol of the order of the universe.

The Italian artist Leonardo da Vinci illustrated this idea in his drawing *Vitruvian Man* (also known as *The Proportions of Man*). People of his time believed that every shape in nature went back to one of the two "perfect" geometrical forms—the square and the circle. Leonardo shows that these forms also relate to the proportions of the human body. Notice that if the man in the drawing stretches out his arms and legs in the shape of an X, his fingers and toes touch the circle. If he closes his legs and spreads his arms to make a T, his fingers and toes touch the square.

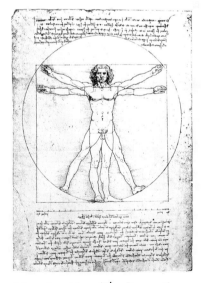

Vitruvian Man (The Proportions of Man), by Leonardo da Vinci.

A New Perspective

By studying mathematics and science, Renaissance artists were able to make important breakthroughs. For example, Renaissance artists wanted to make their paintings look realistic. They wanted people to look at a painting and feel as if they were looking through a window at a scene in the real world. The problem was how to create a sense of depth on a flat surface.

By studying mathematics and the way the eye sees, artists came up with a solution. They noticed that things look bigger when they are close up than when they are far away. In his painting *The Marriage of the Virgin*, Raphael draws the people in the foreground much larger than those in the background—just as we would see them in reality.

Artists also noticed that if a person stands between two parallel lines that stretch way into the distance, the lines look as though they get closer and

Raphael's *The Marriage of the Virgin*.

closer until they seem to come together at a point on the horizon called the vanishing point. Renaissance artists used this new idea—which we call linear perspective—to make their paintings look more real. Notice how Raphael painted the lines on the pavement so that they all seem to come together at the open door of the building in the background.

Leonardo: Renaissance Man

Detail from Leonardo da Vinci, *Mona Lisa*.

You may have heard someone called a "Renaissance man." That means that he can do a surprising number of things very well. Many people think that the term describes Leonardo da Vinci. You've already seen Leonardo's *Vitruvian Man*, but this is only one of many wonderful creations by this many-talented man who lived from 1452 to 1519. Leonardo was a musician, architect, botanist, and student of human anatomy. He was also an inventor who drew designs for machines that were hundreds of years ahead of their time—including a submarine and a flying machine!

But it's as a painter that Leonardo is best known. One of his paintings, the *Mona Lisa*, is probably the best-known painting in the whole history of art. It is a portrait of a young woman gazing calmly at the viewer. Mona Lisa's smile has fascinated people for hundreds of years. Some see it as a satisfied smile, and others feel there is something sad in it. Her haunting smile makes it seem as if Mona Lisa has deep knowledge or wisdom. But knowledge of what? Adding to the puzzle is the lonely landscape in the background. Its jagged mountains give many viewers an ominous feeling. Why is Mona Lisa posed against this background? We don't know, just as we can't solve the mystery of her smile.

The Last Supper

Leonardo's second most famous painting is *The Last Supper*. It depicts a scene from the Bible that takes place shortly before Jesus' crucifixion. His twelve apostles (his main followers) are shown reacting to his shocking statement that one of them will betray him. One apostle throws up his hands in amazement. One reels back in horror. One points to his chest as if to say, "Surely you don't think I am the one?" The way each man reacts shows us something about his character. Leonardo masterfully depicted the apostles as distinct individuals. The real betrayer, Judas, the third figure to the left of Jesus, scowls and clutches the bag of money he got for betraying his master.

Jesus sits in the middle, magnificently calm in contrast to the agitated apostles. To emphasize Jesus' serenity, Leonardo "framed" his head in an open doorway, giving it the stillness of a framed picture. And to make sure that the viewer's eye is drawn to Jesus, Leonardo used linear perspective—the lines made by the room's walls come together at a point just behind Jesus' head.

Leonardo used an experimental technique for *The Last Supper*; instead of painting a traditional fresco on wet plaster, he painted his mural on a dry plaster wall. The experiment was not successful, and the work has not held up well over the years. But despite the damage, it is still a powerful image.

Leonardo da Vinci, *The Last Supper.*

Michelangelo and the Sistine Ceiling

Another Italian artist who lived at the same time as Leonardo became just as famous. His name was Michelangelo Buonarroti. A sculptor, painter, architect, and poet, Michelangelo was almost as well rounded as Leonardo himself. He always preferred sculpture to painting, but when the pope asked him to paint Bible scenes on the ceiling of the Sistine Chapel in Rome, Michelangelo accepted.

It was grueling work. The ceiling was sixty-odd feet above the floor, so every day Michelangelo climbed a tall scaffold. There he painted for hours, his arm reaching upward and his neck stretched painfully back, while paint splattered his face. The ceiling was so large that it took him four years to finish!

The best-known Sistine Chapel painting shows God creating Adam, the first man. Adam is propped up on one elbow and one leg is bent, as though he is trying to push himself up from the ground. Despite his strong-looking body, Adam doesn't have the strength to stand or stretch his hand all the way out (notice his arm resting on his knee).

Michelangelo painted a God who is as powerful as Adam is weak. His hair and clothing stream in the wind as he rushes through the heavens, stretching out his hand toward Adam's. We get the impression that as soon as God's finger touches the man, Adam's body will be flooded with life. Michelangelo focused our attention on the hands by placing them in the center of the painting against a light, empty background.

Detail from Michelangelo's Sistine Chapel paintings, showing the creation of Adam.

Raphael: Painter of Madonnas

A favorite subject of Italian Renaissance painters was the Madonna, or Virgin Mary, with her son, the infant Jesus. Some of the most beautiful Madonnas were painted by Raphael, whose *Marriage of the Virgin* you've already seen.

Raphael was influenced by both Leonardo and Michelangelo, but his work is calmer and gentler than theirs. This gentleness can be seen in the painting called the *Small Cowper Madonna.*

Mary and her baby are depicted as perfectly happy and serene. Notice how both of them seem to be looking at something outside the painting. By showing their chins tilted together, Raphael beautifully conveyed the deep bond between a mother and her baby.

Raphael, *Small Cowper Madonna.*

Renaissance Sculpture

During the Middle Ages, sculpture consisted mostly of carvings on the walls of churches and cathedrals. Renaissance artists rediscovered the art of freestanding sculpture that the viewer can see from every angle. Medieval sculptors weren't very interested in making their human figures seem realistic, but Renaissance sculptors tried to make statues lifelike.

The first important sculptor of the Renaissance was Donatello. Among his many

Donatello, *St. George.*

sculptures is one of Saint George, the Christian warrior-saint who, according to legend, killed a mighty dragon. Donatello carved the face with highly individual features, so that we feel that there is no one else who looks exactly like this young man. By the way he posed the saint's body, Donatello conveys a sense that the statue could move at any moment. Saint George's body is taut and ready for battle, his eyes alert and watchful.

Michelangelo created an even greater statue of a young warrior. Michelangelo's subject is David, the shepherd boy who, according to the Bible, led the Israelites to victory by killing the giant Goliath with a slingshot. Michelangelo shows David when he is preparing for action. His sling is draped over his left shoulder. The muscles in his neck show the tension in his body. Yet if David is

tense, he is also resolute. He stares unflinchingly toward his towering enemy.

Michelangelo chose to depict David nude, like the heroes in classical sculpture. He did this partly to show off his mastery of human anatomy. He carved each part of David's body realistically—even the veins in his hands.

When *David* was unveiled in Florence, it caused a sensation. The statue is thirteen feet, five inches tall, more than twice life size. Michelangelo's *David* still seems to sum up the ambitious spirit of Renaissance art—a spirit as daring as that of David facing Goliath.

Michelangelo, *David.*

Renaissance Architecture

During the Renaissance, building styles changed as much as painting and sculpture styles. The most beautiful buildings of the Middle Ages were great cathedrals built in the Gothic style. Inside the cathedrals, tall columns held up high, vaulted ceilings, and colored light came in through stained-glass windows. Outside, the walls were carved with hundreds of stone decorations. The most impressive parts of the cathedrals were their towering spires that pull the viewer's eye toward heaven.

Renaissance architects moved away from the Gothic style. They looked back instead to ancient Greek and Roman buildings that seemed simple and clean. Their rational, mathematical proportions suggested the underlying harmony of the universe.

In the early 1400s, Filippo Brunelleschi [broo-nuh-LESS-key] designed a dome for the cathedral in Florence. He knew that the ancient Romans had perfected the dome, so he traveled to Rome to study ancient buildings. He came up with an elegant update of Roman design, with a few Gothic elements. At the base of his dome, simple geometric patterns—circles and rectangles—play off one another. The dome itself is made of red brick, divided symmetrically by curved ribs of white marble.

Brunelleschi's dome quickly became a symbol of Florence. Even today a homesick Florentine will say he is "sick for the dome"!

The dome became as characteristic of Renaissance architecture as the spire was of medieval architecture. Michelangelo designed the dome of St. Peter's in Rome, the largest Christian church in the world.

The Florence Cathedral, dome designed by Filippo Brunelleschi.

The Northern Renaissance

The Renaissance began in Italy but soon spread north to Belgium, Holland, and Germany. Northern artists learned linear perspective from Italian artists. In return, Northern artists showed the Italians how to mix pigments with oils made out of plant seeds to make the kind of paint we now call oil paint.

Before the invention of oil painting, artists could show only flat colors. Oil paint allowed artists to lay one color over another, creating an amazing range of hues. Oil paints also make surfaces glow in a way that mimics natural light. A fine example is Jan van Eyck's *Portrait of Giovanni Arnolfini and His Wife*. Notice the different shades of brown in the painting—the fur of the dog, the wood of the floor, the groom's robe. Notice as well how realistically the sunlight falls through the window, illuminating the bride, and how intensely the window's miniature reflection glows in the mirror on the wall.

The Arnolfinis were real people, and van Eyck [van IKE] used traditional symbols to convey his good wishes for the two of them. The dog is a symbol of faithfulness, and the fruit on the table symbolizes the couple's desire to be fruitful and have children.

Jan van Eyck, *Portrait of Giovanni Arnolfini and His Wife.*

Bruegel: Painter of Peasants

The people usually depicted in Renaissance art are the rich and powerful—people like the Arnolfinis. But in Northern Europe, a few painters depicted the day-to-day lives of the common people—a kind of art known as genre painting.

The greatest of the genre painters was Pieter Bruegel [BROY-gull] of the Netherlands. His *Peasant Wedding* shows farmers at a wedding feast. The faces of the people are lined from work and worry. They sit on wooden benches, and servers bring dishes by on wooden planks. The simply dressed bride sits below a paper crown. These are people with hard lives and few possessions, yet they seem to be having as much fun as aristocrats gathered in a palace. Bruegel's treatment of his peasant subjects shows a deep humanity.

Pieter Bruegel, *Peasant Wedding.*

The Proud Artist

In the Middle Ages, an artist was considered a craftsman, like a carpenter or a smith. But in the Renaissance, artists like Michelangelo and Leonardo were famous and well paid. They could talk to—even talk *back* to—noblemen and popes. The pope asked Michelangelo at one point when he would finish painting the Sistine Chapel ceiling, and Michelangelo snapped, "When I can, Holy Father.") Proud of his talent, the Renaissance artist felt inferior to no one.

The greatest German artist of the time was Albrecht Dürer [DUR-er], who made brilliant engravings, woodcuts, watercolors, and oil paintings. Dürer insisted on being treated with the dignity he felt he deserved. In his *Self-Portrait*, Dürer shows himself as a young aristocrat, expensively dressed and with carefully curled hair. He gazes out at us as if he is challenging us to question his high opinion of himself.

Albrecht Dürer, *Self-Portrait.*

AMERICAN ART

The Lives of Americans

Three hundred years after Bruegel, genre painting flourished in the United States. William Sidney Mount painted scenes from Long Island where he lived. Like Bruegel, he depicts people with great sympathy. In *Eel Spearing at Setauket*, the boy and the dog seem spellbound by the African-American woman fishing for eels while standing in a canoe, going about her task with self-assurance. At a time (1845) when blacks were still enslaved in the South and oppressed by bitter racism in the North, Mount gave dignity to all the people in his paintings.

William Sidney Mount, *Eel Spearing at Setauket.*

George Caleb Bingham's painting *Fur Traders Descending the Missouri* also depicts people in a canoe, but its setting is the frontier wilderness. Bingham pulls us into the scene by placing us on eye level with the traders, as if we were gliding down the river beside them in our own canoe. The gray-pink light of dawn envelops the scene, and the river has the calmness of early morning. An indistinct animal is in the prow of the canoe. Some see it as a cat, others as a black fox or a bear cub! Perhaps Bingham meant the animal to represent the mysterious presence of the wilderness through which the trappers journeyed.

George Caleb Bingham, *Fur Traders Descending the Missouri.*

The most popular depictions of ordinary American life in the 1800s were hand-colored prints from the firm of Currier & Ives. These prints show people hunting, farming, sailing, skating on frozen ponds, giving political speeches, racing horses, going to the opera, reading in front of the fireplace, and engaged in hundreds of other activities. The prints are sentimental and stylized, but they show us how varied life was in

Currier & Ives, *Quail Shooting.*

America then. The print above shows hunters shooting quail.

Thomas Cole, *The Oxbow.*

American Landscapes

To other artists of the 1800s, the real drama of America was the land itself. One group of landscape painters, called the Hudson River School, painted the hills and forests of New York and New England. To the most important member of this group, Thomas Cole, America was a kind of Garden of Eden, or paradise. His painting *The Oxbow*, set in Massachusetts, shows a view from the crest of a hill after a thunderstorm. We see America as a place where wild nature (the overgrown hill) lives in harmony with man (the cultivated fields on the right).

As America expanded westward, artists were inspired by the rugged landscapes of places like Colorado. Albert Bierstadt's *Rocky Mountains, Lander's Peak*, does not show a real place, but a composite, or combination, of places that the artist sketched in his travels and painted later in his studio. A group of Native Americans are camped on the edge of a lake. On its far side, a shaft of light illuminates a waterfall—the focal point of the painting. Over the whole landscape, the Rocky Mountains tower mistily, representing the glory and challenge of settling the West.

Albert Bierstadt, *Rocky Mountains, Lander's Peak.*

The Civil War in Art

Before the mid-1800s, in order to picture an event, artists had to draw or paint it. Then photography was invented, and by the 1850s it was recording all sorts of events. The American Civil War was the first major war to be recorded in photographs. The greatest Civil War photographer, Matthew Brady, followed Union troops in a wagon filled with equipment. Looking at Brady's battlefield photographs, civilians far from the front could see the real horrors of war. You can see some Civil War photographs in the History and Geography section of this book.

After the war, artists, especially sculptors, paid tribute to the soldiers who died. Towns all across the country put up statues of Union and Confederate soldiers. One of the most moving memorials, by the sculptor Augustus Saint-Gaudens, is in the Boston park called the Common. The men of the all-black Fifty-fourth Massachusetts Regiment are shown marching to battle, led by their white commander, Colonel Robert Shaw. These were the men who led the assault on Fort Wagner (see page 141).

From his study of Renaissance sculpture, Saint-Gaudens learned how to give his soldiers' faces great nobility but also distinct individuality. And as a Renaissance sculptor might have done, he included a figure from Greek mythology. Flying above them is the Goddess of Victory.

Augustus Saint-Gaudens, Memorial to Robert Gould Shaw
and the Fifty-fourth Massachusetts Regiment.

JAPANESE ART

Buddhism and Japanese Art

In Japan at the time of the early European Middle Ages, many people converted to Buddhism, a religion that began in India and spread across Asia. Buddhists try to reach enlightenment by detaching themselves from the concerns of the world. They believe the best way to do this is by meditating—sitting still and focusing the mind.

The large bronze statue called the Great Buddha of Kamakura, made in the 1200s, shows the Buddha after he reached enlightenment. He sits with an expression of complete serenity on his face. The statue suggests that everyone who follows the Buddha will achieve the same peace.

The Great Buddha of Kamakura.

In Japan, gardens are considered works of art. Japanese gardeners arrange plants and rocks with the care of a painter arranging colors and forms on a canvas. Gardens are also seen as aids to Buddhist meditation. Many Japanese gardens include bridges that arch over ponds and streams, as well as rocks surrounded by carefully raked gravel. The designs of these rock gardens are simple yet mysteriously beautiful, like islands rising out of the sea. By staring at the garden, the monks believed, the viewer could detach his mind from the cares of life.

A Japanese landscape garden.

IV.

Music

Introduction

This chapter introduces some vocabulary, symbols, and concepts that will help children understand and appreciate music. It builds on what students should already know about musical notation and introduces African-American spirituals. It also profiles a few composers and prints the lyrics to some popular songs.

The value and delightfulness of this chapter will be greatly enhanced if children are able to listen to the classical selections described. To facilitate such listening, the Foundation has assembled CD collections of the works discussed here. These are available on our Web site (www.coreknowledge.org). Also on the Web site is Resources to Build On, a free online database that lists more good books on the music topics for this grade.

In music, as in art, students benefit from learning by doing. Singing, playing instruments, following along with musical notation, and dancing all sharpen a child's sense of how music works. We encourage you to share good music with children by playing and/or singing some of the songs presented here, attending concerts, listening to the radio, and playing CDs and tapes.

ELEMENTS OF MUSIC

What All Music Has in Common

What kinds of music do you like to listen to and sing? Do you like classical music played by an orchestra? Church music sung by a choir? Rock music played with electric guitars? These kinds of music can sound very different, but they all have something in common. They can all be written down in a special language called *musical notation* so that others will be able to play the music, too.

Looking at musical notes on a page and singing or playing them is called *reading music*. Once you learn the language of music, you can look at the symbols written down in a piece of music and tell whether to play your instrument loudly or softly and whether to sing high or low.

High Notes and Low Notes

Here's a simple example of musical notation. It shows the notes and words for a song you probably already know.

Music is read from left to right and top to bottom, just like printed English. When musicians write music, they organize the notes on a *staff* made up of five lines and four spaces. When a note is written low on the staff, it has a *low pitch*. When it is written high on the staff, it has a *high pitch*. Can you see how the first two notes of "E-I-E-I-O" are played and sung at a higher pitch than the next two? The last letter in the sequence—"O" —is played at an even lower pitch.

Short Notes and Long Notes

Pitch isn't the only thing you need to know to sing or play a note. It's also important to know how long to hold the note. When composers write music, they use different musical notes to tell you how long a note should sound. A whole note tells you to hold the note for four beats, a half note for two beats, a quarter note for one beat, an eighth note for half a beat, and a sixteenth note for a quarter of a beat.

Notice how the single eighth note shown to the right has a single flag. When two or more eighth notes are written side by side, they are connected by a single bar, like this:

A single sixteenth note has two flags; grouped sixteenth notes have two bars, like this:

Look back at the music for "Old MacDonald." As you sing the first line, can you feel how you hold the note for "farm" longer than the earlier notes? "Farm" gets a half note, whereas the earlier words and syllables get quarter notes.

Sing the line "Here a chick, there a chick, everywhere a chick, chick." Do you notice how you don't stay very long on most of the words in that phrase? When you sing those words, you're singing clusters of eighth notes mixed in with a few quarter notes.

Whole Note

Half Note

Quarter Note

Eighth Note

Sixteenth Note

Dotted and Tied Notes

If a composer wants to make a note last longer than a half note but not as long as a whole note, putting a little black dot to the right of the note will do the job. That dot tells the performers to hold the note half again as long. See how the last half note in "Old MacDonald" is dotted? It's not uncommon for the last note of a song to be held a little longer.

Another special symbol can be used to show that a note should be held for a long time. A composer uses a *tie*, or a curved line that links two notes together, to tell the musician to continue to hold the first note through the time of the second. How many tied notes do you see in the sample below?

Time for a Rest

Rests tell musicians when to be silent. The shapes or position of the various rests tell how long the silence should last. In 4/4 time, a whole rest means silence for four beats, a half rest for two beats, a quarter rest for one beat, and an eighth note for a half beat. Note that a whole rest lasts as long as a whole note, a half rest as long as a half note, etc. The box at the right shows the symbols for rests of different lengths. Can you find any rests in the music for "Old MacDonald"?

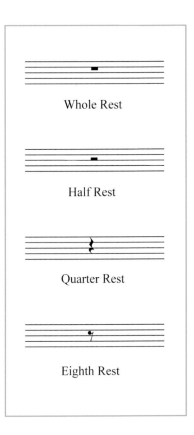

Whole Rest

Half Rest

Quarter Rest

Eighth Rest

Measures and Bar Lines

Look once more at the music for "Old MacDonald." Do you see the vertical (up-and-down) lines that separate the notes into groups? These lines are called *bar lines*. They divide the music into *measures*. How many measures are shown for "Old MacDonald"?

Composers use a single bar line to mark the end of a measure and a double bar line to mark the end of a piece of music.

Could You Repeat That?

Composers use *repeat signs* to tell musicians and singers to go back and play or sing a section again. The section to be repeated is marked off with a begin-repeat sign and an end-repeat sign. The begin-repeat sign is a double bar line with two dots to the right; the end-repeat sign is a double bar line with two dots to the left. When the musicians and singers get to the end-repeat sign, they go back to the begin-repeat sign.

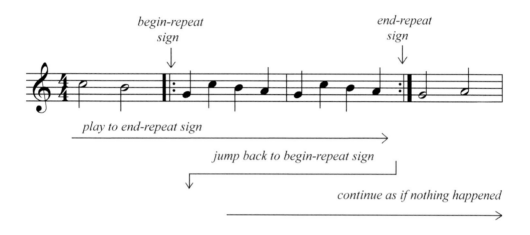

Time Signatures

Do you see the two stacked numbers at the beginning of the music for "Old MacDonald" —the ones that look like a fraction? Those numbers are called the *time signature*. The top number in the time signature tells how many beats are in each measure of a piece of music, and the bottom number tells what kind of note represents one beat.

For "Old MacDonald," the time signature is 4/4. The 4 on top means that there are four beats per measure, and the 4 on the bottom means that each beat lasts as long as a quarter (1/4) note.

You can see that the first measure of "Old MacDonald" is made up of four quarter notes, each of which is held for one beat. The second measure is a little different. It contains only three notes, but the one that goes with the word *farm* is held twice as long—for two beats. So this measure still lasts just as long as four quarter notes. Look at the eleventh measure— the one beginning "Here a chick." In this measure, there are six notes, but since eighth notes last only half as long as quarter notes, the measure is still only as long as four quarter notes would be.

When the time signature is 4/4, we say the song is written in "four-four time." Many popular songs are written in 4/4 time, which is also called "common time" and is sometimes indicated with a large C. But you will also see songs written in 2/4, 3/4, and 6/8 time. Here's an example of a song you probably already know written in 6/8 time. You can see clusters of six eighth notes in the measures that go with "merrily, merrily."

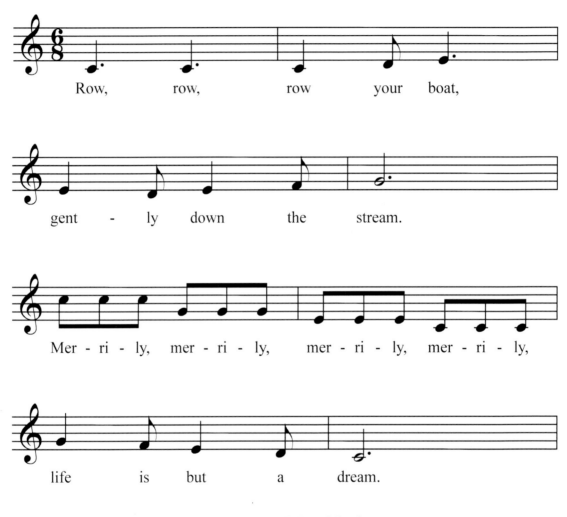

The Treble Clef

You've learned that composers represent sounds by placing musical notes on a staff. The higher a note is on the staff, the higher its pitch. The various pitches are named after the first seven letters of the alphabet: A, B, C, D, E, F, G. Each line and each space on the staff corresponds with one of these letters.

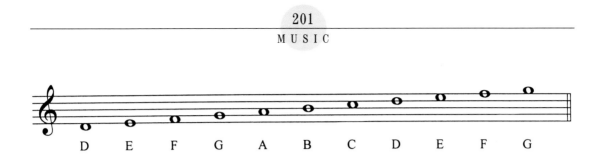

Notice that the letters repeat themselves as they go from low to high. The lowest note shown is D. Then, as the pitches go up, we get E, F, and G. But there is no H. Instead, the series starts over again with A.

How can you remember which positions on the staff correspond with which letters? Notice that the letters that are located on the lines, from bottom to top, are E, G, B, D, F. You can remember these letters by memorizing the following sentence: "Every good boy does fine."

Another way to remember which positions on the staff stand for which letters is to look at the treble clef. The *treble clef* is a fancy, curlicue symbol located at the beginning of a piece of written music. The treble clef is also known as the "G clef," because the innermost circle of the clef circles around the second line on the staff—the line that stands for G. If you remember this, you can figure out all the other pitches above and below G.

The lowest note shown on the diagram above is D. What would happen if the composer wanted to write a note one pitch lower than D? He or she would just draw a short line segment below the staff and place the note on the line segment. This particular note actually has a special name. It is called "middle C," because the key that sounds this note is located in the middle of a piano keyboard.

Middle C

From Sheet Music to Sound

The notes in a piece of music can be played on a keyboard. If you don't have a piano or electronic keyboard at home, you can pretend to play notes on the keyboard on the next page.

On a piano keyboard, every white key has a letter name that matches one of the notes on the staff.

If you wanted to play the first two measures of "Old MacDonald" on this section of a

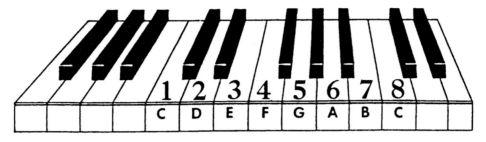

piano keyboard, you would hit the G key three times, then the D key, then the E key twice, and finally the D key again—and you would hold that last D twice as long as the previous notes because it's a half note, while the others are quarter notes. You would read all of this information from the printed sheet music and translate it into finger motions on the keyboard. At first it might take you a long time to translate the notes on the sheet music into finger motions on the keyboard, but if you practice, you will get better. With lots of practice, the process can become automatic.

Sharps and Flats

We've talked about the white keys on the keyboard. But what about the black keys? The black keys get their names from the white keys on either side. Find the G note on the keyboard. The black key to the left of G is called G-*flat*, or G♭. G-flat is a little bit lower in pitch than G. The black key to the right is called G-*sharp*, or G♯. G-sharp is a little bit higher in pitch than G.

A black key can have two names. It can be called a flat of the note to its right or a sharp of a note to its left. No matter what it is called, it sounds the same. F-sharp sounds the same as G-flat.

Italian for Composers

Sometimes just writing down the notes is not enough; sometimes the composer wants to give the performers more specific instructions about how to play the notes. For example, composers write the word *crescendo* [kruh-SHEN-doh] when they want the musicians to begin to play louder, and *decrescendo* [day-kruh-SHEN-doh] when they want them to begin to play more quietly. Both words are Italian. Many composers from all over the world write their musical directions in Italian. This is a tradition that goes back to the 1600s, when Italian opera was very popular throughout Europe.

Composers can create tension and excitement in their music by increasing and decreasing the volume. A good example of this is Beethoven's Fifth Symphony, discussed later in this chapter. Beethoven was a master at changing speeds and creating drama and excitement in his works.

Other Italian words and abbreviations tell musicians how soft or loud they should play the music. Here's a list of terms, arranged from softest to loudest:

> **pp** *pianissimo* [pee-ah-NEES-ee-moe] (very soft)
>
> **p** *piano* [pee-AH-noh] (soft)
>
> **mp** *mezzo piano* [MET-zo pee-AH-noh] (moderately soft)
>
> **mf** *mezzo forte* [MET-zo FOR-tay] (moderately loud)
>
> **f** *forte* [FOR-tay] (loud)
>
> **ff** *fortissimo* [for-TEES-ee-moe] (very loud)

Composers use other Italian words to tell how fast or slow a piece should be played. *Accelerando* [ah-chel-er-AHN-doh] means "go faster," while *ritardando* [RIH-tar-DAHN-do] means "slow down."

Legato [lay-GAH-toh] means that the notes should be played in a smooth, flowing way. The symbol for legato is a curved line connecting two or more notes. *Staccato* [stuh-KAH-toh] means the notes should be played crisply and distinctly.

The Italian words *Da capo al fine* give instructions to go back to the beginning of the piece and finish up where the word *fine* appears. *Da capo* means "from the head," and *al fine* means "to the end."

You Gotta Have Rhythm

Have you ever heard music that makes you want to dance or march across the room? The rhythm in the music is what makes you feel that way. Most music is written in steady beats with the accent falling on the first beat, which is also called the *downbeat*. Have you

ever seen and heard a marching band? Someone calls out a steady beat for them: "ONE two ONE two ONE two." The beat of a march is strong, steady, and predictable.

In most music, the beat stays steady, like the ticking of a clock. Sometimes, however, the composer introduces *syncopation*. In syncopation, the accent moves from the strong beat to the weak beat. The change is like a hiccup. It takes us by surprise and gets our attention. If you've ever heard jazz music, you've heard syncopated music.

Verse and Refrain

To make songs fun to sing, composers often write songs with several verses, each of which is followed by a *refrain*, or chorus. The verses are all different, but the refrain or chorus is the same throughout the song.

When you sing in a crowd, you might notice that most voices come in stronger when they sing the refrain. (It's the part everybody remembers!) When the word *refrain*, or *chorus*, appears at the end of a verse, it means to sing the refrain or chorus again.

In the songs given later in this section, you can see several examples of verse and refrain. For example, in "Sweet Betsey from Pike," the first verse begins "Did you ever hear tell of sweet Betsey from Pike," and the chorus, which follows each verse goes, "Hoodle dang fol-de di-do, hoodle dang fol-de day."

Harmony

Some songs seem meant for just one voice: it might be a song about someone you love or a song you made up that's just for you. But other songs benefit from many voices. If you sing a song about peace or about marching to war, it will send a powerful message if lots of voices sing it together.

Blending voices and sounds can have a powerful effect. When you sing or play two notes at the same time and they have a pleasing sound, you have played *harmony*. If you have a keyboard handy, find C on the keyboard, and then find E, which is two white keys to the right of C. Play C and E together and listen to the sounds blend. You just played a *chord*. A chord makes a richer, fuller sound than one note could make on its own. A chord is one kind of harmony.

Try playing other notes together. How does it sound when you play two white keys that are side by side? How does it sound when you play two white keys that are separated by one key? Two? Three? You will find that some combinations harmonize better than others.

LISTENING AND UNDERSTANDING

Polyphonic Music

During the Middle Ages, most music was created for church. When people sang together at church, they all sang the same melody, and they usually sang *a cappella,* which means they sang without any instruments to accompany them. Indeed, the phrase *a cappella* is an Italian phrase that means "in the chapel style." Since instruments were not allowed in many churches and chapels, singing *a cappella* meant singing in the church-approved manner.

During the Renaissance, polyphonic music became popular. *Polyphony* is a Greek word meaning "many voices." *Polyphonic music* is what you get when, instead of everyone singing the same notes, different voices sing different melodies or words at the same time. When different notes are sung by different voices at the same time, they blend together and *harmonize.*

Canons and Rounds

One kind of polyphonic music is called a *canon.* In a canon, one voice begins singing a melody. After the first few notes, another voice joins in, singing the same melody but maybe at a higher or lower pitch. All the voices sing their parts all the way to the end. The voices mingle and harmonize in a way that can be hauntingly beautiful.

Another kind of polyphonic music is called a *round.* A round is a song that travels around in circles. In rounds, everyone sings the same melody and the same words, but they start at different times. When the first person finishes the first line of the song, the next person joins in. As the various persons sing, their voices overlap and harmonize.

One of the simplest and most beautiful rounds is very old. It's a religious song called "Dona Nobis Pacem," and it was written during the Renaissance. This round has only three Latin words—the title is the whole song! *Dona* means "donate," or "give," *nobis* means "us," and *pacem* means "peace." Doh-nah no-beece pah-chem. "Give us peace."

Rounds are still popular today. "Row, Row, Row Your Boat" and "Frére Jacques" are two rounds you probably know.

Renaissance Composers

One of the greatest Renaissance composers was Josquin Despréz [deh-PRAY]. Despréz lived from around 1450 to 1521. He was born in Northern Europe, but he lived much of his life in Italy, singing and writing music for the pope and other Renaissance noblemen.

Desprez was a great master of polyphonic music. Most of the music he wrote was for use in churches. Desprez wrote music for three to six voices, each voice carrying its own melody. Words and music blend perfectly in his songs.

Lute Music

In the 1500s, almost every musician had a *lute*, a wooden stringed instrument shaped like a half pear with a long neck. People strummed and plucked it in a way similar to playing a guitar. But the lute was more delicate, with a sweeter, softer sound. It was perfect for love songs sung by one voice.

Have you ever heard the song "Greensleeves"? (You might know the melody even if you've never heard the words.) "Greensleeves" was originally a lute song. It was popular in England during the time of Queen Elizabeth I and is mentioned in Shakespeare's plays. It's a lovely tune, but sad. It tells about a man who has loved a woman and given her lots of pretty things, but she no longer cares for him. The first verse explains the situation:

> *Alas, my love, you do me wrong,*
> *To cast me off discourteously.*
> *For I have loved you well and long,*
> *Delighting in your company.*

Then comes the chorus, or refrain:

> *Greensleeves was all my joy*
> *Greensleeves was my delight,*
> *Greensleeves was my heart of gold,*
> *And who but my lady Greensleeves.*

Then another verse:

> *Your vows you've broken, like my heart,*
> *Oh, why did you so enrapture me?*
> *Now I remain in a world apart*
> *But my heart remains in captivity.*

John Dowland

We don't know who wrote "Greensleeves," but we do know that the Englishman John Dowland was responsible for many other smash lute hits of the Renaissance. Indeed, Dowland was probably the greatest composer of lute music who ever lived. He was born in England in 1563. His songs were popular throughout Europe. His biggest hit was "Lachrimae," which means "tears" in Latin.

Dowland based much of his music on two kinds of dance music—a lively dance called a *galliard* [GAL-yerd] and a slow, somber dance called a *pavane* [puh-VAHN]. Most of his music was sad and beautiful at the same time.

Mendelssohn's Midsummer's Night

The German composer Felix Mendelssohn (1809–1847) lived many years after the Renaissance, but he drew inspiration from one of Shakespeare's plays. When Mendelssohn was only seventeen years old, he wrote an *overture*, or introduction, to Shakespeare's comedy *A Midsummer Night's Dream*. The overture tells the story of Shakespeare's play, a funny story about lovers who spend the night in a forest, where fairies play tricks on them.

Mendelssohn.

The music begins with four chords played by woodwinds. The mysterious sound leads us into the world of Oberon and Titania, the king and queen of the fairies. Violins introduce the first melody of the overture. Fairies scurry in and out with the light and distinct *staccato* notes played by violins. Two violins play a melody *fortissimo*, and then other stringed instruments join in to play a theme for lovers *pianissimo*.

Years after Mendelssohn wrote the overture, the King of Prussia wanted Shakespeare's play to be performed at Berlin's royal theater. Mendelssohn wrote a dozen new pieces to follow the overture he had written many years earlier. One of the new pieces was a scherzo. *Scherzo* is the Italian word for "joke." A scherzo is usually a lively, fun piece. Mendelssohn's scherzo captures an argument between Oberon and Titania.

The most famous of the later pieces is the "Wedding March," written for the scene at the end of the comedy in which Duke Theseus marries Hippolyta, Queen of the Amazons. An English princess liked this piece so much she decided to have it played at her own wedding. Ever since, brides have requested it as the recessional, or exit song, for their own weddings.

Beethoven: A Stormy Life Set to Music

Ludwig van Beethoven [LUD-vig vahn BAY-to-ven], one of the greatest composers of all time, was born in Germany in 1770. As soon as he showed promise as a musician, his father forced him to practice constantly. He soon became an accomplished musician.

Beethoven.

With the help of an Austrian prince, Beethoven moved to Vienna to study music. He even met Mozart, the great Austrian composer, who was fourteen years older. After hearing Beethoven play, Mozart said, "Someday he will give the world something to talk about."

Beethoven earned his living as a concert pianist. He performed for royalty and well-to-do people. But he always demanded to be treated as an equal. Once, when a nobleman talked while Beethoven played the piano, the musician jumped up and shouted, "For such pigs I do not play!"

In his late twenties, just as Beethoven began to succeed as both a concert pianist and composer, he realized he was going deaf. He became angry and bitter that the one thing more important to him than anything else was slipping away. In time he went completely deaf—so deaf that he could not give piano concerts or conduct an orchestra. He could communicate only by writing in a little notebook he carried. People wrote notes and he scribbled a response. Beethoven was so miserable he once said that only music kept him alive.

Beethoven took long walks through the countryside surrounding Vienna, imagining music inside his head, waving his arms in time to it and muttering sounds. Every now and then, he'd stop to jot down music in his notebook. People thought he was crazy.

Beethoven wrote many kinds of music, but his Fifth Symphony is probably the best-known symphony in the world. The first four notes—three quick G's and a long E-flat—sound like a knock on the door. Beethoven repeats this four-note *theme* over and over again throughout the first part, or movement, of the work. Then he gives us different *variations* on the theme. That means he changes it in little ways so it stays interesting.

The second movement has a warm and gentle melody. The third movement is a scherzo. Its lively theme begins with strings and wind instruments. The four-note knock at the door comes in again, this time played by horns. The music builds to a crescendo and a glorious melody. It's warm and bright, like the sun breaking through clouds.

The fourth and final movement is very dramatic. It ends with a powerful coda, a special section designed to bring a piece of music to a conclusion. The music in the coda goes faster and faster, surging forward as it speeds toward a dramatic finale.

Beethoven added instruments to the orchestra for a bigger sound: the double bassoon to reach the lowest, fullest notes, the piccolo to reach the highest ones, and three trombones. Listen to the symphony and see if you can hear loud and soft, bright and dark, fast and slow in the music.

Mussorgsky: Painting Pictures with Music

Modest Mussorgsky [muh-SORG-skee] grew up in Russia hearing the colorful folktales of his country. He loved the stories so much that as a toddler he made sounds on the piano to go with them. Soon his mother taught him how to play.

As a young man, Mussorgsky made his first trip to Moscow in 1859. The city thrilled him, and he decided to write music about the Russian people. We call composers who write music for their country *nationalist* composers.

Mussorgsky wrote his most famous composition, *Pictures at an Exhibition*, in 1874 as a tribute to a friend who was a Russian artist. *Pictures at an Exhibition* opens with a stately theme played by a solo trumpet, followed by brasses. The musical theme, repeated throughout the

Mussorgsky.

work, portrays a promenade, or walk, through a gallery. It's a brief *interlude*, a short piece that leads us from picture to picture.

In all, Mussorgsky described ten paintings in his music. Can you hear a part that sounds like children playing in a garden? Here's a clue: a lively clarinet solo runs through the middle. Farther along the gallery walk, there's a silly ballet of chicks hatching with chirping sounds made with a flute and violins. The promenade closes at a Great Gate created to honor a Russian czar. Listen for brass instruments playing a serious tune, voices chanting, then chiming bells, an exciting crescendo, and a return to the promenade theme. What a fine tribute Mussorgsky gave his friend!

SPIRITUALS

Sorrow Songs

Beethoven and Mussorgsky made music for kings and czars. But great music has also been created by the poor and downtrodden. For African-American slaves, music was a source of consolation in their difficult lives, and also a way to express their hopes for the future.

Many slaves became Christians and learned traditional hymns. They blended their way of singing with the Christian hymns to make songs called *spirituals*. The spirituals were sometimes called "sorrow songs" because they were filled with sadness and pain. One famous spiritual (page 211) says that being a slave in America is like being a lost, "motherless child," far, far from home. Another compares the slave's experience to the experiences of a "wayfaring stranger . . . a-travelin' through [a] land of woe" (page 212).

Spirituals weren't just about being sad, though. They also helped people cope with their suffering and sadness. Many songs included a message of hope about the future. The spiritual "Wayfaring Stranger" says that this world is a world of woe, but it also says that things will be better in the life after death promised by Christianity:

> But there's no sickness,
> Toil, nor danger
> In that bright world to which I go.

Many of the spirituals make a comparison between the African-American slaves and the ancient Hebrews. The Old Testament tells the story of the Hebrew people, how they toiled in slavery in Egypt until their leader, Moses, led them out of Egypt, across the Jordan River, and into the "Promised Land" of Canaan. The African Americans found themselves in a similar situation—enslaved, but hoping they might someday reach a Promised Land, where they could be free. So the slaves began to use words and phrases from the Old Testament to describe their own lives.

In some spirituals, going to the Promised Land seems to mean going to heaven, and crossing the Jordan seems to mean dying. In other songs, the Promised Land seems to refer to free territory in the North, and crossing Jordan seems to refer to crossing a river from a slave state to a free state, like the Ohio River. Either way, crossing Jordan and entering the Promised Land were intended to refer to something better than the slaves' present state:

Deep river, my home is over Jordan,
Deep river, Lord, I want to cross over . . .

The spiritual called "Go Down, Moses" was filled with secret meaning for slaves. In this song, Moses may be a code name for Harriet Tubman, the escaped slave who led hundreds of slaves to freedom on the Underground Railroad.

When slave owners heard slaves singing "Go down, Moses" and other spirituals, they heard Bible stories about events that had taken place many years earlier. But the slaves who sang the songs had their minds on the future and on freedom.

Sometimes I Feel Like a Motherless Child

Sometimes I feel like a motherless child,
    Far, far away from home
    A long, long ways from home;
    True believer—a long ways from home

Then I get down on my knees and pray,
Get down on my knees and pray.

Down by the Riverside

Gonna lay down my sword and shield
    Down by the riverside
    Down by the riverside
    Down by the riverside
Gonna lay down my sword and shield
    Down by the riverside
And study war no more

    Refrain:
Ain't gonna study war no more (repeat two more times)

Gonna put on my long white robe
    Down by the riverside
    Down by the riverside
    Down by the riverside
Gonna put on my long white robe
    Down by the riverside
And study war no more.

Wayfaring Stranger

I'm just a poor wayfaring stranger
A-travelin' through this land of woe.
But there's no sickness,
Toil, nor danger
In that bright world to which I go.

I'm goin' there to see my mother.
I'm goin' there no more to roam.
I'm just a-goin' over Jordan,
I'm just a-goin' over home.

We Shall Overcome

This song was sung often during the American Civil Rights movement of the 1960s.

We shall overcome, we shall overcome,
We shall overcome some day.
Oh, deep in my heart I do believe
We shall overcome some day.

We shall live in peace, we shall live in peace,
We shall live in peace some day.
Oh, deep in my heart I do believe
We shall overcome some day.

Civil rights leader Martin Luther King, Jr., speaks at a rally in New York, beneath a banner reading "We Shall Overcome."

SONGS ABOUT WESTWARD EXPANSION

Sweet Betsy from Pike

In the 1800s, thousands of Americans went west, hoping to strike it rich in the Gold Rush.
This song describes the misadventures of Betsy and her lover Ike on the road to California.

Did you ever hear tell of Sweet Betsy from Pike,
Who crossed the wide mountains with her lover Ike,
With two yoke of cattle and one spotted hog,
A tall Shanghai rooster, and an old yellow dog?

> Chorus:
> *Hoodle dang fol-de di-do,*
> *hoodle dang fol-de day.*

They swam the wide rivers and climbed the tall peaks
And camped on the prairies for weeks upon weeks;
Starvation and cholera, hard work and slaughter,
They reached California spite of hell and high water.

They camped on the prairie one bright, starry night;
They broke out the whisky and Betsy got tight.
She sang and she shouted and romped o'er the plain,
And showed her bare bum to the whole wagon train.

The Injuns came down in a wild yelling horde,
And Betsy got skeered they would scalp her adored;
So behind the front wagon-wheel Betsy did crawl,
And fought off the Injuns with musket and ball.

They passed the Sierras through mountains of snow,
Till old California was sighted below.
Sweet Betsy she hollered, and Ike gave a cheer,
Saying "Betsy, my darlin', I'm made millioneer!"

Long Ike and sweet Betsy got married, of course,
But Ike, who was jealous, obtained a divorce,
And Betsy, well satisfied, said with a smile,
"I've six good men waitin' within half a mile!"

Shenandoah

Shenandoah is the name of a river and a valley in Virginia. In this song it is also the name of an Indian chief. The voice we hear is an American trader telling of his love for the chief's daughter and of his plans to travel west.

Oh, Shenandoah, I long to hear you.
Away, you rolling river.
Oh, Shenandoah, I long to hear you.
Away, I'm bound away,
'Cross the wide Missouri.

Oh, Shenandoah, I love your daughter.
Away, you rolling river.
I'll take her 'cross the rolling water.
Away, I'm bound away,
'Cross the wide Missouri.

Git Along, Little Dogies

In this old cowboy song, "dogies" are not dogs but cows. The cowboys who herded the "dogies" were known as "cowpunchers."

As I walked out one morning for pleasure,
I spied a young cowpuncher a-riding along.
His hat was throwed back and his spurs was a-jingling,
And as he approached me he was singing this song.

Whoopee ti yi yo, git along, little dogies,
It's your misfortune and none of my own,
Whoopee ti yi yo, git along, little dogies,
For you know Wyoming will be your new home.

AMERICAN SONGS

God Bless America

God bless America,
Land that I love.
Stand beside her, and guide her
Thru the night with a light from above.
From the mountains, to the prairies,
To the oceans, white with foam
God bless America,
My home sweet home.

If I Had a Hammer

If I had a hammer, I'd hammer in the morning,
I'd hammer in the evening all over this land;
I'd hammer out danger, I'd hammer out a warning,
I'd hammer out love between my brothers and my sisters,
All over this land.

If I had a bell, I'd ring it in the morning,
I'd ring it in the evening all over this land;
I'd ring out danger, I'd ring out a warning,
I'd ring out love between my brothers and my sisters,
All over this land.

If I had a song, I'd sing it in the morning,
I'd sing it in the evening all over this land;
I'd sing out danger, I'd sing out a warning,
I'd sing out love between my brothers and my sisters,
All over this land.

Well, I've got a hammer, and I've got a bell,
And I've got a song all over this land;
It's the hammer of justice, it's the bell of freedom,
It's the song about love between my brothers and my sisters,
All over this land.

SONGS ABOUT LOVE AND LOVERS

Danny Boy

This is an old Irish tune. To "bide" is to wait, or stay.
An "Ave" [AH-vay] is a prayer to Mary, the mother of Jesus.

Oh, Danny Boy, the pipes, the pipes are calling
From glen to glen, and down the mountainside.
The summer's gone, and all the roses fading.
'Tis you, 'tis you must go and I must bide.

But come ye back when summer's in the meadow,
Or when the valley's hushed and white with snow
'Tis I'll be here in sunshine or in shadow.
Oh Danny boy, oh Danny boy, I love you so.

But if ye come when all the flowers are dying
And I am dead, as dead I well may be,
You'll come and find the place where I am lying
And kneel and say an "Ave" there for me.

And I shall hear, though soft you tread above me,
And all my dreams will warmer, sweeter be,
For you will bend and tell me that you love me,
And I shall sleep in peace until you come to me!

Red River Valley

From this valley they say you are going.
We will miss your bright eyes and sweet smile,
For they say you are taking the sunshine
That has brightened our pathways awhile.

Come and sit by my side if you love me.
Do not hasten to bid me adieu,
But remember the Red River Valley
And the girl that has loved you so true.

V.

Mathematics

Introduction

This chapter offers a brief overview of essential math topics for fifth grade, including number sense, ratios and percentages, fractions, decimals, multiplication, long division, measurement, geometry, probability and statistics, and a tiny bit of pre-algebra.

Success in learning math comes through practice: not mindless, repetitive practice but thoughtful practice, with a variety of problems. While it is important to work toward the development of "higher-order" problem-solving skills, such skills depend on a sound grasp of basic facts and an automatic mastery of fundamental operations. Since practice is the secret to mastery, practice is a prerequisite for more advanced problem solving.

Some well-meaning people fear that practice in mathematics—memorizing arithmetic facts or doing timed worksheets, for example—constitutes joyless, soul-killing drudgery for children. Nothing could be further from the truth. It is not practice but *anxiety* that kills the joy in mathematics. And one way of overcoming anxiety is by practicing until the procedures become so easy and automatic that anxiety evaporates.

One effective way to practice is to have children talk out loud while doing problems, explaining computational steps along the way. In this way, the child's mental process becomes visible to you, and you can correct misunderstandings as they happen.

The brief outline presented here *does not constitute a complete math program*, since it does not include as many practice problems as a child ought to do while learning this material. To learn math thoroughly, children need to be shown these concepts and then encouraged to practice, practice, practice. Practice is especially important with the algorithms, or procedures, relating to arithmetic and computation, such as multiplication and long division. We therefore urge that parents and teachers select a math program that allows plenty of opportunities to practice.

The best math programs incorporate the principle of incremental review: once a concept or skill is introduced, it is practiced again and again through exercises of gradually increasing difficulty (including story problems). One result of this approach is that a child's arithmetic skills become automatic. Only when children achieve automatic command of basic facts are they prepared to tackle more challenging problems. Math learning programs that offer both incremental review and varied opportunities for problem solving get the best results.

NUMBERS AND NUMBER SENSE

Billions

One year not long ago, the U.S. government spent $151,874,000,000 more than it took in. That's one hundred fifty-one billion, eight hundred seventy-four million dollars!

You should already know about thousands and millions. Billions may be new to you. A billion is the same as a thousand million. A billion is a very large number. If you counted out one number a second, it would take you more than *thirty years* to count to one billion.

In our number system, groups of digits separated by commas are known as *periods*. Each period contains three columns: a hundreds column, a tens column, and a ones column. Sometimes these columns are called places.

Billions			Millions			Thousands			Ones		
hundreds	tens	ones	hundreds	tens	ones	hundreds	tens	ones	hundreds	tens	ones
1	5	1	8	7	4	0	0	0	0	0	0

Practice writing and reading large numbers. How would you write four hundred and eleven billion? How would you read 32,401,175,013?

Place Value and Expanded Form

You should be able to identify the place and value of specific digits in numbers. In 31,457,018,000, the underlined 3 is in the ten billions place. Its value is 30,000,000,000. The underlined 8 is in the thousands place. Its value is 8,000. What is the value of the underlined 4?

Sometimes it can be useful to write a number in expanded form. This helps you see the value of each digit in the number. Here's what the number 32,401,075,013 looks like in expanded form: 30,000,000,000 + 2,000,000,000 + 400,000,000 + 1,000,000 + 70,000 + 5,000 + 10 + 3.

How would you write 567,892,324,567 in expanded form?

Comparing Large Numbers

Remember that < means "is less than," > means "is greater than," and = means "is equal to." Which symbols would you use to describe the relationships between these numbers?

567,456,321,010	?	99,345,934,999
39,999,999,999	?	42,345,000,000
7,890,000,000	?	489,000,000

Positive and Negative Numbers

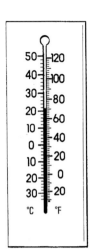

On a Celsius thermometer, 0° (zero degrees) is the temperature at which water freezes. A common room temperature is +20°, and −10° is the outdoor temperature of a very cold winter day.

The number +20, or 20, is a positive number. You read it as "positive 20," or just "20."

The number −10 is a negative number. You read it as "negative 10."

You can write positive numbers with or without a + sign: +3 = 3 ("positive three equals three"). You must always write a negative sign with a negative number.

We can show positive and negative numbers on a number line.

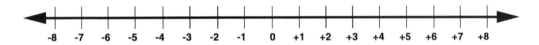

Numbers to the left of 0 on the number line are negative. Numbers to the right of 0 are positive. The number 0 is neither positive nor negative.

Two numbers that are the same distance from zero but in opposite directions are called *opposites*.

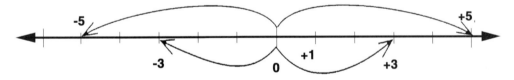

The numbers −3 and +3 are opposites. To find the opposite of a number, simply change its sign: the opposite of −5 is +5; the opposite of +10 is −10.

Zero is its own opposite: +0 = −0 = 0.

Integers

Whole numbers, as opposed to mixed numbers or fractions, are called *integers*. (The word *integer* means "whole.") The positive integers are the numbers +1, +2, +3, . . . The negative integers are the numbers −1, −2, −3, . . . A complete collection, or set, of all the integers would include the positive integers, the negative integers, and zero.

We often use integers in everyday life. For instance, the twenty dollars we earn for doing a job is an example of the positive integer +20; the fifteen dollars we pay for groceries is an example of the negative integer −15. A seven-yard gain in football is an example of the positive integer +7; a twelve-yard loss is an example of the negative integer −12. To mark the sea floor 250 meters below sea level, we can use the negative integer −250; to mark a mountain 4,807 meters above sea level, we can use the positive integer +4,807.

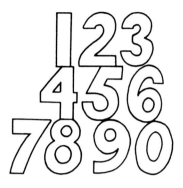

Comparing Integers

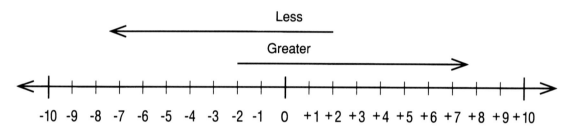

An integer on the number line is greater than those to its left and less than those to its right. $^-7 < {}^-3 < 2$. In general remember the following rules:

- *A positive integer is always greater than a negative integer (1 > $^-$100)*
- *The farther to the left a negative integer is from zero, the smaller its value is ($^-$1 > $^-$100).*

Adding Integers

You can show the sum of two integers by using arrows on a number line. Find the sum of $^+5$ + $^+3$. Starting at 0, first move 5 units to the right and then 3 units to the right.

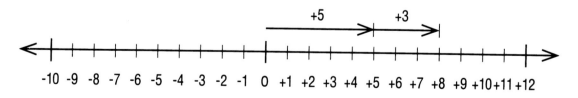

Therefore, $^+5$ + $^+3$ = $^+8$. (Remember, positive integers are most often written without positive signs: 5 + 3 = 8.)

Find the sum of ⁻5 + ⁻3. Starting at 0, first move 5 units to the left and then 3 units to the left.

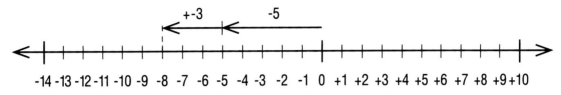

Therefore, ⁻5 + ⁻3 = ⁻8. You can add two negative integers the same way you add two positive integers, but because you are moving in the opposite direction, the sum is negative.

Here are two rules for adding integers:

- *The sum of two positive integers is positive.*
- *The sum of two negative integers is negative.*

We have seen how to add integers that have the same sign. Now let's practice using arrows on a number line to see what happens when you add integers with opposite signs.

To find the sum of ⁻9 + ⁺5, start at 0. First move left nine units and then move right 5 units. ⁻9 + ⁺5 = ⁻4.

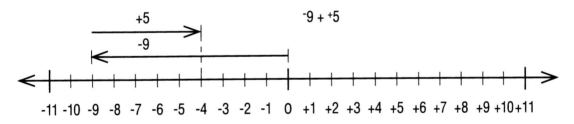

Now find the sum of their opposites. Starting at 0, first move right 9 units and then move left 5 units. 9 + ⁻5 = 4.

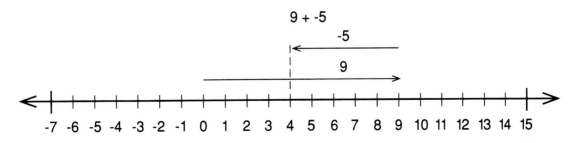

Draw your own number lines to show the sum of $+5 + ^-8$ and $^-5 + ^+8$. See if you can invent your own rules to explain what happens when you add integers with opposite signs. Explain your rules, using examples, to a friend or a parent. Make sure you can find sums such as $^-64 + 41$ or $^+18 + ^-67$.

Notice that $^-6 + ^+6 = 0$ and $3 + ^-3 = 0$. *The sum of an integer and its opposite is always zero.*

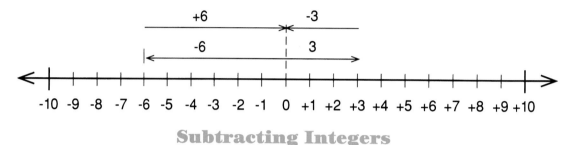

Subtracting Integers

Remember that if $9 - 6 = 3$, then $6 + 3 = 9$. We can also say that the *difference* of 9 and 6 is the number you have to add to 6 to get 9. We can define subtraction with integers the same way. The difference of two integers $a - b$ is the number you have to add to b to get a.

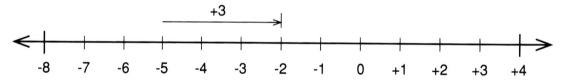

Consider $^-2 - ^-5$. The difference $(^-2 - ^-5)$ is the number you have to add to $^-5$ to get $^-2$. To get from $^-5$ to $^-2$, you add $^+3$. So $^-2 - ^-5 = ^+3$. Notice what happens when instead of subtracting $^-5$, you add its opposite. $^-2 + ^+5 = ^+3$.

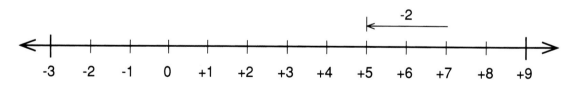

Now try $^+5 - ^+7$. The difference $^+5 - ^+7$ equals the number you have to add to $^+7$ to get $^+5$. $^+5 - ^+7 = ^-2$. Now instead of subtracting $^+7$, add its opposite. $^+5 + ^-7 = -2$. This example shows a general rule that will always work to subtract an integer:

To subtract an integer, add its opposite.

Rounding

To round a number to a certain place, you look at the digit to the right of that place. If the digit to the right is 5 or greater, you round up. If the digit to the right is 4 or less, you round down.

Sometimes rounding a number to a certain place involves changing digits to the left of that place. Round 49,857 to the nearest thousand. 49,857 is between which two thousands? It is between 49 thousand and 50 thousand. The digit to the right of the thousands place is 8. So you round 49,857 up to 50,000.

A good way to practice rounding (especially in problems like the last one) is to write a double inequality first, showing which two round numbers the number is between. To round 2,947,024 to the nearest hundred thousand, you can set it up this way:

$$2,900,000 < 2,947,024 < 3,000,000$$

2,947,024 rounded to the nearest hundred thousand is 2,900,000.

Squares and Square Roots

When you multiply a number by itself, you *square* the number. Since $2 \times 2 = 4$, 2 squared is 4. A shorthand way of writing two squared is 2^2. It is useful to know the squares of the numbers from 1 to 12:

$1^2 = 1$	$4^2 = 16$	$7^2 = 49$	$10^2 = 100$
$2^2 = 4$	$5^2 = 25$	$8^2 = 64$	$11^2 = 121$
$3^2 = 9$	$6^2 = 36$	$9^2 = 81$	$12^2 = 144$

The relationships above can also be expressed using the term *square root*. We say that the square root of 144 is 12, or, using the symbol for square root, $\sqrt{144} = 12$. That means that $12 \times 12 = 144$. What is $\sqrt{64}$? $\sqrt{16}$?

Exponents

When we write 2^2 or 5^2, we are using exponents. An *exponent* is a small, raised number that shows how many times a number is used as a factor in multiplication. For example, 3^4 means the number three is used as a factor four times: $3 \times 3 \times 3 \times 3$. You read 3^4 as "three to the fourth power." The number that is being used as a factor is called the *base*. In 3^4, 3 is the base and 4 is the exponent.

You already learned that when a number has an exponent of 2, we usually read it as "squared." 5^2 is usually read as "five squared," though it is also correct to say "five to the second power." When a number is raised to the 3rd power, we usually read it as "cubed." So 4^3 is read as "four cubed" (or "four to the third power").

$$4^3 = 4 \times 4 \times 4 = 64$$

2^5 is read as "two to the fifth power."

$$2^5 = 2 \times 2 \times 2 \times 2 \times 2 = 32$$

Powers of Ten

The exponents or *powers* of ten are very important in working with place value because the decimal system is based on powers of ten.

$10^1 = 10$
$10^2 = 10 \times 10 = 100$
$10^3 = 10 \times 10 \times 10 = 1,000$
$10^4 = 10 \times 10 \times 10 \times 10 = 10,000$
$10^5 = 10 \times 10 \times 10 \times 10 \times 10 = 100,000$
$10^6 = 10 \times 10 \times 10 \times 10 \times 10 \times 10 = 1,000,000$

Notice that 10^1 equals 10. A number to the first power is usually simply written as the number itself.

The number of zeros in each of the numbers 10, 100, 1,000, 10,000, . . . tells you what power of ten it is. Since 10,000 has 4 zeros, it is 10^4. Furthermore, the exponent in a power of 10 tells you the number of zeros the number has when it is multiplied out. 10^9 has 9 zeros. 10^9 equals 1,000,000,000, or 1 billion.

Sets

A *set* is a collection of things. The things in a set are called its *members*. You list the members of a set inside braces like these: { }. For example, here is a set of the first six odd numbers: {1, 3, 5, 7, 9, 11}. Sets can contain things besides numbers. For instance, here is the set of letters used in the word Mississippi: {m, i, s, p}. How would you record the set of even numbers between 21 and 29?

Prime Numbers

Imagine that you are part of a class of 23 students. One day the teacher asks you to divide up into equal groups. You try to divide into 2 equal groups but find you can't do it because 23 is not evenly divisible by 2. One group is always larger than the other. Then you try to split into 3 equal groups, but that doesn't work either. And neither does 4 or 5, or any of the other numbers you try. That's because 23 is a *prime number*.

A prime number is a number that cannot be divided evenly by any other number except itself and the number 1. The number 23 is prime because it can't be divided evenly by any numbers except 1 and 23. The number 4, on the other hand, is not prime because it can be divided evenly by 1, 2, and 4. Numbers that are not 1 and not prime are called *composite* numbers. A composite number is a number that can be built up by multiplying smaller numbers, called *factors*, together. You can make the number 4 by multiplying 2 × 2. You can make the number 6 by multiplying 2 × 3. So neither of these numbers is a prime number. But what about 7?

More than 2,000 years ago, the Greek mathematician Eratosthenes came up with a clever way of determining which numbers are prime. You can use his method, too. First, make a grid of all the numbers from 2 to 100 in rows of ten, like this:

2	3	4	5	6	7	8	9	10	
11	12	13	14	15	16	17	18	19	20
21	22	23	24	25	26	27	28	29	30, etc.

You want to cross out all the composite numbers, leaving only the prime numbers. First circle the number 2. It is a prime number, evenly divisible only by 2 and 1. Then cross out all the multiples of 2. Each of these numbers is divisible by 2 and therefore not prime. Next, find the smallest number that has not been crossed out: 3. This number is prime, so circle it. Cross out all the multiples of 3 that have not already been crossed out. Continue by circling the smallest remaining number and crossing out its multiples. The circled numbers are the prime numbers. If you did everything right, there should be 25 prime numbers circled.

Prime Factors

Any composite number can be broken down into several prime factors. For instance, the number 6 can be broken down into the factors 3 and 2. When these prime factors are multiplied together, they give the composite number 6. In the same way, the number 16 can be broken down into 4 × 4. But 4 itself can be broken down into 2 × 2. So if we want to break 16 down to its prime factors, we need to do it like this:

$$16 = 2 \times 2 \times 2 \times 2$$

This can be expressed as an exponent:

$$16 = 2^4$$

Can you break the number 32 down into prime factors, expressed as exponents? How about 27?

Greatest Common Factor

Sometimes it is useful to find the largest factor that two numbers have in common. The factors of 12 are 1, 2, 3, 4, 6, and 12. The factors of 16 are 1, 2, 4, 8, and 16. The common factors of 12 and 16 are 1, 2, and 4. The *greatest common factor* (GCF) of 12 and 16 is 4. Many mathematicians prefer the term *divisor* instead of *factor*, so you may also see the abbreviation GCD (greatest common divisor.)

Least Common Multiple

Sometimes it is useful to be able to find common multiples. Suppose you were asked to find the smallest number that is a multiple of both 2 and 3. Multiples of 2 include 2, 4, 6, 8, 10, 12, etc. Multiples of 3 include 3, 6, 9, 12, 15, and so on. Which of these multiples of 3 are also multiples of 2? Six and 12 are both common multiples, but 6 is the smallest. We say that 6 is the *least common multiple* (LCM) of 2 and 3.

COMPUTATION

Properties of Addition

There are certain rules, or properties, that are always true of addition.

1) *Commutative Property of Addition*
   Addends can be added in any order without changing the sum.
   $5 + 3 = 8$ and $3 + 5 = 8$, so $5 + 3 = 3 + 5$

2) *Associative Property of Addition*
   Addends can be grouped in any way without changing the sum.
   $(2 + 6) + 3 = 11$ and $2 + (6 + 3) = 11$, so $(2 + 6) + 3 = 2 + (6 + 3)$

Variables

When a letter stands for a number it is called a *variable*. For example, instead of writing $6 + ? = 8$, we can write $6 + x = 8$. In this equation, $x = 2$. We can also write $x + 4 = 10$. In the second equation, $x = 6$. We call a letter like x a *variable* because it can vary, or change; it can stand for different numbers. Finding what number the variable in an equation stands for is called *solving the equation*.

Inverse Operations, Equations

Remember that addition and subtraction are *inverse*, or opposite, operations. That is why you can write a related subtraction fact from an addition fact, or a related addition fact from a subtraction fact.

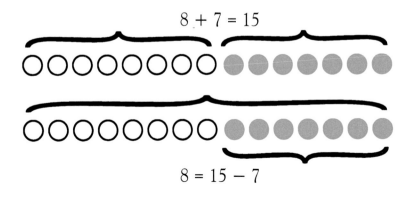

$8 + 7 = 15$ and $8 = 15 - 7$ are two different ways of writing the same problem. You can use addition and subtraction as inverse operations to solve equations. To solve the equation $n + 43 = 74$, rewrite it as a subtraction problem. Subtract 43 from 74.

$$n + 43 = 74$$
$$n = 74 - 43$$
$$n = 31$$

To solve the equation $a - 6 = 8$, rewrite it as an addition problem. Add 6 to 8:

$$a - 6 = 8$$
$$a = 8 + 6$$
$$a = 14$$

Properties of Multiplication

Like addition, multiplication is commutative and associative.

1) *Commutative Property of Multiplication*
   Factors can be multiplied in any order without changing the product.
   $8 \times 6 = 48$ and $6 \times 8 = 48$, so $8 \times 6 = 6 \times 8$

2) *Associative Property of Multiplication*
   Factors can be grouped in any way without changing the product.
   $(4 \times 5) \times 2 = 40$ and $4 \times (5 \times 2) = 40$, so $(4 \times 5) \times 2 = 4 \times (5 \times 2)$

Another property of multiplication involves addition as well.

3) *Distributive Property of Multiplication over Addition*
   When a sum is multiplied by a number, for example $5 \times (3 + 7)$,
   A) you can multiply each addend by the number, and then add the products:
      $(5 \times 3) + (5 \times 7) = 15 + 35 = 50$

   B) or you can add, then multiply: $5 \times (3 + 7) = 5 \times 10 = 50$
      You get the same result either way. So the distributive property tells us that:
      $$5 \times (3 + 7) = (5 \times 3) + (5 \times 7)$$

Learn the names of these three properties and be able to write equations showing what each one means. Also practice using the distributive property to write the answers to problems in two different ways. For example, you could find what $(12 \times 6) + (13 \times 6)$ equals in two ways:

$$(12 \times 6) + (13 \times 6) = \ 72 + 78 \ = 150$$
$$(12 \times 6) + (13 \times 6) = (12 + 13) \times 6 = 25 \times 6 = 150$$

You can use the properties of multiplication to solve problems. For instance, suppose you need to calculate 3×27. You could use the distributive property to divide this multiplication problem into two easier problems, like this:

$$3 \times 27 = (3 \times 20) + (3 \times 7)$$
$$= 60 + 21$$
$$= 81$$

Multiplication and Division as Inverse Operations

Like addition and subtraction, multiplication and division are inverse, or opposite, operations. $6 \times 4 = 24$ and $6 = 24 \div 4$ are two different ways of writing the same problem.

You can use multiplication and division as inverse operations to solve equations. To solve the equation $a \times 12 = 192$, rewrite it as a division problem. Divide 192 by 12:

$$a \times 12 = 192$$
$$a \quad\ \ = 192 \div 12$$
$$a \quad\ \ = 16$$

To solve the equation $n \div 13 = 12$, rewrite it as a multiplication problem. Multiply 12 by 13:

$$n \div 13 = 12$$
$$n \quad\ \ = 12 \times 13$$
$$n \quad\ \ = 156$$

Multiplying Large Factors

You multiply by a number in the thousands using the same methods you have already learned:

```
        5,6 2 7
      × 4,3 3 8
        4 5 0 1 6   ─────────→ 8 × 5,627
      1 6 8 8 1 0   ─────────→ 30 × 5,627
    1 6 8 8 1 0 0   ─────────→ 300 × 5,627
    2 2 5 0 8 0 0 0 ─────────→ 4,000 × 5,627
    2 4,4 0 9,9 2 6
```

First you multiply 8 × 5,627, then 30 × 5,627, then 300 × 5,627, and finally 4,000 × 5,627. Then you add these four subtotals to find the product. Remember that before you multiply by the digit in the tens place, you first write a zero in the product. Before multiplying the digit in the hundreds place, you write 2 zeros, and before multiplying the digit in the thousands place, you write 3 zeros in the product. Using these same methods, you can multiply even larger numbers.

Estimating a Product

Sometimes you don't need to know the exact product. In such cases you can estimate. For instance, suppose you wanted to know about what 3,979 × 509 equals. You could round 3,979 to 4,000 and 509 to 500. Then multiply: 4,000 × 500 = 2,000,000.

Division and Divisibility

You can write a division problem in three ways. 28 divided by 7 can be written in these three ways, which all mean the same thing:

$$28 \div 7 \qquad 7 \overline{)28} \qquad \frac{28}{7}$$

We say that a number is *divisible* by another number if it can be divided by that number without leaving a remainder. For example, 30 is divisible by 2, because 30 ÷ 2 = 15. Thirty is not divisible by 7, because 30 ÷ 7 leaves a remainder of 2.

To find out if one number is divisible by another, you can always divide and see if there is a remainder. There are also rules that let you determine, without dividing, whether a number is divisible by certain numbers.

Here are some tests for divisibility:

A whole number is divisible
- By 2, if it has an even number (0, 2, 4, 6, or 8) in the ones' place. This is called the last-digit test.
- By 5, if it has a 0 or 5 in the ones' place (last-digit test)
- By 10, if it has a 0 in the ones' place (last-digit test)
- By 3, if the sum of its digits is divisible by 3
- By 9, if the sum of its digits is divisible by 9

Short Division

When the divisor is a one-digit number, you can use a shorter form of division, known as short division. Divide, multiply, and subtract in your head. Write the remainder, if there is one, in front of the next place, and continue dividing. For example, to divide 6258 by 8, you go through the following steps:

1) Divide the 62 hundreds.

Think: 8 into 62 goes 7 times.

62 − 56 = 6. Write the

6 hundreds next to the 5 tens.

$$7 \over 8) \, 6\,2_6\,5\,8$$

2) Divide the 65 tens.

8 into 65 goes 8 times.

65 − 64 = 1. Write the 1

ten next to the 8 ones.

$$7\ 8 \over 8) \ \, 6\,2_6\,5_1\,8$$

3) Divide the 18 ones.

$$7\ 8\ 2\ \ R2 \over 8) \, 6\,2_6\,5_1\,8$$

Practice using short division to do division problems with one-digit divisors.

Long Division

When you are dividing by a two-digit divisor, you can use long division. Before you begin to divide, always figure out first how many digits the quotient will have.

Find the quotient of 8150 divided by 26.

First ask: can I divide 26 into 8? No, there are not enough thousands to divide. How about 26 into 81? Yes, there are enough hundreds to divide. The first digit of the quotient goes in the hundreds place. The quotient will have three digits.

As you do the long division, round the divisor to the nearest ten and make an estimate of what each digit in the quotient will be. Sometimes your estimate will be too high or too low; then you have to adjust the quotient. Here are the steps:

1. Divide the hundreds. Round 26 to 30.
   Think: $30\overline{)81}$. $2 \times 30 = 60$. Try 2.

$$\begin{array}{r} 2 \\ 26\overline{)8150} \\ -52 \\ \hline 29 \end{array}$$

Check: is 29 < 26? No.

2. Increase the quotient by 1.
   Try 3.

$$\begin{array}{r} 3 \\ 26\overline{)8150} \\ -78 \\ \hline 3 \end{array}$$

Check: is 3 < 26? Yes.
Now the quotient is correct.

3. Bring down the 5 tens and divide the tens.
   Think: $30\overline{)35}$ or $26\overline{)35}$. Try 1.

$$\begin{array}{r} 31 \\ 26\overline{)8150} \\ -78 \\ \hline 35 \\ -26 \\ \hline 9 \end{array}$$

Check: is 9 < 26? Yes.
The quotient is correct.

4. Bring down zero ones
   Divide the ones.
   Think: $30\overline{)90}$. Try 3.

$$\begin{array}{r} 313 \text{ R12} \\ 26\overline{)8150} \\ -78 \\ \hline 35 \\ -26 \\ \hline 90 \\ -78 \\ \hline 12 \end{array}$$

Check: is 12 < 26? Yes. The quotient is correct; the remainder is 12.

At each step in the division, check to make sure the remainder is less than the divisor. You were dividing by 26 in the last problem. What is the largest remainder you could have had? 25. Why?

You can check division problems by multiplying the divisor and the quotient, and adding the remainder.

MATHEMATICS

```
    3 1 3
  × 2 6
  1 8 7 8
  6 2 6 0
  8 1 3 8
  + 1 2
  8,1 5 0  ✔
```

You can write your answer in the same form as the check, as a multiplication and an addition, followed by an inequality.

$$8,150 = (26 \times 313) + 12 \qquad 12 < 26$$

You can also do a quick mental check of your answer by estimating the quotient. To estimate the quotient of $26 \overline{)8,150}$, round the divisor to the greatest place value. Then round the dividend to a number that makes it easy to divide. Round 26 to 30. Then round 8,150 to 9,000. You could round to 8,000, but you cannot divide 8,000 by 30 easily. You can divide 9,000 by 30 easily:

```
      3 0 0
3 0 )9,0 0 0
```
          $26 \overline{)8,1 5 0}$ is about 300. ✔

More Two-Digit Divisors

Let's try that again. Find the quotient of 227,194 divided by 74. First, figure out how many digits the quotient will have. Can you divide 74 into 2? No, there are not enough hundred thousands to divide. How about $74 \overline{)22}$? No, there are not enough ten thousands to divide. How about $74 \overline{)227}$. Yes, there are enough thousands to divide. The first digit of the quotient goes in the thousands place. The quotient will have 4 digits. Here are the steps for long division.

1) Divide 227 thousands.

```
        3
7 4 )2 2 7,1 9 4
   − 2 2 2
        5 1
  51 < 74  ✔
```

2) Bring down the 1 hundred.
You cannot divide 51 hundreds by 74.
Write 0 in the hundreds place.

```
          3 0
7 4 )2 2 7,1 9 4
   − 2 2 2
        5 1
```

3) Bring down the 9 tens.
   Divide 519 tens.

Think: $70\overline{)519}$

$$
\begin{array}{r}
3\;0\;7 \\
74\overline{)2\,2\,7,1\,9\,4} \\
-2\,2\,2 \\
\hline
5\,1\,9 \\
-5\,1\,8 \\
\hline
1
\end{array}
$$

$1 < 74$ ✔

4) Bring down the 4 ones.
   You cannot divide 14 ones by 74.
   Write 0 in the ones place.

$$
\begin{array}{r}
3\;0\;7\;0\quad \text{R14} \\
74\overline{)2\,2\,7,1\,9\,4} \\
-2\,2\,2 \\
\hline
5\,1\,9 \\
-5\,1\,8 \\
\hline
1\,4
\end{array}
$$

$14 < 74$ ✔

Check:

$$
\begin{array}{r}
3\,0\,7\,0 \\
\times\,7\,4 \\
\hline
1\,2\,2\,8\,0 \\
2\,1\,4\,9\,0\,0 \\
\hline
2\,2\,7,1\,8\,0 \\
+1\,4 \\
\hline
2\,2\,7,1\,9\,4 \quad ✔
\end{array}
$$

$227,194 = (74 \times 3070) + 14 \quad 14 < 74$

Three-Digit Divisors

Practice doing long division problems with three-digit divisors. First decide how many digits the quotient will have; then round the divisor to the nearest hundred to estimate each digit of the quotient.
Divide 163,220 by 321.

1. Think: $321\overline{)163}?$

   Try $321\overline{)1,632}$

No, not enough thousands to divide.
Yes, there are enough hundreds to divide.
The quotient will have three digits.

2. Divide 1,630 hundreds.

   Think: $300\overline{)1,630}.$

Try 5.

```
             5
  321 )1 6 3,2 2 0
      −1 6 0 5
         2 7 2
```

You can't divide 272 tens by 321. Write 0 in the tens place. Then divide 2,720 ones.

Think: 300)2,720.   Try 9.

```
            5 0 9
  3 2 1 )1 6 3,2 2 0
        −1 6 0 5
           2 7 2 0
          −2 8 8 9
```

2,889 is greater than 2,720, so the quotient 9 is too great. Try 8.

```
          5 0 8  R152          Check:     5 0 8
  3 2 1 )1 6 3,2 2 0                     × 3 2 1
        −1 6 0 5                           5 0 8
           2 7 2 0                      1 0 1 6 0
          −2 5 6 8                    1 5 2 4 0 0
             1 5 2                    1 6 3 0 6 8
                                      +     1 5 2
        1 5 2 < 3 2 1                 1 6 3,2 2 0  ✔
```

In this problem, because 300) 2,720 is just barely 9, and you rounded 321 *down* to 300, you might have guessed that 9 was too large a quotient. When making your estimated quotients, always think about whether you rounded the divisor up or down. The more you do long division, the better you will get at estimating quotients.

DECIMALS, FRACTIONS, AND MIXED NUMBERS

Decimals

When you want to indicate a part of an integer, you can use a fraction or you can use a decimal. For example, one way to write five and a half is to use a fraction: $5\frac{1}{2}$. Another way is to use a decimal point: 5.5

The first place to the right of the decimal point is the tenths place; the second place is the hundredths place; the third place is the thousandths place. The fourth place to the right of the decimal point is the ten-thousandths place.

ones		tenths	hundredths	thousandths	ten-thousandths
0	.	5	6	7	2

Places to the right of the decimal point are called decimal places. When a number has four decimal places, you read the decimal places in ten-thousandths. 0.5672 is read: "five thousand, six hundred seventy-two ten-thousandths." People often read decimals in a shorter way. You can read 0.5672 as "point five six seven two." You can read 18.289 as "eighteen and two hundred eighty-nine thousandths" or "eighteen point two eight nine."

Learn to give the value of a digit in a decimal in digits or in words. In 0.6728, the value of the 6 is 0.6 or six tenths; the value of the seven is 0.07 or seven hundredths; the value of the 2 is 0.002 or two thousandths; the value of the 8 is 0.0008 or eight ten-thousandths. You could write this decimal in expanded form, like this:

.6 + .07 + .002 + .0008

Decimals on a Number Line

You can show decimals that come between other decimals on a number line.
This number line shows nine numbers with two decimal places between 2.3 and 2.4.

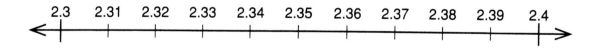

You can also show decimals with patterns. Complete this pattern:

4.73, 4.731, ____, ____, ____, ____, ____, ____, ____, ____, 4.74

With this pattern in mind, think about how many numbers with three decimal places you can write between 2.33 and 2.34. You can write 9. Could you write other decimals between those decimals?

Comparing Decimals

You can add zeros after the last place of a decimal without changing the value. To compare 13.62 and 13.625, you can write 13.62 as 13.620, so that both numbers have the same number of decimal places.

13.620
13.625

Start with the greatest place value, the tens place. All the places are the same from the tens place through the hundredths place. However, 5 thousandths is greater than 0 thousandths, so 13.625 > 13.620 and 13.625 > 13.62.

Decimal Sums and Differences

Remember that addition is commutative. So you can check a decimal sum by adding the decimals in a different order. If you found this decimal sum by adding down, check by adding up.

$$
\begin{array}{r}
9.607 \\
3.23 \\
+\ 18.76 \\
\hline
31.597 \ ✔
\end{array}
$$

Remember that addition and subtraction are opposite, or inverse, operations. Add to check each difference of decimals.

To check this subtraction:

$$
\begin{array}{r}
95.27 \\
-\ 82.96 \\
\hline
12.31
\end{array}
$$

Do this addition:

$$
\begin{array}{r}
12.31 \\
+\ 82.96 \\
\hline
95.27 \ ✔
\end{array}
$$

You can also make a quick check to see if a decimal sum or difference is about right by estimating. To estimate a decimal sum or difference, round each number to its greatest place value and then add or subtract.

To estimate	Round to greatest place value.	To estimate	Round to greatest place value.
9.6 0 7	1 0	9 5.2 7	1 0 0
3.2 3	3	− 8 2.9 6	− 8 0
1 8.7 6	+ 2 0		2 0
	3 3		

One of the things your estimate can tell you is whether you have put the decimal point in the right place or not.

We often estimate by rounding all the numbers to the same place value. Suppose you wanted to know the approximate difference of 95.27 and 82.96 in whole numbers. You would round each number to the nearest whole number and then subtract.

Round to the nearest whole number.

9 5.2 7	9 5
− 8 2.9 6	− 8 3
	1 2

Notice that this estimate of 12 is much closer to the actual difference (12.31) than the estimate you got by rounding each number to its greatest place value.

Multiplying Decimals

Multiplying with different units can help you learn how to multiply a decimal and a whole number. If a small package of cookies costs 69¢, how much do 9 packages cost?

You can multiply 69¢ by 9, or you can write 69¢ with a dollar sign and a decimal point and multiply.

6 9¢	$ 0.6 9 — two decimal places
× 9	× 9
6 2 1¢	$ 6.2 1 — two decimal places

621¢ = $6.21. You get the same product either way you multiply.

Notice that there are the same number of decimal places in the product ($6.21) as in the decimal factor ($0.69). Whenever you multiply a decimal by a whole number, the product will have the same number of decimal places as the decimal factor.

Here is another example. Multiply, and then place the decimal point in the product.

7.63 — two decimal places
$\times 12$
1526
7630
91.56 — two decimal places

Multiplying Decimals by 10, 100, 1000

When you multiply any decimal number by 10, you move its decimal point one place to the right. You make the place value of each digit ten times as large.

$10 \times 2.345 = 23.45$ $0.026 \times 10 = 0.26$

Notice that when you are multiplying a whole number like 6 by 10, moving the decimal point one place to the right is the same as adding one zero.

$10 \times 6.0 = 60.$ $10 \times 6 = 60$

When you multiply a number by 100, you move its decimal point 2 places to the right. You make the place value of each digit 100 times as large.

$100 \times 2.345 = 234.5$ $0.026 \times 100 = 2.6$

When you multiply a number by 1000, you move its decimal point 3 places to the right. You make the place value of each digit 1000 times as large.

$1000 \times 2.345 = 2345$ $0.026 \times 1000 = 26$

Practice multiplying decimal numbers by 10, 100, and 1000, observing how the decimal point moves in each problem. Also practice doing problems like these, in which you must think what the multiplication has been.

$$\underline{\hspace{2cm}} \times 43.82 = 438.2$$
$$\underline{\hspace{2cm}} \times 0.008 = 8$$
$$100 \times \underline{\hspace{2cm}} = 32.56$$

Estimating Decimal Products

You can estimate the product of a decimal and a whole number by rounding each factor to its greatest place value and multiplying. You can use this estimate to see if you have put the decimal point in the right place in the product.

Estimate to check: Round and multiply.

```
     7.6 3                                          8
   ×   1 2                                       × 10
   1 5 2 6                                         80  ✔
   7 6 3 0
   9 1.5 6
```

80 is close to 91.56, so you know you have put the decimal point in the right place. The product is *not* 9.156 or 915.6.

Multiplying a Decimal by a Decimal

When you multiply a decimal by a decimal, the product has the same number of decimal places as the number of decimal places in the factors added together. Here are two examples. Multiply without worrying about the place values. Then place the decimal point in the product.

```
    4 9.6   — 1 decimal place          3.8 6 7   — 3 decimal places
  ×   3.8   — +1 decimal place       ×     8.2   — +1 decimal place
    3 9 6 8                            7 7 3 4
  1 4 8 8 0                          3 0 9 3 6 0
1 8 8.4 8   — 2 decimal places      3 1.7 0 9 4   — 4 decimal places
```

Estimate to make sure the decimal point is in the right place.

50 × 4 = 200   4 × 8 = 32
188.48 is close to 200.   ✔   31.7094 is close to 32.   ✔

Sometimes when you multiply two decimals, you need to add zeros to the product so that it has the right place value.

```
    0.0 3   — 2 decimal places
  × 0.0 2   — 2 decimal places
  0.0 0 0 6   — 4 decimal places
```

There should be 4 decimal places in the product, so you write three zeros to the left of 6 and then the decimal point.

Checking Decimal Products

You can check decimal products by changing the order of the factors. Remember that multiplication is commutative.

To check:

```
   4 9.6
 × 3.8
 ───────
  3 9 6 8
1 4 8 8 0
─────────
1 8 8.4 8
```

Multiply.

```
     3.8
 × 4 9.6
 ───────
   2 2 8
 3 4 2 0
1 5 2 0 0
─────────
1 8 8.4 8   ✔
```

Checking in this way lets you know if you have gotten the digits right, while checking by estimation lets you know if you have gotten the place values right. It can be useful to check a problem in both ways.

Practice multiplying decimals by whole numbers and decimals by decimals. Check each product by estimation or by changing the order of the factors.

Decimal Division

You divide decimals by whole numbers the same way you divide whole numbers by whole numbers. You put the decimal point in the quotient above the decimal point in the dividend.

```
         3.1 4
      ─────────
   6 ) 1 8.8 4
     − 1 8
      ───────
           8
         − 6
         ─────
           2 4
         − 2 4
         ─────
             0
```

You can estimate the quotient by rounding the dividend to a number that is easy to divide.

```
         3
      ──────
   6 ) 1 8   ✔
```

The quotient is about 3, which is close to 3.14. So you know that you have put the decimal point in the right place.

Sometimes you need to put zeros in the quotient so that it has the right place value.

$$\begin{array}{r} 0.0\,3 \\ 3\,2 \overline{)\,0.9\,6} \\ -\,9\,6 \\ \hline 0 \end{array}$$

You can't divide 9 tenths by 32 ($32\overline{)\,0.9}$—no); you can divide 96 hundredths by 32 ($32\overline{)\,0.96}$). Write a zero in the tenths' place to show that the quotient is 3 *hundredths*.

Writing Zeros in the Dividend

When you divide a decimal, you do not usually write a remainder. You continue to divide, adding zeros after the last place of the decimal.

Divide 505.8 by 12. Since 505.8 = 505.80 = 505.800, you can add as many zeros after the last place of the dividend as you need to, in order to complete the division.

1. Divide 50 tens, 25 ones, and 18 tenths.

$$\begin{array}{r} 4\,2.1 \\ 12 \overline{)\,5\,0\,5.8} \\ -4\,8 \\ \hline 2\,5 \\ -2\,4 \\ \hline 1\,8 \\ -1\,2 \\ \hline 6 \end{array}$$

2. You are left with 6 tenths (0.6). Add a zero to the dividend and divide 60 hundredths (0.60).

$$\begin{array}{r} 4\,2.1\,5 \\ 12 \overline{)\,5\,0\,5.8\,0} \\ -4\,8 \\ \hline 2\,5 \\ -2\,4 \\ \hline 1\,8 \\ -1\,2 \\ \hline 6\,0 \\ -6\,0 \\ \hline 0 \end{array}$$

When you get a remainder of zero, the division is complete. When the remainder is zero, it is easy to check the division of a decimal. Multiply the quotient by the divisor to check.

$$\begin{array}{r} 4\,2.1\,5 \\ \times\,1\,2 \\ \hline 8\,4\,3\,0 \\ 4\,2\,1\,5\,0 \\ \hline 5\,0\,5.8\,0 \quad \checkmark \end{array}$$

Dividing Whole Numbers Without Remainders

Instead of writing a remainder, you can continue to divide whole numbers in the same way. Divide 340 by 16.

```
       2 1
16 ) 3 4 0
    − 3 2
      2 0
    − 1 6
        4
```

Remember that 340 = 340.0 = 340.00. Add zeros and continue to divide 40 tenths, then 80 hundredths.

```
       2 1.2 5
16 ) 3 4 0.0 0
    − 3 2
      2 0
    − 1 6
        4 0
      − 3 2
          8 0
        − 8 0
            0
```

Check:
```
   2 1.2 5
   × 1 6
  1 2 7 5 0
  2 1 2 5 0
  3 4 0.0 0  ✔
```

In grade 4 mathematics, you would have written the answer to $16) \overline{340}$ as 21 R4. Or you could have written the quotient as the mixed number $21\frac{4}{16} = 21\frac{1}{4}$. Now you know how to write the quotient in a third way, as a decimal: $340 \div 16 = 21.25$.

Dividing by 10, 100, 1000

When you divide a number by 10, you move its decimal point one place to the left. You make the place value of each digit ten times smaller.

$693.8 \div 10 = 69.38$ $\qquad$ $5.4 \div 10 = 0.54$

When you divide a number by 100, you move its decimal point two places to the left. You make the place value of each digit 100 times smaller.

$693.8 \div 100 = 6.938$ $\qquad$ $5.4 \div 100 = 0.054$

When you divide a number by 1000, you move its decimal point three places to the left. You make the place value of each digit 1000 times smaller.

$$693.8 \div 1000 = 0.6938 \qquad\qquad 5.4 \div 1000 = 0.0054$$

Practice multiplying and dividing decimals by 10, 100, and 1000 until you can move the decimal point and change the place values easily.

Also practice thinking what the divisor or dividend must have been in problems like these:

$$26.2 \div \underline{\hspace{1cm}} = 2.62$$
$$\underline{\hspace{1cm}} \div 100 = 0.084$$
$$670 \div \underline{\hspace{1cm}} = 0.67$$

Rounding Decimal Quotients

Even when you continue to add zeros to the dividend, not all divisions finish exactly. In these division problems, you can round the quotient to a certain place. Sometimes you also round the quotient in problems where the division works out exactly. To round a quotient, divide to one place *beyond* the place to which you are rounding.

Find the quotient of 285 divided by 23, to the nearest tenth. Since you are asked for the nearest tenth, divide until you get a quotient with hundredths, and then round.

```
        1 2.3 9
 2 3 ) 2 8 5.0 0
      −2 3
        5 5
       −4 6
          9 0
         −6 9
          2 1 0
         −2 0 7
              3
```

12.39 rounds to 12.4.

The quotient of 285 ÷ 23 to the nearest tenth is 12.4.

If you'd been asked for a quotient to the nearest hundredth, you would have continued to divide until you had a quotient with thousandths.

```
            1 2.3 9 1
    2 3 ) 2 8 5.0 0 0
        − 2 3
            5 5
          − 4 6
              9 0
            − 6 9
                2 1 0
              − 2 0 7
                    3 0
                  − 2 3
                        7
```

12.391 rounds to 12.39.

The quotient of 285 ÷ 23 to the
nearest hundredth is 12.39.

Often you round quotients because you want to give an
answer to the nearest whole unit. Suppose that 4 liters of oil
weigh 2850 grams. How much does 1 liter of oil weigh, to
the nearest gram?

Divide to the tenths of a gram and then round.

```
            7 1 2.5
    4 ) 2 8 5 0.0
      − 2 8
          0 5
        −   4
            1 0
          −   8
              2 0
            − 2 0
                0
```

712.5 rounds to 713.

To the nearest gram,
1 liter of oil weighs 713 g.

Checking Inexact Division

Remember that to check a division with a remainder, you multiply the quotient by the
divisor and add the remainder. When the quotient is a decimal number, you need to
compare the dividend and the remainder carefully, to find the place value of the
remainder.

To check this division: Multiply and add the remainder.

```
        1 2.3                                  1 2.3
   2 3) 2 8 5.0                                × 2 3
      −2 3                                      3 6 9
        ───                                    2 4 6 0
        5 5                                   ───────
       −4 6                                    2 8 2.9
       ─────                                   +   2.1
         9 0                                  ────────
        −6 9                                   2 8 5.0  ✔
        ─────
          2.1
```

The remainder is 2.1.

Since you can continue to divide 285 by 23 forever without getting an exact answer, you can divide to as many decimal places as you like. Then you can check by multiplying the quotient by the divisor and adding the remainder.

```
        1 2.3 9    Check:                     1 2.3 9 1   Check:
   2 3) 2 8 5.0 0     1 2.3 9             2 3) 2 8 5.0 0 0    1 2.3 9 1
      −2 3            × 2 3                  −2 3             × 2 3
      ─────         ───────                 ─────          ───────
        5 5           3 7 1 7                 5 5             3 7 1 7 3
       −4 6          2 4 7 8 0              −4 6            2 4 7 8 2 0
       ─────        ─────────               ─────         ───────────
         9 0          2 8 4.9 7               9 0            2 8 4.9 9 3
        −6 9          + 0.0 3               −6 9            + 0.0 0 7
        ─────        ─────────               ─────         ───────────
        2 1 0         2 8 5.0 0  ✔           2 1 0           2 8 5.0 0 0  ✔
       −2 0 7                               −2 0 7
       ───────                              ───────
           3                                  3 0
                                            −2 3
The remainder is 0.03.                      ─────
                                               7
```

The remainder is 0.007.

Practice writing answers to division problems that do not finish exactly as a multiplication and an addition. You do not need to write an inequality.

$285 = (23 \times 12.3) + 2.1$

$285 = (23 \times 12.39) + 0.03$

$285 = (23 \times 12.391) + 0.007$

Notice how the answer looks different, depending on how many places you divide to. The more decimal places you find in the quotient, the smaller the remainder will be.

Practice dividing decimals and whole numbers by whole numbers a lot. Finish divisions that are exact by continuing to divide. When the division is not exact, divide to a certain place value. Always check each division by multiplying the quotient by the divisor and adding the remainder, if there is one.

Equivalent Fractions

Equivalent fractions name the same amount. When you multiply or divide the numerator and the denominator of a fraction by the same number, you name an equivalent fraction. Here are two examples.

$$\frac{1 \times 4}{2 \times 4} = \frac{4}{8} \qquad \frac{1}{2} = \frac{4}{8} \qquad\qquad \frac{18 \div 6}{30 \div 6} = \frac{3}{5} \qquad \frac{18}{30} = \frac{3}{5}$$

Practice solving equations like these, so that the fractions are equivalent.

$$\frac{5}{10} = \frac{n}{20} \quad \text{Think:} \quad \overset{\times 2}{\frac{5}{10} = \frac{10}{20}}_{\div 2} \quad \text{so} \quad n = 10 \qquad \frac{18}{24} = \frac{6}{n} \quad \text{Think:} \quad \overset{\div 3}{\frac{18}{24} = \frac{6}{8}}_{\times 3} \quad \text{so} \quad n = 8$$

Lowest Terms

A fraction is in *lowest terms* when its numerator and denominator have no common factor greater than 1. You can write an equivalent fraction in lowest terms by dividing both the numerator and denominator of a fraction by their GCF.

Put $\frac{12}{16}$ in lowest terms. The GCF of 12 and 16 is 4.

$$\frac{12 \div 4}{16 \div 4} = \frac{3}{4} \qquad\qquad\qquad \frac{3}{4} \text{ is in lowest terms.}$$

The numerator and denominator are called the *terms* of a fraction. Putting a fraction in lowest terms is also called putting it in *simplest form*. Because you divide to put a fraction in lowest terms, people often say you *reduce* a fraction to lowest terms.

Comparing Fractions

You can compare two fractions that have the same denominator by comparing the numerator.

$$\frac{4}{5} > \frac{3}{5} \text{, because } 4 > 3$$

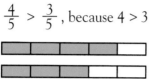

To compare fractions with different denominators, you first give them a common denominator—you make their denominator the same. Once their denominators are the same, you can compare them easily. To give fractions a common denominator, first find the LCM of the two denominators; then write the fractions as equivalent fractions that have this LCM for a denominator.

For example, to compare $\frac{2}{3}$ and $\frac{3}{5}$, first find the LCM of the denominators 3 and 5. The LCM is 15. Write both $\frac{2}{3}$ and $\frac{3}{5}$ as equivalent fractions with a denominator of 15.

$$\frac{2 \times 5}{3 \times 5} = \frac{10}{15} \qquad \frac{3 \times 3}{5 \times 3} = \frac{9}{15}$$

Now compare the fractions. Since $\frac{10}{15} > \frac{9}{15}$, you know that $\frac{2}{3} > \frac{3}{5}$

You can find many common denominator for fractions. Any common multiple of the denominator can be used as a common denominator for fractions. For example, you can also write $\frac{2}{3}$ and $\frac{3}{5}$ with a common denominator of 30, since 30 is a common multiple of 3 and 5.

When you use the LCM to find a common denominator of fractions, you find their *least common denominator* (LCD). Learn to compare fractions by writing them with their LCD.

Comparing Fractions on a Number Line

Seeing fractions on a number line can help you to compare them. Here are number lines divided into twelfths, sixths, fourths, thirds, and halves.

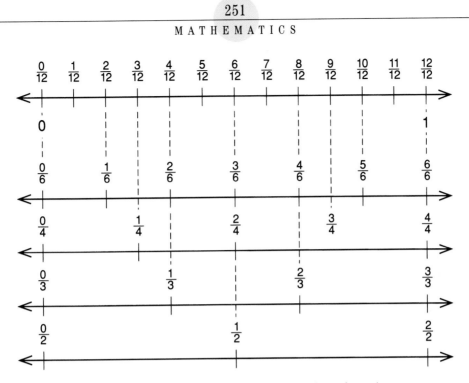

You can see from these number lines that $\frac{2}{3} < \frac{3}{4}$ and that $\frac{3}{6} = \frac{1}{2}$. Practice drawing a number line divided into twelfths in which you also write each fraction in lowest terms.

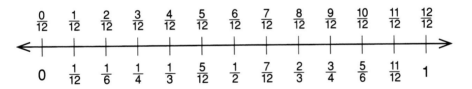

Also practice drawing number lines, divided into eighths or sixteenths. These number lines will help you to get a good mental sense of which fractions are greater, which are less, and which are equivalent.

Notice that a fraction in which the numerator is very small compared to the denominator is close to zero. For example, $\frac{1}{12}$ is close to zero. When the numerator is about half of the denominator, the fraction is about $\frac{1}{2}$. $\frac{5}{12}$ and $\frac{7}{12}$ are both close to $\frac{1}{2}$. When the difference between the numerator and the denominator is small compared to their size, the fraction is close to 1. $\frac{11}{12}$ is close to 1. Practice estimating whether fractions are close to 0, $\frac{1}{2}$, or 1.

Adding Fractions

You add fractions with the same denominator by adding the numerator. You write each sum in lowest terms.

$$\frac{2}{3} + \frac{2}{3} = \frac{4}{3} = 1\frac{1}{3} \qquad\qquad \frac{3}{16} + \frac{5}{16} = \frac{8}{16} = \frac{1}{2}$$

To add fractions with different denominators, you must first write them with a common denominator. Then you can add. You cannot add fractions when their denominators are different, because you would be adding parts of different sizes.

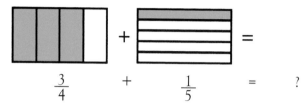

$$\frac{3}{4} \qquad\qquad + \qquad\qquad \frac{1}{5} \qquad\qquad = \qquad ?$$

You cannot add these fractions because their denominators are different. To add, first write $\frac{3}{4}$ and $\frac{1}{5}$ as equivalent fractions with a common denominator. Use the LCM of 4 and 5 to find the LCD. The LCD of $\frac{3}{4}$ and $\frac{1}{5}$ is 20.

$$\frac{3 \times 5}{4 \times 5} = \frac{15}{20} \qquad\qquad \frac{1 \times 4}{5 \times 4} = \frac{4}{20}$$

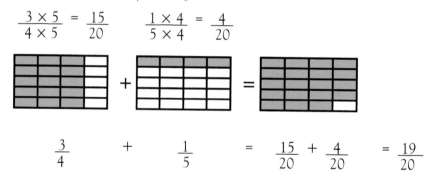

$$\frac{3}{4} \qquad + \qquad \frac{1}{5} \qquad = \qquad \frac{15}{20} + \frac{4}{20} \qquad = \frac{19}{20}$$

Always write a fraction sum as a mixed number or fraction in lowest terms. Sometimes you have to find the LCD of three or more fractions to add them.

The LCD of $\frac{4}{7}$ and $\frac{2}{21}$ is 21.

$$\frac{4}{7} = \frac{12}{21}$$
$$+\frac{2}{21} = +\frac{2}{21}$$
$$\overline{\qquad\quad \frac{14}{21} = \frac{2}{3}}$$

The LCD of $\frac{5}{6}$, $\frac{1}{3}$, and $\frac{5}{8}$ is 24.

$$\frac{5}{6} + \frac{1}{3} + \frac{5}{8} = \frac{20}{24} + \frac{8}{24} + \frac{15}{24} = \frac{43}{24} = 1\frac{19}{24}$$

You can write a fraction addition vertically, as on the left, or horizontally, as on the right, opposite. Practice adding two or more fractions with different denominators lots of times until it seems easy.

Subtracting Fractions

You subtract fractions with the same denominator by subtracting the numerators. You write each difference in lowest terms.

$$\frac{7}{8} - \frac{3}{8} = \frac{4}{8} = \frac{1}{2}$$

To subtract fractions with different denominators, you must first write them with a common denominator. You cannot subtract parts that are of a different size. For example, you cannot take $\frac{1}{4}$ from $\frac{3}{5}$ until you make the parts in the two fractions the same size. To find $\frac{3}{5} - \frac{1}{4}$, write $\frac{3}{5}$ and $\frac{1}{4}$ with their LCD and then subtract. The LCD of $\frac{3}{5}$ and $\frac{1}{4}$ is 20.

$$\frac{3}{5} - \frac{1}{4} = \frac{3 \times 4}{5 \times 4} - \frac{1 \times 5}{4 \times 5} = \frac{12}{20} - \frac{5}{20} = \frac{7}{20}$$

Now try $\frac{5}{6} - \frac{4}{9}$. The LCD of $\frac{5}{6}$ and $\frac{4}{9}$ is 18.

$$\frac{5}{6} = \frac{15}{18}$$
$$-\frac{4}{9} = -\frac{8}{18}$$
$$= \frac{7}{18}$$

You can use any common denominator when you add or subtract fractions with different denominators, but using the LCD as the common denominator will make your work quicker and easier. Practice subtracting fractions with different denominators until you feel like a pro.

Mixed Numbers and Fractions

A mixed number contains an integer and a fraction. $2\frac{1}{2}$ is an example. You can round mixed numbers to the nearest whole number. If the fractional part of a mixed number is less than one-half, round the mixed number down. If the fractional part is one-half or greater, round the mixed number up. A fraction equals one-half if its numerator is half its denominator.

Round to the nearest whole number.

$6\frac{2}{7}$ 2 is less than half of 7, so $\frac{2}{7} < \frac{1}{2}$.

$6\frac{2}{7}$ rounds down to 6.

$7\frac{11}{19}$ 11 is more than half of 19, so $\frac{11}{19} > \frac{1}{2}$.

$7\frac{11}{19}$ rounds up to 8.

$5\frac{7}{14}$ 7 is half of 14, so $\frac{7}{14} = \frac{1}{2}$.

$5\frac{7}{14}$ rounds up to 6.

Decimals, Mixed Numbers, and Fractions

You should know how to write decimals as fractions or mixed numbers. Here are two examples.

$$0.067 = \frac{67}{1,000} \qquad\qquad 8.24 = 8\frac{24}{100}$$

You can also write fractions as decimals. There are two ways you can do this. You can write a fraction as an equivalent fraction with a denominator of 10 or 100 or 1,000. Then write this equivalent fraction as a decimal. For example, to write $\frac{2}{5}$ as a decimal, convert it to an equivalent fraction with a denominator of 10.

$$\frac{2}{5} = \frac{2 \times 2}{5 \times 2} = \frac{4}{10} = 0.4 \qquad \text{Another example: } \frac{17}{25} = \frac{68}{100} = 0.68$$

You can use this method only when the denominator is a power of 10, or 100, or 1000, etc.

You can also remember that the fraction bar is the same as the division sign. To write $\frac{1}{8}$ as a decimal, do the division problem $8\overline{)1}$ until the division finishes.

```
       0.1 2 5
   8 ) 1.0 0 0
      −8
       2 0
      −1 6
         4 0
        −4 0
           0      So ⅛ = 0.125
```

Check:
0.1 2 5
  × 8
1.0 0 0 ✔

For many fractions, this division goes on and on, and the quotient is never exact. These fractions cannot be written as exact decimal numbers.

Write $\frac{1}{3}$ as a decimal to the nearest hundredth.

```
      0.3 3 3
  3) 1.0 0 0
     - 9
        1 0
      - 9
        1 0
      - 9
          1
```

Check:
```
    0.3 3 3
      × 3
    0.9 9 9
  + 0.0 0 1
    1.0 0 0  ✔
```

0.333 rounds to 0.33.

$\frac{1}{3}$ to the nearest hundredth is 0.33.

Notice that this division will continue to give a 3 in each decimal place, as long as you divide. When you discover a pattern like this, you can find the next digit or digits in the quotient without dividing.

To write a mixed number as a decimal, change the fractional part to a decimal. The whole number part remains unchanged.

Write $4\frac{4}{11}$ as a decimal to the nearest thousandth. The whole number 4 remains unchanged. Write $\frac{4}{11}$ as a decimal to the nearest thousandth.

```
       0.3 6 3 6
  1 1) 4.0 0 0 0
      - 3 3
         7 0
       - 6 6
          4 0
        - 3 3
           7 0
         - 6 6
            4
```

Notice the pattern.
If you were to continue to divide,
can you predict what the next two
digits of the quotient would be?

0.3636 rounds to 0.364. To the nearest thousandth, $4\frac{4}{11}$ is 4.364. Practice writing fractions and mixed numbers as decimals.

Adding Mixed Numbers

To add mixed numbers with the same denominator, first add the fractional parts and then add the whole number parts.

Add the fractions.   Add the whole numbers.

$$12 \frac{1}{7}$$ $$12 \frac{1}{7}$$

$$+ 5 \frac{3}{7}$$ $$+ 5 \frac{3}{7}$$

$$\frac{4}{7}$$ $$17 \frac{4}{7}$$

When the denominators of the fractional parts are different, write the fractions with their LCD and then add. Sometimes you will get an improper fraction in the sum. Always *convert*, or change, your answer to a mixed number in lowest terms.

The LCD of $\frac{2}{3}$, $\frac{1}{2}$, and $\frac{1}{6}$ is 6.

$$2 \frac{2}{3} = 2 \frac{4}{6}$$

$$3 \frac{1}{2} = 3 \frac{3}{6}$$

$$+ 6 \frac{1}{6} = + 6 \frac{1}{6}$$

$$11 \frac{8}{6} = 11 + 1 \frac{2}{6} = 12 \frac{2}{6} = 12 \frac{1}{3}$$

Remember that to convert the improper fraction $\frac{8}{6}$ to a mixed number, you do the division:

$$6) \overline{8} \quad 1 \frac{2}{6}$$ So $\frac{8}{6} = 1 \frac{2}{6}$

You can also remember that $\frac{6}{6} = 1$, so $\frac{8}{6} = \frac{6}{6} + \frac{2}{6} = 1 \frac{2}{6}$

Subtracting Mixed Numbers

To subtract mixed numbers, the fractional parts must have a common denominator. Here are two examples.

In the example below, the denominators are the same. First subtract the fractions; then subtract the whole numbers.

$$5 \frac{2}{3}$$ $$5 \frac{2}{3}$$

$$- 2 \frac{1}{3}$$ $$- 2 \frac{1}{3}$$

$$\frac{1}{3}$$ $$3 \frac{1}{3}$$

In the second example, the denominators are different. Write the fractions with their LCD. Subtract the fractions and then the whole numbers.

$$5\frac{5}{6} = 5\frac{10}{12}$$
$$-2\frac{3}{4} = -2\frac{9}{12}$$
$$3\frac{1}{12}$$

Sometimes when you subtract mixed numbers, the fractional part you are subtracting from is too small. Then you need to regroup the number you are subtracting from: you regroup by adding one of the wholes to the fractional part. For example, here is how you subtract a mixed number from a whole number. Suppose that you want to take $2\frac{3}{16}$ from 5.

You can't take $\frac{3}{16}$ from 0.

$$5$$
$$-2\frac{3}{16}$$

You can regroup 1 whole as $\frac{16}{16}$, so that there are sixteenths to subtract.

$$5 = 4\frac{16}{16}$$
$$-2\frac{3}{16} = -2\frac{3}{16}$$
$$2\frac{13}{16}$$

When the fractions have different denominators, write the fractions with their LCD *first*, before you regroup, if you need to. In the problem $5\frac{3}{16} - 2\frac{11}{12}$, the LCD is 48. Write the fractions with a common denominator.

$$5\frac{3}{16} = 5\frac{9}{48}$$
$$-2\frac{11}{12} = -2\frac{44}{48}$$

To subtract, you need to regroup $5\frac{9}{48}$. Add a whole to the fractional part:

$$5\frac{9}{48} = 4 + \frac{48}{48} + \frac{9}{48} = 4\frac{57}{48}$$
$$4\frac{57}{48}$$
$$-2\frac{44}{48}$$
$$2\frac{13}{48}$$

Since you will not always need to regroup, write the fractions with their LCD first.

Multiplying Fractions and Whole Numbers

One way to multiply a fraction and a whole number is by repeated addition. You can think of $6 \times \frac{2}{3}$ as adding $\frac{2}{3}$ six times.

$$\text{So } 6 \times \frac{2}{3} = \frac{2}{3} + \frac{2}{3} + \frac{2}{3} + \frac{2}{3} + \frac{2}{3} + \frac{2}{3} = \frac{12}{3} = 4$$

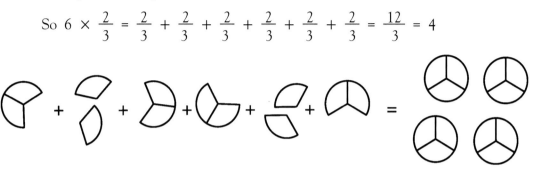

Another way to think of multiplying a fraction and a whole number is taking part of the whole number.

$\frac{2}{3} \times 6$ means $\frac{2}{3}$ of 6

The word *of* means the same thing here as the multiplication sign.

To find $\frac{2}{3}$ of 6, divide 6 into 3 parts and then take 2 of them.

Divide 6 into 3 parts: $6 \div 3 = 2$

Now take 2 of the 3 parts.

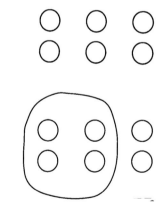

$2 \times 2 = 4$. So $\frac{2}{3}$ of 6 is 4.

Notice that $\frac{2}{3} \times 6 = 4 = 6 \times \frac{2}{3}$. Multiplication is commutative; you will get the same answer whether you think of adding a fraction over and over again or taking part of a whole number.

MATHEMATICS

You can use the following method to multiply a fraction and a whole number. Multiply the whole number and the numerator of the fraction, and write the product over the denominator. Write the product in lowest terms.

$$6 \times \frac{2}{3} = 6 \times \frac{2}{3} = \frac{12}{3} = 4$$

Practice multiplying fractions and whole numbers in this way. Also practice writing a problem like $7 \times \frac{5}{6}$ as repeated addition.

$$7 \times \frac{5}{6} = \frac{5}{6} + \frac{5}{6} + \frac{5}{6} + \frac{5}{6} + \frac{5}{6} + \frac{5}{6} + \frac{5}{6} = \frac{35}{6} = 5\frac{5}{6}$$

Practice solving a problem like finding $\frac{3}{7}$ of 56 in two ways. Remember that $\frac{3}{7}$ **of** 56 is the same as $\frac{3}{7}$ ✗ 56.

1) Multiply: $\frac{3}{7} \times 56 = \frac{3 \times 56}{7} = \frac{168}{7} = 24$

2) Or to find $\frac{3}{7}$ of 56, divide 56 into 7 equal parts. $56 \div 7 = 8$. Now take 3 of the equal parts. $8 \times 3 = 24$. $\frac{3}{7}$ of 56 is 24.

Notice that in the first method, you multiply and then divide. In the second method, you divide and then multiply. You get the same answer either way.

RATIOS, PERCENTS, AND PROBABILITIES

Ratio

A ratio is a way of comparing the size of two numbers. If a family has three dogs and five cats, the ratio of their dogs to cats is 3 to 5. You can write the ratio of their dogs to cats in a number of ways:

$$3 \text{ to } 5 \qquad 3 : 5 \qquad \frac{3}{5}$$

You read each of these ratios "3 to 5." Notice that a ratio can be written as a fraction. You can write equal ratios the same way you write equivalent fractions, by dividing or multiplying both numbers of the ratio by the same number. Here is how you can write two ratios equal to the ratio 4/10 (4 to 10).

$$\frac{4 \div 2}{10 \div 2} = \frac{2}{5} \qquad \frac{4}{10} = \frac{2}{5} \qquad \frac{4 \times 2}{10 \times 2} = \frac{8}{20} \qquad \frac{4}{10} = \frac{8}{20}$$

The ratio 2/5 is in lowest terms. Write ratios as fractions in lowest terms. Practice writing equal ratios.

Solve for a: $\dfrac{8}{21} = \dfrac{24}{a}$

You multiply 8 × 3 to get 24, so you must multiply 21 × 3 to get a.
$a = 21 \times 3$
$a = 63$

Also practice checking to see if two ratios are equal.

Does $\dfrac{5}{9} = \dfrac{10}{14}$?

You multiply 5 × 2 to get 10.

You cannot multiply 9 × 2 to get 14.

So $\dfrac{5}{9} \neq \dfrac{10}{14}$

The sign $\neq$ means "is not equal to."

Scale

A scale drawing uses a ratio, called its *scale*, to shrink or enlarge all the things it shows in the same way. For example, on a map of a city with a scale 1 inch = 2 miles, each inch on the map represents two miles of actual distance in the city. A map is one kind of scale drawing; another example is a plan showing the rooms on a floor of a house.

Meg has made a plan of her room, with the scale 1 inch = 3 feet. On her plan, the side wall is 5 inches long. How long is it actually? To find out, write the scale as a fraction, and then find a fraction equivalent to it.

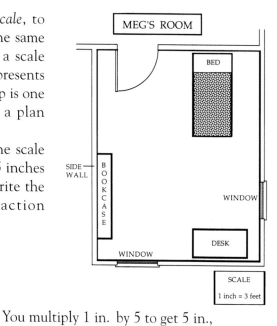

length on the plan — $\dfrac{1 \text{ in.}}{3 \text{ ft.}} = \dfrac{5 \text{ in.}}{n}$ You multiply 1 in. by 5 to get 5 in., so you must multiply 3 ft. by 5 to get n.
actual length

$n = 3 \text{ ft.} \times 5 = 15 \text{ ft.}$

length on the plan — $\dfrac{1 \text{ in.}}{3 \text{ ft.}} = \dfrac{5 \text{ in.}}{15 \text{ ft.}}$
actual length

The side wall is actually 15 feet long.

If her bed is 6 feet long, how long will it appear on the plan? Again find a fraction equivalent to the scale.

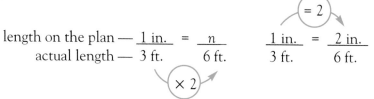

length on the plan — $\dfrac{1 \text{ in.}}{3 \text{ ft.}} = \dfrac{n}{6 \text{ ft.}}$ $\dfrac{1 \text{ in.}}{3 \text{ ft.}} = \dfrac{2 \text{ in.}}{6 \text{ ft.}}$

Her bed would be 2 inches long on the plan.

To find a scale, write a ratio of a plan length to the actual length as a fraction in lowest terms. Here is an example:

On a plan, the length of a school yard is 2 centimeters. It is actually 50 meters long. What is the scale of the plan?

$$\text{plan length —} \frac{2 \text{ cm}}{50 \text{ m}} = \frac{1 \text{ cm}}{25 \text{ m}}$$
$$\text{actual length —}$$

The scale of the plan is 1 cm = 25 m.

Rates and Speed

A *rate* is a ratio between two different quantities. Here are some examples of rates: she was averaging 4 hits in each 10 at bats; he was getting 10 cents for every dollar of apple cider he sold; the car was traveling at 100 kilometers per hour.

One very common rate is speed. Speed is a rate given in distance per unit of time. 100 kilometers per hour is a speed. You can abbreviate it 100 km/hr. Some other units of speed are miles/hour (mi/hr) and miles/minutes (mi/min).

Here is a formula that relates distance, speed, and time.

$D = r \times t$ Distance is equal to the rate times the time.

Remember that speed is a rate. The formula tells you that you multiply the speed by the time spent traveling at that speed to find the distance traveled. For example, an airplane travels at 550 mi/hr for 4 hours. To find how far it has traveled, multiply: $D = 550 \times 4 = 2200$. The plane has traveled 2200 miles in 4 hours.

Sometimes speed is given per minute, or per second. If a train is traveling at 2 km/min, how long will it take to travel 86 km? Remember $D = r \times t$. The distance is 86 km and the rate is 2 km/min.

$$86 = 2 \times t$$
$$86 \div 2 = t$$
$$43 = t \text{ or } t = 43$$

(Use inverse operations.)

It will take the train 43 minutes to travel 86 km.

You can change distance per minute to distance per hour by multiplying the distance by 60. 2 km/min = 120 km/hr.

You can also change distance per hour to distance per minute by dividing by 60. 90 mi/hr = 1.5 mi/min, since 90 ÷ 60 = 1.5.

To find a speed, write the ratio of distance to a single unit of time. For example, if a train travels 195 miles in 3 hours, what has been its speed? The train has traveled 195 mi/3hr. Divide by 3 to find the distance traveled in 1 hour.

$$\begin{array}{r} 65 \\ 3\overline{)195} \end{array}$$ The train has traveled at 65 mi/hr.

Percent

The term *percent* means "per hundred." Percent is a ratio: a percent compares a number to 100. For example, 40 percent means $\frac{40}{100}$ or 40 out of 100. The symbol % stands for percent. You write 11 out of 100 as 11%.

Often a percent is a part of a whole. The whole is 100%. If 45% of a fifth-grade class are boys, then 55% of the class are not boys. They are girls. 100% of the class are either boys or girls.

Boys		Girls		Whole Class				
45%	+	55%	=	100%				

$$\frac{45}{100} \; + \; \frac{55}{100} \; = \; \frac{100}{100}$$

Notice that $100\% = \frac{100}{100} = 1$. When you are talking whole, 100% means "all the parts." For example, if 100% of your friends came to a party, they all came.

Percents and Fractions

Remember that a percent is always in hundredths. So to write a percent as a fraction, write the percent over a denominator of 100. Then reduce the fraction to lowest terms.

$$8\% \; = \; \frac{8}{100} \; = \; \frac{2}{25}$$

8% or $\frac{2}{25}$ of the square is shaded. What would 35% be, written as a fraction in lowest terms?

To write a fraction as a percent, first write an equivalent fraction that has a denominator of 100. Then you can write the percent.

$$\frac{1}{4} \; = \; \frac{1 \times 25}{4 \times 25} \; = \; \frac{25}{100} \; = \; 25\%$$

Percents and Decimals

To write a percent as a decimal, remember that a percent is always in hundredths. 35 percent is the same as 35 hundredths, and 8 percent is the same as 8 hundredths.

$$35\% = \frac{35}{100} = 0.35 \qquad\qquad 8\% = \frac{8}{100} = 0.08$$

To write a decimal as a percent, think of the decimal in hundredths. Then you can write it as a percent. 7 tenths (0.7) is the same as 70 hundredths (0.70), which is the same as 70%.

$$0.7 = 0.70 = \frac{70}{100} = 70\% \qquad 0.04 = \frac{4}{100} = 4\%$$

A quick way to write a decimal as a percent is to multiply the decimal by 100. This method works because percents are already in hundredths.

$$0.70 = 70\% \qquad 0.04 = 04\% = 4\% \qquad \text{(Move the decimal point two places to the right.)}$$

A quick way to write a percent as a decimal is to divide by 100.

$$35\% = \frac{35}{100} = 0.35$$

$$8\% = \frac{8}{100} = 0.08$$

Remember: to divide by 100, simply move the decimal point two places to the left.

Writing Fractions, Decimals, or Percents

Fractions, decimals, and percents are often used interchangeably: people sometimes use a fraction, sometimes a decimal, or sometimes a percent to mean the same thing.

For example, we might say 25% of Jim's marbles are red or $\frac{1}{4}$ of Jim's marbles are red or 0.25 of Jim's marbles are red. ($25\% = \frac{1}{4} = 0.25$) Since we are talking about a part of a whole, we could also say that 75% of Jim's marbles are not red or $\frac{3}{4}$ of Jim's marbles are not red or 0.75 of Jim's marbles are not red. ($75\% = \frac{3}{4} = 0.75$) Practice writing six statements like these for problems like "40% of the pizza was pepperoni."

Also learn to complete a table like this one, writing a number as a fraction, a decimal, or a percent.

Fraction	Decimal	Percent
1/5	____	____
____	0.1	____
____	____	65%
____	0.5	____

You may want to memorize the percent equivalents of some common fractions: $\frac{1}{4}$ is 25%, $\frac{1}{2}$ is 50%, $\frac{1}{10}$ is 10%.

Finding a Percent of a Number

There are 525 students at the elementary school. 44% of them are in fourth or fifth grade. How many students are in fourth or fifth grade?

To solve this problem, you must find a percent of a number: what is 44% of 525? To find a percent of a number, change the percent to a decimal and multiply.

Remember that 44% = 0.44. To find 0.44 *of* 525 you multiply 0.44 × 525.

```
    5 2 5
  × 0.4 4
    2 1 0 0
  2 1 0 0 0
  2 3 1.0 0
```
44% of 525 is 231.

There are 231 fourth and fifth graders at the elementary school.

Finding an Average

To find the average of a set of numbers, you add the numbers together and then divide by the number of addends. This average can give you an idea of how large a typical number in the set is.

For example, Mrs. Tough wants to find the average number of questions out of 20 that Peter has gotten right on his last 5 quizzes. His scores have been 12, 12, 13, 15, and 17. She adds his scores:

```
   12
   12
   13
   15
  +17
   69
```

Then she divides by the number of scores:

```
     1 3.8
  5)6 9.0
```

Peter has averaged 13.8 correct answers on his last five quizzes. Mrs. Tough might round the average and say, "Peter has been getting about 14 questions right out of 20."

Another word for average is *mean*. Practice finding the average price of a gallon of gas in your town if the various gas stations sell it for $1.67, $1.72, $1.78, and $1.54 per gallon.

Probability

Have you ever heard someone say there's a "fifty-fifty chance" that something might happen. Do you ever describe the "chances" of something happening as "one in a million"? Both of these expressions are ways of talking about probability. *Probability* is a measurement of how likely it is that a particular event will happen. A high probability means something is likely to happen; a low probability means it probably won't.

Suppose you have a black bag that contains three red apples and one green apple. If you reach into the bag and pick out one apple without looking, what is the probability that it will be a green apple? The probability is one in four because of the four apples you might pick, only one of them is green. This probability can be written as a fraction: $\frac{1}{4}$. Or it can be written as a percent: there is a 25% chance that you will pick a green apple. Probability can also be expressed as a decimal value between 0 and 1. A probability of 0 means that there is no chance of the event occurring. A probability of 1 means it is certain to occur. In the situation outlined above the probability of choosing a green apple is .25. What is the probability of choosing a red apple?

Now imagine that you have four red apples in the bag: what is the probability of pulling out a green one? What is the probability of pulling out a red one?

GRAPHS, FUNCTIONS, AND WORD PROBLEMS

Circle Graphs

Sometimes the best way to present mathematical information is to draw a graph. There are several different kinds of graphs.

A *circle graph* is good for showing the relationship of different parts to a whole. It is usually divided into fractions or percentages. Circle graphs can be used to show probability. For example, if a bag contains four red apples and two green apples, the probability of choosing a red or green apple can be shown on a circle graph, like this:

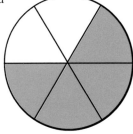

Here the area shaded **yellow** represents the chances that an apple will be red (4 in 6); the unshaded area stands for the chances that an apple will be green (2 in 6). Looking at this graph, you can see why circle graphs are sometimes called pie charts. The chart looks like a pie cut into slices.

Circle graphs can also be used in other ways. The chart below shows how the Brown family spent its income.

The Brown Family Income Last Year (After Taxes)

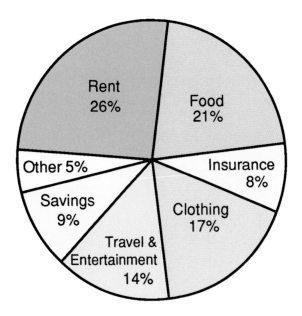

You can see right away from the graph where the Brown family spent most of their money and how much of their total income went to each area. If the Brown family had an income after taxes of $51,860 last year, how much did they spend on insurance? You find 8% of $51,860. 8% = 0.08

$51,860
× 0.08
$4,148.80

The Brown family spent $4,148.80 on insurance last year.

How much money did they save? How much money did they spend on food?

Bar Graphs

A *bar graph* is a good way to show the different sizes of amounts. Here is a table of data and a bar graph based on the numbers in the tables.

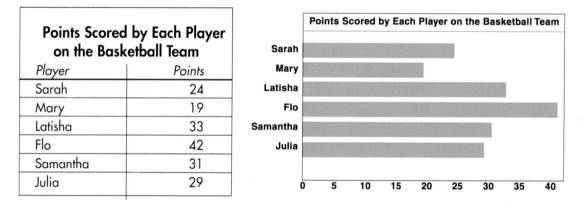

Points Scored by Each Player on the Basketball Team	
Player	*Points*
Sarah	24
Mary	19
Latisha	33
Flo	42
Samantha	31
Julia	29

Along the left side of the graph we listed the players on the team. Along the bottom we listed numbers of points scored. Then we drew a series of bars to mark each player's total points. Lastly, we titled the graph.

You can see right away from this chart that Flo is the top scorer on the team.

Line Graphs

Another kind of graph is the *line graph*. People often use line graphs to show how amounts or numbers change over time. The data opposite shows how the average high temperature in the desert city of Las Vegas, Nevada, changed during the year.

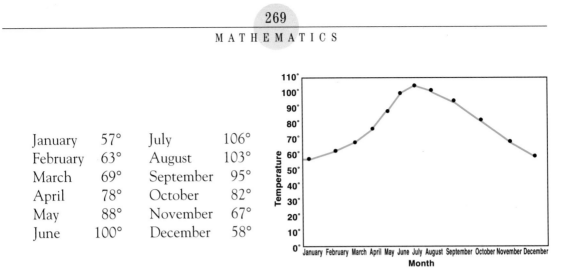

January	57°	
February	63°	
March	69°	
April	78°	
May	88°	
June	100°	

July	106°
August	103°
September	95°
October	82°
November	67°
December	58°

To make our line graph, we put the months along the bottom of the graph. Along the side, we put temperature intervals that would show the data clearly. We gave the graph a title and labels along the bottom and side. When you look at this line graph, you can see at a glance how the temperature heats up in the summer and cools down in the fall and winter.

Practice making your own bar graphs, line graphs, and circle graphs from tables of data. For each chart, you'll need to decide which kind of graph would be the best way to present your data.

Functions and Inverse Operations

add	9	13	21
3	12	16	24

divide	26	57	16	3
by 2	13	28.5	8	1.5

multiply	6	22	5	11
by 7	42	154	35	77

These tables show *functions*. These functions do the same thing to each number you put into them. For example, the first function adds 3 to each number.

Inverse operations can help you to see how functions work. For example, the inverse of the function *add 3* is the function *subtract 3*. If you add 3 to 9 and then subtract 3, you get back to 9 again. An inverse operation undoes the previous operation.

add	9	13	21	subtract
3	12	10	24	3

Addition and subtraction are inverse operations.

multiply by 2	13	28.5	8	1.5	divide by 2
	26	57	16	3	

Multiplication and division are inverse operations.

Practice filling in function tables like these:

divide by 4	16	27	10	18
	4	6.75	?	?

	?	4	7	18	?
		6	?	20	

Graphing Functions

You can make a graph of a function such as <u>add 3</u>.

add 3	0	1	2	3	4
	3	4	5	6	7

Write each pair of numbers as an ordered pair. Define ordered pairs. Then plot the ordered pairs on a grid. (Use graph paper with fairly large squares.) Connect the points to show that they are on the same line. If the points are not on the same line, you have made a mistake.

Graph of function add 3

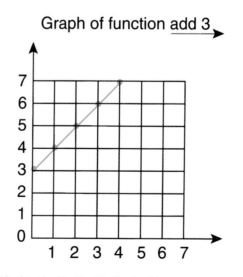

Plot the ordered pairs (0,3), (1,4), (2,5), (3,6), (4,7).

Graph three more functions for practice. Here are the functions:

multiply	0	1	2	3	4
by 2	0	2	4	6	8

subtract	4	5	6	7	8
4	0	1	2	3	4

divide	0	2	4	6	8
by 2	0	1	2	3	4

Writing and Solving Equations for Word Problems

You can write an equation for a word problem, using a variable like x or n to stand for an unknown number. Jennifer goes to the bookstore and buys a mystery and a romance for $8.90; the mystery costs $0.60 more than the romance. How much does each book cost?

Begin with a simple sketch. Draw line segments or bars that will help you write an equation. Be sure to be clear about what the variable or variables in your sketch represent. In the pictures below, r stands for the cost of the romance.

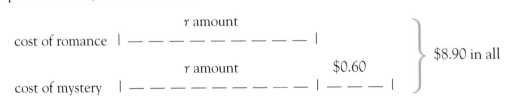

Next write an equation based on the picture. It is customary *not* to include units in an algebraic equation. So, for now, leave out the dollar sign and write your numbers as decimals:

$$r + (r + 0.60) = 8.90$$

Then solve the equation by finding what r is. Use inverse operations.

$$r + r + 0.60 = 8.90$$
$$(2 \times r) + 0.60 = 8.90 \quad — — — — \quad 2 \times r \text{ is the same as } r + r$$
$$(2 \times r) \qquad\quad = 8.90 - 0.60 \quad — — \quad \text{Remember, you can write } 4 + 3 = 7$$
$$2 \times r \qquad\quad = 8.30 \qquad\qquad\qquad \text{as } 4 = 7 - 3$$
$$r \qquad\qquad = 8.30 \div 2 \quad — — — \quad \text{You can write } 2 \times 4 = 8 \text{ as } 4 = 8 \div 2$$
$$r \qquad\qquad = 4.15$$

Now that you have done the calculations and solved the equation, you can restore the dollar sign. The romance costs $4.15, and the mystery costs $0.60 more, or $4.75. You can check your answer by adding: $4.15 + $4.75 = $8.90.

Here is another example. Bill weighs three times as much as his dog Samuel. Together they weigh 128 pounds. How much does each weigh?

1) As before, draw line segments or bars to show the variable.

$$s \text{ lb}$$
Samuel's weight | — — — — |

$$s \text{ lb} \qquad\qquad s \text{ lb} \qquad\qquad s \text{ lb}$$
Bill's weight | — — — — | — — — — | — — — — |

} 128 lb in all

2) Set aside the units and write an equation.

$$s + (s + s + s) = 128$$

3) Solve the equation.
$$4 \times s = 128$$
$$s = 128 \div 4$$
$$s = 32$$

Finally, identify your units. Samuel weighs 32 pounds. Bill weighs 3×32 pounds, or 96 pounds. You can check your answer by adding: $32 + 96 = 128$.

Now you try one. Susan paid $20 for two mice and a goldfish. The goldfish cost $4. What did each mouse cost?

When solving word problems, bear in mind that the solution to your equation may sometimes be mathematically correct but not realistic as a solution for the original word problem. For example, suppose you wanted to find out how many buses are needed to transport the students in your school to a museum. There are 135 students, and each bus holds 30 students. Write an equation, where b stands for the number of buses you need:

$$b \times 30 = 135$$
$$b = \frac{135}{30} = 4.5$$

The math says you need 4.5 buses, but since you can't travel in half a bus, you'll actually need 5 buses.

GEOMETRY

Angles

Now let's learn some geometry. You remember that *geometry* is the study of points, lines, and angles—and of the shapes and forms that can be constructed using points, lines, and angles.

Whenever two lines, line segments, or rays meet at a common point, they form an *angle*. The place where they come together is called a *vertex*.

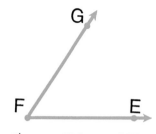

This is ∠EFG or ∠GFE.

You measure an angle by measuring the size of its opening in units called *degrees*. You can do this with a measuring tool called a *protractor*. First, place the protractor's center on the vertex of the angle and the zero mark along one ray. Then you can read the number of degrees in the angle, where the second ray crosses the protractor. Angle EFG has a measure of 56 degrees. You write m∠EFG = 56°. The symbol ° stands for degrees, and the letter *m* stands for "the measure of."

You can also use a protractor to draw an angle with a certain measure. Use a ruler to draw a ray. Then place the protractor's center on the endpoint and the zero mark along the ray. Mark a point at the right number of degrees, and draw a second ray from the vertex of the angle through this point.

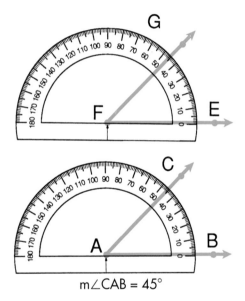

m∠CAB = 45°

Kinds of Angles

A *right angle* has a measure of 90°. ∠BAD is a right angle.

An *acute angle* has a measure less than 90°. ∠BAC is an acute angle. Remember that acute angles are smaller than right angles.

An obtuse angle has a measure greater than 90° but less than 180°. ∠BAE is an obtuse angle. Obtuse angles are greater than right angles.

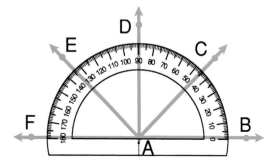

A *straight angle* is formed when its two rays are part of the same line. A straight angle has a measure of 180°. ∠BAF is a straight angle.

Practice drawing right, acute, and obtuse angles using a protractor. Practice estimating about how large some angles are, using right angles (90°) and straight angles (180°) as mental guides. For example, a 30° angle would have an opening about one-third as wide as a right angle.

Kinds of Triangles

Triangles have three interior angles. An *equilateral triangle* has three sides of the same length.

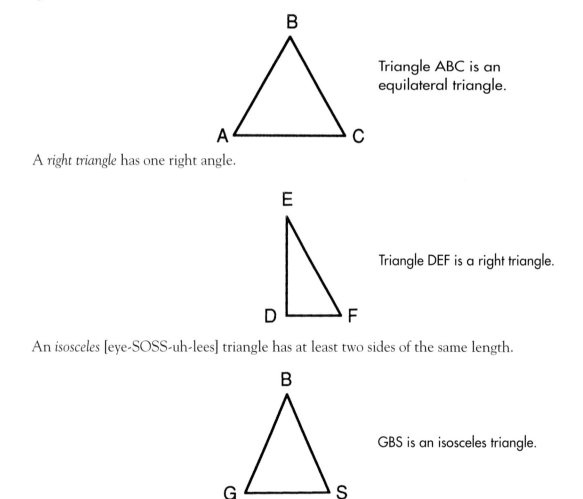

Triangle ABC is an equilateral triangle.

A *right triangle* has one right angle.

Triangle DEF is a right triangle.

An *isosceles* [eye-SOSS-uh-lees] triangle has at least two sides of the same length.

GBS is an isosceles triangle.

With some simple tools, you can construct a triangle with sides of a certain length. You'll need a ruler and a compass. A *compass* is a special tool that is used for drawing circles and parts of circles.

To construct triangle DGC with sides of 6 inches, $4\frac{1}{2}$ inches, and 3 inches, first draw a segment 6 inches long.

Label the endpoints D and G. Now, take your compass and expand it so the pencil point is 3 inches from the needle point. Place the needle point on endpoint D and scoot the pencil point around to draw an arc (part of a circle) 3 inches from D. Drawing an arc 3 inches from D is like drawing part of a circle with radius 3 inches and center D.

Now draw another arc, this time $4\frac{1}{2}$ inches from G. Where the two arcs intersect, mark point C. Use your ruler to draw segments DC and GC and complete the triangle.

A compass.

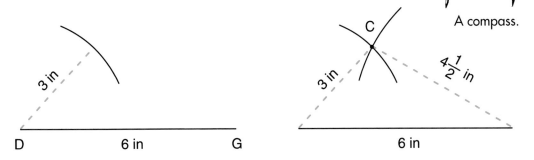

If you have a compass, you can use this method to construct equilateral and isosceles triangles. For example, construct an equilateral triangle with sides of 8 centimeters; construct two different isosceles triangles with sides of 5 centimeters and 7 centimeters.

Whenever two triangles are the same shape and size, they are *congruent*. These two triangles are congruent.

If you cut out the triangle on the right and rotate it, you could place it right on top of the triangle on the left, and you would see that the two triangles have the same shape and size.

These two triangles are not congruent: they do not have the same shape and size.

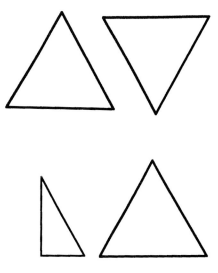

Polygons

A *polygon* is a closed figure made out of three or more line segments. Triangles are three-sided polygons. Four-sided polygons are called *quadrilaterals*. You probably already know some kinds of quadrilaterals. A rectangle is a quadrilateral in which all the angles are right angles and the opposite sides are the same length.

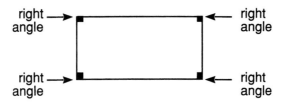

A *square* is a special kind of rectangle in which all four sides are equal in length.

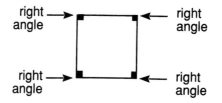

A *trapezoid* is a quadrilateral in which only two of the four sides are parallel.

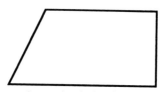

A *parallelogram* is a quadrilateral in which both pairs of opposite sides are parallel. They are also of equal length.

A *rhombus* is a special kind of parallelogram in which all four sides are of equal length. The diagonals of a rhombus are *perpendicular*, and divide each other in half where they intersect.

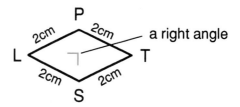

Parallelogram PTSL is a rhombus. All of its sides have the same length.

A square is a special kind of rhombus: it has four sides of the same length, *and* four right angles. A square is both a rhombus and a rectangle.

A polygon with five sides is called a *pentagon*.

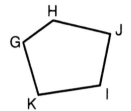

Polygon GHIJK is a pentagon.

A polygon with six sides is called a *hexagon*.

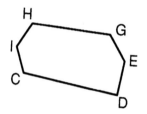

Polygon HGEDCI is a hexagon.

A polygon with eight sides is called an *octagon*.

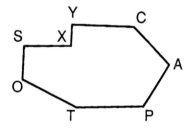

Polygon YCAPTOSX is an octagon.

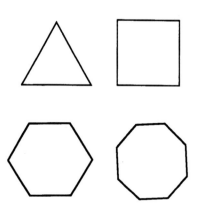

A *regular* polygon has sides of equal length and angles of equal measure.

A regular triangle is also called an equilateral triangle and a regular quadrilateral is also called a square. A stop sign has the shape of a regular octagon.

Diagonals

A *diagonal* is a line segment that joins two vertices of a polygon but is not one of the sides of that polygon. A quadrilateral has two diagonals. How many diagonals does a pentagon have?

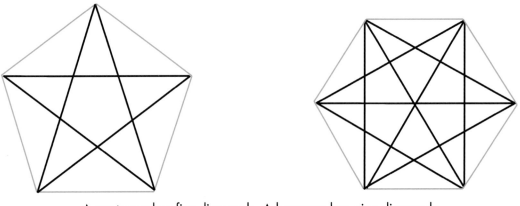

A pentagon has five diagonals. A hexagon has nine diagonals.
How many diagonals does an octagon have?

Practice drawing in all the diagonals on a pentagon, a hexagon, a seven-sided polygon, and an octagon. See if you can find a pattern.

Circles

Earlier you learned how to draw a triangle using a compass. A compass can also be used to draw a circle. Simply keep the needle point fixed in one place and guide the pencil point all the way around until it ends where it began.

A line segment joining two points on a circle is called a *chord*. Segments DC and TS are chords of the circle with center P.

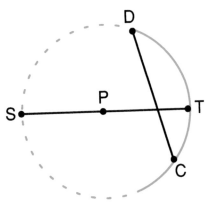

The *diameter* of a circle is the length of a chord that passes through the center of the circle. TS is both a chord and a diameter of the circle. A diameter is the longest possible chord of a circle. The *radius* is the distance from the center of a circle to the circle. It is the same wherever you measure it and is always equal to half the diameter. PS is a radius of this circle, and so is PT.

An *arc* is a part of the circle. It has two endpoints on the circle.

arc DC

The distance around a circle—or the distance traveled by the pencil end of the compass while drawing the circle—is called its *circumference*. You can measure the circumference of a circle (or of any other flat figure) by placing a piece of string along the circle and then measuring the length of the string that you used. You can also find the circumference of a circle using a formula.

$$\text{Circumference of a circle} = \pi \times \text{diameter}$$
$$C = \pi \times d$$

The symbol π is a letter from the Greek alphabet. It is pronounced and spelled out "pi." π is a number: it is the number of diameter lengths there are in the circumference of a circle. For example, if you had pieces of string the length of the diameter, it would take you π number of these pieces of string to go all the way around a circle. You cannot write the number π exactly as a finite decimal. To the nearest hundredth, π is 3.14. It would take a little more than three pieces of string the length of the diameter to go all the way around a circle.

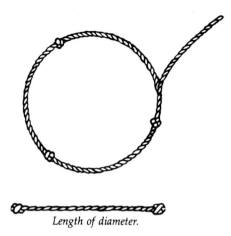

Length of diameter.

Using the value 3.14 for π, practice finding the circumference of a circle. For example, find the circumference of a circle with a diameter of 13 centimeters. Round your answer to the nearest tenth of a centimeter.

$C = \pi \times d$
$\approx 3.14 \times 13$ (the symbol $\approx$ means "approximately equal to")
≈ 40.82 40.82 rounds to 40.8

The circumference of a circle with a diameter of 13 cm is *approximately* 40.8 cm.

Since the diameter of a circle is twice its radius, you can also write the circumference formula with the radius.

$C = \pi \times 2 \times r$ (r stands for radius)

Practice using $C = \pi \times 2 \times r$ to calculate the circumference of a circle given its radius. Also practice using a compass to construct circles that have a certain radius.

Area

Remember that the area of a rectangle is its length times its width. The formula for the area of a rectangle is $A = l \times w$. So the area of a rectangle with sides 7 feet and 5 feet is 35 square feet, or 35 ft^2. ($7 \times 5 = 35$)

You can measure area in common units or in metric units. The common units in the United States include square inches (in^2), square feet (ft^2), square yards (yd^2), and square miles (mi^2). Metric units (used in most of the rest of the world) include square millimeters (mm^2), square centimeters (cm^2), square meters (m^2), and square kilometers (km^2).

Suppose you wanted to paint a wall in your room that was a rectangle 10 feet long and 8 feet tall. Would a can of paint that covers 100 ft² be big enough?

$A = l \times w$ (here the width is really height)
$A = 10 \text{ ft} \times 8 \text{ ft}$
$A = 80 \text{ ft}^2$
$80 < 100$, so you should have enough paint.

Now try a more difficult problem. Suppose you wanted to buy squares of fabric to make a small quilt. You want the quilt to be 13 square feet and each square to be 9 square inches. Each square costs 10 cents. How many squares will you need to buy?

The problem here is that some of your numbers are measured in square feet and others are measured in square inches. Before you can solve the problem you need to convert either the inches to feet or the feet to inches. Start by converting 13 square feet to square inches. If you know how many inches are in a foot, you can figure out how many square inches are in a square foot. Since there are 12 inches in a foot, a square foot contains 12 × 12 square inches, or 144 square inches.

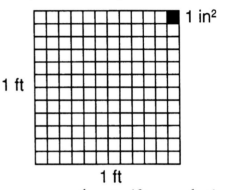

So if there are 144 square inches in 1 square foot, how many are there in 13 square feet? 13 × 144 = 1872. 13 square feet = 1872 square inches. The quilt has an area of 1872 square inches. Now divide by 9 square inches to find how many squares are needed.

$$\frac{208}{9)\,1872}$$

You will need 208 squares. At 10¢ a square, they will cost you $20.80.

$$\begin{array}{r} \$0.10 \\ \times\ 208 \\ \hline \$20.80 \end{array}$$

You can practice the same kind of question with metric numbers. For instance, how many square tiles measuring 10 centimeters on each side would you need to cover a wall that is 4 meters by 5 meters?

Finding the Area of a Triangle

To find the area of a triangle, you need to learn to measure the height of a triangle. Start by calling any side of the triangle its base. The height of a triangle is the perpendicular distance from the vertex opposite the base to the line containing the base. Here are examples of heights of triangles.

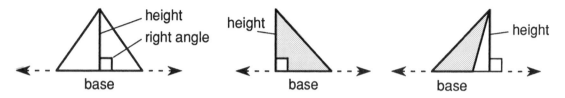

Practice drawing and measuring the heights of different triangles.

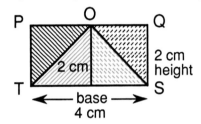

Study the rectangle above. The area of rectangle PQST is 8 square centimeters (4 × 2 = 8). Triangle OST is half of rectangle PQST: you can see that when you divide triangle OST into two right triangles, there are two matching right triangles left in rectangle PQST. Since triangle OST is half of rectangle PQST, the area of triangle OST must be half of 8 square centimeters, which is 4 square centimeters.

So you can find the area of triangle OST by multiplying its base (4 cm) times its height (2 cm), and then dividing by 2.

$$A = (4 \times 2) \div 2$$
$$= 8 \div 2 = 4 \quad \text{The area of triangle OST is 4 cm}^2.$$

You can find the area of any triangle by multiplying its base times its height and then dividing by 2.

Formula for the area of a triangle: $A = (b \times h) \div 2$

Practice finding the area of a triangle. For example, construct a triangle with sides of 6 cm, 7 cm, and 8 cm, and draw its three different heights using each side as a base. (Notice that the heights all intersect each other at the same point.) Measure the heights in centimeters, and calculate the area of the triangle in square centimeters in three different ways.

Finding the Area of a Parallelogram

You can call any side of a parallelogram its base. The height of a parallelogram is the perpendicular distance from its base to the opposite side. The pictures below show you how you can find the area of a parallelogram.

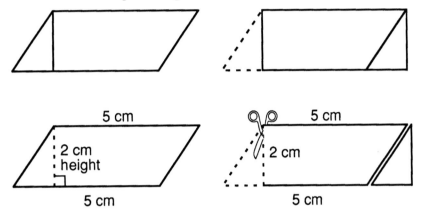

The parallelogram has the same area as a rectangle with the same base and height. $5 \times 2 = 10$. So the area of the parallelogram is 10 cm^2.

You can always find the area of a parallelogram in the same way, by multiplying its base times its height.

Formula for the area of a parallelogram: $A = b \times h$

Practice using this formula to find the area of parallelograms.

Finding Areas of Other Figures

Sometimes you have to find the area of a figure by dividing it into smaller areas that you know how to find. For example, you can find the area of this trapezoid by dividing it into smaller areas. Here is one way.

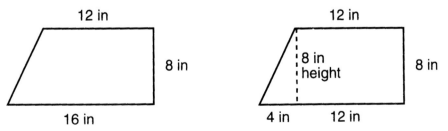

Divide the trapezoid into a rectangle and a right triangle. Find the area of each and add to find the total area.

Area of rectangle: $12 \times 8 = 96$
Area of triangle: $(4 \times 8) \div 2 = 16$
Add the two areas: $96 + 16 = 112$
The area of the trapezoid is 112 in^2.

See if you can find the area of the trapezoid on the previous page by dividing it into two triangles.

Rectangular Prisms

So far the figures you have been working with have been flat, or *plane* figures. But it is also possible to use your geometry skills to measure three-dimensional shapes.

The figure to the right is a rectangular prism. A rectangular prism has six faces that are rectangles, and twelve edges. Each edge is parallel to three other edges, and all four of these edges have the same length. The opposite faces of a rectangular prism are congruent.

A *cube* is a special rectangular prism: all of its edges have the same length, and all of its faces are congruent. The illustrations below show what a cube would look like with all its surfaces opened out flat.

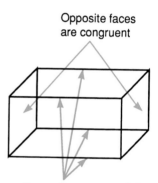

Opposite faces are congruent

Four edges are parallel and of equal length

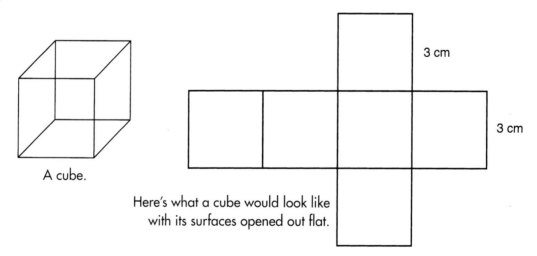

A cube.

Here's what a cube would look like with its surfaces opened out flat.

3 cm

3 cm

You can make a cube by making a copy of this page, cutting out the cross-shaped figure, and folding it along the lines so that all of the edges are touching each other. You can hold the figure together with tape.

Volume

Volume is measured in cubic units. Cubic units tell you how much space something occupies. Cubic units have three dimensions: usually length, width, and height.

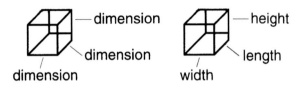

Some common cubic units are a cubic centimeter (cm^3), a cubic meter (m^3), a cubic inch (in^3), and a cubic foot (ft^3).

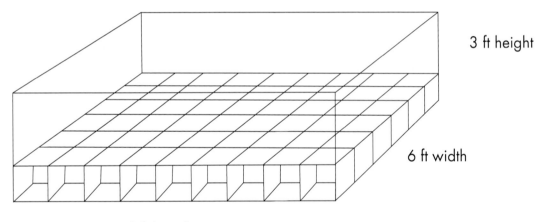

The volume of this rectangular prism is 9 x 6 x 3 or 162 cubic feet.

You can count by layers to find the volume of a rectangular prism.

On one layer you can fit 9 cubic feet along the length and 6 cubic feet along the width. You can fit 9 × 6 or 54 cubic feet on one layer. Since the prism is 3 feet tall, you can fit 3 layers of cubic feet. Altogether you can fit 54 × 3 or 162 cubic feet in the rectangular prism. Its volume is 162 cubic feet.

You can always find the volume of a rectangular prism by multiplying its length times its width times its height—even if the length, width, and height are not in whole number units.

Formula for the volume of a rectangular prism: $V = l \times w \times h$

An easy way to remember this is as the area of its base (l × w) times its height: The same formula gives the volume of a cylinder as well.

V = (area of the base) × height

For example, to find the volume of a box that has for its dimensions 4.3 cm, 3.6 cm, and 3.9 cm, you multiply 4.3 × 3.6 × 3.9.

```
    4.3           1 5.4 8
  × 3.6           × 3.9
    2 5 8         1 3 9 3 2
  1 2 9 0         4 6 4 4 0
  1 5.4 8         6 0.3 7 2     The volume of the box is 60.372 cm³.
```

The volume of a box that is 4.3 centimeters by 3.6 centimeters by 3.9 centimeters is 4.3 cm × 3.6 cm × 3.9 cm. Notice that the word *by* represents multiplication; to find the volume of a rectangular prism, multiply its three dimensions.

Volume and Surface Area

You can also find the *surface area* of a three-dimensional figure. The surface area is the area, in square units, occupied by all of the faces of a solid figure. Suppose you want to paint your toy box with a special bright blue paint. The paint comes in small cans that each hold enough paint to cover 50 square feet. If the box has a length of 4 feet, a width of 2 feet, and a height of 3 feet, will one can of paint be enough to cover it completely?

Remember that each face of a rectangular prism has an opposite congruent face. The top and the bottom are congruent. The area of each is l × w. The front and back are congruent. The area of each is l × h. The two sides are congruent. The area of each is w × h.

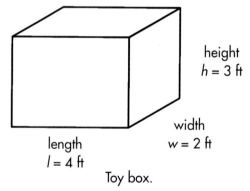

length
l = 4 ft

height
h = 3 ft

width
w = 2 ft

Toy box.

Surface Area of a Rectangular Prism
SA = (2 × l × w) + (2 × l × h) + (2 × w × h)
 top and bottom   front and back   two sides

SA = (2 × 4 × 2) + (2 × 4 × 3) + (2 × 3 × 2)
  = 16 + 24 + 12
  = 52

The surface area of the toy box is 52 square feet, so you'll need more than one can of paint. If you decide not to paint the bottom of the box, will you still need more than one can?

Practice finding the volume and surface area of rectangular prisms. Remember that you measure volume in cubic units and surface area in square units. For example, find the volume and surface area of a box with a length of 8 cm, a width of 6 cm, and a height of 5 cm. Then find the volume and surface area of this box if each dimension is doubled. By what number do you multiply the surface area of the box, when you double each of its dimensions? By what number do you multiply the volume?

Changing U.S. Customary Units of Volume

If you know the equivalences among the U.S. customary units of length, you can find the equivalences among the U.S. customary units of volume.

There are 12 inches in 1 foot. There are $(12 \times 12 \times 12)$ in^3 in 1 ft^3
$$1728 \text{ in}^3 = 1 \text{ ft}^3$$

There are 3 feet in 1 yard. There are $(3 \times 3 \times 3)$ ft^3 in 1 yd^3
$$27 \text{ ft}^3 = 1 \text{ yd}^3$$

Practice changing from one U.S. customary unit of volume to another. For example, a small truck has 400 cubic feet of storage space. To the nearest cubic yard, how many cubic yards is that?

$27 \text{ ft}^3 = 1 \text{ yd}^3$ So to find how many cubic yards there are in 400 ft^3, divide 400 by 27.

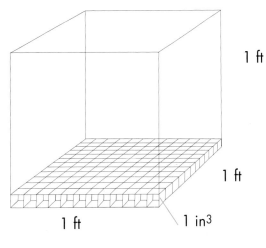

One cubic foot.

$$
\begin{array}{r}
1\,4.8 \\
27\overline{)4\,0\,0.0} \\
-2\,7 \\
\hline
1\,3\,0 \\
-1\,0\,8 \\
\hline
2\,2\,0 \\
-2\,1\,6 \\
\hline
4
\end{array}
$$

14.8 rounds to 15.

400 ft^3 is 15 yd^3, to the nearest cubic yard.

Changing Metric Units of Volume

Changing units in the metric system is easy, because all you have to do is move the decimal points. Remember m stands for meter, dm for decimeter, and cm for centimeter.

$$1 \text{ m} = 10 \text{ dm, so } 1 \text{ m}^3 = (10 \times 10 \times 10) \text{ dm}^3$$
$$= 1000 \text{ dm}^3$$

$$1 \text{ dm} = 10 \text{ cm, so } 1 \text{ dm}^3 = (10 \times 10 \times 10) \text{ cm}^3$$
$$= 1000 \text{ cm}^3$$

How many dm^3 are in 3.23 m^3? 3.23 m^3 = 3230 dm^3 (multiply by 1000)

How many dm^3 are in 237 cm^3? 237 cm^3 = 0.237 dm^3 (divide by 1000)

Notice that a decimeter is 10 times as long as a centimeter, but a cubic decimeter is *1000* times as large as a cubic centimeter!

Volume and Capacity

Remember that units of capacity, such as cups and quarts in the U.S. customary system, and liters in the metric system, measure how much a container (for example, a bottle) can hold. When you measure the capacity of a container, you are measuring the space inside the container, that is, the volume of the inside of the container. So units of capacity are also units of volume. In the U.S. customary system there is no easy equivalence between units of capacity (such as cups) and units of volume (such as in^3). But in the metric system 1 liter = 1 cubic decimeter (1 L = 1 dm^3). Since 1 m^3 = 1000 dm^3, you also know that 1 m^3 = 1000 L.

Practice converting measures that are in cubic centimeters, decimeters, and meters to liters. For example, 35 dm^3 = 35 L; 750 cm^3 = 0.75 L; 800 m^3 = 800,000 L.

VI.

Science

Introduction

The pages that follow outline what fifth graders should know about science. Students will be introduced to chemistry and atoms. They will also learn about the classification of living things, cells, plants, life cycles, the human body, and the physical changes they experience as they enter adolescence. In addition, they will read brief biographies of four important scientists.

Parents and teachers can supplement this chapter with various science activities. Students who have studied the classification of animals will find trips to zoos more interesting. They will see how different animals in the zoo are grouped together and how species are linked by common features. Students who have studied plants and seeds may enjoy gardening, collecting leaves and seeds, and examining plant life with a magnifying glass. An inexpensive home microscope will allow children to see cells and other tiny structures, and a chemistry set (properly supervised) will allow them to perform some basic experiments. Many books collecting simple and safe science experiments are now available. For book recommendations, consult the Core Knowledge Foundation's searchable database, Resources to Build On (www.coreknowledge.org).

Hands-on scientific experience is so important that some educators have come to reject the very idea of teaching young children about science from books. But book learning should not be neglected altogether. It helps bring system and coherence to a young person's developing knowledge of nature and provides essential building blocks for later study. Book learning also provides knowledge not likely to be gained by simple observations; for instance, books can tell us about things that are not visible to the naked eye, like cells, eggs and sperm, hormones, and atoms. And we should not forget that some children enjoy book learning even more than they enjoy experiments and field trips. Both kinds of experience are necessary to ensure that gaps in knowledge will not hinder later understanding.

CHEMISTRY: MATTER AND CHANGE

Atoms

Suppose you had a nugget of pure gold in your hands. With the right tools, you could cut the nugget in half. And you could cut one of the halves in half, too. But how long could you keep dividing like this? If you had very good tools, maybe even microscopic tools, could you keep going forever? Or would you eventually come up with a particle of gold so tiny that you could no longer divide it?

Many years ago, the ancient Greek philosophers wondered about this. Some philosophers claimed that you could go on dividing anything forever. Others thought there must be some limit, some particle so small that it cannot be divided. The philosopher Democritus thought that there must be such a particle and he named it *atomos*, which is Greek for "indivisible." That's where our idea of atoms comes from.

Although Democritus came up with the name *atom*, he couldn't prove that atoms exist. Atoms are much too small to see with the human eye or even with a regular microscope, and how can you study something that you can't see? Despite this difficulty, scientists now know a great deal about these basic building blocks of matter.

It turns out that atoms can be divided, but if you divide an atom of gold, it is no longer gold, and if you divide an atom of lead, it is no longer lead. So an atom is the smallest piece of a substance that retains the qualities and characteristics of that substance.

Atoms themselves are made of smaller particles, called *sub-atomic particles*. These sub-atomic particles are called protons, neutrons, and electrons. *Protons* have a positive (+) electrical charge. *Electrons* have a negative (−) charge. *Neutrons* have no charge: they are neutral. The protons and neutrons are located in the center of the atom, called the *nucleus*, while the electrons swirl around them.

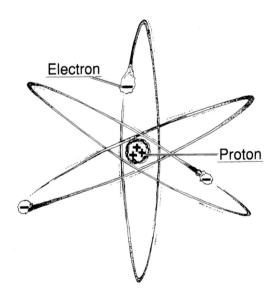

Electron

Proton

There are several ways of drawing models of atoms. This model of a lithium atom shows protons with positive charges in the nucleus and electrons with negative charges circling the nucleus.

John Dalton

Although Democritus believed more than 2,000 years ago that atoms must exist, it wasn't until the 1800s that scientists investigated atoms in a scientific way. One of the earliest scientists to work on the subject was John Dalton (1766–1844). Dalton analyzed the experiments done before his time and concluded that Democritus might have been right: perhaps all matter really is composed of atoms. Scientists had already discovered that chemical reactions cannot break down certain substances, now called *elements*, into anything simpler. Gold is an element, and so are lead, silver, hydrogen, and oxygen.

Dalton figured out that elements are composed of tiny particles called atoms, and that the atoms of each element are identical to each other, but different from the atoms of other elements. Even during dramatic chemistry experiments, the atoms themselves did not change, Dalton said; they just rearranged themselves.

The Parts of Atoms

Dalton's basic ideas proved to be correct, but it wasn't until the 1930s that scientists began to figure out how atoms work. Several theories were proposed, and it was difficult to prove which one was right.

Scientists discovered that most of the mass of an atom is in its nucleus. The electrons surrounding the nucleus are much lighter. They discovered that the nucleus has a positive charge that exactly balances the negative charges on the electrons. Once scientists formed this picture of the atom's structure, they began to understand how chemical elements work.

Mendeleev and the Periods

By the late 1800s, scientists had identified most of the elements, from hydrogen, the lightest and most plentiful element in the universe, to lead and other heavy elements. But they did not understand why the elements interact with each other as they do.

A very important step in understanding elements was the discovery by a Russian chemist, Dmitri Mendeleev, that the properties of the elements repeated themselves at regular intervals, or periodically.

Mendeleev discovered that when you arrange the elements in horizontal rows, from lightest to heaviest, after a while you find another element that has similar properties to the first atom in the row. If you put the similar elements in vertical columns you can arrange all the elements in related groups.

Here is one such column:

element #3 lithium
element #11 sodium
element #19 potassium

These three elements have many similar characteristics. They are all metals, which means that they are shiny and good conductors of heat and electricity; these particular metals are all soft, low in density, and solid at room temperature. They can be hammered or drawn into different shapes. They also react with other substances in very similar and sometimes dramatic ways. It's much too dangerous for anyone to do at home, but if you were to place these elements on a pool of water, you would see that they float and skitter around on bubbles of hydrogen that are created. Sometimes the hydrogen even burns or explodes!

Mendeleev made a chart of the repetitions he saw, and a version of his chart, called the *periodic table of the elements*, has been used ever since to show similarities and differences among the elements. Although no one doubted that Mendeleev had discovered something very important, it took many years to figure out why the elements can be arranged this way.

Here's a simplified periodic table. Can you find some of the elements
you've been reading about?

Explaining the Periods

In the 1920s, Niels Bohr, a Danish scientist, proposed that what gives each element its distinctive characteristics and determines how it can combine with other elements is mainly one thing: the number of electrons in a single atom of the element. Scientists had already assigned a number to each element according to the number of electrons in a single atom. Lithium, the third element, has three electrons; sodium, the eleventh element, has eleven electrons, and so on.

Bohr had the inspired idea that the electrons arrange themselves in something like shells, or energy levels, around the nucleus. When there were a certain number of electrons in a shell, that made the shell stable and complete, and another outer shell would form.

Bohr was basically right. The chart below shows the number of electrons in the shells of lithium, sodium, and potassium.

	Shell #1	Shell #2	Shell #3	Shell #4
element #3 lithium:	2	1		
element #11 sodium:	2	8	1	
element #19 potassium:	2	8	8	1

Notice that the total number of electrons is the same as the number of the element. Notice also that each element has a single electron in the outer shell of its atoms. It's that single electron that gives the element many of its chemical and electrical properties.

In general, all chemical reactions are determined by the electrons in the outer shells of atoms. Some elements, such as sodium, can give off an electron easily. Other elements like oxygen can take on electrons easily. That's why these types of elements tend to come together, one giving electrons, one taking electrons, to stabilize the outer shells of both kinds of atoms.

Sodium is the eleventh element on the periodic table. It has eleven electrons—two in its inner shell, eight in its middle shell, and one in its outer shell. It can give off the single electron in its outer shell easily.

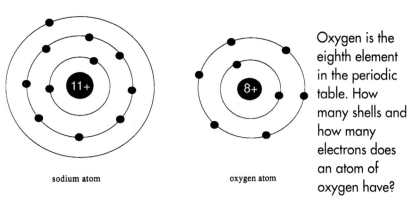

sodium atom

oxygen atom

Oxygen is the eighth element in the periodic table. How many shells and how many electrons does an atom of oxygen have?

Elements and Abbreviations

There are more than one hundred known elements. Scientists often refer to these elements using a set of abbreviations known as *atomic symbols*. Some symbols consist of a single capital letter. Others consist of two letters, the first a capital and the second a small letter. Many are easy to remember because they correspond with the first few letters or sounds of the English names:

H = Hydrogen	He = Helium	C = Carbon
N = Nitrogen	O = Oxygen	Al = Aluminum
Si = Silicon	Cl = Chlorine	

Some other abbreviations are a little harder to remember because they are based on the Latin names of the elements:

Abbreviation	Latin name	English name
Fe	ferrum	Iron
Cu	cuprum	Copper
Ag	argentum	Silver
Au	aurum	Gold

Can you find these elements on the periodic table on page 294? Can you find elements that are in the same vertical column, called a group?

Metals and Non-Metals

Two important categories of elements are metals and non-metals. About two-thirds of the elements are metals. Lithium, sodium, potassium, iron, copper, silver, lead, and gold are all metals. Carbon, oxygen, hydrogen, and chlorine are some nonmetallic elements.

How is a metal different from a non-metal? Metals are usually shiny and *malleable*, which means they can be beaten into different shapes. Metals are also usually *ductile*, which means they can be stretched out into wires. Finally, most metals *conduct* electricity—that is, they allow electricity to flow through them. Some metals are better conductors than others. Silver and copper are very good conductors of electricity. Since copper is less expensive than silver, it is commonly used in electric wires and motors.

This serving piece is made from element 47 on the periodic table. Can you figure out what element that is?

Molecules

If the atoms of the elements always stayed by themselves, nothing much would happen. There would be no chemical reactions—and no life.

A *molecule* is created when two or more atoms join together—either atoms of different elements or atoms of the same element. For example, you know that humans need oxygen to survive. The oxygen in the air you breathe is actually in the form of molecules, that is, as two oxygen atoms joined together. The symbol for oxygen is "O," and the double oxygen molecule can be represented like this:

The way chemists indicate a regular molecule of two oxygen atoms is by the symbol O_2. The number means that there are two atoms of oxygen together in a molecule. Sometimes, though, lightning bolts can cause this oxygen molecule to break up into its individual atoms:

Many of these single oxygen atoms quickly combine with O_2 molecules to produce a form of oxygen molecules called "ozone." Ozone molecules are made of three oxygen atoms.

Chemists indicate an ozone molecule by writing O_3. Sometimes you can smell ozone after a thunderstorm. Because ozone is unstable, many ozone molecules break apart after a while, and regular oxygen molecules (O_2) form again.

Compounds

Compounds are molecules made up of atoms of different elements. Here is the scientific formula for the most important compound in the world: H_2O. That is the chemical formula for water. The way you say this formula is "H-two-Oh". It means that two hydrogen atoms are joined with one oxygen atom to make one molecule of water. Here is one way to show a water molecule.

Another famous compound is carbon dioxide, or CO_2. Carbon dioxide is made up of two atoms of oxygen joined to one atom of carbon. Carbon dioxide is a colorless, odorless gas. Your body is a carbon dioxide factory. Every time you exhale, you breathe out millions of molecules of carbon dioxide. Some of this carbon dioxide is used by plants for a process called photosynthesis. Plants, in turn, give off oxygen needed by human beings.

Physical and Chemical Changes

Scientists distinguish between two kinds of changes that can happen to a substance. A *physical change* changes the properties or the appearance of a substance but does not change what it is made of. If you saw a piece of wood in half, you have made a physical change: the wood is still the same stuff, but now it's in two pieces. If you hit a baseball through your neighbor's window, you will physically change the windowpane, but the pieces of glass on the floor will still have the same chemical makeup. When water freezes it is still made up of the same H_2O molecules, but its physical properties change from a liquid to a solid.

In a *chemical change*, the atoms and molecules of the reacting substances are rearranged to create new substances. All the original atoms are still present, but there are new molecules with different properties and different chemical formulas. If, instead of cutting a piece of wood, you burn it, you change the wood in a chemical way. The molecules of the wood are transformed into different substances, including carbon dioxide, water vapor, and carbon. Rust is another example. You may have noticed that iron rusts when it gets wet. When iron combines with oxygen, a chemical reaction takes place and a compound called iron oxide, or rust, is created.

These campers are using the chemical reaction we call *fire* to stay warm.

The chemical formula for table salt is NaCl. You can say it either "N-A-C-L," or "sodium chloride," which is what the letters stand for. Scientists can make NaCl by joining together HCl (hydrochloric acid) with NaOH (sodium hydroxide) when these substances are dissolved in a water solution. In these solutions, the atoms have either gained or lost electrons, which gives them an electrical charge. These charged atoms are called *ions*. When HCl and NaOH are combined, a chemical reaction takes place, in which the ions get new partners. The result will be table salt and water. Chemists write a chemical equation to show what happened:

$$HCl + NaOH \longrightarrow NaCl + H_2O$$

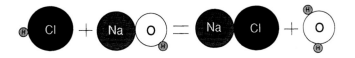

The chemical reaction is stated as follows: hydrochloric acid plus sodium hydroxide yields sodium chloride plus water. Notice that this equation is something like a mathematical equation. All the elements on the left side still appear on the right, but the sodium atom (Na) has joined the chlorine atom (Cl), and the first hydrogen atom has combined with the OH to make H_2O. This shows us that no atoms disappear and no new ones are created.

Chemical changes are essential for life. When your body uses the food you eat, it uses chemical reactions that give off the energy you need to do everything you do. It's this chemical energy that keeps you breathing and keeps your heart pumping blood through your body. Without chemical energy, there could be no life!

CLASSIFYING LIVING THINGS

Why Classify?

If someone asked you how to find apples in the grocery store, you'd probably send her to the fruits and vegetables aisle or tell her to look near the oranges and watermelons. Where would you tell a friend to look if he wanted to borrow a pair of your socks? You'd tell him to look in the drawer where you keep your socks.

Grouping things that are alike makes it easier for us to find them and easier to add similar new things to the group. Would you find frozen French-fried potatoes in the snack-food aisle? No, although French-fried potatoes and potato chips have potatoes as ingredients, frozen French fries, unlike chips, need to be in a freezer. So we put these products in different places in the grocery store. We group things together or separate them according to certain similarities or differences. When we group things together because they are alike in certain ways, we are *classifying* them.

If you go to school, you and your fellow students are probably grouped in a fifth-grade class. You are placed in that class because your teachers think you are ready to do fifth-grade work. Within your class, you could think of other classifications. Boys could be one group, for example, or the people who have freckles. There are many ways to divide people and things into classes, and it's important to remember that there is generally no single right way to divide up and name things. Still, classes and our names for them are indispensable both for everyday life and for science. We classify and name things for our convenience in talking about them. In fact, we could not talk about most things without using classifications, because the very name we use for a thing is often the word for a whole class of things. A fancy recliner and a simple folding chair both belong to the class of things called "chairs."

Classifying Organisms

You've already read how chemists classify elements by their properties. Scientists who study living things, or *organisms*, also use classifications. One of the features scientists look at when they want to classify an organism is how it gets its food. Plants usually make their own food from sunlight, water, and air, while animals do not. Animals can usually move themselves around, while plants can't. Based on features like these, scientists have classified living things into large groups called *kingdoms*.

The first two kingdoms that scientists agreed on are the plant and animal kingdoms. Within these large kingdoms we can classify organisms into smaller groups. For instance, we put all flowering plants in one large group, and all non-flowering plants into another. We put all animals that have hair and give milk into one class, and all animals that have feathers and beaks into another.

Once the microscope was invented and we could see more creatures, the classifier's job became more difficult. Scientists discovered many new organisms that seemed to be neither plants nor animals and needed new classifications. Their observations led to the naming of three new kingdoms: the fungus [FUN-gus], protist [PRO-tist], and prokaryote [pro-CARE-ee-oat] kingdoms. To see why scientists thought these microscopic organisms couldn't be classified as plants or animals, we need to learn about cells.

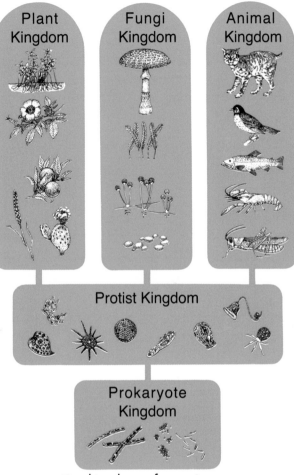

Five kingdoms of organisms.

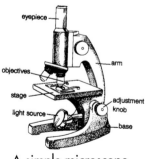

A simple microscope.

Cells

Cells are the tiny building blocks that make up all living things. Most cells are so small we can see them only with a microscope. Cells were discovered over 300 years ago when an English scientist named Robert Hooke was looking through his microscope at thin slices of cork—the material from the bark of the cork tree that can be used to seal bottles. Hooke noticed a regular pattern of small, boxlike squares in the cork, which reminded him of little rooms. He named these "cells," after the Latin word for room, *cella*. When scientists developed even stronger microscopes, they were able to study the insides of cells and see various structures. Let's look at a picture of a cell and learn what its parts do.

Robert Hooke drew this sketch of the cork cells he saw under his microscope.

The Parts of a Cell

The cell *membrane* is a thin covering around the cell that separates it from its surroundings. The cell membrane helps give the cell its shape and controls what goes into it (food, water, and oxygen) and out of it (waste). Inside the cell is the *cytoplasm* [SY-toh-plaz-um], a jellylike liquid that surrounds all the other cell parts. Inside the cytoplasm is the nucleus [NOO-klee-us], the cell's control center. The nucleus is surrounded by the nuclear membrane, which controls what goes into and comes out of the nucleus. The nucleus contains all the instructions for running the cell. To reproduce, a cell splits into two cells. But before the cell splits, the instructions in the nucleus are copied and the two copies separate to form two nuclei, so that each new cell has a nucleus with a copy of the cell's instructions.

Also inside the cytoplasm are tiny *organelles*, small structures that carry out the chemical activities of the cell. These organelles include *vacuoles* [VAK-you-ohlz], spherical structures that store food, water, or wastes, and *mitochondria* [my-toh-KAHN-dree-uh], small structures shaped like kidney beans that help break down food to release energy the cell can use.

The cells in both plants and animals, though they may differ in shape and size, have the features you've been reading about: a cell membrane, cytoplasm, a nucleus, a nuclear membrane, vacuoles, and mitochondria. As hard as it may be to believe, the cells that make up our body have all these things in common with the cells in a blade of grass!

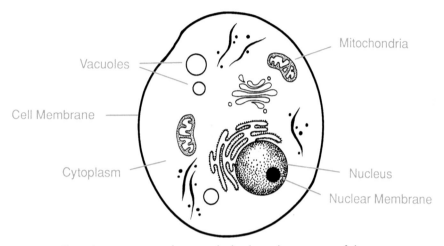

A cell and its parts, as they might look under a powerful microscope.

Living versus Non-living

How do we know if something is alive? Sometimes it's easy: you know that you are alive and a rock is not. But sometimes it's hard to tell. What about a cloud, a fire, or a tiny virus? Scientists say all living things do six activities. They take in nutrients, use energy to do work, reproduce, grow, get rid of wastes, and react to outside changes. Is a cloud alive? What about a fire? Do you think cells inside living organisms are alive? Why, or why not? Can one cell be a living organism?

Different Kinds of Cells

Cells can be different shapes depending on the jobs they do. Muscle cells are long and thin so they can relax or contract and move the body. Red blood cells are tiny, round, and flat so they can pass through blood vessels and bring oxygen to other cells. Cells in a tree trunk are long and thin and form tubes to transport food and water up and down the tree. The cells on the surface of a plant's leaves are flat and tightly connected to form a type of "skin" that keeps water in.

In complex organisms like human beings, cells are often organized into tissues, organs, and systems. A *tissue* is a collection of similar cells that work together. If you feel your upper arm, you touch skin tissue. If you "make a muscle," you can feel muscle tissue under the skin.

Tissues that have similar functions combine to make *organs*, like the heart, the stomach, or the brain. Organs can work together to form *systems*. For instance, the stomach, the large intestine, and the small intestine are parts of your digestive system. All of these tissues, organs, and systems are built from cells.

The job a cell does has a lot to do with its shape. See how differently the cells from a tree's trunk and a tree's leaf are shaped.

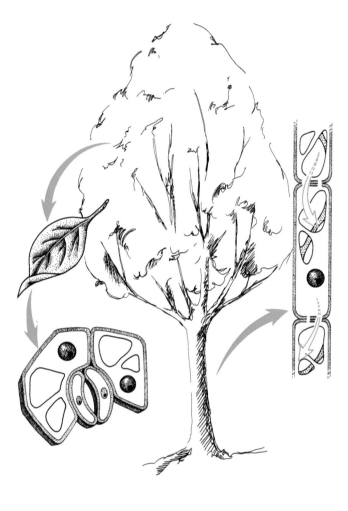

How Plant Cells Differ from Animal Cells

Plant cells have two additional parts that animal cells don't have. Unlike animal cells, plant cells have cell walls. The *cell wall* is a sturdy layer around the cell membrane that supports and protects the cell. The cell wall helps the plant cell to be stiff when it has enough water and cytoplasm inside, and this helps the plant remain upright. Robert Hooke was looking at the cell walls of tree bark cells when he made his discovery. The inside of the cells had died and dried up, leaving the pattern of "boxes" he saw.

Another structure that plant cells have that animal cells don't is the *chloroplast* [KLOR-uh-plast]. Chloroplasts contain chlorophyll [KLOR-uh-fill], a green substance that traps the energy from sunlight, enabling plants to make food in a process called *photosynthesis*.

Remember that one of the basic differences between plants and animals is that plants usually make their own food while animals don't. It's the chloroplasts that allow plants to do this.

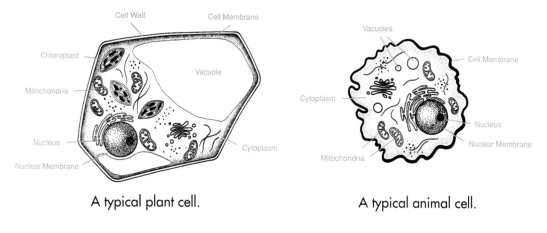

A typical plant cell.   A typical animal cell.

Fungi

Have you ever seen a mushroom at the grocery store? If so, you've seen a fungus. If there were different kinds of mushrooms on display, you probably saw several kinds of fungi [FUN-jie]. Fungi were once thought to be part of the plant kingdom because they have cell walls and produce spores (which plants also produce). But they were separated into a distinct kingdom because they get their energy not from sunlight but by breaking down material from dead plants and animals. The mushrooms you can buy at the grocery store are created by colonies of fungi that feed on decaying plant material. From time to time, the fungi send up mushrooms. When they are mature, or fully grown, the mushrooms release millions of tiny spores, which are cells with a protective coat. The wind blows the spores to distant places, where they start new fungus colonies.

The yeast that makes bread rise is a type of fungus. So is the green mold that forms on bread when it is exposed to moist air. And so is the white, powdery mildew that can appear on houseplants and in moist places.

One of the most exciting fungi known to scientists is Pilobolus, also known as "the shotgun fungus." Pilobolus grows on cow manure. When the fungus is ready to spread its spores, its cap explosively pops off and flies through the air, sometimes traveling up to six feet!

A puffball fungus dispersing its spores into the air.

Protists

The fourth kingdom is the protists. Some protists are so tiny they are only one cell. They can be seen only with a microscope. Others are quite large. Some protists have animal features, others have plant features, and still others have features of both! For years, scientists were confused about how to classify these organisms. Finally, scientists decided that these organisms should make up their own kingdom.

Protists that are single-celled and that act like animals are called protozoans [proh-toh-ZOH-unz]. *Proto* means "early" in Greek and *zoan* means "animal." Protozoans can move around. They can also capture food they find in their environment. Some are found in fresh water, some in salt water. Some live in soil, and some live inside other organisms.

One protozoan you may have heard about is called an *amoeba* [uh-MEE-buh]. An amoeba is a bloblike protozoan that is one large cell. It can stretch its body around tiny organisms that it wants to eat. Once the prey is surrounded, the amoeba brings it inside its one-celled body. This forms a vacuole, in which the prey is digested.

Other protists are plantlike and are called *algae* [AL-jee]. Some of these are single cells and some have many cells. You may have seen algae growing as a film on top of a pond or lake. Seaweed, or kelp, is also a type of algae. These organisms do photosynthesis and their cells contain chloroplasts.

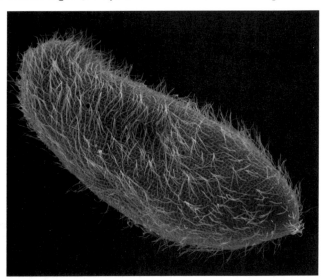

Euglena [you-GLEE-nah] are single-celled protists that have both plant and animal features. Like plants, *euglena* contain chloroplasts, but unlike plants, *euglena* can move around. *Euglena* can make food through photosynthesis, but when there is no sunlight, they can eat bacteria or other protists.

This picture, taken with an electron microscope, shows a single, ciliated protozoan—a kind of protist. The protist is covered with *cilia*, tiny hairlike projections that help the organism move in liquids.

Prokaryotes

Prokaryotes (formerly called monerans) are small, single-celled organisms that are very simple. Until high-powered microscopes were developed, scientists thought that prokaryotes were very small protists, and they had a hard time classifying them. But once they could see prokaryotes more clearly under high-powered microscopes, scientists found that they have a very important characteristic that puts them in a group by themselves: prokaryotes have no cell nucleus! The material normally found in a cell nucleus is clumped together, but has no nuclear membrane around it.

Prokaryotes are also called *bacteria*. They have both a cell wall and a cell membrane. They are classified according to their shape: some are long rods or capsules, some look like spiral tubes, and some are spherical. They get their food from other organisms or from decaying matter. They are found just about everywhere: in the air, water, and soil, and even inside other organisms, including you!

Some bacteria cause diseases. (Perhaps you've taken medicine to get rid of a bacterial disease like strep throat or bronchitis.) Other bacteria are very useful to life. Like fungi, they help break down decaying material so nutrients are free to be used by plants. Certain types of bacteria are necessary for proper digestion in humans. Scientists have even been able to develop bacteria that "eat" oil and help clean up oil spills.

Cyanobacteria are prokaryotes found in water or soil. They do photosynthesis but they do not have chloroplasts; instead, their chlorophyll is contained in membranes spread throughout the cell. Cyanobacteria used to be called blue-green algae. About half of them are bluish-green, but the rest are other colors, including red! Cyanobacteria are the beginning of the food chain for many animals that live in water. They also produce oxygen in the water and in the air we breathe.

The classification on page 301 shows all prokaryotes in one kingdom. However, a growing number of scientists divide prokaryotes into two kingdoms, called Eubacteria ("true bacteria") and Archaebacteria ("ancient bacteria"). This is an area where ideas about classification are changing rapidly as scientists learn more about these tiny organisms.

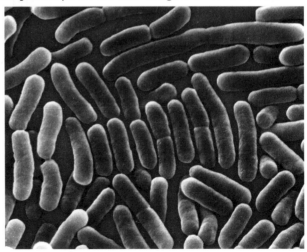

These are *Salmonella typhi* prokaryotes, seen under an electron microscope and magnified to more than 3,000 times their actual size. These prokaryotes cause the disease typhoid fever.

Taxonomy

Scientists first classify living things by placing them in one of the kingdoms. But these are very large categories, so scientists have divided them into a series of smaller groupings:

Kingdom
    Phylum (plural: phyla)
       Class
          Order
             Family
                Genus (plural: genera)
                   Species
                      (Variety)

Each kingdom can contain several phyla, and each phylum can contain several classes, and so on. (You can remember these categories, in the correct order by size, by memorizing the sentence "King Philip came over for good spaghetti.")

Here's how scientists would classify a collie dog.

Kingdom: Animalia (an animal)
    Phylum: Chordata (an animal with a type of internal skeleton)
      Subphylum: Vertebrata (a vertebrate, an animal with a backbone)
        Class: Mammalia (a mammal, an animal that is warm-blooded, has
            hair, and makes milk)
          Order: Carnivora (a carnivore, or meat-eater)
            Family: Canidae (a group with dog-like characteristics)
              Genus: Canis (a coyote, wolf, or dog)
                Species: familiaris (a domestic dog)
                  Variety: Collie (a specific breed of dog)

Can you see how this description gets more specific as it goes along? It begins by classifying the collie as an animal and then says: "But it's not just any kind of animal. It's an animal with a backbone." Gradually, more and more details are introduced and the description "closes in" on the exact kind of animal. This system of classifying living things is called *taxonomy*.

Did you notice that there is one extra stage in the classification of the Collie? In addition to phylum and class, this classification also includes a subphylum. Some phyla are divided into subphyla, which are then divided into classes.

Genus: Canis; Species: familiaris; Variety: Collie.

Latin Names

When taxonomy was just getting started, Latin was a language spoken by educated people in many different countries. It enabled a Frenchman, an Englishman, and a Dutchman to communicate with one another. So the early taxonomists used Latin. Today scientists still use Latin names so everyone will know which plants and animals they are talking about.

When scientists want to specify an animal, they don't usually list all the categories it belongs to. It would not be very convenient to refer to a dog as an *Animalia Chordata Vertebrata Mammalia Carnivora Canidae Canis familiaris*. Scientists usually use only the genus name and species name. So the scientific name for a dog is *Canis familiaris*. Do you know the scientific name for our species? It's *Homo sapiens* [HO-mo SAY-pee-ins]. *Homo* is the genus name, which means "man," and *sapiens* is the species name, which means "wise." So *Homo sapiens* means "wise man." We always capitalize the genus and never the species name.

Meet the Vertebrates

One thing the taxonomic description of a collie tells you is that collies are vertebrates. That's another way of saying that collies have backbones. In fact, most of the animals you see at the zoo are vertebrates. Fish, amphibians, reptiles, birds, and mammals are five different groups of vertebrates.

A fish is a vertebrate that lives in water and uses gills to get oxygen from water. Its body temperature is the same as the temperature of the surrounding water, so we sometimes say that it is "cold-blooded." Most fish are covered with small scales. Most of them also lay soft, jelly-coated eggs. Salmon, trout, and tuna are different kinds of fish.

Amphibians are also vertebrates, and they also cannot adjust their body temperature. They live part of their lives in the water and part on land. (The word *amphibian* means "living in two places.") Amphibians have gills and live mostly in water when they are young, but most of them develop lungs when they grow up. Frogs and salamanders are amphibians.

Reptiles are vertebrates that hatch from eggs and breathe with lungs. The eggs have a hard shell to protect them and keep them from drying out. Like fish and amphibians, their body temperature depends on the temperature of their surroundings. Snakes, lizards, and turtles are all reptiles.

This lizard is a reptile.

Birds are warm-blooded vertebrates, which means that they always keep their body at a certain warm temperature. To do this, they release heat when they break down food. Birds have lungs, as well as feathers and wings. Most birds can fly, but a few, like ostriches and penguins, cannot. Most birds build nests in which to lay their hard-shelled eggs.

Mammals are another class of warm-blooded vertebrates. They breathe with lungs and usually have hair on their bodies. Female mammals produce milk to feed their babies. Human beings are mammals, and so are dogs, kangaroos, giraffes, and lions.

With most animals, it's not hard to guess what kind of vertebrates they are. But a few are tricky. For instance, what category would you guess whales and dolphins belong in? Did you say fish? That's a logical guess, but have you ever noticed that both whales and dolphins come to the surface a lot and blow out big puffs of air? That's because whales and dolphins have lungs, not gills. They are warm-blooded and feed their babies milk. That means they are mammals, not fish!

PLANTS

Plants and Photosynthesis

Animals like whales and dolphins and human beings have to eat food to keep their energy levels up. Plants, on the other hand, are able to make food from carbon dioxide and water, using sunlight energy.

All plants (as well as some types of prokaryotes and protists) contain chlorophyll, a molecule that makes some or all of their cells appear green. The word *chlorophyll* comes from two Greek words—*chlor*, meaning "green," and *phyllo*, meaning "leaf." In fact, chlorophyll can be found in other green parts of a plant besides the leaves. Protists and prokaryotes containing chlorophyll have no leaves. But all of these organisms use chlorophyll to trap the energy they need to make food. The process they use to make food is called *photosynthesis* [foh-toh-SIN-thu-sis].

Photo means "light." *Synthesis* means "putting together." So photosynthesis means "putting together with light." Organisms that contain chlorophyll combine water and carbon dioxide using energy from sunlight. The end products of photosynthesis are sugars, which the organisms use for food, and oxygen gas.

How is this done? Where do the water and carbon dioxide come from, and where do the oxygen and sugars go? Let's start with a diagram of how water and carbon dioxide get into a celery leaf, and a description on page 312.

Photosynthesis in a celery plant.

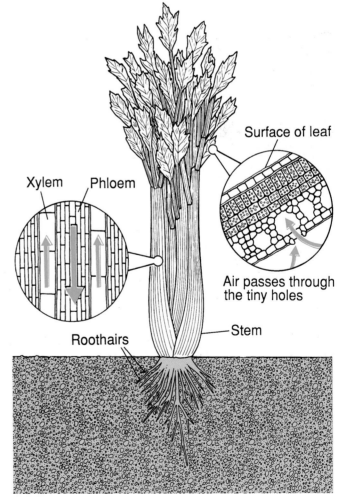

Xylem Phloem

Surface of leaf

Air passes through the tiny holes

Roothairs

Stem

Step One: Transporting Water and Nutrients: Cars, buses, and subways are all systems of transportation we use to move from one place to another. Many plants transport things internally too, in order to make and store food. Look at the drawing of a celery plant. The plant takes in water and nutrients from the soil through tiny hairs on its roots. The water and nutrients are transported through the root hairs to the roots, and then up the stem (or "stalk") of the celery through tubes arranged in bundles.

There are two types of tubes in plants: *xylem* [ZYE-lem] and *phloem*. Xylem tubes carry water and nutrients from the soil up the stem to the leaves where most photosynthesis occurs. Phloem tubes carry sugars from the leaves to every part of the plant that is not green (like the roots, trunk, and flowers) and also to the growing tips and to the fruits.

Step Two: Light Energy from the Sun: Look at the cross section of the celery leaf, as seen through a microscope, in the illustration. Note the layer of cells just below the top surface of the leaf. These cells contain chloroplasts, where chlorophyll is found. Sunlight shines through the top of the leaf, and the light energy is trapped by the chlorophyll and stored in special molecules for later use.

Step Three: Carbon Dioxide from the Air: In this step, food is made. Air passes in through tiny holes on the bottom surface of the leaf called *stomata*. (A single hole is called a stoma; many holes are called stomata.) Carbon dioxide from the air reaches the cells where chlorophyll has trapped energy from sunlight. This energy causes a chemical reaction that combines water and carbon dioxide to make various kinds of sugars.

Step Four: Back to the Transport System: The sugars created in the leaves are transported down the celery plant in phloem tubes, to be stored as sugar or very large molecules called starch, in other parts of the plant. The plant's cells use this food later to grow and do work.

The sugars and starches stored in a plant are necessary for the plant to survive, but they can also make the plant taste good to humans and animals. Doesn't an orange taste sweet? That sweetness comes from the sugars the orange tree stored in its fruit—sugars created by photosynthesis. Many plants—potatoes and corn, for example—change the sugar they make into starch before it is stored.

We eat many plants to get their stored sugar and starch. And just like plants, we convert this stored food into energy for our cells to do their work.

Water Transportation: See for Yourself.

Collect the following materials: a glass large enough to hold a stalk of celery upright, water, blue food coloring, a stalk of celery with leaves, scissors, a magnifying glass or hand lens. Cut about an inch off the bottom of the celery stalk. Place the stalk upright in a glass. Fill the glass half full of water and add a few drops of food coloring. Let the celery sit for about an hour. What do you observe at the end of the hour? Take the stalk out of the water and with scissors cut it above the water line. Observe the bottom end with the magnifying glass. What do you see?

Vascular and Non-vascular Plants

Scientists divide plants into two categories: vascular and non-vascular. Most of the plants you are familiar with are vascular plants. Vascular plants have roots, stems, and leaves. Inside the stems and leaves are xylem and phloem that allow water and nutrients to move through the plant. But other plants don't have these tube-like structures and can't move nutrients as well. These are the non-vascular plants.

Moss is an example of a non-vascular plant. A moss relies on photosynthesis just like a celery plant, but it has to make do without the transportation network provided by stems and branches. Non-vascular plants are small and low to the ground, and they can grow only in moist places.

LIFE CYCLES AND REPRODUCTION

The Replacements

All living things are born, grow during their lifetime, and eventually die. Tadpoles are born, grow, change into frogs, and eventually die, but female frogs lay eggs that will hatch into new tadpoles. Chicks hatch, grow to be adult chickens, and eventually die, but hens lay eggs that hatch into new chicks, so the life cycle continues. What would happen if no new chickens were born to replace those that died? There would be no chickens in the world—they'd be extinct. To keep from dying out, all living things reproduce themselves. *Reproduce* means "to make again," or "to make a copy." Reproduction is the process of making again.

"The life cycle of a frog."   "The life cycle of a chicken."

The cells in your body reproduce themselves and increase in number, which is how you grow. Every day, for example, some of your skin cells reproduce themselves and some of them die. As you grow bigger, your skin cells reproduce faster than they die, so your skin can continue to cover your whole body. As you grow taller, cells in your bones reproduce and make longer, thicker bones. When you become an adult, cells reproduce more slowly, so slowly, in fact, that at about age twenty you stop growing bigger. From then on, cells are created at about the rate they die, so the number of cells stays about even.

Organisms reproduce in different ways. Some plants make seeds. Mushrooms and other fungi make spores. Frogs and chickens lay eggs. Dogs have litters of puppies. What about protists and bacteria? Let's read about two categories of reproduction: asexual and sexual.

Asexual Reproduction

One way that organisms copy themselves is through *asexual reproduction*. Asexual means "non-sexual," that is, reproduction without using males and females. The organism simply copies itself through cell division.

Asexual reproduction can be very simple. Bacteria (the simplest of all organisms) and many protists reproduce by splitting. After duplicating their genetic material (the cell's set of instructions), bacteria simply split their single cell in half. Each half becomes a new cell. Under the right conditions, some bacteria can double their numbers every twenty minutes and quickly form colonies large enough to see without a microscope! That's why it's important to keep food in refrigerators. Most food contains some bacteria, but not enough to make you sick. Cold temperatures

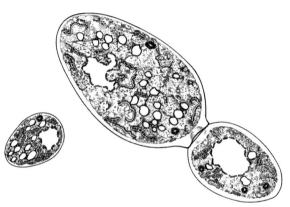

This yeast cell is reproducing by budding. See how a small bud is forming on the side of the parent cell?

keep bacteria from growing and dividing. However, if you leave some types of food out for too long, the bacteria will start reproducing until your food is full of millions of bacteria and is not safe to eat.

Mildews, molds, and mushrooms are fungi that reproduce by forming spores. Spores are single cells that are often protected by a hard covering. Spores drop off the parent and grow into fungi if there is enough water and food for them to live. On the other hand, most yeasts, which are single-celled fungi, reproduce by budding. A "bud" forms on one side of the cell, and eventually pinches off to form a new yeast cell.

Asexual Reproduction in Larger Animals and Plants

Some plants and animals can reproduce themselves *asexually*. In plants, the most familiar example of such reproduction is called *cloning*, where a piece of the plant—a leaf or stem cutting—is put into some moist material, and a whole new plant forms—a new plant that is just like the parent. Some plants do this naturally, like strawberries that send out "runners" or daffodil bulbs that divide in two underground. Only simple animals like sponges, flatworms, and jellies (also known as jellyfish) reproduce asexually. Some simple animals just split in two, and some grow a new, smaller copy on their side that eventually falls off and grows on its own.

Most animals do not reproduce asexually. However, many animals have the ability to replace lost cells or even lost body parts. This is called *regeneration*. The amount of regeneration that can occur depends on the type of organism. You regenerate skin cells when you cut your finger and the wound heals. But if you cut off your whole finger, it won't grow back.

Other animals have a much greater ability to regenerate. Have you ever seen a starfish, or sea star? A sea star can grow a whole new arm if one is cut off. The lost arm, if it still has a piece of the center of the sea star, can even grow into a new sea star! When some kinds of worms are cut in half, each half grows into a new worm. Salamanders can regenerate a leg if they lose one. But the leg can't regenerate a new salamander. In general, more complex animals like salamanders and humans have a more limited ability to regenerate.

A starfish, or sea star, can regenerate amputated limbs.   Salamanders.

Sexual Reproduction in Mosses and Ferns

Sexual reproduction requires special male and female cells to combine. These special cells are called *gametes*. In sexual reproduction, male and female gametes join to form a fertilized egg.

Mosses, which you may have seen growing in shady spots, reproduce by making spores. Look at the drawing of the moss's life cycle. In the first step, shown on the lower right, a spore has just landed in a moist, nutrient-rich spot and germinated. Next it grows into a moss plant that is green and often forms a soft mat. After a time, something amazing happens. Buds near the tips of the moss plant begin making gametes. If the buds make gametes that are eggs, the moss plant is female. If the buds make gametes that can swim, called *sperm*, the moss plant is male. When a male and female plant are close enough together, and there is some water present, a male gamete (the sperm) swims to a female gamete (the egg) and fertilizes it. This fertilized egg divides and grows into a stalk on top of the female moss plant. The cells continue to divide to form a capsule at the tip of the stalk and to

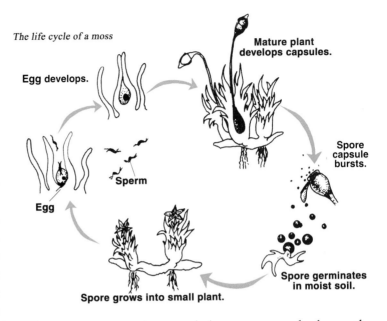

The life cycle of a moss

Egg develops.

Sperm

Egg

Spore grows into small plant.

Mature plant develops capsules.

Spore capsule bursts.

Spore germinates in moist soil.

form spores inside that capsule. When it is mature, the capsule bursts open and releases the spores. If the spores fall on moist ground, they germinate and the process starts over again.

The life cycle of a fern is similar to that of a moss, but there are some differences. When the fern spore gets wet it germinates, turning into a tiny, heart-shaped plant that produces both male and female gametes. When these male and female gametes come together, the

fertilized egg grows into a totally new and different plant that will become the large fern you can find in the woods. The leaves of a fern are called fronds. On the bottom of some of the fronds of a mature fern, there are special cells that produce capsules full of spores. These capsules burst open and release the spores to start the cycle over again.

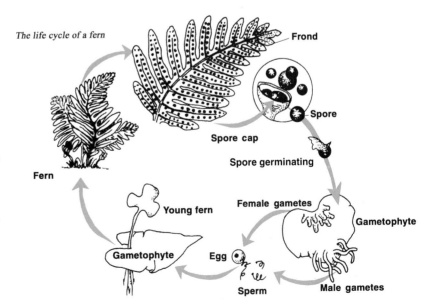

The life cycle of a fern

Frond

Spore

Spore cap

Spore germinating

Female gametes

Gametophyte

Male gametes

Sperm

Egg

Gametophyte

Young fern

Fern

Conifer Seeds Are Naked

Most large plants reproduce by combining a male and female gamete to make a fertilized egg that grows into an embryo. This *embryo*, or baby plant, is protected inside a seed. Some of the simplest of these seed plants are the *conifers*, a name that means "cone carriers." Have you wondered what a pine cone is for? It is the reproductive part of the pine tree.

If you can find a big pine tree, you may be able to see that there are both big and small cones on it. These two kinds of cones are usually found on the same plant. The small cone carries the male cells. That's because it doesn't take much space to store millions of tiny grains of pollen, each of which carries a male gamete.

Pollen from the male pine cone is carried by the wind and sticks to the larger female pine cone. Tubes grow from the grains of pollen to reach the eggs inside the female cone, and a male gamete joins with the egg to fertilize it. The fertilized egg then divides and grows into an embryo. In addition to the embryo, the seed also contains a supply of food on the inside and a seed coat on the outside. The seed coat keeps the embryro from drying out. The seed drops to the ground when the cone opens. If the soil is moist, the seed germinates, using the stored food to help the embryo grow. The embryo grows into a new tree if there is enough water plus enough nutrients in the soil.

The seed from a conifer is called a naked seed, because it has nothing on except its own seed coat. There is no fruit that surrounds it. Conifers belong to the group of plants called *gymnosperms*, which means "naked seeds."

Pollen from the male cone is carried through the air to the larger female pine cone.

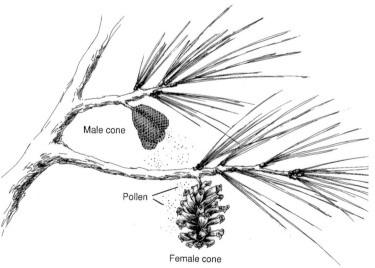

Male cone

Pollen

Female cone

Seeds of Flowering Plants Have Clothes

Most plants clothe the seeds they make with some sort of covering. The fruit of a cherry is the covering for the seed inside it. Tomatoes have seeds inside, and so do cucumbers, green peppers, and oranges. All of these are fruits! You're probably more interested in the fruit than the seeds, but for the purpose of reproduction, the tomato or the orange are just coverings for seeds.

These plants with covered seeds are called *angiosperms*, which in Greek means "covered seeds." All these plants have one thing in common: they have flowers. The seed covers, hard or soft, big or small, sweet or sour, all come from the same place —a flower.

Flowers

Many plants you are familiar with, including most trees, shrubs, vines, grasses, and garden plants, produce flowers. They can be as large and showy as sunflowers or as tiny as the flowers on a grass plant, but most flowers have essentially the same parts.

Let's look at a diagram of a typical flower to see how seeds are formed. Typically the flower is formed as a series of rings, one inside the other. The outer ring is made up of *sepals*, which are usually green and look like leaves attached to the stem at the base of a flower. Inside the sepals, the *petals* make the next ring. The colorful petals attract insects, which are often important for bringing pollen carrying the male gamete to the egg.

Inside the petals, in the center of the flower, lie the reproductive parts. The *stamens* are the male reproductive organs. Each stamen has an *anther* on its tip, where millions of tiny pollen grains, each with a male gamete, are made. At the very center of most flowers is the *pistil*, with the female reproductive organs. The pistil is a tube that leads down to the ovary with its egg or eggs.

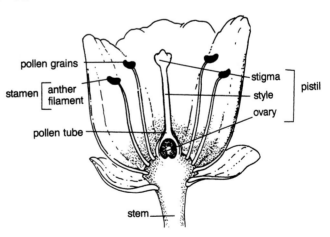

A typical flower and its parts.

What is an *ovary*? In Latin it means a "place for eggs." This place for the egg or eggs is completely protected, which is one of the great advantages of a flower. Sometimes, when there is just one egg, the ovary is called an *ovule*, which means "small ovary." For instance, when there is just one seed inside a fruit, you know it came from a single ovule. When there are several eggs, then there will be several ovules inside a larger ovary. And later when that ovary develops into a fruit, there will be several seeds inside, as in a tomato, orange, or apple.

Flower Fertilization

The first step of flower fertilization is *pollination*, the movement of pollen from the anther to the sticky top of the pistil. But how does the pollen make that trip? Insects or birds are responsible for pollinating many flowers. But wind and rain also help. Look at the bee in the picture. When the bee sips nectar from the flower, it also picks up some pollen that sticks to its back or legs. When it visits another flower to get more nectar, the pollen can fall off and stick onto the pistil.

In the second step of fertilization, a tube grows out of the pollen grain that is stuck to the pistil. A pollen tube cannot grow unless the pollen comes from the same kind of plant as the pistil it lands on. Inside the pollen tube is the male gamete. The tube grows down the pistil and into the ovule at the bottom.

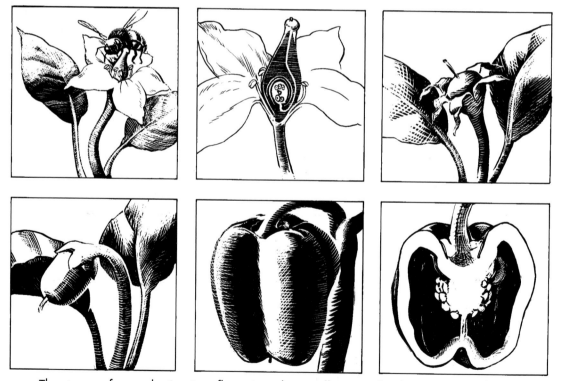

The stages of reproduction in a flowering plant: pollination, fertilization, ovary begins to grow as flower petals die, ovary continues to grow, mature fruit or vegetable houses seeds for next generation.

In the last step, the male gamete joins the egg cell in the ovule, and fertilization occurs. The fertilized egg cell begins to divide and form an *embryo*, or young plant. The ovule grows into a seed coat that protects what is now the seed. As the seed forms in the parent plant, the flower changes. The sepals and petals die and fall off, and the ovule or the ovary grows into a covering or fruit—into beans or berries or tomatoes or the hard shells of nuts. The covering protects the seed or seeds inside it and also helps scatter the seed. These coverings are often juicy and nutritious. Animals eat fruits, but they often do not digest the seeds. When the seeds pass through the animal's body, they may end up in a new location where they can germinate. If the fruit falls from the parent plant but is not eaten, it starts to decay and the seed is uncovered. This allows the seed to reach the soil, where it can germinate and grow into a new plant.

Plant Development

What happens to a seed once it reaches the soil? Let's look at the development of a bean plant. The two drawings below show the outside and inside of a young bean seed. In the drawing on the right, you can see the young plant or embryo inside. Notice the large area where food is stored. This is called the *endosperm*; it contains food for the young plant— and also for animals, including humans, who eat seeds. This food keeps the embryo alive and helps it germinate and grow until it is big enough to make its own food. See the seed coat? It protects the seed and keeps it from drying out.

When a seed falls to the ground, it is sometimes pushed into the soil by heavy rainfall. Certain seeds are buried by animals, like squirrels that want to eat them later. When seeds are planted in moist soil, they absorb water. This softens the seed coat and makes the inside of the seed swell up and burst through the seed coat. If temperatures are warm enough, the cells of the embryo inside the seed begin to divide, and the embryo grows. The tiny embryo continues to use the stored food inside the seed to grow and breaks through the seed coat. The embryo sprouts roots and is now a new plant. This sprouting of the new plant is called *germination*.

The roots of the new plant take in water and minerals from the soil that the plant uses to grow. As the stem grows upward,

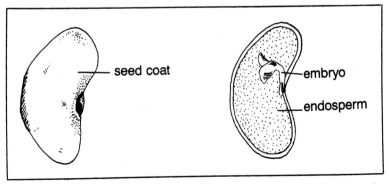

A tough seed coat surrounds and protects the tender embryo and the endosperm of the bean seed.

leaves appear. Leaves help the plant make its own food by photosynthesis, which helps the plant grow into an adult plant. Later, the adult plant develops flowers, the flowers develop seeds, and the cycle begins again.

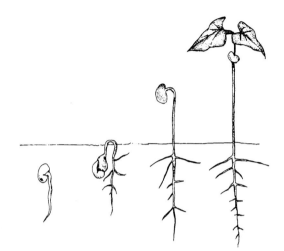

Stages of germination in a bean seed. The growing embryo breaks through its seed coat and sprouts roots. The roots grow bigger, pushing the new plant above ground. The plant grows leaves that help it make its own food as an adult.

Examining a Bean Seed

Materials: One bean seed, a cup of water, one magnifying glass
Method: Soak the bean seed in water overnight. Remove the seed from the water and examine the soaked bean seed. Remove the seed coat and note its thickness. Carefully separate the two halves of the bean seed with your fingernail. Can you find the embryo inside? Draw a picture of the inside of your seed. Can you find the stored food?

Monocots and Dicots

There are two kinds of flowering plants: monocots and dicots. Grass is an example of a monocot. If you plant a grass seed and water it, in a few days a single seed leaf will break out of the seed and push its way through the soil. This seed leaf is called a *cotyledon* [kah-tuh-LEE-dun]. Because each grass seed produces only one cotyledon, grass is called a *monocotyledon*, or *monocot* for short. (The word *monocotyledon* means "one-seed leaf.") If you plant a bean seed, it will send up two seed leaves. That's why bean plants are classified as *dicots*, or plants with two seed leaves.

There are other differences between monocots and dicots, too. The total number of flower parts on a monocot is often a multiple of three. So a monocot flower might have three petals, or six, or nine. By contrast, the total number of flower parts on a dicot is often a multiple of four, like eight or twelve, or a multiple of five, like ten or fifteen. Monocots usually have long narrow leaves, with veins running parallel to one another. Dicots tend to have broader leaves with veins that look like nets.

Grains like wheat, corn, and rice are all monocots, as are some flowers, like lilies and tulips. Most fruits and vegetables are dicots, as are many garden flowers.

MONOCOTS

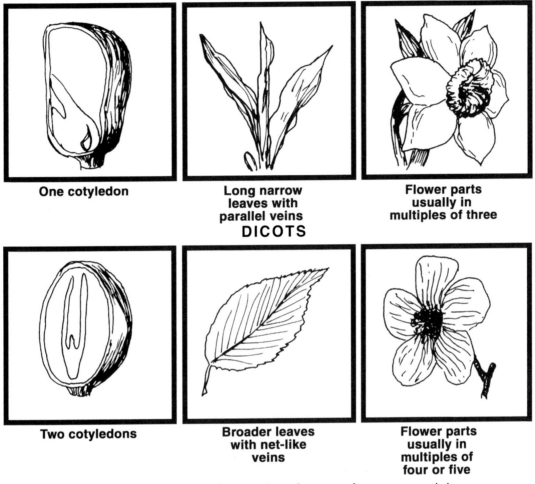

One cotyledon

**Long narrow
leaves with
parallel veins**

DICOTS

**Flower parts
usually in
multiples of three**

Two cotyledons

**Broader leaves
with net-like
veins**

**Flower parts
usually in
multiples of
four or five**

This diagram shows some distinguishing features of monocots and dicots.

Reproduction in Animals

Most animals reproduce sexually. Just as plants produce male and female gametes, so do animals. In animals, the male gametes, or *sperm*, are produced in special organs called the *testes*, while the female gametes, or *eggs*, are produced by *ovaries*. In some simpler animals —earthworms, for example—the sperm- and egg-making organs are in one creature. But in most animals, male and female gametes are made by separate male and female individuals.

If the sperm and egg join outside the bodies of the parents, the process is called *external fertilization*. When the sperm and egg join inside the body of the female, as with humans, it is called *internal fertilization*.

Have you ever seen video of fish spawning? *Spawning* is a form of external fertilization. During spawning, female fish and male fish come very close together in the water. The female releases her eggs into the water, and the male releases his sperm. The sperm swim to the eggs and fertilize them.

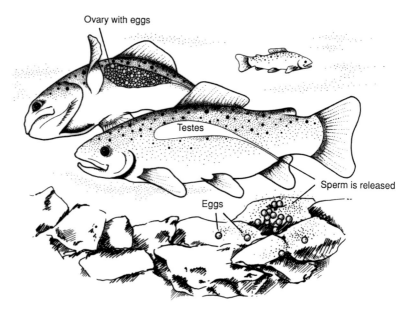

During spawning season, adult fish release eggs and sperm into the water, where fertilization takes place.

Birds and also mammals like horses and humans reproduce by internal fertilization. The female releases an egg from her ovary, and it travels down a tube that leads from the ovary. During mating, the male releases sperm inside the female. The sperm travels to the tube where the egg is located and fertilizes it. If no sperm joins an egg, it is unfertilized, and it leaves the female's body.

Have You Ever Seen a Koalaroo?

What makes a species? Scientists use information about reproduction along with other information to classify organisms into smaller and smaller groups. One very important group is called a *species*. For species that reproduce sexually, members of a species usually mate and produce offspring only with other members of the same species. For example, when a female koala bear mates and produces a baby koala bear, we know that her mate must have been a male of the same species as the female. Koala bears do not and cannot mate with kangaroos and produce young; that means koalas and kangaroos are different species. And that's why you've never seen a koalaroo!

Development of the Embryo

Once the egg is fertilized, it is called a *zygote* [ZYE-goat]. The zygote begins to divide and grow, and after several days or weeks, depending on the animal, it becomes an *embryo* [EM-bree-oh]. An embryo, remember, is a developing organism. In most mammals, the embryo develops inside the mother's body in an organ called the *uterus* [YOO-ter-us]. The zygote travels down the tube from the ovary and attaches to the wall of the uterus. The developing embryo gets its food and water from the mother. In the later stages of development, the embryo is called a *fetus*. When it has developed enough to live outside the mother's body, the *fetus* is born.

The amount of time it takes an animal to develop before birth depends on the species. Horses take eleven months to develop inside their mothers. Sheep take only five months. It takes a human embryo nine months to develop.

Care and Growth of Young

Different species have different ways of looking after their young. Fish do not take care of their young at all. Nor do sea turtles. Female sea turtles lay fifty to one hundred eggs in a hole in the sand and then return to the ocean. Their young hatch, crawl out of their nest, and crawl to the sea with no protection or help from

A sea turtle in the ocean.

their mothers. Before reaching the ocean they are often eaten by hungry gulls or crabs. If they do reach the water, they may be swallowed by hungry fish. But because the sea turtle lays fifty to one hundred eggs, there is a chance some of them will survive.

Other newborn animals are cared for by one or more parents until they can survive on their own. Usually, birds tend their young until they are old enough to fly. Lion cubs stay with their parents for about four years, until they are old enough to defend themselves and to find food. Humans stay with their parents even longer.

Growth Stages

The development of an organism from birth through reproduction and death is called the *life cycle*. Usually there are noticeable stages of development during an organism's life cycle. Look at the drawing of the horse life cycle. Reproduction occurs inside the mother when egg and sperm unite, and an embryo develops. The embryo grows into a fetus, which looks almost like a full-grown horse in miniature. Soon after birth, when he can stand, the young foal drinks milk from his mother's teat. After a year, the foal is now a colt. He no longer needs his mother's milk and eats grass beside her. In four years, the colt is a mature horse.

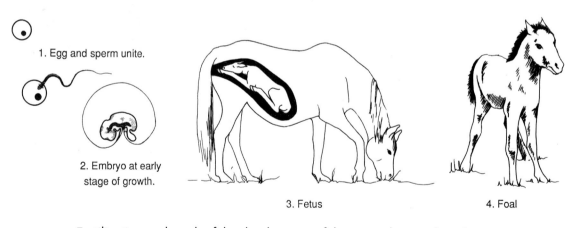

1. Egg and sperm unite.

2. Embryo at early stage of growth.

3. Fetus

4. Foal

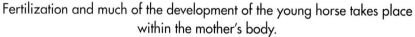

Fertilization and much of the development of the young horse takes place within the mother's body.

SCIENCE

THE HUMAN BODY

Human Growth Stages

Humans also show stages in their growth. You developed into an embryo and then a fetus inside your mother's uterus. When you were a newborn baby, also called an infant, you were bottle-fed or you drank breast milk. You grew and developed fairly rapidly until, when you were about a year old, you learned to walk. Between the ages of eight and seventeen, most of you will experience a period of rapid growth, and your bodies will begin changing as you reach *puberty*, the age at which you become capable of reproducing. By age twenty-one, you will stop growing. At about forty, your metabolism will begin to slow down, and at sixty or later, you will reach old age.

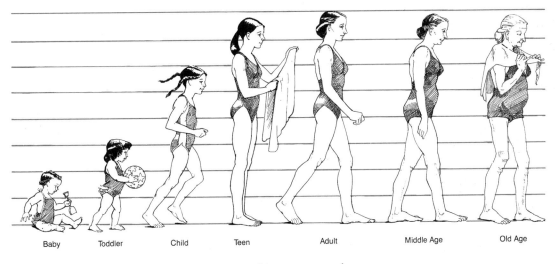

| Baby | Toddler | Child | Teen | Adult | Middle Age | Old Age |

Stages of human growth.

Adolescence and Puberty

The period of growth and change in the human body that occurs between eight and seventeen is known as *adolescence* [add-uhl-ES-ens). During adolescence, powerful chemicals called *hormones* are released into the bloodstream from glands in your body. These hormones cause physical, mental, and emotional changes. The process usually begins earlier in girls than it does in boys.

As an adolescent, you may experience an increase in your appetite; you may be hungry all the time. You may also require more sleep at night. Some people experience a very rapid change in height and weight, sometimes called a "growth spurt." Their muscles and bones get larger, and their favorite clothes don't fit anymore. They may feel awkward, because their hands and feet are growing faster than the other parts of their body.

Girls start to develop breasts, and their hips begin to round out. Boys' shoulders widen, and their voices change, sometimes cracking as they begin to deepen. Both boys and girls grow hair under their arms and around their genitals. These changes are normal, and they happen to every human being, though there is variation in the age at which people begin adolescence.

The Human Reproductive System

The changes in a person's body during adolescence are in preparation for *puberty*, the time when male and female humans are able to produce children. Human reproduction is very similar to reproduction in other mammals. In females, an egg cell is released each month from one of two ovaries. The egg then passes into one of the *Fallopian* [fah-LOW-pee-en] tubes, where it could be fertilized by sperm from a male. If it is not fertilized, it passes into the uterus and then out of the body along with the lining of the uterus. The uterus lining and egg pass through the *vagina* [vuh-JIE-nuh] on their way out of the body. This monthly process of shedding the egg and the lining of the uterus is called *menstruation* [men-stroo-AY-shun]—from the Latin word *mensis*, meaning "month."

How does the sperm reach the egg in the Fallopian tube? First we need to learn about the male reproductive organs. Sperm are produced in the testes, egg-shaped glands that are contained in a pouch of skin, the *scrotum*, which hangs below the penis. The sperm travel through tubes in the testes in a whitish fluid called *semen*. When the male is sexually aroused, the semen exits the male's body through the *urethra*, a tube in his penis.

During sexual intercourse, the male places his penis inside the female's vagina. The semen shoots out of his penis and into her vagina, and the sperm swim toward her uterus. After reaching the uterus, they swim toward the Fallopian tubes, where one sperm cell breaks through the egg's outer covering and then fuses with the egg and fertilizes it.

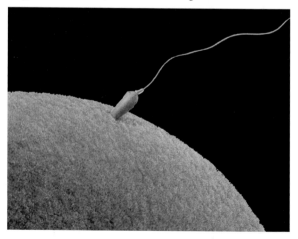

A microscope captures the moment of union between a sperm and an egg.

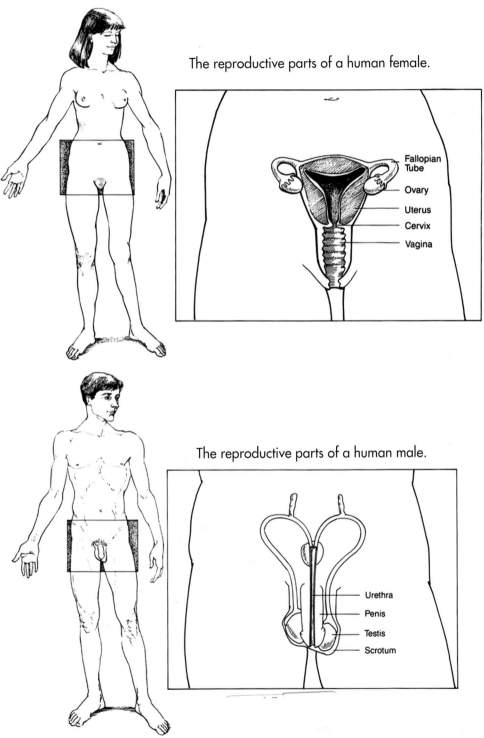

The reproductive parts of a human female.

Fallopian Tube
Ovary
Uterus
Cervix
Vagina

The reproductive parts of a human male.

Urethra
Penis
Testis
Scrotum

If the egg is fertilized, it develops into a zygote, which travels down the Fallopian tube and implants itself in the wall of the uterus. Once this happens, we say the woman is pregnant. In the uterus, the zygote grows into an embryo and further develops into a fetus. The fetus grows inside the mother for nine months, until it has developed enough to live in the outside world. At that point, the mother's uterus pushes the fetus out of her body. The process of pushing the baby out is called *labor and delivery*. Sometimes the baby is delivered by cesarean section, an operation in which an incision is made in the abdomen and the uterus and the baby is removed through this incision.

Once it is born, a human baby needs constant care and attention. Left alone, a human infant would die.

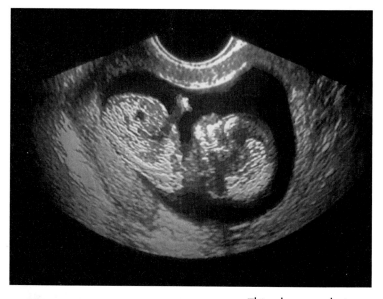

This ultrasound picture shows a baby in its mother's womb. You can see the baby's hand and head.

A baby boy with his mother.

The Endocrine System

Earlier you learned that the changes that take place during puberty are caused when glands inside the body secrete hormones into the bloodstream. Humans have two different kinds of glands: duct glands and ductless glands. *Duct glands* secrete their products outside the body or directly into the digestive system. Sweat glands are an example. When you run around or play sports, your sweat glands secrete perspiration outside your body to help keep you cool.

Ductless glands also secrete chemicals, but they secrete them *inside* the body. They secrete hormones that travel through the blood stream, carrying chemical messages to various parts of the body. These ductless glands are also known as *endocrine glands*, and together they make up the endocrine system.

Sweat glands help keep us cool when we exercise.

Meet the Glands

The *pituitary gland* is a tiny gland located at the bottom of the brain, near where the brain meets the spinal cord. It is sometimes called the "master gland," because it secretes hormones that tell the other endocrine glands what to do. The pituitary also secretes the hormone that makes you grow, as well as the hormones that trigger the beginning of puberty.

The *thyroid gland* is located in the front of the neck, just below the larynx, or voice box. It secretes a hormone that controls the rate at which the body burns energy and uses food.

The *pancreas* is located behind the stomach. It is divided into two parts. One part has ducts, while the other is ductless. The part with ducts releases chemicals that help the digestive system break down food. The ductless part secretes hormones into the blood, including the hormone *insulin*, which regulates how the body uses sugar.

When a person's pancreas does not produce enough insulin, that person has a disease called *diabetes*. Fortunately, diabetes can be treated. Some diabetic people give themselves shots of insulin to make sure their blood sugar levels don't get too high.

The *adrenal glands* are small glands located above the kidneys. They give off a hormone called *adrenaline* that speeds up the heart and allows blood to flow more rapidly to muscles and the brain. If you've ever gotten scared or angry and felt your breathing and heart rate speed up, you've experienced what people call an "adrenaline rush." This is your body's way of getting you prepared for an emergency situation, in which you might have to fight or run away.

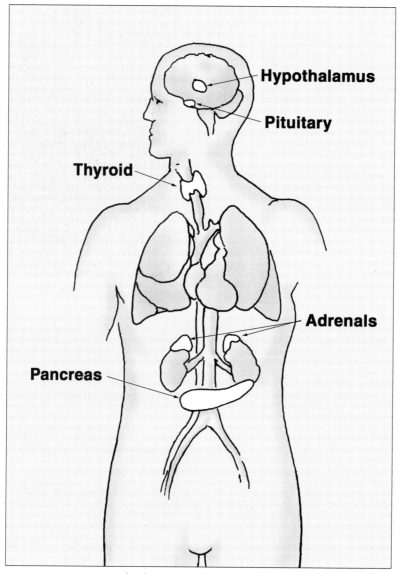

The human endocrine system.

SCIENCE BIOGRAPHIES

Galileo

During the Renaissance, an Italian mathematician named Galileo Galilei became interested in the stars and planets. At that time, people still believed that Earth was at the center of the universe and that the sun and the other planets moved around Earth. Galileo read a book by the Polish astronomer Nicolaus Copernicus, who argued that the sun was at the center and that Earth and other planets actually move around the sun.

Galileo was intrigued by Copernicus's theory. He knew that a Dutch inventor had built a primitive telescope. Galileo built a telescope of his own. When he looked through it, he made some important discoveries. For example, he saw that the Milky Way is not a band of light but clusters of stars—more stars than anyone could possibly count.

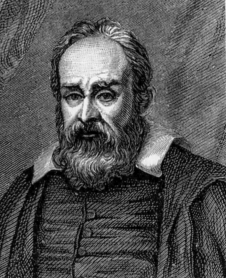

Galileo.

One night, Galileo looked at Jupiter and saw a row of three moons: two to the right of the big planet and one to the left. The next night, all three moons were to the left of Jupiter. Galileo concluded that the moons must circle around Jupiter—and if that was true, then not *every* object in the sky was circling Earth! Galileo began to think maybe Copernicus was right, and he said so in some letters.

At this point Galileo got in trouble with the Church. The Church insisted that Earth was at the center of the universe. There were passages in the Bible that seemed to say as much. Therefore, the Church put the works of Copernicus on its list of forbidden books and ordered Galileo to stop arguing for the Copernican theory.

Galileo kept silent for several years, but eventually he published a book called *A Dialogue Concerning the Two Chief World Systems*. A *dialogue* is a kind of book in which two or more people discuss ideas. Many ancient writers used dialogues to describe their theories without revealing which of the speakers in the dialogue they agreed with. One person in Galileo's dialogue said that the sun and the other planets circled Earth. Another defended the Copernican theory.

When they saw the book, Church officials felt that Galileo had broken his promise not to promote Copernican ideas. Galileo was ordered to go to Rome for a trial. During the trial, he was ordered to take back his support for the Copernican system. Galileo knew that if he refused he might be executed or imprisoned. He agreed to sign a paper denying "the false opinion that the Sun is the center of the world." He was also forced to deny that Earth moved around the sun. However, according to legend, Galileo was heard to murmur under his breath: "But it *does* move!"

Galileo's last years were difficult. He was not allowed to talk about his theories, or even leave his house. The Church banned his book. As if this weren't enough, the man who loved to gaze at the stars went blind. When Galileo died in 1644, it seemed he had been defeated. But in the long run, Galileo's ideas were victorious. Today we know that Earth goes around the sun—and not the other way around.

Carl Linnaeus

Earlier you learned how scientists classify living things and give them special scientific names, using the Latin language. The man who did more than anyone else to develop this system of classification was the Swedish scientist Carl Linnaeus.

Linnaeus was born in 1707. His father and grandfather were Lutheran priests, and they hoped that Carl would follow in their footsteps. But from an early age Linnaeus was more interested in botany than theology. In his mind, however, religion and nature were closely connected. He believed that God had created the world and all the plants and animals in it. So by studying these wonderful creations, he was learning about God.

Linnaeus went to school to become a doctor. This allowed him to learn even more about plants, because many medicines came from plants. He began traveling around gathering unusual plants. Once he had a large collection, he set about organizing it. In the process, he developed a new, improved way of classifying plants.

Linnaeus.

In 1735, Linnaeus published the work that made him famous, *The System of Nature*. In this book he laid out a classification system for all living things.

Linnaeus became a professor, and he sent his students all around the world to gather plants and animals: one student went to the American colonies, another to Japan. A third visited Australia and the South Pacific. Each time a student returned to Sweden with exotic plants and animals, Linnaeus had additional material to make his book bigger and better. By the time Linnaeus died, *The System of Nature* had expanded to fill several volumes.

Linnaeus gave the various species he identified a *genus* name and a *species* name. The genus name was more general. For instance, both the lion and the tiger were members of the genus *Felis*, which is Latin for "cat." But the lion was *Felis leo*, the tiger *Felis tigris*. Linnaeus also developed larger categories called orders, classes, and kingdoms. Although scientists have modified Linnaeus's system over the years, much of it is still used today.

Ernest Just

Some scientists conduct experiments just because they want to know why things are the way they are, not because they expect an immediate benefit. We call this kind of experimentation "pure" research. Ernest Just was a pure research scientist who wanted to understand how individual cells function.

Just was born in South Carolina in 1883. Because schools for African-American children in the South were poor, Just's mother sent him north to finish his education. There was a school in New Hampshire that accepted African-American boys who couldn't pay tuition. Just enrolled there and did so well that he went on to Dartmouth College, where he studied biology and fell in love with the subject.

From Dartmouth, Just went to Howard University, a university for African Americans in Washington, D.C., where he became a teacher. In the summers, he worked at the Marine Biological Laboratory in Woods Hole, Massachusetts, probably the most famous marine lab in the world. (A marine lab studies life in the sea.) At Woods Hole, Just began his lifelong

Ernest Just.

investigation of how cells work. He used the eggs of marine animals like sea urchins and sandworms to study how cells reproduce and divide.

As you've learned, cells are the most basic units of life. When Just was conducting his research, most scientists focused their attention on the nucleus because they thought it was the only part of the cell that was important for development and reproduction. As Just studied the eggs he collected, keeping track of how they developed under different conditions, he saw something amazing. He discovered that cell activity depended not just on the nucleus but also on the cytoplasm, especially the outer part of the cytoplasm, called the *ectoplasm*. Because the ectoplasm is the part most influenced by the environment outside the cell, Just realized, it helps determine whether or not the cell develops normally, and how a particular cell will be different from other cells.

Just's research changed the way scientists think about cells. His ideas led scientists to think about how the outer layers of the egg influence the process of fertilization.

Just also worked hard to improve the quality of scientific education available to African Americans. For his scientific and civil rights work, the National Association for the Advancement of Colored People (NAACP) awarded Just its first Spingarn Medal, given to an African American for extraordinary achievement.

Percy Lavon Julian

Have you ever known anyone who suffered from arthritis, the painful and crippling disease that attacks the body's joints? Many people who suffer from arthritis use cortisone, one of a group of hormones called steroids, to keep their arthritis under control. Cortisone is cheap and easily available now. But because it once had to be extracted from animals, cortisone cost so much—up to fifty dollars a pill—that only the rich could afford it. Then a brilliant chemist named Percy Lavon Julian figured out how to synthesize cortisone and other important steroids from an unlikely source: soybeans.

Percy Julian was born in Montgomery, Alabama, in 1899, a time when most African-American children had no chance of getting a good education. But Julian's father and mother were determined that all their children would be educated. The family had a long tradition of schooling. When Julian's grandfather was a slave, his master cut off two of his fingers because he had dared to learn to read and write.

Percy Lavon Julian.

It wasn't easy for Percy Julian, but his hard work paid off. When he entered DePauw University in Indiana in 1921, he had to enroll in remedial classes, along with his regular college courses, to catch up. By the time he graduated, however, he was at the top of his class.

Julian's favorite subject was chemistry, and he decided he wanted to get his Ph.D. and become a research scientist. But he found that in the 1920s, very few American universities were willing to admit an African American into their graduate programs. So Julian took a teaching job at Fisk University, a black college in Nashville, Tennessee. After two years, Harvard University awarded him a fellowship in chemistry. Julian completed his master's degree at Harvard, with the highest grades in his program. In 1929, Julian began working on his Ph.D. in Vienna, Austria, because European universities were then more open to African-American students than American universities.

In Vienna, Julian studied soybeans to find out what useful products they might produce. In 1935, while working at his old school, DePauw, Julian became the first person to synthesize from soybean proteins a drug called physostigmine, used to treat the eye disease glaucoma.

Despite his brilliant success, Julian found that as an African American he was denied academic positions he deserved. Eventually Julian became director of research for the Glidden manufacturing company. This was a turning point in American science—the first time an African American headed a major laboratory.

With the freedom Glidden gave him, Julian continued his research on soybeans. He found a way to make a fire-fighting foam out of soybeans. The U.S. navy called it "bean soup" and used it in World War II to put out fires on navy ships. Julian also manufactured large amounts of synthetic progesterone and testosterone from soy protein. Progesterone is a hormone that prevents miscarriages among pregnant women; doctors also use it to help fight cancer. Then Julian created something called cortexolone, or Substance S, from soybeans. Substance S was almost the same as cortisone from animals; it lacked only one oxygen molecule. Julian figured out how to introduce the missing molecule into Substance S, producing the first manmade cortisone. Julian's techniques for synthesizing cortisone and other steroids from soybeans made these important substances widely and cheaply available, and earned Julian his reputation as one of the most brilliant research chemists of the twentieth century. In 1947, Julian followed in the footsteps of Ernest Just when he received the Spingarn Award from the NAACP.

Illustration and Photo Credits

Every effort has been taken to trace and acknowledge copyrights. The editors tender their apologies for any accidental infringement where copyright has proved untraceable. They would be pleased to insert the appropriate acknowledgment in any subsequent edition of this book. Trademarks and trade names are shown in this book for illustrative purposes only and are the property of their respective owners. The references to trademarks and trade names given herein do not affect their validity.

American Museum of Natural History
  Tenochtitlàn. 326597, courtesy the Library, American Museum of Natural History: 85
AnthroArcheArt.org
  Tikal © Philip Baird/www.anthroarcheart.org: 83
  Stele © Philip Baird/www.anthroarcheart.org: 84
  Machu Picchu © Philip Baird/www.anthroarcheart.org: 88
Art Resource
  Dürer Self-Portrait © Erich Lessing/Art Resource, NY: 185
  St. George © Nimatallah/Art Resource, NY: 181(a)
  Mona Lisa © Reunion des Musees Nationaux/Art Resource, NY: 177
  Last Supper © Scala/Art Resource, NY: 178
  Mussorgsky © Scala/Art Resource, NY: 209
  Marriage of Virgin © Scala/Art Resource, NY: 176
Buffalo Soldier Education Committee
  William Jennings, Licensee. Buffalo Soldier Educational and Historical Committee. Distributor/Dormail, Inc., 117 Delaware Street, Leavenworth, KS 66048.
Corbis
  Lake Michigan © Alan Schein Photography/CORBIS: 81
  Japanese Landscape Garden © Richard Cummins/CORBIS: 191(b)
  Kamakura Buddha © Royalty-Free/CORBIS: 191(a)
  Samurai Warrior. © Bettmann/CORBIS: 121
Denver Public Library
  Chinese Worker. Denver Public Library/Western History Collection/Neg. X-21515: 155(a)
Leslie Evans
  Original drawings: 4, 12
Jonathan Fuqua
  Original art: 240, 247, 292
Julie Grant
  Original art: 312, 316(all), 319(a), 321, 322
Harvard University Art Museums/Fogg
  Bierstadt, *Rocky Mountains, Lander's Peak.* Courtesy of the Fogg Art Museum, Harvard University Art Museums, Bequest of Mrs. William

Hayes Fogg, Photo: Kallsen, Katya, Image Copyright © President and Fellows of Harvard College: 189.
Phillip Jones
  Original art: 301(a), 311,
Bob Kirchman
  Original maps and illustrations: 72, 73, 74(a&b), 75, 76, 77, 82, 95(a), 96, 98, 117, 120, 123, 135, 153, 159, 168(a), 221(b&c), 267(a), 268, 269, 278(diagonals), 314(a&b), 317(a&b), 323, 332
Library of Congress
  Abraham Lincoln. Library of Congress, Prints and Photographs, LCBH8277-242:132
  Abraham Lincoln portrait, by Alexander Gardner, Meserve no. 97; Library of Congress Prints and Photographs, LC-USZ61-1938: 147
  African-American Troops. Library of Congress, Prints and Photographs, LC-262-2048. 140(b)
  Annie Oakley with gun Buffalo Bill gave her, 1922; Library of Congress, Prints and Photographs, LC-USZ62-126783: 157(b)
  Aztec priest performing sacrificial offering, 1904, Codex Magliabecchi, XIII, II, 3. 1904 ed., p. 70; Library of Congress, Prints and Photographs, LC-USZ62-43569: 86
  Baldassare Castiglione, Steel engraving by John J. Wedgwood after a painting by Raffaelle; Library of Congress, Prints and Photographs, LC-USZ62-78543: 106
  Blacks Voting, Library of Congress, Prints and Photographs, LC-US262-29247: 151
  Bronze statue of Amida Nyorai (Amitabha) in the Kondo. Library of Congress, Prints and Photographs, LC-USZ62-98646: 122
  Buffalo Bill (William Frederick Cody) portrait (full length); Library of Congress, Prints and Photographs, LC-USZC4-3116: 157(a)
  Carpetbagger by Carl Schurz, cartoon, 1872; Library of Congress, Prints and Photographs, LC-USZ62-77793: 149
  Catherine the Great; Library of Congress, Prints and Photographs, LC-USZ62-9090: 119
  Champion Sunnybank Sigurdson (collie owned

Library of Congress (continued)

by Albert Payson Terhune); Library of Congress, Prints and Photographs, LC-USZ62-119728: 308

Charles I, King of Great Britain, 1600-1649; Library of Congress, Prints and Photographs, LC-USZ62-77770: 115(a)

Chief Joseph half-length portrait, 1900, Smithsonian Institution, Bureau of American Ethnology, Photo: Library of Congress, Prints and Photographs, LC-USZ61-2087: 165

Christopher Columbus at the court of Ferdinand and Isabella, Library of Congress, Prints and Photographs, LC-USZ62-3939: 93

Church at Lancaster, NH, Library of Congress, Prints and Photographs, LC-USF34-002400-C: 168(b)

Cowboy. Library of Congress, Prints and Photographs, LC-USZ62-13227: 156

Dr. King addressing crowd in Lakeview, NY, 5/12/65, Library of Congress, Prints and Photographs, LC-USZ62-111162: 212

Dr. Percy L. Julian portrait, 1949; Library of Congress, Prints and Photographs, LC-USZ62-121585: 336

Emancipation Proclamation; Library of Congress, Prints and Photographs, LC-USZ62-2356: 140(a)

Federal soldier from New York; portrait between 1860-1865; Library of Congress, Prints and Photographs, LC-B8184-10086: 138(a)

Five Ute women posed for picture by Rose & Hopkins, Denver, 1899; Library of Congress, Prints and Photographs, LC-USZ62-111566: 161

Fort Sumter, Library of Congress, Prints and Photographs, LC-USZ62-5500: 134

Frederick Douglass portrait; Library of Congress, Prints and Photographs, LC-USZ62-126782: 28

Front of the Alamo, San Antonio, TX 1922; Library of Congress, Prints and Photographs, LC-USZ62-87798: 128

Gen. George A. Custer portrait, Matthew Brady photo; Library of Congress, Prints and Photographs, LC-B8172-1613: 164(b)

Ivan IV, Czar of Russia, 1530-1584; Library of Congress, Prints and Photographs, LC-USZ62-128730: 118(a)

John Brown by John Steuart Curry; Library of Congress, Prints and Photographs, LC-USZC4-6116: 133

Latter-day Saint with his six wives, 1885; Library of Congress, Prints and Photographs, LC-USZ62-83877: 125(a)

Longstreet at Gettysburg, July 2, 1863, by H. A. Ogden; Library of Congress, Prints and Photographs, LC-USZ62-77370: 142

Martin Luther engraving; Library of Congress, Prints and Photographs, LC-USZC4-6894: 108

Michel-Ange by J. L. Potrelle, engraving; Library of Congress, Prints and Photographs, LC-USZ62-123050: 105

Native American on horseback spearing buffalo, 1901, "Doomed"; Library of Congress, Prints and Photographs, LC-USZ62-115188: 162

Native Americans posed outside of Carlisle Indian School, 1890; Library of Congress, Prints and Photographs, LC-USZ62-124294: 167

Native standing by Inca masonry wall, Cuzco, Peru, 1907; Library of Congress, Prints and Photographs, LC-USZ62-101895: 89

New Mexico Desert highway, June 1938, by Dorothea Lange; Library of Congress, Prints and Photographs, LC-USF34-018272-C: 169

Newspaper ad, "To be sold on board the ship Bance Island," 1780s?; Library of Congress, Prints and Photographs, LC-USZ62-10293: 129

Parliament offering the crown to William III and Mary, from a picture by James Northcote, R.A.; Library of Congress, Prints and Photographs, LC-USZ62-111990: 116

Peter the Great, Emperor of Russia, portrait; Library of Congress, Prints and Photographs, LC-USZ62-92347: 118(b)

Pvt. Philip Carper, 35th Battalion, Virginia Cavalry, CSA portrait; Library of Congress, Prints and Photographs, LC-B8184-10018: 138(b)

Quail shooting, Currier & Ives scene showing American life in the 1800s; Library of Congress, Prints and Photographs, LC-USZC2-2940: 188(a)

Robert E. Lee. Library of Congress, Prints and Photographs, LC-USZ62-3794: 137(b)

Sitting Bull, Library of Congress, Prints and Photographs, LC-USZ62-112177: 164(a)

Sod House, McKenzie County, ND, 1937, Nov.; Library of Congress, Prints and Photographs, LC-USF342-T-031035-A: 154

Spaniards burning Atahualpa, Inca river, at stake with monk holding crucifix to right of Inca (Execution of the Inca by A. B. Greene); Li-

Text Credits and Sources

Index

References to illustrations appear in italics.

Abolitionists, 130, 133, 139
A cappella singing, 205
Acute angles, 273, 273
Addition, 230
    of fractions, 251–53, 252
    of integers, 222–24
    inverse operations, 229–30,
      239
    of mixed numbers, 255–56
    properties of, 229
Adjectives, 56, 64
Adolescence and puberty, 327–28,
    331
Adrenal glands, 332, 332
Adrenaline, 332
Adventures of Tom Sawyer, The
    (Twain), 19–20, 56
Adverbs, 56, 64
Africa, 91, 92, 93, 94, 95
    Cape of Good Hope, 92, 95, 97,
      99
African Americans, 186
    Black Codes and, 148–49
    Freedmen's Bureau and, 150
    Julian, Percy Lavon, 336–37,
      336
    Just, Ernest, 335–36, 335
    Ku Klux Klan and, 152
    slaves. See Slavery
    soldiers, 140–41, 140, 145, 155,
      155, 190
    voting rights for, 148, 149, 151,
      152
Alamo, 127–28, 128
Alaska, 158, 170
Alberti, Leon Battista, 104
Alcott, Louisa May, 24–27
Alexander VI, Pope, 94
Algae, 306, 307
Algebra, 103
Ali, Muhammad, 46
Alliteration, 49

Amendments to the Constitution,
    133, 150–51, 151, 152
American geography. See Geogra-
    phy, U.S.
American history. See History, U.S.
American Revolution, 116
Americas, early civilizations of,
    82–90, 82
    Aztecs, 82, 82, 84–87, 85, 86,
      88, 97, 99, 100
    Incas, 82, 82, 88–90, 88, 89,
      90, 100
    Maya, 82–84, 82, 83, 84
Amoeba, 306
Amphibians, 309
Angles, 273, 273
    kinds of, 273–74, 273
Animals, 301
    regeneration in, 316, 316
    sexual reproduction in, 314,
      323–25, 324
Antarctic Circle, 74, 74, 75
Antietam, 149
Apache, 160
Appomattox Courthouse, 145–46,
    146
Appositives, 61
Arapaho, 162, 163, 164
Arc, 279, 279
Archaebacteria, 307
Architecture, 104, 182–83
Arctic Circle, 74, 74, 75, 75
Area, 280–84, 281, 283
    of parallelogram, 283, 283
    of triangle, 282, 282
Aristotle, 103
Arithmetic, 219. See also Mathe-
    matics
Arizona, 160
"Arrow and the Song, The"
    (Longfellow), 5
Art, 104, 173, 174–91

    American, 186–90
    Japanese, 191
    Renaissance, 174–85
Arthritis, 336
Asia, 91, 99
Atahualpa, 89–90
Atomic symbols, 296
Atoms, 292, 292, 293
    chemical reactions, 293, 297,
      298–99, 298, 299
    compounds, 297–98, 298
    molecules, 297, 297
Austin, Stephen, 127
Averages, 265–66
Aztecs, 82, 82, 84–87, 85, 86, 88,
    97, 99, 100

Babies, 327, 330, 330
Bacteria, 307, 315
Balboa, Vasco Núñez de, 89
"Barbara Frietchie" (Whittier), 14
Bar graphs, 268, 268
Bar lines and measures, in music,
    196, 198
"Battle Hymn of the Republic,
    The," 139
Bean seeds, 321–22, 321, 322
Bees, 320, 320
Beethoven, Ludwig van, 203,
    208–9, 208, 210
Bible, 104, 107, 108, 108, 109, 110
    in art, 175, 178, 179
    Galileo and, 333
    King James, 114
    Lincoln and, 132
    spirituals and, 131, 210, 211
Bibliographies, 63
Bierstadt, Albert, 189, 189
Billions, 220, 220
Bill of Rights, 116
Billy the Kid, 156–57
Bingham, George Caleb, 187, 187

"Bird came down the Walk, A" (Dickinson), 11
Birds, 310, 326
Birthday suit, 65
Birth of Venus, The (Botticelli), *174*, 175
Bite the hand that feeds you, 65
Black Americans. *See* African Americans
Black Codes, 148–49
Black Kettle, Chief, 163
Blake, William, 12, 13, 48
Body, human, 327–32
    adolescence and puberty, 327–28, 331
    embryo development, 325, 327, 330
    endocrine system, 331–32, *332*
    glands, 331–32, *332*
    growth stages, 327, *327*
    reproductive system, 327, 328–30, *328, 329, 330*
Bohr, Niels, 295
Boleyn, Anne, 112
Books and printing, 107–8, *107*, 109
Boone, Daniel, 123
Booth, John Wilkes, 147
Botticelli, Sandro, 105, *174*, 175
Bowie, Jim, 128
Brady, Matthew, 190
Brazil, 96, 99, 101
Brooks, Gwendolyn, 10
Brown, John, 133, *133*, 136
Bruegel, Pieter, 184, *184*, 186
Brunelleschi, Filippo, 182, *182*
Buddha, 122, *122*, 191, *191*
Buddhism, 122, 191
Budding, 315
Buffalo, 161–62, *162*, 163, 165
Buffalo Bill, 157, *157*
Buffalo Soldiers, 155, *155*
Bull Run, 135–36
Burnett, Frances Hodgson, 29–33
Byzantine Empire, 91

Cabral, Pedro, 96, 99
Calvin, John, 97, 110, 111
Calvinism, 97, 110, 111, 113, 115
Canons and rounds, 205
Capacity, 288
Cape of Good Hope, 92, 95, 97, 99
Carbon dioxide, 298, 311, 312
Carlisle Indian School, 166, *167*
Carpetbaggers, 149, *149*
Carroll, Lewis, 18
Case, pronoun agreement in, 57–60
"Casey at the Bat" (Thayer), 16–17
Castiglione, Baldassare, 106, *106*
Catch forty winks, 65
Cathedrals, 182
Catherine of Aragon, 112
Catherine the Great, 119, *119*
Catholicism, 110, 111, 112–13, 114, 115, 116
Celery plant, photosynthesis in, 311–12, *311*, 313
Cell division, 315
Cell membrane, 302, 303, *303*, 304, *305*, 307
Cells, 302, *302*
    Just's investigation of, 335–36, *335*
    nucleus of, 302, 303, *303*, 305, 307, 336
    parts of, 302–3, *303*
    plant versus animal, 304–5, *305*
    types of, 303–4, *304*
Cell wall, 304, *305*, 307
Cervantes, Miguel de, 21–23
Cervix, *329*
Charles, King of Spain, 97
Charles I, King, 114–15, *115*
Charles II, King, 115–16, *115*
Checks and balances, 150
Chemical reactions, 293, 297, 298–99, *298, 299*
Chemistry, 292–99
    atoms, 292, *292*, 293
    chemical reactions, 293, 297, 298–99, *298, 299*
    compounds, 297–98, *298*

Dalton, John, 293
    element abbreviations, 296
    metals, 294, 296, *296*
    molecules, 297, *297*
    periodic table of the elements, 293–94, *294*, 295, *295*, 296
Cheyenne, 162, 163, 164
Chickens, 314, *314*, 315
China, 91, 95, 96
Chip on your shoulder, 65
Chivington, J. M., 163
Chlorophyll, 304–5, 307, 311, 312
Chloroplasts, 304–5, *305*, 306, 307, 312
Chords, in geometry, 278, 279
Chords, in music, 204
Choruses, 204
Christianity, 104, 175
    Bible in. *See* Bible
    explorers and, 90, 91, 93
    Galileo and, 333–34
    Reformation and, 97, 108–11, 112
    slaves and, 131, 210
Church of England, 112, 113, 115
Cilia, 306, *306*
Circle graphs, 267–68, *267*
Circles, 278–80, *278, 279, 280*
Circumference, 279, 280
"Civil Disobedience" (Thoreau), 128
Civil War, 24, 28, 129–47, *134, 135*
    in art, 190
    beginning of, 134
    Gettysburg, 142–43, *142*
    Grant, Ulysses S., 137, *137*, 142, 145–46, *146*, 147
    ironclad ships, 142
    Lee, Robert E., 136, 137, *137*, 139–40, 142–43, 145–46, *146*, 147
    Lincoln and. *See* Lincoln, Abraham
    Reconstruction after, 148–52
    Richmond, 145

Sherman, William Tecumseh, 144–45, *144*, 150
slavery. *See* Slavery
soldiers, 138, *138*, 139, 140–41, *140*, 145, 155, *155*, 190
Clark, William, 124, 161
Classes, in taxonomy, 308, 335
Classifying living things, 300–310
    cell parts, 302–3, *303*
    cells, 302, *302*
    cell types, 303–4, *304*
    fungi, 301, *301*, 305, *305*, 315
    Linnaeus and, 334–35, *334*
    organisms, 301, *301*
    plant cells versus animal cells, 304–5, *305*
    prokaryotes, 301, *301*, 307, *307*, 311
    protists, 301, *301*, 306, *306*, 307, 311, 315
    taxonomy, 308, 309
    vertebrates, 309–10
Clemens, Samuel (Mark Twain), 19–20
Climate zones, 75, *75*
Cloning, 315–16
"Clouds" (Rossetti), 46, 47
Cody, William F. (Buffalo Bill), 157, *157*
Cole, Thomas, *188*, 189
Collie, 308, *308*, 309
Colonies, 99–100, 101, 102, 114, 123
Colons, 61
Columbus, Christopher, 92–94, *93*, 98, 99, 101
Comanche, 162
Comedies, 49, *49*
    of Shakespeare, 51, 207
Commas, 53, 54, 60–61
Common nouns, 56
Compass, 275, *275*, 278, 279
Composite numbers, 227
Compounds, 297–98, *298*
Confederacy, 135–46
    Reconstruction and, 148–52

See also Civil War
Congress, 150
Conifers, 318, *318*
Conjunctions, 54
    coordinating, 54, 60
Constantinople, 117
Constitution, 150
    amendments to, 133, 150–51, *151*, 152
Copernicus, Nicolaus, 333–34
Core knowledge, need for, xxii–xxiii
Core Knowledge Foundation, xix–xx, xxi, xxiv, xxvi
    Web site of, 3, 71, 173, 195
Core Knowledge Sequence, xix, xxiii–xxiv, xxv, xxvi
Core Knowledge Series, xxi, xxiii, xxiv, xxvi
    nature of, xxv
Cork cells, 302, *302*
Cortés, Hernando, 84, 86–87, 90, 91, 97, 99
Cortisone, 336, 337
Cotyledon, 322, *323*
Council of Trent, 111
Counter-Reformation, 111
Count your blessings, 65
Courtiers, 106
Cowboys, 156, *156*, 157
"Coyote Goes to the Land of the Dead," 43–44, *43*
Crazy Horse, 164
Crockett, Davy, 128
Cromwell, Oliver, 115
Crow Indians, 162
Cubed numbers, 226
Cubes, 284, *284*
Cubic units, 285, 287, *287*
Cullen, Countee, 9
Cumberland Gap, 123
Curricula, xix, xxi–xxiii, xxv
Currier & Ives, *188*, 188
Custer, George Armstrong, 164, *164*
Cyanobacteria, 307

Cytoplasm, 302, 303, *303*, 304, *305*, 336

Da Gama, Vasco, 95–96, *95*
Dalton, John, 293
"Danny Boy," 216
David (Michelangelo), 181, *181*
Davis, Jefferson, 136, *136*, 145
Decimals, 238–49
    checking sums and differences, 239–40
    comparing, 239
    dividing, 243–49, 254–55
    estimating products, 242
    multiplying, 240–41, 242, 243
    on number line, 238–39, *238*
    percents, fractions, and, 264–65
Declaration of Independence, 144
Degrees, 273
Democritus, 292, 293
Despréz, Josquin, 205–6
Diabetes, 331
Diagonals, 278, *278*
Dialogues, 333
Diameter, 279, *280*
Dias, Bartolomeu, 92, 93
Dickinson, Emily, 10, 11, 45, 47
Dicots, 322, *323*
Direct objects, 54
Distance, speed, and time, 262
Division and divisibility, 232–37
    of decimals, 243–49, 254–55
    inverse operations, 231
    long division, 233–37
    short division, 233
"Dixie," 139
"Dona Nobis Pacem," 205
Donatello, 180–81, *181*
Don Quixote (Cervantes), 21–23
Douglas, Stephen A., 132
Douglass, Frederick, 28–29, *28*, 130, 140, 141
Dowland, John, 207
"Down by the Riverside," 211
Doyle, Arthur Conan, 34–38

Drake, Francis, 114
Drama, 49
"Dreams" (Hughes), 47
Dürer, Albrecht, 185, *185*
Dutch (Netherlands), 91, 95,
     97–99, 113

"Eagle, The" (Tennyson), 4
Earth's movement around sun,
     Galileo and, 333–34
Eastern Hemisphere, 72, *72*
Eastern Orthodox Church, 117
Eat crow, 65
Ectoplasm, 336
Education. *See* Schools and educa-
     tion
Edward VI, King, 112
Eel Spearing at Setauket (Mount),
     186, *186*
Eggs
     of animals, 323, 324, *324*, 326,
        326
     fertilization of, 317, 318, 321,
        323–26, *324, 326,* 328, *328,*
        330, 336
     of humans, 328, *328,* 330
     ovaries for, 319–20, *319, 320,*
        321, 323, 324, *324,* 328, *329*
     of plants, 317, *317,* 318, 321
Egypt, 91
Electricity, 296
Electrons, 292, *292,* 293, 295
Elements, 293
     atomic symbols for, 296
     periodic table of, 293–94, *294,*
        295, *295, 296*
Eleventh hour, 65
Elizabeth I, Queen, 99, 113, *113,*
     114, 206
Emancipation Proclamation, 140,
     141
Embryo
     animal, 325, 326, *326*
     human, 325, 327, 330
     plant, 318, 321, *321, 322*
Emerson, Ralph Waldo, 7

Endocrine system, 331–32, *332*
Endosperm, 321, *321*
England, 112–16
     Bill of Rights, 116
     Charles I, 114–15, *115*
     Charles II, 115–16, *115*
     Civil War, 115
     Elizabeth I, 99, 113, *113,* 114,
        206
     explorers, 91, 95, 99, 114
     Henry VIII, 112, *112*
     James I, 114
     James II and the Glorious Rev-
        olution, 116
     Protestants and Catholics,
        112–13
     Spanish Armada and, 113–14
Equator, 72, *72,* 73, *73,* 74, 75, *75*
Equilateral triangles, 274, *274,* 275,
     277, *277*
Erasmus, Desiderius, 104
Eratosthenes, 227
Erie Canal, 124
Eubacteria, 307
Euglena, 306
Eureka!, 65
European exploration, 82, 91–102,
     96, 174
     Columbus, Christopher, 92–94,
        93, 98, 99, 101
     English, 91, 95, 99, 114
     Portuguese, 91, 92, 94–99, 101
     Spanish, 84–95, 99, 100, 101,
        159, 160
European Renaissance. *See* Renais-
     sance
Everett, Edward, 143
Every cloud has a silver lining, 65
Execution of the Inca, The (Greene),
     90
Exponents, 225–26, 228

Factors, 227
     greatest common (GCF), 228,
        249
     prime, 227–28

Fallopian tubes, 328, *329,* 330
Family, in taxonomy, 308
Ferdinand, King, 93, *93,* 94, 112
Ferns, reproduction in, 316–17,
     317
Fertilization, 317, 318, 336
     in animals, 323, 324, *324,* 325,
        326, *326*
     in flowers, 320–21, *320*
     in humans, 328, *328,* 330
Fetus, 325, 326, *326,* 327, 330
Few and far between, 66
Ficino, Marsilio, 105
Fifth Symphony (Beethoven), 203,
     208–9
Figurative language, 45–48
Figures of speech, 45
Fire, 298, *298*
Fish, 309, 310, 325, 326
     spawning of, 324, *324*
Flats and sharps, in music, 202
Florence, 104–5, 174
     Cathedral of, 182–83, *182*
Flowering plants, 301
     monocots and dicots, 322, *323*
     seeds of, 318–19, 321, 322
Flowers, 319–20, *319,* 322
     fertilization of, 320–21, *320*
"Fog" (Sandburg), 46
Fort Sumter, 134, *134,* 135
Forty-niners, 125, *125*
Fractions, 238, 249–59
     adding, 251–53, *252*
     comparing, 250–51, *250, 251*
     decimals and, 264–65
     equivalent, 249
     lowest terms, 249
     in mixed numbers, 253–57
     multiplying whole numbers
        and, 258–59, *258*
     percents and, 263, *263,* 264–65
     ratios as, 260
     subtracting, 253, *253*
France, 95, 123
Freedmen's Bureau, 150
Frigid zones, 75, *75*

Frontier, 158
Frogs, 314, *314*, 315
Frost, Robert, 6, 48
Fruits, 318–19, 320, *320*, 321
Functions, 269–71, *269*, *270*, *271*
Fungi, 301, *301*, 305, *305*, 315
Fur trade, 124
Fur Traders Descending the Missouri (Bingham), 187, *187*

Galilei, Galileo, 333–34, *333*
Gametes, 316–17, *317*, 318, 319, 320–21, 323
Gardens, Japanese, 191, *191*
Garrett, Pat, 156–57
Garrison, William Lloyd, 130
Gender, pronoun agreement in, 59
Genre painting, 184, 186
Genus, 308, 335
Geography, U.S., 168–70, *168*
    Alaska, 170
    Hawaii, 170, *170*
Geography, world, 71, 72–81
    Arctic and Antarctic Circles, 74, *74*, 75, *75*
    lakes, 80–81, *81*, 124
    latitude, 73, *73*, 74, 75, 76
    longitude, 73, *73*, 76
    maps, 71, 78–80, *79*, *80*
    reference points, 72
    seasons, 76, *76*
    time of day, 76–78
    tropical, temperate, and frigid zones, 75, *75*
Geometry, 273–88
    angles, 273–74, *273*
    area, 280–84, *281*, *282*, *283*
    capacity, 288
    circles, 278–80, *278*, *279*, *280*
    diagonals, 278, *278*
    parallelograms, 283, *283*
    polygons, 276–77, *276*, *277*
    rectangular prisms, 284, *284*
    surface area, 286–87, *286*
    triangles, 274–75, *274*, *275*, 276, 277, 282, *282*

volume, 285–87, *285*, *286*, *287*, 288
George III, King, 116
Germination, 321, *322*
Gettysburg, 142–43, *142*
Gettysburg Address, 143–44
Ghost Dance, 165–66
"Git Along, Little Dogies," 214
Glands, 331–32, *332*
Globe, 78
Globe Theater, 51, *51*
Glorious Revolution, 116
"God Bless America," 215
"Go Down, Moses," 211
Gold
    as element, 292, 293, 296
    prospecting for, 125, 153, 158, 163, 164, 213
Grammar, 3. *See also* Language
Grant, Ulysses S., 137, *137*, 142, 145
    Lee's surrender to, 145–46, *146*, 147
Graphs, 267
    bar, 268, *268*
    circle, 267–68, *267*
    of functions, 270–71, *270*, *271*
    line, 268–69, *269*
Grass, 322
Grass is always greener on the other side of the hill, the, 66
Great Plains, 169
Greeks, 103, 104, 175, 182, 190
Greeley, Horace, 153
Greene, A. B., 90
"Greensleeves," 206, 207
Growth, 325–26
    stages of, 326, *326*, 327, *327*
Guatemala, 82, *83*
Gutenberg, Johannes, 107–8

Harmony, 204, 205
Harpers Ferry, 133, 136
Hawaii, 170, *170*
Hemingway, Ernest, 46
Hemispheres, of Earth, 72, *72*

Henry VIII, 112, *112*
Henry the Navigator, Prince, 92, *92*
Hexagons, 277, *277*, 278, *278*
"Hills Like White Elephants" (Hemingway), 46
History, U.S., 71, 123–67
    Civil War. *See* Civil War
    Native Americans. *See* Native Americans
    Reconstruction, 148–52
    westward expansion before the Civil War, 123–28, *126*
    westward expansion following the Civil War, 153–58, *153*
History, world, 71, 82–120
    early civilizations of the Americas. *See* Americas, early civilizations of
    England. *See* England
    European exploration. *See* European exploration
    Japan. *See* Japan
    Reformation, 97, 108–11, *112*
    Renaissance. *See* Renaissance
    Russia. *See* Russia
Holmes, Sherlock, 34–38
Homesteading, 153–54, 163
Hooke, Robert, 302, 304
Hormones, 327, 331, 336
Horses, life cycle of, 326, *326*
Howe, Julia Ward, 139
Huáscar, 89–90
Hudson River School, 189
Hughes, Langston, 9, 47
Human body. *See* Body, human
Humanists, 104
Human sexual reproduction, 323, 328–30
Hydrogen, 293, 294, 296

"I, Too" (Hughes), 9
Ibn Sina, 103, *103*
"If I Had a Hammer," 215
Ignatius of Loyola, Saint, 111, *111*
"I Hear America Singing" (Whitman), 8

"I like to see it lap the Miles—"
  (Dickinson), 10, 47
Imagery, 46
Impeachment, 150
Incas, 82, *82*, 88–90, *88*, *89*, *90*,
  100
"Incident" (Cullen), 9
Indexes, 62
India, 92, 93, 94, 95, 96, 99
Indians. *See* Native Americans
Indies, 91, 93, 94, 99, 100, 101
Indirect objects, 54–55
Indonesia, 91, 98, 99
Insulin, 331
Integers (whole numbers), 221–22
  adding, 222–24
  comparing, 222
  in mixed numbers, 253–57
  multiplying fractions and,
    258–59, *258*
  subtracting, 224
Interjections, 57
International date line, 78
Inverse operations, 229–30, 231,
  239, 269–70
Ions, 299
Iron, 296, 298
Ironclad ships, 142
Isabella, Queen, 93, *93*, 94, 112
Islam. *See* Muslims and Islam
Isosceles triangles, 274, *274*, 275
Italics, 61
Italy
  Renaissance in, 104–5, 174,
    175, 183
  trade and, 91–92
It's never too late to mend, 66
Ivan the Great, 117
Ivan the Terrible, 118, *118*

"Jabberwocky" (Carroll), 18
Jackson, Thomas J. "Stonewall,"
  135–36
James, Frank, 156
James, Jesse, 156
James I, King, 114

James II, King, 116
Japan, 120, *120*
  art in, 191
  feudal, 121
  religions in, 122
  "Samurai's Daughter, The,"
    38–40, *39*
Jefferson, Thomas, 123–24
Jesuits, 111
Jesus, 178, 180
John, King, 93
Johnson, Andrew, 148, 149, 150
  impeachment of, 150
Joseph, Chief, 165, *165*
Julian, Percy Lavon, 336–37, *336*
Jupiter, 333
Just, Ernest, 335–36, *335*

Kentucky, 123
Keyboard, 201–2
Kill two birds with one stone, 66
Kilmer, Joyce, 48
King, Martin Luther, Jr., 212, *212*
Kingdoms, in classification, 301,
  308, 335
Ku Klux Klan, 152

Labor and delivery, 330
Lakes, 80–81, *81*, 124
Lakota (Sioux), 162, 164, *164*,
  165–66
Landscapes, *188*, *189*, 189
Language, 3, 52–67
  adjectives and adverbs, 56, 64
  agreement in case, 57–60
  agreement in gender, 59
  agreement in number, 59–60
  colons, 61
  commas, 53, 54, 60–61
  direct objects, 54
  indirect objects, 54–55
  interjections, 57
  italics, 61
  literal and figurative, 45–48
  nouns, 56, 61
  personal pronouns, 57–60

possessive case, 57, 59, 60
predicates, 55
prefixes, 63–64
run-on sentences, 53–54
sayings and phrases. *See* Sayings
  and phrases
sentence fragments, 53
subjects, 52, 55
suffixes, 64
verbs, 52–53
writing, 3, 62–63
Las Casas, Bartolomé de, 100, *100*
Last Supper, The (Leonardo da
  Vinci), 178, *178*
Latitude, 73, *73*, 74, 75, 76
Lead, 292, 293, 296
Learning, xxi, xxii, xxv
Lee, Robert E., 136, 137, *137*,
  139–40, 142–43, 145
  surrender of, 145–46, *146*, 147
Leo X, Pope, 105, 109
Leonardo da Vinci, 105, 179, 180,
  185
  Last Supper, The, 178, *178*
  Mona Lisa, 177, *177*
  Vitruvian Man, 175, *175*
Lewis, Meriwether, 124, 161
Life cycles, 314, *314*, 326
Lincoln, Abraham, 132, *132*, 133,
  134, 135, 137, 139, *147*
  assassination of, 147
  Emancipation Proclamation of,
    140, 141
  Gettysburg Address of, 143–44
  Reconstruction plans of, 148
  reelection of, 145
Linear perspective, 104, 176, 178,
  183
Line graphs, 268–69, *269*
Linnaeus, Carl, 334–35, *334*
Lion cubs, 326
Literal and figurative language,
  45–48
Literature, 3, 4–51
  alliteration, 49
  drama, 49

imagery, 46
literal and figurative language, 45–48
onomatopoeia, 48–49
personification, 48
poetry. *See* Poetry
Shakespeare, William, 50–51, *50*, 113, 206, 207
simile and metaphor, 46–47
stories. *See* Stories, myths, and legends
symbols, 48
Lithium, 292, *292*, 294, 295, 296
Little Big Horn, 164
Little Women (Alcott), 24–27, 57
Living things
classification of. *See* Classifying living things
non-living things versus, 303
Lizards, 309, *309*
Lock, stock, and barrel, 66
Long Drive, 156
Longfellow, Henry Wadsworth, 5
Longitude, 73, *73*, 76
Longstreet, James, 142, *142*
Louisiana Purchase, 123–24, *123*
Love, songs about, 216
Lute music, 206, 207
Luther, Martin, 108–10, *108*, 111

Machiavelli, Niccolò, 106–7
Machu Picchu, 88, 88
Madonnas, 180
Magellan, Ferdinand, 97, *97*
Make a mountain out of a molehill, 66
Mammals, 310
Manassas, 135–36
Manco Capac, 89
Manifest destiny, 127
Maps, 71, 78–80, *79*, *80*
Marriage of the Virgin, The (Raphael), 176, *176*, 180
Mary I, Queen, 112–13, 116
Mason-Dixon Line, 130

Mathematics, 103, 219, 220–88
adding fractions, 251–53, *252*
adding integers, 222–24
adding mixed numbers, 255–56
addition properties, 229
angles, 273–74, *273*
area, 280–84, *281*, *282*, *283*
averages, 265–66
billions, 220, *220*
capacity, 288
circles, 278–80, *278*, *279*, *280*
comparing large numbers, 220
computation, 229–37
decimal division, 243–49, 254–55
decimals, 238–49, 254–55, 264–65
decimals on a number line, 238–39, *238*
diagonals, 278, *278*
division and divisibility, 231, 232–37, 243–49, 254–55
estimating products, 232, 242
exponents, 225–26, 228
fractions, 238, 249–59, 260, 263, 264–65
fractions on a number line, 250–51, *251*
functions, 269–71, *269*, *270*, *271*
geometry, 273–88
graphs, 267–69, *267*, *268*, *269*, 270–71, *270*, *271*
greatest common factor (GCF), 228, 249
integers (whole numbers), 221–24, 258–59, *258*
inverse operations, 229–30, 231, 239, 269–70
least common multiple, 228
mixed numbers, 253–57
multiplication properties, 230–31
multiplying decimals, 240–41, 242, 243

multiplying fractions and whole numbers, 258–59, *258*
multiplying large factors, 232
numbers and number sense, 220–28
parallelograms, 283, *283*
percents, 263–65
place value and expanded form, 220, 226
polygons, 276–77, *276*, *277*
positive and negative numbers, 221
powers of ten, 226
prime factors, 227–28
prime numbers, 227
probability, 266
rates and speed, 262
ratios, 260–65
rectangular prisms, 284, *284*
rounding, 225, 240, 242
scale, 261–62, *261*
sets, 226
squares and square roots, 225–26
subtracting fractions, 253, *253*
subtracting integers, 224
subtracting mixed numbers, 256–57
surface area, 286–87, *286*
triangles, 274–75, *274*, *275*, 276, 277, 282, *282*
variables, 229
volume, 285–87, *285*, *286*, *287*, 288
word problems, equations for, 271–72
Maya, 82–84, *82*, *83*, *84*
Measurement, units of, 280
of capacity, 288
cubic, 285, 287, *287*
of volume, 285–86, *285*, *287*, *287*, 288
Measures and bar lines, in music, 196, 198
Medici family, 104–5, 109, 174

Memorial to Robert Gould Shaw and the Forty-fourth Massachusetts Regiment (Saint-Gaudens), 190, *190*

Mendeleev, Dmitri, 293–94

Mendelssohn, Felix, 207, *207*

Menstruation, 328

Mercator projection, 79, *79*, 80

Meridians, 73
180°, 72, 76, 77
prime, 72, *72*, 73, *73*, 76, 77

Merrimack, 142

Metals, 294, 296, *296*

Metaphor and simile, 46–47

Metric units, 280, 285, 288

Mexican-American War, 128, 136, 137

Mexico, 82, 84, 86–87, 101
Texas and, 127–28

Michelangelo Buonarroti, 105, *105*, 179, 180, 182, 185
David, 181, *181*
Sistine Chapel, 179, *179*, 185

Microscope, 301, *301*, 302, *302*

Mid-Atlantic, 168–69

Midsummer Night's Dream, A (Shakespeare), 207

Midwest, 169

Mildew, 305, 315

Miss is as good as a mile, a, 66

Missouri Compromise, 129–30, 131

Mitochondria, 302, 303, *303*, 305

Mold, 305, 315

Molecules, 297, *297*
chemical reactions, 293, 297, 298–99, *298, 299*
compounds, 297–98, *298*

Mona Lisa (Leonardo da Vinci), 177, *177*

Monitor, 142

Monocots, 322, *323*

Montezuma, 86, 87, 90

Mormons, 124–25, *125*

Mosses, 313
reproduction in, 316–17, *317*

Mount, William Sidney, 186, *186*

Mozart, Wolfgang Amadeus, 208

Multiple, least common, 228

Multiplication
of decimals, 240–41, 242, 243
estimating a product, 232
exponents, 225–26, 228
of fractions and whole numbers, 258–59, *258*
inverse operations, 231
of large factors, 232
properties of, 230–31
squares and square roots, 225–26

Mushrooms, 305, 315

Music, 195, 196–216
American songs, 215
Beethoven, Ludwig van, 203, 208–9, *208*, 210
canons and rounds, 205
dotted and tied notes, 198, *198*
Dowland, John, 207
elements of, 196–204
harmony, 204, 205
Italian directions in, 202–3
keyboard, 201–2
listening and understanding, 205–9
lute, 206, 207
measures and bar lines, 196, 198
Mendelssohn, Felix, 207, *207*
Mussorgsky, Modest, 209, *209*, 210
notes, 196–98, *196, 197, 198*
polyphonic, 205, 206
Renaissance, 205–7
repeat signs, 199, *199*
rests, 198, *198*
rhythm, 203–4
sharps and flats, 202
songs about love and lovers, 216
songs about westward expansion, 213–14
spirituals, 131, 210–12

time signatures, *196*, 199–200, *200*
treble clef, 200–201, *201*
verse and refrain, 204

Muslims and Islam, 91, 93, 95, 96
scholars, 103–4, *103*

Mussorgsky, Modest, 209, *209*, 210

"Narcissa" (Brooks), 10

Narrative of the Life of Frederick Douglass (Douglass), 28–29

Native Americans, 126–27, 159–67, *159*
"Coyote Goes to the Land of the Dead," 43–44, *43*
Ghost Dance, 165–66
Joseph, Chief, 165, *165*
Little Big Horn, 164
reservations, 163, 165, 166–67
Sand Creek Massacre, 163–64
"Sun Dance, The," 40–43

Navajo, 160

Negative and positive numbers, 221

Netherlands (Dutch), 91, 95, 97–99, 113

Neutrons, 292

New England, 168, *168*

New Mexico, 160, *160*

New York City, 124

Nez Percé, 43, 161, 165

Nominative case, 57, 58–59, 60

Northern Hemisphere, 72, *72*, 74, *74*, 76

North Pole, 72, *72*, *73*, 74, *74*, 76

Northwest, 169

Notes, musical, 196–98, *196, 197, 198*
dotted and tied, 198, *198*

Nouns, 56
appositives, 61

Nuclear membrane, 302, 303, *303*, 305, 307

Nucleus, of atom, 292, 293, 295

Nucleus, of cell, 302, 303, *303*, 305, 307, 336

Number, pronoun agreement in, 59–60
Number lines
    adding integers on, 222–24, 222, 223, 224
    comparing fractions on, 250–51, 251
    decimals on, 238–39, 238
    positive and negative numbers on, 221, 221
Numbers, 220–28
    billions, 220, 220
    exponents, 225–26, 228
    factors, 227, 228
    integers, 221–24
    large, comparison of, 220
    mixed, 253–57
    multiples, 228
    place value and expanded form, 220, 226
    positive and negative, 221
    powers of ten, 226
    prime and composite, 227
    prime factors, 227–28
    rounding, 225, 240, 242
    squares and square roots, 225–26
    variables, 229
    See also Mathematics

Oakley, Annie, 157, 157
Objective case, 57, 58–59, 60
Objects
    direct, 54
    indirect, 54–55
Obtuse angles, 273, 273
"O Captain! My Captain!" (Whitman), 15, 147
Octagons, 277, 277
Oil painting, 183
"Old McDonald," 196, 197, 198, 199, 201–2
180° meridian, 72, 76, 77
Onomatopoeia, 48–49
"Opposites" (Wilbur), 5
Orders, in taxonomy, 308, 335

Organelles, 302
Organs, 304
Osceola, 127
Ottomans, 91–92
Out of the frying pan and into the fire, 66
Ovaries
    in animals, 323, 324, 324
    in humans, 328, 329
    in plants, 319–20, 319, 320, 321
Ovule, 319–20, 321
Oxbow, The (Cole), 188, 189
Oxygen, 293, 295, 295, 296, 297, 297, 307, 311
    in carbon dioxide, 298
Ozone, 297, 297

Pacific Islands, 98, 98
Pacific Ocean, 97, 98
Pancreas, 331, 332
Parallelograms, 276, 276
    finding area of, 283, 283
Parallels, in geography, 73, 75
Parliament, 114, 115, 116, 116
Peasant Wedding (Bruegel), 184, 184
Penny saved is a penny earned, a, 66
Pentagons, 277, 277, 278, 278
Percents, 263–65
    decimals and, 264–65
    fractions and, 263, 263, 264–65
Periodic table of the elements, 293–94, 294, 295, 295, 296
Periods, in number system, 220, 220
Personal pronouns, 57–60
Personification, 48
Perspective, linear, 104, 176, 178, 183
Peru, 89
Petals, 319, 321
Peter the Great, 118–19, 118
Philip II, King, 113

Philippines, 97, 98
Phloem, 312, 313
Photography, 190
Photosynthesis, 298, 304, 306, 307, 311–13, 311, 322
Phylum, 308
Physical change, 298
Phrases. See Sayings and phrases
Pi (π), 279, 280
Pickett, George, 143
Pictures at an Exhibition (Mussorgsky), 209
Pike, Zebulon, 124
Pine cones, 318, 318
Pistil, 319, 319, 320
Pituitary gland, 331, 332
Pizarro, Francisco, 89, 90, 91
Place value, 220
    powers of ten, 226
Plains Indians, 40, 161–62, 162
Plants, 301, 311–13
    cells of, versus animal cells, 304–5, 305
    development of, 321–22, 321, 322
    flower fertilization, 320–21, 320
    flowering, 301, 318–20, 319, 322, 323
    monocots and dicots, 322, 323
    oxygen and, 298
    photosynthesis in, 298, 304, 306, 307, 311–13, 311, 322
    seeds of, 315, 318–19, 318, 321–22, 321, 322
    sexual reproduction in mosses and ferns, 316–17, 317
    vascular and non-vascular, 313
    water transportation in, 311, 312, 313
Plateau Indians, 161
Plato, 105
Plays, 49
    of Shakespeare, 50–51, 206, 207
Plural pronouns, 59–60

Poetry, 3, 4–18
    alliteration in, 49
    "Arrow and the Song, The"
        (Longfellow), 5
    "Barbara Frietchie" (Whittier),
        14
    "Bird came down the Walk, A"
        (Dickinson), 11
    "Casey at the Bat" (Thayer),
        16–17
    "Eagle, The" (Tennyson), 4
    "I, Too" (Hughes), 9
    "I Hear America Singing"
        (Whitman), 8
    "I like to see it lap the Miles—"
        (Dickinson), 10, 47
    imagery in, 46
    "Incident" (Cullen), 9
    "Jabberwocky" (Carroll), 18
    literal and figurative language
        in, 45–48
    "Narcissa" (Brooks), 10
    "O Captain! My Captain!"
        (Whitman), 15, 147
    "Opposites" (Wilbur), 5
    personification in, 48
    "Poison Tree, A" (Blake), 13,
        48
    "Road Not Taken, The"
        (Frost), 6, 48
    of Shakespeare, 50
    simile and metaphor in, 46–47
    "Snowstorm, The" (Emerson),
        7
    symbols in, 48
    "Tyger, The" (Blake), 12
    "Wise Old Owl, A" (Richards),
        4
"Poison Tree, A" (Blake), 13, 48
Polk, James, 128
Pollen, 318, 319, 319, 320
Pollination, 320, 320
Polo, Marco, 91, 92
Polygons, 276–77, 276, 277
    diagonals in, 278, 278
Polyphonic music, 205, 206

Portrait of Giovanni Arnolfini and
    His Wife (van Eyck), 183–84,
    183
Portugal, explorers from, 91, 92,
    94–99, 101
Positive and negative numbers, 221
Possessive case, 57, 59, 60
Potassium, 294, 295, 296
Powers of ten, 226
Predicates, 55
Prefixes, 63–64
Pregnancy, 330
Prime factors, 227–28
Prime meridian, 72, 72, 73, 73, 76,
    77
Prime numbers, 227
Princes, 106
Printing and books, 107–8, 107,
    109
Probability, 266
Progesterone, 337
Prokaryotes, 301, 301, 307, 307,
    311
Pronouns, personal, 57–60
Proper nouns, 56
Proportions of Man, The (Leonardo
    da Vinci), 175, 175
Protestant Reformation, 97,
    108–11, 112
Protestants, 111, 112–13, 114, 116
Protists, 301, 301, 306, 306, 307,
    311, 315
Protons, 292, 292
Protozoans, 306, 306
Protractor, 273
Puberty, 327–28, 331
Pueblos, 160, 160
Puritans, 113, 114–15

Quadrilaterals, 276, 276, 277
Quail Shooting (Currier & Ives),
    188, 188
Quotation marks, 61–62

Radical Republicans, 148, 149, 150
Radius, 279, 280

Railroads, 154–55, 155, 156, 162,
    163, 165
Raphael, 105
    Marriage of the Virgin, The, 176,
        176, 180
    Small Cowper Madonna, 180,
        180
Rates and speed, 262
Ratios, 260–62
    percent, 263–65
    rate, 262
    scale, 261–62, 261
Read between the lines, 67
Reconstruction, 148–52
Rectangles, 276, 276, 277
Rectangular prisms, 284, 284
    surface area of, 286–87, 286
    volume of, 285–86, 285, 287
"Red-Headed League, The"
    (Doyle), 34–38
"Red River Valley," 216
Reference points, in geography, 72
Reformation, 97, 108–11, 112
Refrains and verses, 204
Regeneration, 316, 316
Religion, 104
    Buddhism, 122, 191
    Christianity. See Christianity
    Islam, 91, 95
Renaissance, 21, 104–8, 112, 117
    architecture, 182
    art, 174–85
    books, 107
    Galilei, Galileo, 333–34, 333
    Medici family, 104–5, 109, 174
    music, 205–7
    princes and courtiers, 106–7
    printing press, 107–8, 107
Repeat signs, in music, 199, 199
Reproduction, 314–26
    in animals, 323–25, 324
    asexual, 315–16, 315
    care and growth of young,
        325–26
    embryo development, 318, 321,

321, 322, 325, 326, 326, 327, 330
flower fertilization, 320–21, *320*
flowers, 319–20, *319*
growth stages, 326, *326*
in humans, 327, 328–30, *328, 329, 330*
monocots and dicots, 322, *323*
in mosses and ferns, 316–17, *317*
plant development, 321–22, *321, 322*
seeds, 315, 318–19, *318,* 321–22, *321, 322*
Reptiles, 309, *309*
Researching and writing a report, 62–63
Reservations, Indian, 163, 165, 166–67
Rests, in music, 198, *198*
Rhombuses, 276, *276,* 277
Rhythm, 203–4
Richards, Edward Hersey, 4
Richmond, fall of, 145
Right angles, 273, *273*
Right triangles, 274, *274*
Rivers, 81
"Road Not Taken, The" (Frost), 6, 48
Rocky Mountain, Lander's Peak (Bierstadt), 189, *189*
Romans, 103, 104, 117, 175, 182
Rossetti, Christina, 46, 47
Rounding numbers, 225, 240, 242
Rounds and canons, 205
"Row, Row, Row Your Boat," *200,* 205
Russia, 117–19, *117*
    Alaska sale, 158
    Catherine the Great, 119, *119*
    Ivan the Great, 117
    Ivan the Terrible, 118, *118*
    Peter the Great, 118–19, *118*

Sacagawea, 124, 161

Saint-Gaudens, Augustus, 190, *190*
St. George (Donatello), 181, *181*
St. Peter's, 182
Salamanders, 316, *316*
Salmonella, 307, *307*
Salt, 299
Salt Lake City, 125
Samurai, 121, *121*
"Samurai's Daughter, The," 38–40, *39*
Sandburg, Carl, 46
Sand Creek Massacre, 163–64
Santa Anna, Antonio López de, 127–28
Sayings and phrases, 3, 65–67
    birthday suit, 65
    bite the hand that feeds you, 65
    catch forty winks, 65
    chip on your shoulder, 65
    count your blessings, 65
    eat crow, 65
    eleventh hour, 65
    Eureka!, 65
    every cloud has a silver lining, 65
    few and far between, 66
    grass is always greener on the other side of the hill, the, 66
    it's never too late to mend, 66
    kill two birds with one stone, 66
    lock, stock, and barrel, 66
    make a mountain out of a molehill, 66
    miss is as good as a mile, a, 66
    out of the frying pan and into the fire, 66
    penny saved is a penny earned, a, 66
    read between the lines, 67
    sit on the fence, 67
    steal his/her thunder, 67
    take the bull by the horns, 67
    till the cows come home, 67
    time heals all wounds, 67
    Tom, Dick, and Harry, 67
    vice versa, 67

    watched pot never boils, a, 67
    well begun is half done, 67
    what will be will be, 67
Scalawags, 149
Scale, 261–62, *261*
Schools and education
    curricula in, xix, xxi–xxiii, xxv
    what you can do to help improve, xxv–xxvi
Science, 291, 292–337
    adolescence and puberty, 327–28, 331
    atoms, 292, *292,* 293
    biographies, 333–37
    care and growth of young, 325–26
    cells, 302–5, *302, 303, 304, 305*
    chemical reactions, 293, 297, 298–99, *298, 299*
    chemistry, 292–99
    classification, 300–310
    compounds, 297–98, *298*
    Dalton, John, 293
    element abbreviations, 296
    embryo development, 318, 321, *321, 322,* 325, 326, *326,* 327, 330
    endocrine system, 331–32, *332*
    flower fertilization, 320–21, *320*
    flowers, 319–20, *319*
    fungi, 301, *301,* 305, *305,* 315
    Galilei, Galileo, 333–34, *333*
    glands, 331–32, *332*
    growth stages, 326, *326,* 327, *327*
    human body, 327–32
    Julian, Percy Lavon, 336–37, *336*
    Just, Ernest, 335–36, *335*
    life cycles, 314, *314,* 326
    Linnaeus, Carl, 334–35, *334*
    living versus non-living things, 303
    metals, 294, 296, *296*

Science (*continued*)
    molecules, 297, *297*
    monocots and dicots, 322, *323*
    periodic table of the elements, 293–94, *294*, 295, *295*, 296
    plant development, 321–22, *321*, *322*
    plants and photosynthesis, 298, 304, 306, 307, 311–13, *311*, 322
    prokaryotes, 301, *301*, 307, *307*, 311
    protists, 301, *301*, 306, *306*, 307, 311, 315
    reproduction in animals and plants, 314–26, *315*, *317*, *324*
    reproduction in humans, 327, 328–30, *328*, *329*, *330*
    seeds, 315, 318–19, *318*, 321–22, *321*, *322*
    taxonomy, 308, 309
    vertebrates, 309–10
Scott, Dred, 131, *131*
Sculpture, 180–81, *181*, 190
Seasons, 76, *76*
Sea star, 316, *316*
Sea turtles, 325–26, *325*
Secession, 133, 134, 136
Secret Garden, The (Burnett), 29–33, 56
Seeds, 315, 318, 321–22, *321*, *322*
    conifer, 318, *318*
    of flowering plants, 318–19, 321, 322
Self-Portrait (Dürer), 185, *185*
Senate, 150
Sentences
    fragments, 53
    predicates in, 55
    run-on, 53–54
    subjects in, 52–53
    verbs in, 52–53
Sepals, 319, 321
Sets, 226
Seward, William H., 158

Sexual reproduction
    in animals, 314, 323–25, *324*
    in humans, 327, 328–30, *328*, *329*, *330*
    in mosses and ferns, 316–17, *317*
Shakespeare, William, 50–51, *50*, 113, 206, 207
Sharps and flats, in music, 202
Shaw, Robert Gould, 141
"Shenandoah," 214
Sherman, William Tecumseh, 144–45, *144*, 150
Shintoism, 122
Shoshone, 161
Silver, 293, 296
Simile and metaphor, 46–47
Singular pronouns, 59–60
Sioux (Lakota), 162, 164, *164*, 165–66
Sistine Chapel, 179, *179*, 185
Sit on the fence, 67
Sitting Bull, 164, *164*, 166
Slavery, 92, 100–102, 128, 129–34, 136, 139–40, 145, 148, 186
    abolitionists and, 130, 133, 139
    Brown, John, 133, *133*, 136
    Constitutional amendments and, 150–51, *151*, 152
    Emancipation Proclamation, 140, 141
    Freedmen's Bureau, 150
    Missouri Compromise, 129–30, 131
    Narrative of the Life of Frederick Douglass (Douglass), 28–29
    poster for a slave sale, *129*
    Scott, Dred, 131, *131*
    slave ships, 102, *102*
    spirituals, 131, 210–12
Small Cowper Madonna (Raphael), 180, *180*
"Snowstorm, The" (Emerson), 7
Sod houses, 154, *154*
Sodium, 294, 295, *295*, 296, 299
Soldiers, in Civil War, 138, *138*

African-American, 140–41, *140*, 145, 155, *155*, 190
    songs of, 139
"Sometimes I Feel Like a Motherless Child," 210, 211
Songs
    American, 215
    about love and lovers, 216
    of soldiers, 139
    spirituals, 131, 210–12
    about westward expansion, 213–14
South, 169
    Secession of, 133, 134, 136. *See also* Confederacy
South America, 82, 88, 90, 96, 97, 99, 101
Southern Hemisphere, 72, *72*, 74, *74*, 76
South Pole, 72, *72*, *73*, 74, *74*, 76
Southwest, 169, *169*
Soybeans, 336, 337
Spain, 93, 97–99
    Armada, 113–14
    explorers, 84–95, 99, 100, 101, 159, 160
Spawning, 324, *324*
Species, 308, 325, 335
Speed and rates, 262
Sperm
    of animals, 323, 324, *324*, 326, *326*
    of humans, 328, *328*
    of plants, 317, *317*
Spice Islands, 97, 98, *98*
Spirituals, 131, 210–12
Spores, 305, *305*, 315, 316, 317, *317*
Squares, 276, *276*, 277, *277*
Squares and square roots of numbers, 225–26
Staff, musical, 200
Stamens, 319, *319*
Starfish, 316, *316*
Stars, 333
Steal his/her thunder, 67

Steroids, 336, 337

Stories, myths, and legends, 3, 19–44

Adventures of Tom Sawyer, The (Twain), 19–20, 56

"Coyote Goes to the Land of the Dead," 43–44, *43*

Don Quixote (Cervantes), 21–23

dramas, 49

imagery in, 46

literal and figurative language in, 45–48

Little Women (Alcott), 24–27, 57

Narrative of the Life of Frederick Douglass (Douglass), 28–29

"Red-Headed League, The" (Doyle), 34–38

"Samurai's Daughter, The," 38–40, *39*

Secret Garden, The (Burnett), 29–33, 56

"Sun Dance, The," 40–43

symbols in, 48

Stowe, Harriet Beecher, 130, *130*

Straight angles, *273, 274*

Sub-atomic particles, 292

Subjects, 52, 55

Subtraction

of fractions, 253, *253*

of integers, 224

inverse operations, 229–30, 239

of mixed numbers, 256–57

Suffixes, 64

Sun, movement of planets around, 333–34

"Sun Dance, The," 40–43

Sunlight, in photosynthesis, 311, 312

Surface area, 286–87, *286*

Sweat glands, 331, *331*

"Sweet Betsy from Pike," 204, 213

Symbols, 48

Syncopation, 204

Systems, 304

Take the bull by the horns, 67

Taxonomy, 308

Latin names in, 309

Taylor, Zachary, 128

Tecumseh, 127

Telescope, 333

Temperate zones, 75, *75*

Ten, powers of, 226

Tenochtitlán, 84–85, *85*, 87

Tennyson, Alfred, Lord, 4

Tense, 52

Testosterone, 337

Tetzel, Johann, 109

Texas, 127–28

Thayer, Ernest Lawrence, 16–17

Thoreau, Henry David, 128

Thyroid gland, 331, *332*

Tikal, 82–83, *83*, 84

Till the cows come home, 67

Time, distance, and speed, 262

Time heals all wounds, 67

Time signatures, *196*, 199–200, *200*

Time zones, 76–78, *77*

Tissues, 304

Tom, Dick, and Harry, 67

Totem poles, *160*, 161

Trade, 89, 91–92, 93, 95–96, 99, 174

fur, 124

Tragedies, 49, *49*, 51

Trapezoids, 276, *276*

finding area of, 283–84, *283*

Treaties with Native Americans, 127

Treaty of Tordesillas, 93–94, *95, 96*, 97

Treble clef, 200–201, *201*

"Trees" (Kilmer), 48

Triangles, 276

congruent, 275, *275*

finding areas of, 282, *282*

kinds of, 274–75, *274, 275, 277*

Tropical zone, 75, *75*

Tropic of Cancer, 75, *75*

Tropic of Capricorn, 75, *75*

Tubman, Harriet, 140, 211

Turks, 91–92, 117, 119

Turtles, sea, 325–26, *325*

Twain, Mark, 19–20

"Tyger, The" (Blake), 12

Uncle Tom's Cabin (Stowe), 130, *130*

Underground Railroad, 140, 211

Units of measurement. *See* Measurement, units of

Universities, 104

Urethra, 328, *329*

U.S. geography. *See* Geography, U.S.

U.S. history. *See* History, U.S.

Ute, 161, *161*

Uterus, 325, 327, *329*, 330

Vacuoles, 302, 303, *303, 305*, 306

Van Eyck, Jan, 183, *183*

Variables, 229

Variety, in taxonomy, 308

Verbs, 52–53

Verses and refrains, 204

Vertebrates, 309–10

Vertex, 273

Vice versa, 67

Victoria, Queen, 157

Visual arts. *See* Art

Vitruvian Man (Leonardo da Vinci), 175, *175*

Vitruvius, 104

Volume, 285–86, *285*

capacity and, 288

units of, 287, *287*

Watched pot never boils, a, 67

Water, 297–98, *298*

plants and, 311, 312, 313

"Wayfaring Stranger," 210, 212

Well begun is half done, 67

"We Shall Overcome," 212, *212*

West, 169

West (*continued*)
    Wild, 156–57
Western Hemisphere, 72, *72*
Westward expansion, 159
    before Civil War, 123–28, *126*
    following Civil War, 153–58,
       153
    songs about, 213–14
What will be will be, 67
Whitman, Walt, 8, *8*, 15, 147
Whittier, John Greenleaf, 14
Wichita Indians, 162

Wilbur, Richard, 5
Wilderness Trail, 123
Wild West, 156–57
William and Mary, 116, *116*
Williams, Cathay, 155, *155*
"Wise Old Owl, A" (Richards), 4
Word problems, equations for,
    271–72
Words. *See* Language
World geography. *See* Geography,
    world
World history. *See* History, world

Wounded Knee, 166
Writing, 3, 62–63. *See also* Language

Xylem, 312, 313

Yeast, 305, 315
Young, Brigham, 125
Young, care and growth of, 325–26

Zygote, 325, 330